T0366097

# E–Commerce in Regional Small to Medium Enterprises

Robert MacGregor
*University of Wollongong, Australia*

Lejla Vrazalic
*University of Wollongong in Dubai, UAE*

A volume in the Advances in
Electronic Commerce (AEC)
Book Series

| | |
|---|---|
| Acquisition Editor: | Kristin Klinger |
| Senior Managing Editor: | Jennifer Neidig |
| Managing Editor: | Sara Reed |
| Assistant Managing Editor: | Sharon Berger |
| Development Editor: | Kristin Roth |
| Copy Editor: | Larissa Vinci |
| Typesetter: | Michael Brehm |
| Cover Design: | Lisa Tosheff |

Published in the United States of America by
    Idea Group Publishing (an imprint of IGI Global)
    701 E. Chocolate Avenue
    Hershey PA 17033
    Tel: 717-533-8845
    Fax: 717-533-8661
    E-mail: cust@igi-global.com
    Web site: http://www.igi-global.com

Library of Congress Cataloging-in-Publication Data

MacGregor, Robert C., 1951-
  E-commerce in regional small to medium enterprises / Robert MacGregor and Lejla Vrazalic, authors.
    p. cm.
  Summary: "This book presents detailed studies of e-commerce in multiple regions focusing on business size, sector, market focus, gender of CEO, and education level of CEO as driving forces for e-commerce adoption. Results show that regional SMEs in developed countries have low e-commerce adoption rates, and strategic alliances by SMEs play a key role in overcoming the low rate"--Provided by publisher.
  Includes bibliographical references and index.
  ISBN 978-1-59904-123-0 (hardcover) -- ISBN 978-1-59904-125-4 (ebook) 1. Electronic commerce. 2. Small business. 3. Strategic alliances (Business) I. Vrazalic, Lejla. II. Title.
  HF5548.32.M327 2007
  381'.142--dc22
                        2007007266

This book is published in the IGI Global book series Advances in Electronic Commerce (AEC) Book Series (ISSN: 1935-2921; eISSN: 1935-293X)

British Cataloguing in Publication Data
A Cataloguing in Publication record for this book is available from the British Library.

# Advances in Electronic Commerce (AEC) Book Series

*Mehdi Khosrow-Pour (Information Resources Management Association, USA)*

ISSN: 1935-2921
EISSN: 1935-293X

## MISSION

The impact of information technology on commerce is a dynamic and perpetually evolving field of research, most notably as electronic approaches for business transactions shift to the Internet and other telecommunication networks. Given the rapid advancements in the field, research addressing e-commerce and its related areas needs an outlet to reach its audience.

The **Advances in Electronic Commerce (AEC)** series provides comprehensive coverage and understanding of the social, cultural, organizational, and cognitive impacts of e-commerce technologies. The series provides accounts from both the consumer perspective and the organization perspective. AEC aims to expand the body of knowledge regarding e-commerce technologies and applications, thus assisting researchers and practitioners to develop more effective systems.

## COVERAGE

- Commerce strategy
- Digital economy
- Electronic banking
- Mobile commerce
- Online marketplaces
- Social media & e-commerce
- Virtual marketplaces
- Virtual storefronts
- Web commerce

IGI Global is currently accepting manuscripts for publication within this series. To submit a proposal for a volume in this series, please contact our Acquisition Editors at Acquisitions@igi-global.com or visit: http://www.igi-global.com/publish/.

# Titles in this Series

*For a list of additional titles in this series, please visit: www.igi-global.com*

*Virtual Worlds and E-Commerce Technologies and Applications for Building Customer Relationships*
Barbara Ciaramitaro (Ferris State University, USA)
Business Science Reference • copyright 2011 • 399pp • H/C (ISBN: 9781616928087) • US $180.00 (our price)

*Consumer Behavior, Organizational Development, and Electronic Commerce Emerging Issues for Advancing Modern Socioeconomies*
Mehdi Khosrow-Pour (Information Resources Management Association, USA)
Information Science Reference • copyright 2009 • 410pp • H/C (ISBN: 9781605661261) • US $195.00 (our price)

*Outsourcing and Offshoring of Professional Services Business Optimization in a Global Economy*
Amar Gupta (University of Arizona, USA)
Information Science Reference • copyright 2008 • 438pp • H/C (ISBN: 9781599049724) • US $180.00 (our price)

*Commerce in Space Infrastructures, Technologies, and Applications*
Phillip Olla (Madonna University, USA)
Information Science Reference • copyright 2008 • 400pp • H/C (ISBN: 9781599046242) • US $180.00 (our price)

*E-Commerce in Regional Small to Medium Enterprises*
Robert MacGregor (University of Wollongong, Australia) and Lejla Vrazalic (University of Wollongong in Dubai, UAE)
Idea Group Publishing • copyright 2007 • 428pp • H/C (ISBN: 9781599041230) • US $99.95 (our price)

www.igi-global.com

701 E. Chocolate Ave., Hershey, PA 17033
Order online at www.igi-global.com or call 717-533-8845 x100
To place a standing order for titles released in this series,
contact: cust@igi-global.com
Mon-Fri 8:00 am - 5:00 pm (est) or fax 24 hours a day 717-533-8661

# E-Commerce in Regional Small to Medium Enterprises

## Table of Contents

Foreword......................................................................................................... xi

Preface......................................................................................................... xiv

Acknowledgments ........................................................................................ xx

**Chapter I**
**SMEs and Electronic Commerce:**
**An Overview of Our Current Knowledge**..................................................... 1
*The Nature of SMEs* .................................................................. 2
*SMEs in Regional Areas*............................................................ 7
*Pre E-Commerce Acquisition of IT by SMEs* ............................ 8
*IT Adoption Criteria*................................................................ 11
*The Diversity of the SME Sector* ............................................. 12
*Electronic Commerce*.............................................................. 13
*E-Commerce and SMEs* ......................................................... 14
*Conclusion*.............................................................................. 17
*References* ............................................................................. 18

**Chapter II**
**General Research Methodology and Procedures:**
**An Overview of How the Study was Undertaken** .................................................. **25**

*Overall Goals of the Study* .......................................................................... 25
*Choice of Location for Data Gathering* ...................................................... 27
*Mode of Data Collection* ............................................................................. 31
*Development of the Survey Instrument* ...................................................... 31
*E-Commerce Criteria, Barriers, Benefits, and Disadvantages* ................. 35
*Pilot Study* ................................................................................................... 37
*Statistical Analysis* ..................................................................................... 37
*Conclusion* ................................................................................................... 39
*References* .................................................................................................... 40

**Chapter III**
**Profile of SMEs in Sweden, Australia, and the USA:**
**Associations Between Various Business Characteristics** ........................ **42**

*Survey Instrument* ........................................................................................ 43
*Response Rates* ............................................................................................ 45
*Profile of Respondents in Sweden* .............................................................. 46
*Associations Between Business Characteristics in Sweden* ....................... 51
*Associations Between Business Characteristics and*
*    E-Commerce Adoption in Sweden* ........................................................... 63
*Summary of Swedish Findings* .................................................................... 67
*Profile of Respondents in Australia* ........................................................... 68
*Associations Between Business Characteristics in Australia* ................... 71
*Associations Between Business Characteristics and*
*    E-Commerce Adoption in Australia* ......................................................... 73
*Summary of Australian Findings* ................................................................ 73
*Profile of Respondents in the USA* .............................................................. 74
*Associations Between Business Characteristics in the USA* ...................... 78
*Associations Between Business Characteristics and*
*    E-Commerce Adoption in the USA* ........................................................... 79
*Summary of USA Findings* ........................................................................... 80
*A Comparison of Sweden, Australia, and the USA* ..................................... 81
*Conclusion* ................................................................................................... 83
*References* .................................................................................................... 83

**Chapter IV**
**Criteria for the Adoption of E-Commerce:**
**Why Do SMEs Decide to Implement E-Commerce?** ............................... **86**

*Background* .................................................................................................. 87
*E-Commerce Adoption Criteria and Business Characteristics* .................. 90
*Research Questions* ..................................................................................... 92
*Methodology* ................................................................................................ 93
*Business Characteristics and E-Commerce Adoption*
*    Criteria in Swedish SMEs* ....................................................................... 94
*Groupings of E-Commerce Adoption Criteria in Sweden* .......................... 98

*Summary: E-Commerce Adoption Criteria in Swedish SMEs* ....................... 110
*Business Characteristics and E-Commerce Adoption Criteria in Australia*.... 111
*Groupings of E-Commerce Adoption Criteria in Australia* .......................... 112
*Summary: E-Commerce Adoption Criteria in Australian SMEs*..................... 115
*Business Characteristics and E-Commerce Adoption Criteria in the USA* ..... 115
*Groupings of E-Commerce Adoption Criteria in the USA*............................ 117
*Summary: E-Commerce Adoption Criteria in USA SMEs* ............................ 118
*Comparison of Results: A Discussion* ....................................................... 118
*E-Commerce Adoption Criteria: Implications* ............................................ 122
*E-Commerce Adoption Criteria: Key Findings*........................................... 124
*References* .......................................................................................... 125

**Chapter V**
**Barriers to E-Commerce Adoption:**
**Why are SMEs Staying Away from E-Commerce?**................................**129**
*Background* .......................................................................................... 130
*Research Questions*............................................................................... 133
*Methodology*........................................................................................ 134
*Business Characteristics and E-Commerce Adoption Barriers in Sweden*...... 135
*Groupings of E-Commerce Adoption Barriers in Sweden* ............................ 135
*Summary: Adoption Barriers in Swedish SMEs*.......................................... 140
*Business Characteristics and E-Commerce Adoption Barriers in Australia*.. 141
*Groupings of E-Commerce Adoption Barriers in Australia*........................... 145
*Summary: Adoption Barriers in Australian SMEs*........................................ 147
*Business Characteristics and E-Commerce Adoption Barriers in the USA*..... 147
*Groupings of E-Commerce Adoption Barriers in the USA* ........................... 149
*Summary: E-Commerce Adoption Barriers in USA SMEs* ........................... 150
*Comparison of Results: A Discussion*........................................................ 151
*E-Commerce Adoption Barriers: Implications* ............................................ 155
*E-Commerce Adoption Barriers: Key Findings*............................................ 155
*References* .......................................................................................... 156

**Chapter VI**
**Benefits of E-Commerce Adoption:**
**What Can SMEs Expect to Gain from E-Commerce Adoption?** ..........**160**
*Background* .......................................................................................... 161
*Research Questions*............................................................................... 163
*Methodology*........................................................................................ 163
*Business Characteristics and E-Commerce Benefits in Sweden*..................... 165
*Groupings of E-Commerce Benefits in Sweden*........................................... 165
*Summary: E-Commerce Adoption Benefits in Swedish SMEs*........................ 172
*Business Characteristics and E-Commerce Benefits in Australia*................... 172
*Groupings of E-Commerce Adoption Benefits in Australia*............................ 174
*Summary: E-Commerce Benefits in Australian SMEs* .................................. 175
*Comparison of Results: A Discussion*........................................................ 175
*E-Commerce Benefits: Implications*.......................................................... 177
*E-Commerce Adoption Benefits: Key Findings*............................................ 177
*References* .......................................................................................... 178

**Chapter VII**
**Disadvantages of E-Commerce Adoption:**
**What Types of Problems do SMEs Face from E-Commerce?** ............................. 180
    *Background* ................................................................................. 181
    *Research Questions* ...................................................................... 182
    *Methodology* ................................................................................ 183
    *Business Characteristics and E-Commerce Disadvantages in Sweden* ........... 184
    *Groupings of E-Commerce Disadvantages in Sweden* ......................... 186
    *Summary: E-Commerce Disadvantages in Swedish SMEs* ....................... 192
    *Business Characteristics and E-Commerce Disadvantages in Australia* ........ 193
    *Groupings of E-Commerce Disadvantages in Australia* ......................... 194
    *Summary: E-Commerce Disadvantages in Australian SMEs* ......................... 195
    *Comparison of Results: A Discussion* ........................................... 196
    *E-Commerce Disadvantages: Implications* ....................................... 197
    *E-Commerce Adoption Disadvantages: Key Findings* ......................... 197
    *References* ................................................................................. 198

**Chapter VIII**
**Strategic Alliances and E-Commerce Adoption:**
**Does Partnering with Other SMEs Affect E-Commerce Adoption?** ..................... 200
    *Background* ................................................................................. 200
    *The Role of Strategic Alliances* ................................................... 201
    *The Role of Alliances E-Commerce Adoption* ................................... 205
    *Research Questions* ...................................................................... 206
    *Methodology* ................................................................................ 206
    *Business Characteristics and Strategic Alliance Membership* ..................... 207
    *Strategic Alliances and E-Commerce Adoption* ................................... 211
    *Comparison of Differences Between the Three Locations: A Discussion* ........ 221
    *Groupings of E-Commerce Criteria, Barriers, Benefits, and*
        *Disadvantages and Alliance Membership* ................................... 222
    *Comparison of Results: A Discussion* ........................................... 243
    *E-Commerce and Strategic Alliances: Implications* ......................... 247
    *E-Commerce and Strategic Alliances: Key Findings* ......................... 249
    *References* ................................................................................. 252

**Chapter IX**
**The Role of Gender in E-Commerce Adoption:**
**Does Having a Male or Female CEO Affect E-Commerce Use?** ......................... 256
    *Background* ................................................................................. 257
    *Research Questions* ...................................................................... 260
    *Methodology* ................................................................................ 260
    *Gender and E-Commerce Adoption* ............................................... 261
    *Comparison of Differences Between the Three Locations: A Discussion* ........ 266
    *Groupings of E-Commerce Criteria, Barriers, Benefits, and Disadvantages*
        *and CEO Gender* ......................................................... 267
    *Comparison of Results: A Discussion* ........................................... 279
    *E-Commerce and Gender: Implications* ......................................... 284
    *E-Commerce and Gender: Key Findings* ......................................... 285
    *References* ................................................................................. 287

**Chapter X**
**The Role of Education in E-Commerce Adoption:**
**Does the CEO's Level of Education Affect E-Commerce Adoption?**...................291
    *Background* ................................................................................................291
    *Research Questions* ....................................................................................292
    *Methodology*..............................................................................................293
    *Education and E-Commerce Adoption*......................................................294
    *Groupings of E-Commerce Criteria, Barriers, Benefits, Disadvantages,*
        *and CEO Education* ............................................................................298
    *Comparison of Results: A Discussion* ........................................................318
    *E-Commerce and CEO Education: Implications* .......................................319
    *E-Commerce and CEO Education: Key Findings*.......................................319
    *References* .................................................................................................326

**Chapter XI**
**Interaction of Adoption Factors:**
**Do SMEs Achieve the Desired Benefits from E-Commerce Adoption?** ..............328
    *E-Commerce Criteria and Benefits in Sweden*...........................................329
    *Summary of Criteria and Benefits in Sweden*............................................334
    *E-Commerce Criteria and Disadvantages in Sweden*.................................336
    *Summary of Criteria and Disadvantages in Sweden*..................................337
    *E-Commerce Criteria and Benefits in Australia* .......................................338
    *Summary of Criteria and Benefits in Australia*.........................................340
    *E-Commerce Criteria and Benefits/Disadvantages Associations*
        *and Strategic Alliance Membership*.....................................................341
    *E-Commerce Criteria and Benefits/Disadvantages Associations*
        *and Business Size* ................................................................................344
    *E-Commerce Criteria and Benefits/Disadvantages Associations*
        *and Business Sector*.............................................................................346
    *E-Commerce Criteria and Benefits/Disadvantages Associations*
        *and Market Focus* ................................................................................348
    *E-Commerce Criteria and Benefits/Disadvantages Associations*
        *and Type of E-Commerce* .....................................................................349
    *Comparison of the Two Locations and Implications*..................................350
    *E-Commerce Criteria and Resulting Benefits/Disadvantages:*
        *Key Findings* .......................................................................................352
    *References* .................................................................................................354

**Chapter XII**
**Current Barriers and Future Drivers:**
**Why SMEs Don't Use E-Commerce Today and What Potential Benefits May**
**Lead Them to Use E-Commerce in the Future** ......................................................355
    *E-Commerce Barriers and Potential Drivers in Sweden*.............................356
    *Summary of Barriers and Potential Drivers in Sweden*..............................363
    *E-Commerce Barriers and Potential Drivers in Australia* ..........................365
    *Summary of Barriers and Potential Drivers in Australia*............................367
    *E-Commerce Barriers and Potential Drivers in the USA*.............................368
    *Summary of Barriers and Potential Drivers in the USA*..............................373

   *Comparison of the Three Locations and Implications*.....................................374
   *E-Commerce Barriers and Potential Drivers: Key Findings*..........................378
   *References* ..................................................................................................379

**Chapter XIII**
**E-Commerce Adoption in Sweden, Australia, and the USA:**
**A Comparison**..........................................................................................................**381**
   *A Comparison of E-Commerce Criteria*..............................................................382
   *A Comparison of E-Commerce Barriers*.............................................................386
   *A Comparison of E-Commerce Benefits*..............................................................389
   *A Comparison of E-Commerce Disadvantages*...................................................390
   *Comparison of Three Locations: Implications*....................................................391
   *Comparison of Three Locations: Key Findings*..................................................391
   *References* ..................................................................................................393

**Chapter XIV**
**Implications for E-Commerce Adoption by SMEs:**
**How Can These Results Help with E-Commerce Adoption by SMEs?** ..............**395**
   *E-Commerce in Sweden* .....................................................................................396
   *E-Commerce in Australia*...................................................................................398
   *E-Commerce in the USA*.....................................................................................399
   *Final Remarks* ...................................................................................................401
   *References* ..................................................................................................402

**About the Authors**...................................................................................................**404**

**Index** .........................................................................................................................**405**

# Foreword

Most of us who are connected with the rapidly expanding field of small business research feel privileged to engage the opportunities and challenges provided by the Internet and related information and communication technologies (ICTs). Indeed, these are extraordinary times in the working lives of small business owner/managers, their supporters, suppliers, and customers as well as the researchers that focus on this exciting topic of academic endeavour.

During the last decade, we have witnessed the emergence of the World Wide Web (WWW) and the birth of electronic commerce (e-commerce), events that have radically altered the economic activities of most small, medium, and large organisations as well as the purchasing habits of their customers, both private and corporate. No aspect or strata of the socio-economic and political structure of our society escaped untouched by these relatively recent developments. Even the most conservative bastions of government and politics have now yielded to the influence, connectivity, and efficiencies afforded by the Internet.

In the context of small business economic activity, e-commerce has provided owner/managers with a wide range of online, innovative, and collaborative approaches to product manufacturing, service provision, and knowledge sharing. The ongoing e-commerce revolution in this important sector of economic activity reflects the accelerating pace of change that is currently affecting the market place at local, regional, national, and international levels. Furthermore, a wide spectrum of evolutionary and revolutionary innovations and technological developments have opened new market places and radically altered existing ones. At the same time, long-standing, traditional local and national entrepreneurial outlets have been increasingly replaced by global *e*-Markets, which bring geographically dispersed producers and consumers into close, cost-efficient, and mutually beneficial proximity. Typically, such innovations also reduced significantly the barriers that have traditionally affected market performance, including imperfect information relating to the willingness and ability to supply or purchase, at a given price, a vast portfolio of goods and services. As a result, a variety of collaborative strategies have emerged to assist small business owner/managers in their efforts to achieve and maintain sustainable competitive advantage. Nevertheless, and despite the burgeoning mass of related research and dissemination, the full strategic impact of e-commerce upon small business operation and competitiveness is yet to be fully investigated. In this context, this book goes a long way toward redressing the knowledge imbalances that plague most research that focuses specifically upon e-commerce in small businesses.

During the last few years, as the editor of the *Journal of Small Business and Enterprise Development (JSBED)*, I have assisted and encouraged the authors to disseminate the results of their internationally acclaimed research. This book incorporates the results of three of their large international studies (Sweden, Australia, and the USA) and provides an in-depth analysis of the most important and relevant aspects of e-commerce in smaller firms. In addition to a comprehensive and critical literature review and analysis of existing knowledge, the authors outline the main criteria for the adoption of e-commerce, and its advantages and disadvantages to small business owner/managers. There are also chapters relevant to e-commerce adoption barriers and strategic alliances as well as the role of gender and education upon the implementation of related strategies. Importantly, the authors compare and contrast issues related to e-commerce adoption in small businesses across the three international locations, setting the groundwork for valuable comparative and regional research in an international context.

There is no doubt in my mind that this book represents a valuable and timely contribution to a pertinent aspect of small business research and development. As such, I would recommend it as compulsory reading to all the stakeholders that are interested in supporting and facilitating a thriving small business sector, at both micro- and macro-economic levels. Similarly, I would recommend it as a core, research-based text for the growing population of undergraduate and postgraduate students involved in small business and entrepreneurship education. Researchers all over the world would benefit considerably from the mass of knowledge and experience encapsulated in this empirically rigorous book. I congratulate the authors for their expert work and unfailing commitment to the international small business community, and the publishers for facilitating the publication of relevant and cutting edge knowledge.

*Dr. Harry Matlay*

*Professor of Small Business and Enterprise Development*

*UCE Birmingham Business School*

*Birmingham UK*

*Editor*

*Journal of Small Business and Enterprise Development*

*Harry Matlay is a professor of small business and enterprise development at UCE Business School in Birmingham (West Midlands, UK). He specialises in e-entrepreneurship and small e-business development as well as in training and human resource development issues in smaller firms. Matlay holds three degrees from Warwick University, UK: BSc (Hons), MEd, and PhD (1984, 1993, and 1997, respectively). Prior to joining the UCE Business School, he worked in senior positions in industry and commerce, as an entrepreneur and business consultant, and at Warwick University, where he undertook teaching, supervision and various small business related projects. He edited the English language EC SME Observatory (1997) and has contributed an extensive chapter on Health and Safety in European SMEs.*

*Matlay joined the UCE Business School (January 1998) and contributed to the research activities of the Knowledge Management Centre (KMC) and the Enterprise Research and Development Centre (ERDC). He is the editor of the* Journal of Small Business and Enterprise Development, *guest editor of* Education and Training *and on the editorial boards of the* International Journal of Entrepreneurship and Industry Higher Education. *He was awarded the Golden Page prize in the research relevance category for his editorial work on JSBED (2003). He has written over 100 articles and conference papers, published in refereed and practitioner journals as well as in the proceedings of prestigious national and international conferences. His contribution to research is internationally recognised and he is the holder of several national and international research awards.*

# Preface

SMEs have been an object of academic study for decades. Despite their small size, they are considered to be the cornerstone of national economic development and a significant contributor to the economic wealth and prosperity of a country. The European Commission views SMEs as the backbone of the European economy (Europa, 2003). Similarly, the Australian government recognises that SMEs are a "powerhouse" of economic potential, whose employees account for almost five million members of the workforce (NOIE, 2002) making them a major source of jobs.

In recent years, SMEs have faced a number of challenges. With the establishment of Free Trade Agreements between countries worldwide, SMEs are increasingly competing in global markets. This has been made possible by several developments most notably in the area of information technology. With the advent of electronic commerce (e-commerce), SMEs found themselves in position to enter new markets, expand their organisation, and utilise technology for competitive advantage. Indeed, apart from academic research confirming this development, anecdotal evidence from SME owners suggests that the Internet and e-commerce have stretched their business horizons beyond expectations. Numerous SME owners have reported receiving orders for their products and services from all over the world, despite deciding to use technology to improve services to their local market.

E-commerce involves the application of Web-based information technologies toward automating business processes, transactions, and workflows, and buying and selling information, products, and services using computer networks (Kalakota & Whinston, 1997). E-commerce technology has the potential to become a major source of competitive advantage to SMEs because it is a cost effective way of reaching customers globally and competing on par with larger counterparts. Governments worldwide have recognised this and created funding schemes and initiatives to facilitate e-commerce adoption in SMEs. These are evident in highly developed countries in particular where government organisations are investing millions in programs and incentives to promote IT and e-commerce adoption in SMEs.

Regional areas have come under particular scrutiny for these programs in order to encourage economic growth. Regional areas are geographic locations that are outside the greater boundaries of metropolitan areas and large cities. In recent years, there has been a significant demographic trend of migration from regional to metropolitan areas, which has placed a burden on social systems in large cities and raised questions about the sustainability of both smaller townships (where the population is dwindling) and cities (which are increasingly overcrowded). Inevitably, this has led to initiatives to reverse the trend with government funding being channelled to regional areas in an attempt to promote their economic growth. A significant amount of this funding has been invested in developing IT infrastructure, particularly for SMEs, which dominate the regional landscape. However, we still do not have reliable data about the success of these initiatives. The exploratory study presented in this book aims to open the door for further research in this field by providing empirical evidence about the use of e-commerce in SMEs located in regional areas.

# Research Objectives

The key aim of the study presented in this book is to determine how SMEs located in regional areas are going about e-commerce adoption. The study was undertaken over a period of three years in three highly developed nations all belonging to the OECD and with comparable per capita GDPs and levels of Internet penetration. These included Sweden, Australia, and the USA. In each country, one regional area was surveyed—Varmland (Sweden), Illawarra (Australia), and Salt Lake City (USA).

In each location, we examined SMEs that were e-commerce adopters as well as non-adopters. For adopters, we considered the following aspects:

- The reasons why they had adopted e-commerce (we have termed these "criteria")
- The advantages they gained from e-commerce adoption (we have termed these "benefits")
- The difficulties they experienced following e-commerce adoption (we have termed these "disadvantages")

For the non-adopters, we were interested in two aspects of e-commerce adoption:

- Their reasons for not using e-commerce (termed "barriers")
- The potential benefits that would be an incentive to adopt e-commerce in the future (these were termed "criteria" and mirror the criteria used by adopters)

In addition to the previous, we also collected data about the SMEs in order to develop a profile of the respondents. Some of the information we collected included the size of the business (defined in terms of the number of employees), the age of the business (in years), the business sector, the market focus (i.e., where the majority of the customers come from), the gender and educational level of the CEO, whether they were members of an alliance, and others. We use the term "business characteristics" to refer to this information. In addition to examining the aspects of e-commerce, we have also examined the correlations between business characteristics and e-commerce criteria, barriers, benefits, and disadvantages, in an attempt to answer questions such as the following:

- Are SMEs with a male or female CEO more likely to adopt e-commerce to increase their sales?
- Are SMEs, which are between 3 and 5 years old, more likely to experience reduced costs as a result of e-commerce adoption?
- Are those SMEs that have not adopted e-commerce because it doesn't suit their products/services more likely to have between 10 and 19 employees?

A list of specific research goals is included in Chapter II. However, the broad objectives of the research can be summarised as follows:

- To determine the levels of e-commerce adoption in regional SMEs located in developed countries.
- To define the main reasons for e-commerce adoption (and non-adoption) in regional SMEs.
- The understand the benefits and disadvantages of e-commerce adoption in regional SMEs.
- To determine the effects of business characteristics such as the gender and education of the CEO on e-commerce adoption.
- To examine the effects of belonging to an alliance on e-commerce adoption.
- To discuss the implications of the research findings for government initiatives in regional areas.

# Methodology

A survey instrument was used in all three locations to collect data. Depending on the likely response rate, different modes of data collection were implemented. A total of 589 responses were received and used to undertake different statistical analyses in order to address the previous research objectives. The amount of data collected was substantial and this book presents only a portion of the total data collected and analysed over a four-year period in the three locations previously described. Chapter II provides a detailed explanation of the research methodology used.

# Outcomes and Implications

The primary outcome of this research is empirical evidence of e-commerce adoption in regional SMEs. Eleven chapters of this book (Chapters III to XIII) provide detailed accounts of every aspect of e-commerce adoption, including the effects of various business characteristics. For simplicity, each chapter is treated as separate and can be read as a stand-alone chapter.

This book is primarily aimed at academics and researchers and has been presented accordingly. However, the results of the statistical analyses have an inherent practical value and to allow both government organisations and e-commerce providers to benefit from the findings, we have provided a summary at the end of each chapter highlighting the key issues arising as well as the implications of the results. The book is rich in data and those practitioners who are familiar with statistical techniques may refer to a specific table to examine the results of a specific analysis if required. As such, this book can be used as a reference and the wealth of information contained within it can be used to focus on certain aspects of e-commerce adoption. Therefore, this book is a piece of empirical research and a reference at the same time.

One of the key outcomes of the research is the finding that SMEs are not homogeneous and that there are very few similarities even between businesses located in relatively comparable areas. The differences between SMEs with fewer and more employees, for example, are significant when it comes to e-commerce adoption. As are the differences between SMEs located in Sweden and Australia.

The main message of this study is that SMEs can not be treated as a single entity. Any government program that aims to promote technology must take into account a range of factors and provide tailored solutions for different categories of SMEs. This book contains a plethora of findings, which aims to assist with this customised approach. Similarly, e-commerce software developers will benefit from the findings by designing and developing custom made solutions for different SMEs.

# Limitations

It should be noted that the study presented here has several limitations. The choice of variables selected for the study is somewhat problematic because of the complex nature of e-commerce, which changes over time. Furthermore, according to Sohal and Ng (1998), the views expressed in the surveys are of a single individual from the responding organisation and only those interested in the study are likely to complete and return the survey. However, previous empirical studies (Raymond, 2001) have demonstrated the survey methodology to be a valid instrument for this type of research. It should be noted that the results presented in the study are the *perceptions* and *beliefs* of the individuals who completed the survey. When asked to rate e-commerce benefits, for example, the respondents are providing their personal views and it is not always possible to attribute the various benefits and problems in the organisation to e-commerce specifically.

The number of respondents in Australia that had adopted e-commerce was small, reducing the generalisability of certain findings. Due to a low response rate to certain questions, there was insufficient data from some of the U.S. surveys to undertake the full range of statistical analyses. Although statistically valid, some results are derived from a small sample size. As such, they may be a function of the response rate and should be treated with caution.

Finally, this is a quantitative study, and further qualitative research is required to gain a better understanding of the key issues.

We are not providing the reader with infallible results and findings that can be taken on board and used in practice. Our study provides a "snap shot" of e-commerce adoption issues in regional areas in three countries and the differences between these. Technology progresses at a rapid pace and that is always one of the pitfalls of doing research in the area. However, to overcome this we have focused on the organisational issues of e-commerce adoption, as opposed to the technical issues. From this point of view, it can be argued that the findings presented in this book are probably still valid today even though the last survey was carried out in 2004.

# Structure of the Book

The following thirteen chapters provide the context to our study and contain the results of the research. They are organised as follows:

**Chapter I** provides an overview of SMEs and electronic commerce as a background to the research. A review of the literature is presented in order to situate the present study and demonstrate its significance and the knowledge gap it aims to fill.

**Chapter II** describes the research methodology in detail, including the specific research goals, data collection (survey) instrument, and the statistical analyses undertaken.

**Chapter III** consists of general findings from the study. It presents a profile of the respondents and examines the interactions between different business characteristics. E-commerce adoption at the broadest level (i.e., the number of adopters and non-adopters) is examined briefly.

**Chapter IV** commences a detailed treatment of e-commerce by examining e-commerce adoption criteria. First, we look at the associations between various business characteristics (i.e., business size, age, sector, etc.) and various e-commerce adoption criteria to determine which types of businesses are more likely to adopt e-commerce for certain reasons. This is followed by a factor analysis to identify the groupings of e-commerce criteria, which will tell us the overarching reasons for adoption in each of the three locations. The three subsequent chapters follow the same format.

**Chapter V** presents the results of the analyses concerning e-commerce barriers, including the associations between business characteristics and specific e-commerce barriers and a factor analysis to understand the main reasons for lack of e-commerce adoption.

**Chapter VI** is concerned with the benefits of e-commerce adoption. Several business characteristics were found to be associated with certain benefits and different groupings of benefits were found in each of the three locations.

**Chapter VII** examines the final aspect of e-commerce—disadvantages. Each disadvantage is analysed in relation to business characteristics and to identify groupings, as in the previous chapters.

**Chapter VIII** provides the results of analysing the relationship between alliance membership and e-commerce adoption. As mentioned previously, alliances have been promoted as a catalyst for e-commerce adoption, among other things. This chapter presents empirical evidence of how this trend is developing in regional areas.

**Chapter IX** looks at the effects of gender on e-commerce adoption. Previous research has found strong correlations between the gender of the CEO and IT adoption. We examine whether this is applicable to e-commerce adoption in regional SMEs.

**Chapter X** mirrors Chapter IX, but looks at the effects of education on e-commerce adoption. Our aim is to determine to what extent the education level of the CEO is associated with e-commerce adoption.

**Chapter XI** only examines e-commerce adopters and specifically the relationship between adoption criteria and adoption benefits/disadvantages. This chapter answers two very important questions:

- Did SMEs that adopted e-commerce for specific reasons experience the matching benefits? (i.e., if an SME adopted e-commerce to increase sales, did this benefit materialise?)
- What disadvantages did SMEs that had adopted e-commerce for a specific reason experience? (i.e., if an SME adopted e-commerce to reduce costs did it experience increased costs as a result.)

**Chapter XII** is similar to Chapter XI in that it examines only non-adopters, and specifically the relationship between current adoption barriers and future adoption criteria. The chapter aims to determine which barriers are associated with which criteria.

**Chapter XIII** zooms out from the detailed level of analysis in the previous chapter to make a broad comparison of the results across the three locations and determine the differences between criteria, barriers, benefits, and disadvantages.

**Chapter XIV** provides a summary of the key findings and the main conclusions of the study. It also discusses the implications of the results and highlights the areas where action is required in order to promote e-commerce adoption by SMEs located in regional areas.

# References

Europa – The European Commission. (2003). *Small to medium enterprises.* Retrieved December 15, 2003, from http://europa.eu.int/comm/enterprise/enterprise_policy/sme_definition/index_en.htm

Kalakota, R., & Whinston, A. (1997). *Electronic commerce: A manager's guide.* Wesley, Reading: Addison.

NOIE – The National Office for the Information Economy. (2002). *e-business for small business.* Retrieved December 10, 2003, from http://www.noie.gov.au/projects/ebusiness/Advancing/SME

Raymond L. (2001) Determinants of Web Site Implementation in Small Business Internet Research. *Electronic Network Applications and Policy, 11*(5), 411 - 422

Sohal, A. S., & Ng, L. (1998). The role and impact of information technology in Australian business. *Journal of Information Technology, 13*(3), 201-217.

# Acknowledgments

The writing of a book such as this is never a solo, or in this case a duo effort, it requires the assistance, skill, patience, and good will of many people.

We would firstly like to thank Professor Sten Carlsson and Monika Magnusson from Karlstad University in Sweden for their diligence in developing the Swedish questionnaire used in this study. We would also like to thank Sten's students for the distribution, gathering, and coding of the data from SMEs in and around Karlstad.

For the U.S. section of this study, we are indebted to Dr. Jean Pratt and Mark Harris from Utah State University who oversaw the distribution of questionnaires and the gathering of data from U.S. regional SMEs.

The Australian "leg" of the study required many hours of sweet-talking and cajoling SME owner/managers over the phone. This, sometimes difficult task was handled professionally and patiently by Sheila Matete, Connie Nielsen, and Tarcita Heaven.

The authors would like to give a special thanks to Danielle Stern for her knowledge and insights into the world of statistics. While we knew of many of the techniques available to us, Danielle opened our eyes to many other exciting possibilities that have given these studies a far greater depth than we might have first imagined possible.

Our gratitude also goes out to Dr. Deborah Bunker at the University of New South Wales for her support and involvement in certain aspects of this research study.

The production of a book such as this not only requires the skills of data gathering and analysis, it requires a knowledgeable publishing team to guide, referee, and produce a final product that is useful to the reader. The authors have nothing but praise for the team at IGI Global, and particularly Kristin Roth, who have advised us on every step of the journey from having some interesting insights into SMEs and e-commerce to producing a manuscript that is useful to both researchers and practitioners in the field.

Particular thanks goes to Professor Harry Matlay for his ongoing support of our work and for writing the foreword to this book. Harry has always been a leading light in the study of SMEs and his endorsement means a lot to us.

A book such as this cannot be written without data. The authors would like to thank all of the owner/managers who took time away from their busy schedules to answer questions concerning their experiences and views of e-commerce. There is no substitute for practical experience.

Finally, we would like to thank our respective partners, Connie and Diniz, who have listened, smiled, nodded, and kept us going throughout this project.

*Rob MacGregor & Lejla Vrazalic*
*March 2007*

## Chapter I

# SMEs and Electronic Commerce:
## An Overview of Our Current Knowledge

Small to medium enterprises (SMEs) are generally regarded as the cornerstone of developed economies. Most governments view the SME sector as a major driver of the economy and a source of employment opportunities. It is widely recognised that SMEs are not simply scaled down versions of large organisations. SMEs have their own unique characteristics, which can either lead to improved competitiveness or inhibit growth depending on how they are managed. Increasingly, the emphasis has been on promoting the use of information and communication technologies (ICTs) in SMEs in order to encourage the advancement of the sector and underpin the development of a knowledge-based economy. In recent times, the emphasis has been on the adoption of electronic commerce (e-commerce) technology.

Unlike previous technological initiatives, however, e-commerce is a "disruptive" innovation that is radically changing the way organisations do business. Where previous innovations have sought to minimise dependency on other firms, allowing the business to dictate production, marketing, and other business functions, e-commerce has forced organisations to reassess their boundaries and to focus their attention interorganisationally rather than organisationally. As SMEs confront an environment that is increasingly complex, technologically uncertain, and globally focused, there is a growing need to be flexible and pro-active in business dealings. An e-commerce business strategy may seem to be the ideal solution to this. But how well are SMEs equipped to implement e-commerce, what kinds of benefits can they expect, and what are the problems they are likely to face? These are questions to which we have only partial answers. The study presented in this book aims to add new information to this body of knowledge so that government organizations can promote e-commerce uptake by SMEs more effectively, particularly in regional areas, which are located outside major metropolitan cities and do not have the same infrastructure and resources available in highly urbanized areas.

This chapter will set the context for the study described in this book by presenting an overview of the relevant literature about SMEs and e-commerce. It should be noted that existing knowledge about e-commerce adoption by SMEs in the traditionally disadvantaged, regional areas is limited. Most of the literature presented here pertains to SMEs in metropolitan areas where access to IT infrastructure and resources is readily available. These findings by previous studies, therefore, represent the backdrop for our study and our aim is to add to the findings and extend the knowledge about e-commerce adoption to SMEs located in regional areas.

The chapter will begin with an examination of the nature of SMEs and an outline of the business characteristics that are unique to this sector. An overview of regional areas will then be given in order to provide an insight into the issues that affect these areas. This will be followed by a discussion about general IT adoption in SMEs in order to identify the broader adoption issues. The final part of this chapter will focus on e-commerce technology and e-commerce adoption issues in SMEs.

# The Nature of SMEs

The nature of SMEs can be understood from the perspectives of how they are formally defined and the characteristics that are unique to this sector.

## Defining an SME

There are a number of definitions of what constitutes an SME. Some of these definitions are based on quantitative measures, while others employ a qualitative approach. Meredith (1994) suggests that any definition of an SME must include a quantitative component that takes into account staff levels, turnover, and assets together with financial and non-financial measurements, but that the description must also include a qualitative component that reflects how the business is organised and how it operates.

The lack of a formal means of defining an SME has lead to diverse approaches by governments and other organisations in different countries. In Australia in the 1960s, the federal government commissioned a report from a committee known as the Wiltshire Committee. This report suggested a flexible definition of an SME as (Meredith, 1994, p. 31) "one in which one or two persons are required to make all of the critical decisions (such as finance, accounting, personnel, inventory, production, servicing, marketing, and selling decisions) without the aid of internal (employed) specialists and with owners only having specific knowledge in one or two functional areas of management." The Wiltshire Committee concluded that this definition could normally be expected to apply to the majority of enterprises in Australia with fewer than 100 employees. This recommendation has remained in use to the present day with the Australian Bureau of Statistics (ABS) defining a small business as an enterprise employing up to 99 people. A medium enterprise employs between 100 and 199 individuals and organisations with more than 200 employees are considered large businesses. The ABS definition has become the de-facto definition of SMEs in Australia. In 2001, more than 1.2 million organisations fell into this category according to the ABS.

The United States bases its definition on the position of the organisation within the overall marketplace. According to the United States Small Business Administration (SBA), Section 3 of the Small Business Act of 1953 defines an SME as "one which is independently owned and operated and which is not dominant in its field of operation." The SBA defines different size standards for each industry in the USA. For example, in manufacturing the standard is 500 employees, while the standard for the services industry is defined in terms of annual receipts (US$6 million in this instance).

By comparison, the United Kingdom took a similar approach to Australia and rather than defining SMEs by industry, a common standard of having fewer than 50 employees and not being a subsidiary of any other company was laid out in the UK Companies Act (1989) to define a small business. The UK definition is in agreement with the European Commission's definition of less than 50 employees (Europa, 2006). More than 99% of all businesses in Sweden are classified as small to medium enterprises (SMEs), which means they employ less than 250 people. Of those, 94% are micro businesses with less than 10 employees (MIEC, 2003).

Owing to these differences across countries, researchers have applied diverse SME definitions in their own studies, which have implications for cross-study comparisons. A study of Canadian SMEs by Montazemi (1988) based its definition on the number of employees, this being in accordance with the Canadian Small Business Guide. Other studies (for example Bradbard, Norris, & Kahai, 1990; Chen, 1993) have based their studies on the UK Companies Act.

There has been a tendency for researchers to simply utilise a mailing list of SMEs supplied by a government agency such as a local Chamber of Commerce, thus making decisions about the definitions of an SME the responsibility of government agencies, rather than the researcher. Examples of this approach can be seen in studies by Pendegraft, Morris, and Savage (1987) and DeLone (1988). However, it is not simply the number of employees that sets apart an SME from a larger organisation. SMEs have their own unique characteristics.

## Unique Characteristics of SMEs

Not only has the definition of SMEs been the subject of both government and academic debate, the special circumstances of the SME sector has been the topic of investigation by both government and academic researchers. Perhaps most important in the ongoing discussion of SMEs is the view, best summarised by Westhead and Storey (1996) that:

*... the small firm is not a scaled down version of a large firm. In short, theories relating to SMEs must consider the motivations, constraints and uncertainties facing smaller firms and recognise that these differ from those facing large firms.* (Westhead et al., 1996, p. 18)

Indeed, there are many factors influencing enterprise scale including economies of scale, transaction costs, and market structure. This apparent inappropriateness of applying large firm concepts to small organisations presents the researcher with the critical question: just how do small firms differ from their larger counterparts?

Brigham and Smith (1967) found that SMEs tended to be more risky than their larger counterparts. This view was supported in later studies (DeLone, 1988; Walker, 1975) and is still in evidence today with high failure rates in the SME sector. Cochran (1981) agreed that SMEs tended to be subject to higher failure rates while Rotch (1987) suggested that they maintained inadequate records of transactions. Welsh and White (1981), in a comparison of SMEs with their larger counterparts, found that they suffered from a lack of trained staff and had a short-range management perspective. They termed these traits "resource poverty" and suggested that their net effect was to magnify the effect of environmental impact, particularly when information systems were involved.

These early suggestions have been supported by more recent studies that have found most SMEs lack technical expertise (Barry & Milner, 2002) and adequate capital to undertake technical enhancements (Gaskill, Van Auken, & Kim, 1993; Raymond, 2001), and also suffer from inadequate organisational planning (Miller & Besser, 2000; Tetteh & Burn, 2001). Many small organisations also differ from their larger counterparts in the extent of the product/service range available to customer (Reynolds, Savage, & Williams, 1994).

A number of recent studies (Bunker & MacGregor, 2000; Murphy, 1996; Reynolds et al., 1994) have examined the differences in management style between large and small businesses. These studies have shown that among other characteristics, SMEs tend to have a smaller management team (often one or two individuals), they are strongly influenced by the owner and the owner's personal idiosyncrasies, they have little control over their environment (this is supported by the studies of Westhead et al. (1996) and Hill & Stewart (2000)), and they have a strong desire to remain independent (this is supported by the findings of Dennis (2000) and Drakopoulou-Dodd, Jack, & Anderson (2002)).

Based on our review of the literature, a summary of the features unique to SMEs was derived (Table 1). An analysis of the features revealed that they could be classified as being internal or external to the business. Internal features include management, decision-making, and planning processes, and the acquisition of resources, while external features are related to the market (products/services and customers) and the external environment (risk taking and uncertainty). These features have significant implications for an SME's ability, and indeed, desire to adopt new technology (including e-commerce).

Perhaps central to the characteristics distinguishing SMEs from their larger counterparts are the views of Westhead et al. (1996) and Hill et al. (2000) who suggest that uncertainty is the key difference between small and large businesses. They suggest that while "internal" uncertainty is more a characteristic of large business, it is "external" uncertainty that characterises smaller organisations.

While some of this external uncertainty may be attributable to those factors termed external features (see Table 1), Hill et al. (2000) suggest that the major reason for external

*Table 1. Features unique to SMEs*

| Features Unique to SMEs | Reported By | |
|---|---|---|
| **Features Related to Management, Decision Making, and Planning Processes** | | |
| SMEs have small and centralised management with a short range perspective. | Markland (1974) <br> Reynolds et al. (1994) <br> Bunker et al. (2000) <br> Welsh et al. (1981) | |
| SMEs have poor management skills. | Blili & Raymond (1993) | |
| SMEs exhibit a strong desire for independence and avoid business ventures, which impinge on their independence. | Dennis (2000) <br> Reynolds et al. (1994) | |
| SME owners often withhold information from colleagues. | Dennis (2000) | |
| The decision making process in SMEs is intuitive, rather than based on detailed planning and exhaustive study. | Reynolds et al. (1994) <br> Bunker et al. (2000) | |
| The SME owner(s) has/have a strong influence in the decision making process. | Reynolds et al. (1994) <br> Murphy (1996) <br> Bunker et al. (2000) | |
| Intrusion of family values and concerns in decision making processes. | Dennis (2000) <br> Bunker et al. (2000) <br> Reynolds et al. (1994) | INTERNAL FEATURES |
| SMEs have informal and inadequate planning and record keeping processes. | Reynolds et al. (1994) <br> Tetteh et al. (2001) <br> Miller et al. (2000) <br> Markland (1974) | |
| SMEs are more intent on improving day-to-day procedures. | MacGregor, Bunker, & Waugh (1998) | |
| **Features Related to Resource Acquisition** | | |
| SMEs face difficulties obtaining finance and other resources, and as a result have fewer resources. | Cragg & King (1993) <br> Welsh et al. (1981) <br> Gaskill & Gibbs (1994) <br> Reynolds et al. (1994) <br> Blili et al. (1993) | |
| SMEs are more reluctant to spend on information technology and therefore have limited use of technology. | Walczuch, Van Braven, & Lundgren (2000) <br> Dennis (2000) <br> MacGregor & Bunker (1996) <br> Poon & Swatman (1997) <br> Abell & Lim (1996) <br> Brigham et al. (1967) | |

*continued on following page*

*Table 1. Continued*

| Features Unique to SMEs | Reported By | |
|---|---|---|
| SMEs have a lack of technical knowledge and specialist staff and provide little IT training for staff. | Martin & Matlay (2001) <br> Cragg et al. (1993) <br> Bunker et al. (2000) <br> Reynolds et al. (1994) <br> Welsh et al. (1981) <br> Blili et al. (1993) | INTERNAL FEATURES |
| **Features Related to Products/Services and Markets** | | |
| SMEs have a narrow product/service range. | Bunker et al. (2000) <br> Reynolds et al. (1994) | EXTERNAL FEATURES |
| SMEs have a limited share of the market (often confined towards a niche market) and therefore heavily rely on few customers. | Hadjimonolis (1999) <br> Lawrence (1997) <br> Quayle (2002) <br> Reynolds et al. (1994) | |
| SMEs are product oriented, while large businesses are more customer oriented. | Reynolds et al. (1994) <br> Bunker et al. (2000) <br> MacGregor et al. (1998) | |
| SMEs are not interested in large shares of the market. | Reynolds et al. (1994) <br> MacGregor et al. (1998) | |
| SMEs are unable to compete with their larger counterparts. | Lawrence (1997) | |
| **Features Related to Risk Taking and Dealing with Uncertainty** | | |
| SMEs have lower control over their external environment than larger businesses and therefore face more uncertainty. | Westhead et al. (1996) <br> Hill et al. (2000) | |
| SMEs face more risks than large businesses because the failure rates of SMEs are higher. | Brigham et al. (1967) <br> DeLone (1988) <br> Cochran (1981) | |
| SMEs are more reluctant to take risks | Walczuch et al. (2000) <br> Dennis (2000) | |

uncertainty is the lack of influence over the market environment. In order to cope with the changing market place, SMEs are often obliged to operate in a regime that is far more short term. While this short term strategy may provide the advantage of flexibility of response to external changes, Hill et al. (2000) suggest that very often it is "like plate spinning, waiting to see which one comes down first" (p. 107). Most of the characteristics summarised in Table 1 can be viewed in this light—as opportunities or constraints. More often than not, they are constraints that limit the expansion and growth of SMEs. SMEs in regional areas are particularly susceptible to these types of constraints.

# SMEs in Regional Areas

SMEs located in regional areas are affected by circumstances inherent to their location. Regional areas are defined as geographical areas located outside metropolitan centres and major cities. Regional areas can be classified into inner and outer regions, remote and very remote areas (ABS, 2001). Determining the classification of a region is usually based on a formula, which primarily relies on the measures of proximity to services in terms of physical distance and population size. Rather than remote and rural areas (which are sparsely populated), the research presented in this chapter focuses on inner and outer regional areas (which are more urbanised than rural areas).

Regional areas are of particular interest to governments because they are characterised by high unemployment rates (Larsson, Hedelin, & Gärling, 2003), a shortage of skilled people, limited access to resources, and a lack of infrastructure (Keniry, Blums, Notter, Radford, & Thomson, 2003). Yet, at the same time, businesses located in regional areas often play a major role in developing these areas. This potential has not gone unnoticed by government organisations. The European Union views SMEs as a catalyst for regional development (Europa, 2006). In 2001, the Swedish Parliament passed legislation that resulted in the creation of Regional Development Councils (Johansson, 2003). The Councils have a mandate to promote a positive business climate and sustainable growth in their respective regions. SMEs have been earmarked as playing an important role in promoting growth because they are seen as a key source of jobs and employment prospects (Keniry et al., 2003; Larsson et al., 2003).

To encourage growth and development in regional areas, government organisations have been heavily promoting the adoption of information and communication technology by SMEs in these areas. This has primarily been undertaken through funding projects that assist SMEs with implementing Internet and e-commerce technologies. These projects have ranged from simple Internet adoption to the establishment of virtual business networks (Damanpour, 2001; Jeffcoate, Chappell, & Feindt, 2002; Papazafeiropoulou, Pouloudi, & Doukidis, 2002).

In Sweden, the Swedish Business Development Agency (NUTEK) runs a national program known as IT.SME, which provides skills training in ICT for SMEs. The program targets regional SMEs in particular (MIEC, 2003). The agency also runs a similar program that concentrates on increasing the use of ICT in SMEs located in regional areas to strengthen their competitiveness on the global market. Specifically on the e-commerce front, the Swedish Alliance for Electronic Business set an objective of having 80% of SMEs starting to use e-commerce tools by the end of 2004 (MIEC, 2003). (The results from our research indicate that they are likely to have met this target.)

In Australia, the initiatives have been just as forthcoming. In 2002, the Federal Government announced a $6.5 million scheme over two years to accelerate the uptake of e-commerce in SMEs (NOIE, 2002). Similarly, the information technology online (ITOL) funding program offered up to $200,000 to support the adoption of collaborative e-business by SMEs.

However, unlike their "city cousins" and despite government promises of "telecommunication enhanced communities," there has been a resistance by many regional SMEs to adopt and use e-commerce (Martin et al., 2001a). A number of barriers have been noted in the literature that are inherent to regional areas. These include poor cabling and frequent line outages compared to major cities (Wilde, Swatman, & Castleman, 2000), deterioration of long established client links and business practices (Wilde & Swatman, 2001), and geographic separation from vital infrastructure (Martin, Halstead, & Taylor, 2001b). These differences between metropolitan and regional SMEs mean that they are disadvantaged by any application of a "homogeneous approach" to e-commerce, which fails to take these inherent limitations into account.

Before we examine e-commerce adoption in SMEs, it is important to examine how these organisations acquired pre e-commerce technology in order to provide a view of how technology is historically introduced into an SME organisation.

# Pre E-Commerce Acquisition of IT by SMEs

E-commerce is not just another mechanism to sustain and enhance existing business practices. It is a paradigm shift that is radically changing traditional ways of doing business. This premise is well supported in the literature (Fuller, 2000; Kendall & Kendall, 2001; Kuljis, Macredie, & Paul, 1998). Lee (2001), who describes e-commerce as a "disruptive technology," suggests that the focus has shifted from lean manufacturing and total quality management, within the organisation, to synthesis and distribution of information outside the organisation. He terms the shift in focus as moving from "economics of scarcity" to "economics of abundance."

The premise is important for several reasons. Firstly, e-commerce has altered the day-to-day practices of many businesses (Fuller, 2000). According to Lee (2001), where once a company used raw materials, transformed those raw materials into products, displayed those products, and ultimately sold those products to customers, with e-commerce this has changed. Now, the raw materials are information about the customer, the transformation is the synthesis and packaging of this information, the products are designed, very often, by the customer and are sold with information services to entice future interaction.

Secondly, the focus of technology acquisition has altered from production within the organization to marketing between organizations. Indeed, Treacy and Wiersema (1997) have suggested that e-commerce transforms organizations that were "geared towards" production excellence into organizations "geared towards" customer intimacy.

Thirdly, in a pre e-commerce environment, the benefits or disadvantages of technology were planned, tangible, and controllable by the organization. With e-commerce, many of the benefits and disadvantages have become less tangible and far more difficult to plan for and manage. Added to this is the fact that many of the benefits, as well as the disadvantages, are unique to e-commerce. Some of the benefits are externally sourced. For example, new customers and markets (Quayle, 2002; Raymond, 2001; Ritchie & Brindley, 2001; Vescovi, 2000), improved marketing techniques (Sparkes & Thomas, 2001), and improved relations with business partners (Poon et al., 1997) would not have been the typical benefits derived from internal (back room) IT support systems.

Perhaps the most important reason for distinguishing e-commerce from other technologies is the notion that the adoption and use of e-commerce cannot be based on the same criteria as was used for other technology adoption. As already stated, a number of authors suggest that to base e-commerce adoption and use on criteria used in other technology adoption produces a naïve, over-simplistic, linear model, whose focus is organizationally based rather than inter-organisationally directed (Culkin & Smith, 2000; Martin et al., 2001a).

In line with the views of Faia-Correia, Patriotta, Brigham, and Corbett (1999), who suggest that technology shapes and is shaped by the organization, it is appropriate to consider the organizational context prior to the advent of e-commerce, and in turn, the acquisition and use of technology in that context.

Prior to the introduction of e-commerce, most organizations were essentially hierarchical in nature. They exhibited a unity of purpose and were primarily concerned with extending control over resources considered essential to the quality of their products. Communications within such a structure was essentially uni-dimensional (i.e., information flowed in a single direction only), and technology introduced into the business was normally focused on production. As such, the acquisition of technology could be evaluated against tangible inputs and outputs. Thus, while technology might have re-shaped the organisation, these changes were predictable and planned, reinforcing rather than disrupting organisational boundaries.

Organizations relied primarily on a product base that was supported by stand-alone technology (Lee, 2001). The products themselves were tangible, requiring physical inputs and processes, which could be clearly evaluated. This meant that the introduction of technology into these processes could be evaluated and directed toward aggregated financial effects, and outcomes were related to the revenue goals of the entire organization (Dignum, 2002). Technology was designed to embody existing organisational values and practices, power relationships, and conventions. As such, strategies were fixed and controllable (Treacy et al., 1997). While technology supported these strategies and the products offered by the organisation, it was bounded by the nature of those same products. Its role was simply to increase efficiency within the boundaries of the products at a procedural level (Lee, 2001).

Organizations were also able to utilise technology to enforce the use of specific products and product boundaries. This was achievable by limiting the number and types of products and by placing the boundaries within the operational level of the organisation. Factors that might be termed "informal social ties" (customers, competitors, environmental trends) were "shadows" to the formal organisation. The focus, instead, was on computerising procedures to achieve low-level operational competence, and the decision to invest in computer technology was primarily concerned with improvements in efficiency and effectiveness. Investment decisions were carried out in terms of strict boundaries and were judged on rigid internal perspectives. An organisation considering the adoption of technology examined the return on investment (ROI) of such technology where the ROI was defined within a pre-stated set of strategic guidelines. Willcocks, Graeser, & Lester et al. (1998) consider that, under such organisational models, the metrics used in the acquisition of computer technology remained static and were still able to give a valid picture of organisational requirements.

Many of the studies carried out on the adoption of computer technology by SMEs attempted to portray differences between these organisations and their larger counterparts. These studies are summarized in Table 2.

Not only are many of the processes of adoption and use of pre e-commerce IT different for SMEs, but many of the criteria used by SMEs in the decision-making process about IT differ from larger businesses.

*Table 2. Summary of IT adoption and use in SMEs*

| IT adoption issues in SMEs | Reported By |
|---|---|
| Decision making on IT adoption differs from those made by large businesses. | Bunker et al. (2000) |
| IT decisions are not based on detailed planning. | Bunker et al. (2000)<br>Tetteh et al. (2001) |
| IT decisions are usually made by the owner. | Bunker et al. (2000) |
| SMEs are more reluctant to spend on technology. | Walczuch et al. (2000)<br>Dennis (2000) |
| SMEs lack technical staff and IT expertise. | Martin et al. (2001a)<br>Bunker et al. (2000)<br>Neergaard (1992) |
| Limited use of technology. | MacGregor et al. (1996)<br>Poon et al. (1997)<br>Abell et al. (1996) |
| Little IT training. | Bunker et al. (2000)<br>MacGregor & Cocks (1994)<br>Wood & Nosek (1994) |
| IT more often used for better record keeping. | Fink & Tjarka (1994)<br>Neergaard (1992)<br>MacGregor et al. (1996) |
| Vendors are surrogates for an IT department. | Yap, Soh, & Raman (1992)<br>MacGregor et al. (1996)<br>Wood et al. (1994) |
| Informal and inadequate IT planning. | Reynolds et al. (1994)<br>Tetteh et al. (2001)<br>Miller et al. (2000) |
| User information satisfaction is a surrogate for IS success. | Yap et al. (1992)<br>McDoniel, Palko, & Cronan (1993)<br>Bailey & Pearson (1983)<br>Ives, Olsen, & Baroudi (1983)<br>Doukidis, Smithson, & Naoum (1992)<br>Igbaria (1993) |
| User attitudes impact on their behaviour with new systems. | Ginzberg (1981)<br>Desanctis (1983)<br>Amoaka-Gyampah & White (1993)<br>MacGregor et al. (1996) |
| Management involvement is essential to IT success. | Bergeron, Rivard, & De Serre (1990)<br>Yap et al. (1992)<br>Black & Porter (2000) |

# IT Adoption Criteria

A combined study of Danish, Irish, and Greek SMEs carried out in the early 1990s by Neergaard (1992) concluded that there were four main reasons for the acquisition of IT. These were increased productivity, streamlining work procedures, better client service, and better record keeping. Fink et al. (1994) in a study of Australian executives collapsed two of the categories (streamlining work procedures and better client services) but provided similar reasons to Neergaard for IT acquisition. They described their three reasons for acquisition as "doing the right thing," "doing things right," and "improving the bottom line." Figure 1 provides a mapping of the two sets of categories.

Fink et al. (1994) concluded that while larger businesses were demonstrating a shift from "doing things right" to "doing the right thing" this shift was less visible in SMEs. This conclusion is supported by a number of other studies (see Amer & Bain, 1990; Chen, 1993; MacGregor et al., 1996).

Several explanations were provided to explain SMEs' continued focus on the operational use of technology. MacGregor et al. (1996), in line with the findings of Welsh et al. (1981), suggested that most SMEs tended to have a short-range management perspective and appeared more concerned with improving the day-to-day internal nature of the business than with seeking new markets or customers. They added that control mechanisms were often informal, were centralised, and were coupled with reluctance, by most SMEs, to take risks. This reduced the need for long-term decision-making. Added to this was a management that, more often than not, was product oriented rather than customer oriented (Bunker et al., 2000; MacGregor et al., 1998; Reynolds et al., 1994).

It is interesting to note that Fink et al. (1994) posit a gradual movement from "doing things right" to "doing the right thing" in larger businesses. MacGregor et al. (1996) found that SMEs that had based their IT acquisition criteria on "doing the right thing" or "improving the bottom line" reported significantly less success than those that based their acquisition criteria on "doing things right." Although the reasons for introducing technology into the organisation were diverse, the environment into which the technology was being introduce was also equally diverse.

*Figure 1. IT adoption criteria from two studies (Source: Fink et al., 1994; Neergaard, 1992)*

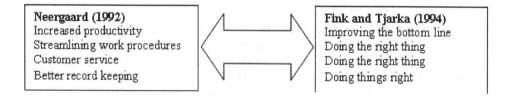

# The Diversity of the SME Sector

Martin et al. (2001a) suggest that many initiatives aimed at promoting IT acquisition and use in SMEs fall into the trap of viewing the sector as a homogeneous group that is able to take a well ordered, sequential approach to technology adoption. They continue by suggesting that:

*the targets and, in particular, the way in which they are defined, point towards a 'generalist' view of small business operation that largely fails to differentiate between businesses of varying business sizes, ethnic origin, stages of adoption, etc.* (Martin et al., 2001a, p. 400)

There are a number of studies in the literature that point to a variety of business characteristics affecting the adoption and use of IT in SMEs. Indeed, several researchers (Hyland & Matlay, 1997; Poon et al., 1997) stress that the differing effects of some of these business characteristics often makes it impossible to generalise findings across the entire SME community. Business characteristics include the size of the organisation, its location, age, the sector it operates in, market focus, level of IT skill, and others, which are discussed subsequently.

Several studies (Culkin et al., 2000; Fallon & Moran 2000; Lal, 2002; Matlay, 2000; Matlay & Fletcher, 2000; Riquelme, 2002) have found that business size (in terms of the number of employees as well as turnover) is significantly associated with the adoption of IT. Culkin et al. (2000) suggest that larger SMEs are by nature inherently more complex and thus decisions concerning IT acquisition require more detailed examinations of the impact of IT. These organisations tend to adopt more sophisticated systems and very often are more likely to "computerise" far more of their business than smaller ones. Matlay et al. (2000) noted that these findings did not appear to be localised or country-specific.

Recent studies (Martin et al., 2001b) have examined SMEs in terms of location. These studies suggest that those SMEs in rural or regional locations often report lower levels of success with IT adoption when compared to those in capital cities or large economic centres. A number of explanations have been put forward, including a heavier reliance on vendors in regional areas than in larger centres and the failure of vendor groups to fully understand the nature of the business they are servicing.

Kai-Uwe Brock (2000), in a study of SME adoption of IT, suggests that another important business characteristic appears to be business age. Businesses that have a long-established set of work practices will very often avoid any form of IT intervention that threatens to disrupt those long-held practices.

Studies by Dibb (1997), MacGregor and Bunker (1999), Meikle and Willis (2002), and MacGregor et al. (2002) have found that business sector is significantly associated with the level and type of IT use in SMEs. These studies found that the manufacturing and retail sectors tended to adopt IT far more quickly than professional or service related businesses. Unlike the studies relating to business size, the business sector studies cannot be considered "global." For example, while Australian studies (MacGregor et al., 1999; MacGregor et al., 2002) found a higher uptake of IT in the manufacturing and retail sectors, Riquelme (2002), in a study of adoption of technology in China found that service related businesses were adopting IT at the same rate as retail groups.

Other studies (Blackburn & Athayde, 2000; Donckels & Lambrecht, 1997; Poon et al., 1997) have examined the impact of internationalisation on SMEs in their adoption of IT. While all studies have been prescriptive, enunciating the steps to be taken in order to utilise technology in an international market each identifies market focus as being a business characteristic associated with the level and depth of IT adoption and use.

Another business characteristic that appears to be significantly associated with IT adoption and use is the level of IT expertise. Studies in Singapore (Yap et al., 1992; Thong et al., 1996) and Australia (MacGregor et al., 1996; MacGregor et al., 1998) have shown that the level of IT skill within the SME community is a strong determinant of the type of IT acquired as well as the ongoing success with that IT.

Thus, it can be argued that a number of business characteristics, including business size, business age, business sector, market focus, and level of IT expertise are associated with adoption and use of IT in SMEs. Does this hold equally true for e-commerce? Although e-commerce is a primarily a business strategy, it is also a technological innovation. There-fore, by extension, we can posit that e-commerce adoption will also be affected by certain characteristics of the business. Before we examine e-commerce adoption, it is appropriate that we consider the nature of e-commerce itself.

# Electronic Commerce

There are nearly as many definitions of e-commerce as there are contributions to the litera-ture. Turban, Lee, King, and Chung (2002) define e-commerce as:

*... an emerging concept that describes the process of buying, selling, or exchanging services and information via computer networks.* (Turban et al., 2002, p. 4)

Choi et al. (1997, cited in Turban et al., 2002) draw a distinction between what they term pure e-commerce and partial e-commerce. According to Choi et al., "pure e-commerce" has a digital product, a digital process, and a digital agent. All other interactions (including those that might have one or two of the three nominated by Choi et al. are termed "partial e-commerce." Raymond (2001) defines e-commerce as:

*... the functions of information exchange and commercial transaction support that operate on telecommunications networks linking business partners (typically customers and sup-pliers).* (Raymond, 2001, p. 411)

Damanpour (2001), by comparison, defines e-commerce as:

*... any "net" business activity that transforms internal and external relationships to cre-ate value and exploit market opportunities driven by new rules of the connected economy.* (Damanpour, 2001, p. 18)

For the purposes of this study, which examines changes to the organisation, brought about by involvement in e-commerce, the definition provided by Damanpour is used. While it may be argued that other definitions do not preclude organisational transformation, only the definition of Damanpour "demands" those transformations and it is consistent with the concept in the literature, generally. It is these organisational changes, rather than the definition, that needs to be addressed.

The roots of e-commerce can be found in electronic data interchange (EDI). EDI is a set of standards that allowed businesses to connect electronically in order to exchange information about customers, place orders, submit invoices, and undertake other business transactions. Traditional EDI systems were implemented through private, third-party managed networks, which were known as "value-added networks." EDI enabled organisations to handle different types of procurement transactions with ease and through standardised formats, which were introduced in the early 1980s when the ASC X 12 standard, was established.

With the advent of the Internet and Web protocols, traditional EDI systems were replaced with Internet-based EDI systems (Turban et al., 2006) and electronic commerce systems. This was particularly beneficial for SMEs, which did not usually have the resources to implement value-added networks and use EDI. Being able to conduct business transactions securely on a public network created new opportunities for SMEs to compete. The growth of e-commerce was fuelled by the introduction of high-speed ADSL connections, as more and more customers joined the Internet revolution.

Although relatively new in comparison with other business models and strategies, e-commerce is a mature technology that has been used successfully by both large and small organisations. There are several different types of e-commerce and a variety of e-commerce business models, however, a discussion of these is beyond the scope of this book. The reader is referred to the following sources of information for a detailed description of e-commerce: Turban et al. (2006), Kalakota & Whinston (1997), Plant (2000), Laudon and Traver (2006). The focus in this book is on the organisational issues related to e-commerce adoption by SMEs. Rather than replicating general e-commerce concepts and issues, which are readily available in excellent books such as the ones previously listed, we present the results of an empirical study, which examined e-commerce adoption in regional SMEs.

# E-Commerce and SMEs

The use of e-commerce by SMEs is not a recent phenomenon. Typically regarded as innovators, SMEs have been known to adopt new technologies as soon as they are available. Studies carried out at the onset of e-commerce (Acs, Morck, Shaver, & Yeung, 1997; Auger & Gallaugher, 1997; Gessin, 1996; McRea, 1996; Murphy, 1996; Nooteboom, 1994) predicted that, since SMEs had always operated in an externally uncertain environment, they were more likely to benefit from e-commerce. Other authors, while agreeing in principle with this viewpoint, did so with a degree of caution. Hutt and Speh (1998) felt that most areas of the SME sector, with the exception of those organisations involved in the industrial market, would benefit from e-commerce. They suggest that the industrial SMEs already concentrated on an established base of customers and product offerings. Swartz and Iacobucci (2000), by contrast, felt that the service industries would benefit far more than other areas of the SME community.

Regardless of the industry, however, a number of benefits were predicted for SMEs, which took the plunge and adopted e-commerce. These included:

- A global presence presenting customers with a global choice (Barry et al., 2002)
- Improved competitiveness (Auger et al., 1997)
- Mass customisation and "customerisation," presenting customers with personalised products and services (Fuller, 2000)
- Shortening of supply chains, providing rapid response to customer needs (Barry et al., 2002)

Recent studies have found that these predictions have not necessarily eventuated and that it has been the larger businesses that have been more active with respect to e-commerce (see Barry et al., 2002; Riquelme, 2002; Roberts & Wood, 2002). A number of reasons have been put forward including poor security, high costs, and lack of requisite skills. However, some researchers have begun to examine how decisions concerning IT adoption and use are made in the SME sector.

As already stated, there have been many governmental as well as privately funded projects attempting to further the cause of adoption of e-commerce by SMEs. One of the most well known initiatives is the so called "adoption ladder" that was put forward by the Department of Trade and Industry (DTI) in the UK in the early 2000s. DTI's aim was to have one million SMEs trading online by 2002 in the UK. To achieve this, SMEs would go through a six-stage process toward full e-commerce, starting with (1) messaging or e-mail, through (2) online marketing, (3) ordering, and (4) payments, followed by (5) online sales support and finally, a full-fledged (6) e-commerce strategy. This linear progression, however, fails to take into account the very nature of doing business online. It is not possible to conduct online transactions such as ordering and payments without some effect on other organizational systems. Any initiative, which seeks to promote e-commerce adoption, must factor in a complete organizational change process, rather than a gradual implementation of technical components that will eventually become an e-commerce system.

Many of these types of projects relied on pre e-commerce criteria and focused on internal systems within the SME rather than inter-organisational interaction (Fallon et al., 2000; Martin et al., 2001a; Poon et al., 1997). Not only are these models based on inappropriate or oversimplified criteria (Kai-Uwe Brock, 2000), but they recommend the adoption of e-commerce prior to any form of organisational change to render the SME "e-commerce ready." Since e-commerce brings with it changes in communication (Chellappa, Barua, & Whinston, 1996), business practices (Henning, 1998), market structure, and approaches to marketing (Giaglis, Klein, & O'Keefe, 1999), as well as changes in day-to-day activities (Doukidis et al., 1998), a major organizational change is implicit in the adoption of e-commerce. This change, however, is problematic in the SME sector as many businesses have no overall plan and, for the most part, fail to understand the need for competitive strategies (Jeffcoate et al., 2002).

For SMEs, the changes associated with e-commerce have produced both positive and negative effects. Studies by Raymond (2001) and Ritchie et al. (2000) found that, while e-commerce adoption has eroded trading barriers for SMEs, this has often come at the price of altering or eliminating commercial relationships and exposing the business to external risks. Lawrence (1997), Tetteh et al. (2001), and Lee (2001) contend that e-commerce adoption fundamentally alters the internal procedures within SMEs. For those who have developed an organisation-wide strategy (in anticipation of e-commerce), these changes can lead to an increase in efficiency in the business for those who have not, this can reduce the flexibility of the business (Tetteh et al. 2001) and often lead to a duplication of the work effort (MacGregor et al., 1998).

The introduction of e-commerce into an SME is also affected by the SME itself—its size, sector, market focus, and other characteristics. Fallon et al. (2000) found significant links between the size of the SME and the level of Internet adoption. Matlay (2000) showed that the business sector was significantly associated with e-commerce adoption. Both studies showed that the same results were achievable despite varying geographic spread or market focus. These studies indicated that smaller businesses (fewer than 10 employees) were less likely to adopt e-commerce technology than larger SMEs. They also found that service organisations were more likely to adopt e-commerce than manufacturing or retail based SME's. Blackburn et al. (2000) identified not only size and sector but also the level of international marketing as a factor associated with adoption of e-commerce technology. Table 3 provides a summary of some of the research carried out in this area.

*Table 3. Business characteristics affecting the adoption of e-commerce by SMEs*

| Business Characteristics | Reported By |
| --- | --- |
| Business size (number of employees). | Hawkins, Winter, & Hunter (1995) |
| | Hawkins & Winter (1996) |
| | Hyland et al. (1997) |
| | Fallon et al. (2000) |
| | Blackburn et al. (2000) |
| | Matlay (2000) |
| Age of the business. | Kai-Uwe Brock (2000) |
| | MacGregor et al. (2002) |
| | Donckels et al. (1997) |
| Business sector. | Matlay (2000) |
| | MacGregor et al. (2002) |
| | Schindehutte & Morris (2001) |
| | BarNir & Smith (2002) |
| | Blackburn et al. (2000) |
| Market focus (local, national, international). | Blackburn et al. (2000) |
| | Schindehutte et al. (2001) |
| | BarNir et al. (2002) |
| Level of IT expertise/skill. | Tetteh et al. (2001) |
| | O'Donnell, Gilmore, Cummins, & Carson (2001) |

We will examine various aspects of e-commerce adoption in SMEs, including the reasons why organisations adopt e-commerce (criteria), the reasons they don't (barriers), the advantages that e-commerce brings (benefits), and the problems it creates (disadvantages) in grater detail in subsequent chapters. Our aim in this chapter was to situate our research study in the context of previous similar work done in the area and highlight the organisational issues stemming from e-commerce adoption. These will be revisited again at the end of the book when the findings from our research will be compared to previous studies and the implications of the results will be presented.

# Conclusion

By way of a conclusion, we will emphasise some of the key issues related to the successful adoption and use of e-commerce in SMEs that have been identified through previous research. Many of these points will appear self-evident, however they are often disregarded in an attempt to reach a wider range of customers and markets as quickly as possible. These include the following:

- The development of any form of e-commerce must be preceded by a full development of competitive strategies within the organisation (Straub & Klein, 2001).
- The goals of e-commerce must be clearly defined and must be progressive (Straub et al., 2001).
- Sales management must be counterbalanced by improvements to purchasing management (Calkins, Farello, & Shi, 2000).
- Organisations must develop and clearly state search prices, terms and agreements, return policies, etc. (Korper & Ellis, 2001).
- As most SMEs cannot engage in price matching with larger organisations, hybrid strategies, which incorporate price and product differentiation are crucial (Miller & Toulouse, 1986).
- Any development of an e-commerce site must include due attention to supply chain management and logistics (Karagozoglu & Lindell, 2004; Korper et al., 2001; Phan, 2003).
- Web sites must be designed with the customer in mind and must be continually user tested (Pavlou, 2003; Savin & Silberg, 2000; Schneider & Perry, 2000).

This book is concerned with e-commerce implementation in regional SMEs. To examine this process more closely, we will present empirical data about adoption drivers and barriers, as well as the benefits and disadvantages of using e-commerce. We have presented an overview of the literature in this chapter to set the context for this study and demonstrate that previous research has resulted in divergent and at times, inconclusive, findings. We attempt to fill some of the gaps that continue to exist in our knowledge about e-commerce adoption in SMEs and provide a clearer picture of e-commerce use in regional areas. The following chapter will describe how we set out to do this by describing the research methodology, before we begin elaborating our results in subsequent chapters.

# References

Abell, W., & Lim, L. (1996). Business use of the Internet in New Zealand: An exploratory study. In *Proceedings of AUSWeb 96*. Retrieved from http//www.scu.edu.au/sponsored/ausweb96

ABS. (2001). *Australian Bureau of Statistics*. Retrieved from www.abs.gov.au

Acs, Z. J., Morck, R., Shaver, J. M., & Yeung, B. (1997). The internationalisation of small and medium sized enterprises: A policy perspective. *Small Business Economics, 9*(1), 7-20.

Amer, T. S., & Bain, C. E. (1990, July). Making small business planning easier. *Journal of Accountancy, 170*, 53-60.

Amoaka-Gyampah, K., & White, K. B. (1993). User involvement and satisfaction an exploratory contingency model. *Information & Management, 25*(1), 1-10.

Auger, P., & Gallaugher, J. M. (1997). Factors affecting adoption of an Internet-based sales presence for small businesses. *The Information Society, 13*(1), 55-74.

Bailey, J. E., & Pearson, S. W. (1983). The development of a tool for measuring and analysing computer user satisfaction. *Management Science, 29*(5), 530-545.

BarNir, A., & Smith, K. A. (2002). Interfirm alliances in the small business: The role of social networks. *Journal of Small Business Management, 40*(3), 219-232.

Barry, H., & Milner, B. (2002). SME's and electronic commerce: A departure from the traditional prioritisation of training? *Journal of European Industrial Training, 25*(7), 316-326.

Bergeron, F., Rivard, S., & De Serre, L. (1990). Investigating the support role of the information centre. *MIS Quarterly, 14*(3), 246-260.

Black, J. S., & Porter, L. W. (2000). *Management: Meeting new challenges*. NJ: Prentice Hall.

Blackburn, R., & Athayde, R. (2000). Making the connection: The effectiveness of Internet training in small businesses. *Education and Training, 42*(4/5).

Blili, S., & Raymond, L. (1993). Threats and opportunities for small and medium-sized enterprises. *International Journal of Information Management, 13*, 439-448.

Bradbard, D. A., Norris, D. R., & Kahai, P. H. (1990). Computer security in small business: An empirical study. *Journal of Small Business Management, 28*(1), 9-19.

Brigham, E. F., & Smith, K. V. (1967). The cost of capital to the small firm. *The Engineering Economist, 13*(1), 1-26.

Bunker, D. J,. & MacGregor, R. C. (2000). Successful generation of information technology (IT) requirements for small/medium enterprises (SME's)—Cases from Regional Australia. In *Proceedings of SMEs in a Global Economy*, Wollongong, Australia (pp. 72-84).

Calkins, J. D., Farello, M. J., & Shi, C. S. (2000). From retailing to e-tailing. *The McKinsey Quarterly, 1*, 4-11.

Chellappa, R., Barua, A., & Whinston, A. (1996). Looking beyond internal corporate Web servers. In R. Kalakota & A. Whinston (Eds), *Readings in electronic commerce* (pp. 311-321). Reading: Addison Wesley.

Chen, J. C. (1993). The impact of microcomputers on small businesses: England 10 years later. *Journal of Small Business Management, 31*(3), 96-102.

Cochran, A. B. (1981). Small business mortality rates: A review of the literature. *Journal of Small Business Management, 19*(4), 50-59.

Cragg, P. B., & King, M. (1993). Small-firm computing: Motivators and inhibitors. *MIS Quarterly, 17*(1), 47-60.

Culkin, N., & Smith, D. (2000). An emotional business: A guide to understanding the motivations of small business decision takers. *Qualitative Market Research: An International Journal, 3*(3), 145-157.

Damanpour, F. (2001). E-business e-commerce evolution: Perspective and strategy. *Managerial Finance, 27*(7), 16-33.

DeLone, W. H. (1988). Determinants for success for computer U.S.A.ge in small business. *MIS Quarterly, 12*(1), 51-61.

Dennis, C. (2000). Networking for marketing advantage. *Management Decision. 38*(4), 287-292.

Desanctis, G. (1983). Expectancy theory as an explanation of voluntary use of a decision support system. *Psychological Reports, 52*, 247-260.

Dibb, S. (1997). How marketing planning builds internal networks. *Long Range Planning, 30*(1), 53-64.

Dignum, F. (2002). E-commerce in production: Some experiences. *Integrated Manufacturing Systems, 13*(5), 283-294.

Donckels, R., & Lambrecht, J. (1997). The network position of small businesses: An explanatory model. *Journal of Small Business Management, 35*(2), 13-28.

Doukidis, G., Poulymenakou, A., Terpsidis, I., Themisticleous, M., & Miliotis, P. (1998). *The impact of the development of electronic commerce on the employment situation in European Commerce.* Athens University of Economics and Business.

Doukidis, G. I., Smithson, S., & Naoum, G. (1992). Information systems management in Greece: Issues and perceptions. *Journal of Strategic Information Systems, 1*, 139-148.

Drakopoulou-Dodd, S., Jack, S., & Anderson, A. R. (2002). Scottish entrepreneurial networks in the international context. *International Small Business Journal, 20*(2), 213-219.

Europa (2006). *SME definition.* Retrieved from http://europa.eu.int/comm/enterprise/ enterprise_policy/sme_definition/index_en.htm

Faia-Correia, L., Patriotta, G., Brigham, M., & Corbett, J. M. (1999). Making sense of telebanking information systems: The role of organisational backup. *Journal of Strategic Information Systems, 8*, 143-156.

Fallon, M., & Moran, P. (2000). Information communications technology (ICT) and manufacturing SMEs. In *Proceedings of the 2000 Small Business and Enterprise Development Conference*, University of Manchester (pp. 100-109).

Fink, D., & Tjarka, F. (1994). Information systems contribution to business performance: A study of information systems executives' attitudes. *Australian Journal of Information Systems*, *2*(1), 29-38.

Fuller, T. (2000). The small business guide to the Internet: A practical approach to going online. *International Small Business Journal*, *19*(1), 105-107.

Gaskill, L. R., & Gibbs, R. M. (1994). Going away to college and wider urban job opportunities take highly educated youth away for rural areas. *Rural Development Perspectives*, *10*(3), 35-44.

Gaskill, L. R., Van Auken, H. E., & Kim, H. (1993). The impact of operational planning on small business retail performance. *Journal of Small Business Strategy*, *5*(1), 21-35.

Gessin, J. (1996, January-February). Impact of electronic commerce on small and medium sized enterprises. *Management*, 11-12.

Giaglis, G. M., Klein, S., & O'Keefe, R. M. (1999). Disintermediation, reintermediation, or cybermediation? The future of intermediaries in electronic marketplaces. In *Proceedings of the 12th Bled Electronic Commerce Conference on Global Networked Organizations*, Bled Slovenia (pp. 389-407).

Ginzberg, M. J. (1981). Key recurrent issues in MIS implementation program. *MIS Quarterly, 5*(2), 47-59.

Hadjimonolis, A. (1999). Barriers to innovation for SMEs in a small less developed country (Cyprus). *Technovation*, *19*(9), 561-570.

Hawkins, P., & Winter, J. (1996). The self reliant graduate and the SME. *Education and Training*, *38*(4), 3-9.

Hawkins, P., Winter, J., & Hunter, J. (1995). *Skills for graduates in the 21st Century*. Report Commissioned from the Whiteway Research, University of Cambridge, Association of Graduate Recruiters, Cambridge.

Henning, K. (1998). *The digital enterprise. How digitisation is redefining business.* New York: Random House Business Books.

Hill, R., & Stewart, J. (2000). Human resource development in small organisations. *Journal of European Industrial Training*, *24*(2/3/4), 105-117.

Hutt, M. D., & Speh, T. W. (1998). *Business marketing management: A strategic view of industrial and organisational markets.* Fort Worth, TX: Dryden Press.

Hyland, T., & Matlay, H. (1997). Small businesses, training needs, and VET provisions. *Journal of Education and Work*, *10*(2).

Igbaria, M. (1993). User acceptance of microcomputer technology: An empirical test. *International Journal of Management Science*, *21*, 73-90.

Ives, B., Olsen, M. H., & Baroudi, J .J. (1983). The measurement of user information satisfaction. *Communications of the ACM*, *26*(10), 785-793.

Jeffcoate, J., Chappell, C., & Feindt, S. (2002). Best practice in SME adoption of e-commerce. *Benchmarking: An International Journal*, *9*(2), 122-132.

Johansson, U. (2003). *Regional development in Sweden: October 2003.* Svenska Kommunförbundet. Retrieved from http://www.lf.svekom.se/tru/RSO/Regional_development_in_Sweden.pdf

Kai-Uwe Brock, J. (2000). Information and technology in the small firm. In S. Carter & Jones-Evans (Eds.), *Enterprise and the small business* (pp. 384-408). Prentice Hall.

Kalakota, R., & Whinston, A. (1997). *Electronic commerce: A manager's guide.* Wesley, Reading: Addison.

Karagozoglu, N., & Lindell, M. (2004). Electronic commeroc stiategy, operations, and performance in small and medium-sized enterprises. *Journal of Small Business and Enterprise Development, 11*(3), 290-301.

Kendall, J. E., & Kendall, K. E. (2001). A paradoxically peaceful coexistence between commerce and ecommerce. *Journal of Information Technology, Theory, and Application, 3*(4), 1-6.

Keniry, J., Blums, A., Notter, E., Radford, E., & Thomson, S. (2003). *Regional business--A plan for action.* Department of Transport and Regional Services. Retrieved from http://www.rbda.gov.au/ action_plan

Korper, S., & Ellis, J. (2001). *The e-commerce book.* San Diego: Academic Press.

Kuljis, J., Macredie, R., & Paul, R. J. (1998). Information gathering problems in multinational banking. *Journal of Strategic Information Systems, 7*, 233-245.

Lal, K. (2002) Institutional environment and the development of information and communication technology in India. *The Information Society, 17*(2), pp 105–117

Larsson, E., Hedelin, L., & Gärling, T. (2003). Influence of expert advice on expansion goals of small businesses in rural Sweden. *Journal of Small Business Management, 41*(2), 205-212.

Laudon, K., & Traver, C. (2006). *E-commerce: business, technology, society* (3rd ed.). NJ: Prentice Hall.

Lawrence, K. L. (1997). Factors inhibiting the utilisation of electronic commerce facilities in tasmanian small-to-medium sized enterprises. In *Proceedings of the 8th Australasian Conference on Information Systems* (pp. 587-597).

Lee, C. S. (2001). An analytical framework for evaluating e-commerce business models and strategies. *Internet Research: Electronic Network Applications and Policy, 11*(4), 349-359.

MacGregor, R. C., & Bunker, D. J. A (1999). Comparison of real estate brokers' computer training needs with other small business sectors: An Australian perspective. *Journal of Real Estate Practice and Education*, 1-12.

MacGregor, R. C., & Bunker, D. J. (1996). The effect of priorities introduced during computer acquisition on continuing success with IT in small business environments. In *Proceedings of the Information Resource Management Association International Conference*, Washington (271-277).

MacGregor, R. C., & Cocks, R. S. (1994). Veterinary computer education requirements: A survey. *Australian Veterinary Practitioner, 24*(1), 41-46.

MacGregor, R. C., Bunker, D. J., & Waugh, P. (1998). Electronic commerce and small/medium enterprises (SME's) in Australia: An electronic data interchange (EDI) pilot study. In *Proceedings of the 11th International Bled Electronic Commerce Conference*, Slovenia.

MacGregor, R. C., Vrazalic, L., Carlsson, S., Bunker, D. J., & Magnusson, M. (2002). The impact of business size and business type on small business investment in electronic commerce: A study of Swedish small businesses. *Australian Journal of Information Systems, 9*(2), 31-39.

Markland, R. E. (1974). The role of the computer in small business management. *Journal of Small Business Management, 12*(1), 21-26.

Martin, L. M., & Matlay, H. (2001a). "Blanket" approaches to promoting ICT in small firms: Some lessons from the DTI ladder adoption model in the UK. *Internet Research: Electronic Networking Applications and Policy, 11*(5), 399-410.

Martin, L. M., Halstead, A., & Taylor, J. (2001b). Learning issues in rural areas. *Contemporary Readings in Post-compulsory Education*, Triangle.

Matlay. H. (2000). Training in the small business sector of the British Economy. In S. Carter & D. Jones (Eds.), *Enterprise and small business: Principles, policy, and practice.* London: Addison Wesley Longman.

Matlay, H., & Fletcher, D. (2000). Globalisation and strategic change: Some lessons from the UK small business sector. *Strategic Change, 9*(7), 437-449.

McDoniel, P. L., Palko, J., & Cronan, T. P. (1993). Information systems development: Issues affecting success. *Journal of Computer Information Systems*, Fall, 50-62.

McRea, P. (1996, January-February). Reshaping industry with the Internet. *Management*, 7-10.

Meikle, F., & Willis, D. (2002). A pilot study of regional differences e-commerce development in UK SMEs. In *Proceedings of IRMA* (pp. 1142-1143).

Meredith, G. G. (1994). *Small business management in Australia* (4th ed.). McGraw Hill.

MIEC—Ministry of Industry Employment and Communications. (2003). *The European charter for small enterprises: A review of relevant actions and measures in Sweden.* Retrieved from http://europa.eu.int/comm/enterprise/enterprise_policy/charter/index.htm

Miller, D., & Toulouse, J. (1986). Strategy, structure, CEO personality, and performance in small firms. *American Journal of Small Business*, Winter, 47-62.

Miller, N. L., & Besser, T. L. (2000). The importance of community values in small business strategy formation: Evidence from rural Iowa. *Journal of Small Business Management, 38*(1), 68-85.

Montazemi, A. R. (1988). Factors affecting information satisfaction in the context of the small business environment. *MIS Quarterly, 12*(2), 239-256.

Murphy, J. (1996). *Small business management.* London: Pitman.

Neergaard, P. (1992). Microcomputers in small and medium-size companies: benefits achieved and problems encountered. In *Proceedings of the 3rd Australian Conference on Information Systems,* Wollongong, Australia (pp. 579-604).

Nooteboom, B. (1994). Innovation and diffusion in small firms: Theory and evidence. *Small Business Economics, 6*(5), 327-347.

O'Donnell, A., Gilmore, A., Cummins, D., & Carson, D. (2001). The network construct in entrepreneurship research: A review and critique. *Management Decision, 39*(9), 749-760.

Papazafeiropoulou, A., Pouloudi, A., & Doukidis, G. J. (2002). A framework for best practices in electronic commerce awareness creation. *Business Process Management Journal, 8*(3), 233-244.

Pavlou, P. A. (2003). Consumer acceptance of electronic commerce: Integrating trust and risk with the technological acceptance model. *International Journal of Electronic Commerce, 7*(3), 101-134.

Pendegraft, N., Morris, L., & Savage, K. (1987). Small business computer security. *Journal of Small Business Management, 25*(4), 54-60.

Phan, D. D. (2003). E-business development for competitive advantages: A case study. *Information & Management, 40*, 581-590.

Plant, R. (2000). *E-commerce: Formulation of strategy.* Prentice Hall PTR.

Poon, S., & Swatman, P. (1997). The Internet for small businesses: An enabling infrastructure. In *Proceedings of the 5th Internet Society Conference* (pp. 221-231).

Quayle, M. (2002). E-commerce: The challenge for UK SMEs in the Twenty-First Century. *International Journal of Operations and Production Management, 22*(10), 1148-1161.

Raymond, L. (2001). Determinants of Web site implementation in small business. *Internet Research: Electronic Network Applications and Policy, 11*(5), 411-422.

Reynolds, W., Savage, W., & Williams, A. (1994). *Your own business: A practical guide to success.* London: ITP.

Riquelme, H. (2002). Commercial Internet adoption in China: Comparing the experience of small, medium, and large business. *Internet Research: Electronic Networking Applications and Policy, 12*(3), 276-286.

Ritchie, R., & Brindley, C. (2000). Disintermediation, disintegration, and risk in the SME global supply chain. *Management Decision, 38*(8), 575-583.

Roberts, M., & Wood, M. (2002). The strategic use of computerised information systems by a micro enterprise. *Logistics Information Management, 15*(2), 115-125.

Rotch, W. (1987). *Management of small enterprises: Cases and readings.* University of Virginia Press.

Savin, J., & Silberg, D. (2000). There's more to e-business than point and click. *Journal of Business Strategy, 21*(5), 11-18.

Schindehutte, M., & Morris, M. H. (2001). Understanding strategic adaptation in small firms. *International Journal of Entrepreneurial Behaviour and Research, 7*(3), 84-107.

Schneider, G. P., & Perry, J. T. (2000). *Electronic commerce.* Cambridge: Course Technology.

Sparkes, A., & Thomas, B. (2001). The use of the Internet as a critical success factor for the marketing of Welsh Agri-food SMEs in the twenty first century. *British Food Journal, 103*(4), 331-347.

Straub, D., & Klein, R. (2001). E-competitive transformations. *Business Horizons, 44*(3), 3-12.

Swartz, T. A., & Iacobucci, D. (2000). *Handbook of services marketing and management.* California: Sage.

Tetteh, E., & Burn, J. (2001). Global strategies for SME-business: Applying the SMALL framework. *Logistics Information Management, 14*(1-2), 171-180.

Thong J. Y. L., Yap C. S., & Raman K. S. (1996) Top management support, external expertise and information systems implementation. *Small Business Information Systems Research, 7*(2), pp 248 – 267

Treacy, M., & Wiersema, F. (1997). *The discipline of market leaders.* Cambridge: Perseus Press.

Turban, E., Lee, J., King, D., & Chung, H. (2002). *Electronic commerce: A managerial perspective.* NJ: Prentice Hall.

Turban, E., Lee, J., King, D., & Chung, H. (2006). *Electronic commerce: A managerial perspective.* NJ: Prentice Hall.

Vescovi, T. (2000). Internet communication: The Italian SME case. *Corporate Communications: An International Journal, 5*(2), 107-112.

Walczuch, R., Van Braven, G., & Lundgren, H. (2000). Internet adoption barriers for small firms in the Netherlands. *European Management Journal, 18*(5), 561-572.

Walker, E. W. (1975). Investment and capital structure decision making in small business. In E. W. Walker (Ed), *The dynamic small firm: Selected readings.* TX: Austin Press.

Welsh, J. A., & White, J. F. (1981, July-August). A small business is not a little big business. *Harvard Business Review*, 18-32.

Westhead, P., & Storey, D. J. (1996). Management training and small firm performance: Why is the link so weak? *International Small Business Journal, 14*(4), 13-24.

Wilde, W. D., & Swatman, P. A. (2001). *Studying R-3 communities: An economic lens* (Deakin University Working paper No. 3).

Wilde, W. D., Swatman, P. A., & Castleman, T. (2000). Investigating the impact of IT&T on rural, regional, and remote Australia. In *Proceedings of CollECToR 2000*, Breckenbridge.

Willcocks, L., Graeser, V., & Lester, S. (1998). "Cybernomics" and IT productivity: Not business as usual. *European Management Journal, 16*(3), 272-283.

Wood, J. G., & Nosek, J. T. (1994). Discrimination of structure and technology in a group support system: The role of process complexity. In *Proceedings of the International Conference on Information Systems,* Vancouver (pp. 187-199).

Yap, C. S., Soh, C. P. P., & Raman, K. S. (1992). Information system success factors in small business. *International Journal of Management Science, 20*, 597-609.

## Chapter II

# General Research Methodology and Procedures:
## An Overview of How the Study was Undertaken

An examination of the Table of Contents of this book would indicate to the reader that the research presented in the book is multi-faceted. This has led to a necessary careful consideration of the approach to the research, the methods employed to gather the data, and the methods to present the data in a meaningful way. These will be detailed in this chapter.

## Overall Goals of the Study

Based on the literature review presented in Chapter I, we have identified a gap in our understanding of the organisational issues related to e-commerce adoption in SMEs located specifically in regional areas. The present research is concerned primarily with regional areas in developed countries with a mature infrastructure and technology that enable e-commerce adoption and use. We chose Australia, the USA, and Sweden as the location of our research because all three countries are members of the Organisation for Economic Cooperation and Development (OECD) with comparable per capita GDPs and household Internet penetration rates of approximately 55% in 2003/2004. The locations will be described in more detail later.

Our overall aim was to address the very broad issue of "what are SMEs in regional areas doing about e-commerce adoption?" However, this aim was broken down into a number of specific research goals related to the organisation itself and the use of e-commerce, including the following:

1. To examine whether business characteristics such as business age, business size (as defined by the number of employees), business sector, gender of the CEO, educational level of the CEO, level of IT skill within the business, the existence or non-existence of an enterprise wide business system, the use of product planning, market focus, or membership of an alliance are associated with the adoption/non-adoption of e-commerce in SMEs

2. To compare the adoption levels of e-commerce in regional SMEs across the three locations

3. To examine the effects of the business characteristics previously listed on e-commerce adoption criteria, barriers, benefits, and disadvantages

4. To determine the key underlying reasons why SMEs adopt or do not adopt e-commerce

5. To find out the main benefits and disadvantages that SMEs experience after implementing e-commerce

6. To determine whether being a member of an SME alliance is associated with e-commerce adoption in order to understand whether alliances promote or hinder e-commerce

7. To examine whether the gender and education level of the CEO have any bearing on e-commerce adoption

8. To compare and contrast e-commerce adoption in general across the three locations in order to identify similarities and differences

It should be noted that since limited research had been carried out into e-commerce adoption by SMEs in regional areas, our study was conceived as exploratory in nature, although we adopted an empirical approach. One approach to meeting these goals might have been to conduct a series of in-depth case studies of SMEs in the three locations. While such an approach might provide substantial detail concerning the various questions raised, there are just too many permutations that need to be considered. Attempting to include all the permutations would require application of decisions as to which SMEs should be included or excluded from the study, resulting in a potentially biased view of regional SMEs that was not generalisable beyond the samples used in the study.

A second approach was to undertake a large data gathering survey. This approach allowed for differing business characteristics and perceptions of e-commerce and reduced bias brought about by decisions concerning inclusion/exclusion of candidate SMEs for the study.

# Choice of Location for Data Gathering

An examination of the literature concerned with e-commerce adoption by SMEs shows that findings differ from location to location. Where, for example, in Australia, Poon and Swatman (1997) found that e-commerce improved relationships with business partners; a similar study in Canada (Raymond, 2001) found the opposite. Similarly, where in a U.K. study by Quayle (2002) found that a benefit of e-commerce adoption was reduced costs, studies in Australia (MacGregor, Bunker, & Waugh, 1998; Stauber, 2000) showed cost was increased. It appears, then, that the location of the study may have some bearing on the findings, rendering them inapplicable to other groups of SMEs in a different location.

Our main concern lies with businesses located in regional areas, which (as mentioned in Chapter I) do not have access to the same infrastructure, resources, and technology that their counterparts in metropolitan areas and large cities do. In order to select a region in each country, a set of location guidelines was developed. These were as follows:

* The location must be a large regional centre rather than a major/capital city or a remote (rural) area.

* A viable government initiated chamber of commerce must exist and be well patronised by the SME community.

* The location should have the full range of educational facilities, including a university.

* The business community must represent a cross-section of the business characteristics listed previously.

* The SME community must include e-commerce adopters and non-adopters.

The locations chosen were the Varmland region in Sweden, the Illawarra region in Australia, and Salt Lake County (Utah) in the USA.

## Varmland Region (Sweden)

Despite covering a large area of 450,000 km$^2$, only 9 million people call Sweden home. According to the official reports, the Swedish economy is "characterised by high internationalisation, a broad business sector, and a large element of public sector activity, especially in the service sector" (Sweden.se, 2006). With a GDP of US$270 billion in 2005 and an annual growth rate of 3%, Sweden is a skilled nation with an extensive welfare system. Although an exporter of electrical and telecommunications equipment, along with cars, paper, pharmaceuticals, iron, and steel (*ibid*), 70% of the Swedish economy is based on the service sector. Sweden also has more than $7 million Internet users (CIA, 2006). Of the three countries studied, Sweden currently has the highest Internet penetration of almost 75% (Internetworldstats, 2006).

*Figure 1. Varmland region in Sweden (Source: wikipedia.com)*

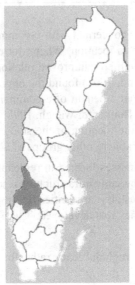

Our study was situated in the Varmland region (see Figure 1). Located in the central-west, the region of Varmland has a population of approximately 320,000 people and is rich in the natural landscape with lakes, forests, and rivers, which is a tourist attraction. The largest town in the region is Karlstad with a population of 82,000 of which the majority is employed in trade and communications, and mining and manufacturing (Karlstad Municipality, 2006).

## Illawarra Region (Australia)

Australia is similar to Sweden in that it covers a vast geographical area (almost 7.7 million km$^2$), yet it only has a population of 20 million. A member of the Commonwealth, Australia is a capitalist economy comparable to the four dominant Western European economies (CIA, 2006). Although Australia has a similar annual growth rate to Sweden, the value of the economy in terms of GDP is over $600 billion (*ibid*). The service sector dominates, but Australia is also a major exporter of raw materials and agricultural products. The Internet penetration rate is high with more than 70% of the population online (Internetworldstats, 2006).

We selected the Illawarra for our study (see Figure 2), a coastal region approximately 80km south of Sydney in the state of New South Wales. Despite it's proximity to Sydney, the Illawarra has a distinct economy of its own, which was dominated by the steel industry until recently. Now largely based around the service industry (tourism and education), the Illawarra is still known as an industrial heartland with a population of approximately 300,000 people. The largest city in the region and the third largest in New South Wales is Wollongong.

*Figure 2. Illawarra region in Australia (Source: wikipedia.com)*

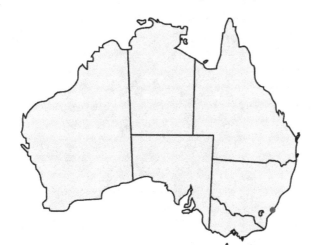

## Salt Lake County (USA)

The United States of America is more densely populated than Sweden or Australia, with almost 300,000 million people living on 9.6 million km² (CIA, 2006). The U.S. economy is the "largest and most technologically powerful in the world" and has an annual growth of 3% and a per capita GDP of US$42,000, compared to $30,000 in Sweden and $32,000 in Australia (*ibid*). However, based on recent statistics, the U.S. lags behind Sweden and Australia on the level of Internet penetration with less than 70% of the population online (Internetworldstats, 2006). The service industry dominates the economy with almost 80% of businesses operating in this sector.

Our study was set in the Salt Lake County (see Figure 3) in the state of Utah. Salt Lake City, the state capital, is the largest city in the region and has a population of approximately 200,000 (U.S. Census Bureau, 2006). Originally, an industrial (mining) region, since playing host to the 2002 Winter Olympics, Salt Lake City has developed a tourist industry.

*Figure 3. Salt Lake County in Utah (USA) (Source: wikipedia.com)*

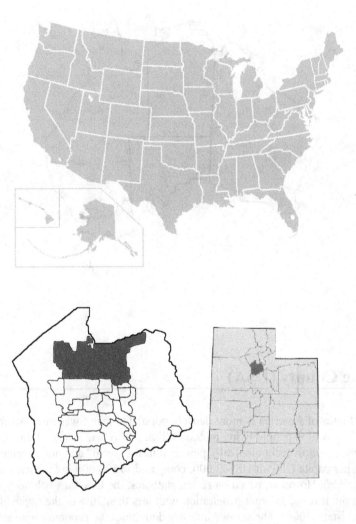

In summary, all three locations have some distinct similarities. The regions selected are located in developed, Western countries with comparable populations (between 200,000 and 320,000), similar Internet penetration rates (between 70 and 75%), and the same dominant business sectors (service, including tourism) and annual economic growth rates (3%). This makes it possible to compare the results from the three regions and draw conclusions about e-commerce use in each one.

# Mode of Data Collection

The mode of the data collection was selected based on previous research by de Heer (1999), which indicated that Scandinavian countries (including Sweden) had historically high survey response rates (although he notes that this is declining). Subsequently, the Swedish survey was administered by mail. Businesses surveyed were randomly selected from a government-produced list and all businesses were from one of four towns in Varmland: Saffle, Arvika, Filipstad, and Karlstad

The Australian survey was re-developed from the Swedish questionnaire so that it could be administered by phone because mail survey response rates in Australia were found to be poor, and to ensure higher rates of participation.

The U.S. survey was administered using a mix of the two methods. Potential participants were first contacted by phone and invited to participate. Those who agreed to do so were sent a copy of the survey by mail.

# Development of the Survey Instrument

Two sets of questions needed to be developed to address the goals of the study. These included:

- Questions about the business characteristics such as business age, business size, business sector, gender of the CEO, educational level of the CEO, level of IT skill within the business, the existence or non-existence of an enterprise wide business system, product planning, market focus, and alliance membership
- Questions about e-commerce adoption criteria (or drivers), benefits, and disadvantages for e-commerce adopters, and questions about e-commerce barriers for non-adopters

## Business Size

A number of authors (Hawkins, Winter, & Hunter, 1995; Hawkins & Winter, 1996) have noted that the business size (in terms of the number of employees) appears to be significantly associated with the level and type of adoption of e-commerce technology. While most studies categorise SMEs with less than five employees as micro businesses, a number of studies (Fallon & Moran, 2000; Matlay, 2000) suggest that SMEs with fewer than ten employees is a far more significant subdivision than comparing "micro" to "small." Similar views were found in the two previous pilot studies carried out by the authors. In both cases, significant differences were found when business with ten or fewer employees were compared to businesses with more than ten employees. The pilot studies carried out as part of this study support these findings, but add a separate category for single owner-operated businesses (termed sole trader). The pilot studies also suggested that SMEs with 20 to 50 employees tended to operate similarly and thus did not need to be split into smaller groupings. Thus, the following categories of business size are adopted. These are:

- Sole proprietorship (0 employees)
- 1 to 9 employees
- 10 to 19 employees
- 20 to 49 employees
- 50 to 199 employees
- 200 or more employees

# Business Age

A number of studies (Donckels & Lambrecht, 1997; Martin & Matlay, 2001) have indicated that there appears to be some association between the business age of the SME and decisions regarding e-commerce adoption and use. Many studies have simply categorised business age in "sets of five" (0 to 5 years, 6 to 10 years, etc.). The pilot study found that within the first of these groups (0 to 5 years), three subsets existed. The first was the very new businesses (less than one year in business), the second included a number of businesses that had joined the "online revolution" and were usually one to two years old. The second group also included SMEs that were acting as outsourcers to larger businesses. The third group was the residue (3 to 5 years in business). The pilot study showed that all three of these groups acted very differently where IT or e-commerce adoption and use were concerned. The pilot studies also found that for older businesses, subgroups of 6 to 10 years, 11 to 20 years and over 20 years were adequate groupings.

Thus, six categories of business age are used. These are:

- Very new business (less than 1 year)
- 1 to 2 years
- 3 to 5 years
- 6 to 10 years
- 11 to 20 years
- Over 20 years

# Business Sector

A study examining Internet training in SMEs carried out by Blackburn and Athayde (2000) found an association between business sector and e-commerce adoption and use. Subsequently, we asked survey respondents to indicate their business sector as one of the following:

- Industrial (this includes manufacturing, engineering, and transport)
- Service (this includes professional SMEs such as lawyers, doctors, etc.)
- Retail (this includes both business to business as well as business to customer retail)
- Finance (insurance, banking, accounting)
- Other (must be specified)

It should be noted that while previous studies (Blackburn et al., 2000) have placed finance respondents into the service category, the results from the two previous pilot studies in Wollongong (Bunker & MacGregor, 2000; MacGregor & Bunker, 1996; MacGregor et al., 1998) suggested that the financial sector was sufficiently different to warrant a separate category.

## Market Focus

Market focus refers to the major "push" of the organization to attract customers/clients and to sell its products/services. A number of studies (Achrol & Kotler, 1999; Blackburn et al., 2000) suggest that market focus is associated with the level of adoption of e-commerce in SMEs. Based on the pilot study findings, location of major customer base was found to be an adequate surrogate for market focus. Four distinct location bases were found. These were:

- Local (customer normally in a boundary of 5 to 10 kilometres)
- Regional (customers within a 50 kilometre radius)
- National (trading extends across the whole nation)
- International (products and services are exported)

## Level of IT Skill

MacGregor et al. (1998) have suggested that the level of IT skill within the organisation is associated with the level of adoption of e-commerce in SMEs. Based on the pilot studies, five levels of IT skill were identified and used in the survey. These are:

- No computer knowledge
- Low computer knowledge
- Average computer knowledge
- Advanced computer knowledge
- Expert computer knowledge

## Gender of the CEO

The gender of the CEO (owner/manager) was required due to studies by Rosa, Hamilton, Carter, and Bums (1994), Sonfield, Lussier, Corman, and McKinney (2001) and Carter (2000), which found that the gender of the CEO may be associated with e-commerce. Therefore, we asked respondents to indicate the gender of their CEO.

## Education Level of the CEO

Previous studies (Fusilier & Durlabhji, 2003; Mitra & Matlay, 2000) have suggested that the level of formal education of the CEO may be associated with patterns of adoption and use of e-commerce. Therefore, three levels were chosen to describe the level of education:

- No formal education
- Trade/high school qualification
- University qualification

We did not make a distinction between undergraduate and postgraduate university qualifications.

## Enterprise-Wide Business System

Research (Blackburn et al., 2000; Tetteh & Burn, 2001) suggests that the development of an enterprise-wide business system prior to e-commerce adoption often raises the level of success of that adoption. We asked respondents to indicate whether their organisation had an enterprise-wide business system in place.

## Product Planning

Studies by Savin and Silberg (2000), Karagozoglu and Lindell (2004), and Korper and Ellis (2001) have stressed the need to plan product offerings prior to the adoption of e-commerce. Therefore, we asked respondents if they engaged in any form of advance product planning.

## Alliance Membership

SME alliances have been promoted as a driver of e-commerce adoption. We discuss this trend in detail in Chapter VIII. One of our major research goals was to examine the effect of these alliances on e-commerce. Subsequently we asked respondents to indicate whether they belonged to any type of formal or informal network or alliance.

# E-Commerce Criteria, Barriers, Benefits, and Disadvantages

The second part of the survey asked respondents about their experience with e-commerce, namely for the adopters:

- Why they adopted e-commerce (criteria, drivers, or expectations)
- What benefits they experienced by adopting e-commerce
- What setbacks they encountered following e-commerce adoption (disadvantages)

For non-adopters, we asked about e-commerce barriers or constraints that prevented them from using e-commerce. Each of these four aspects of e-commerce (criteria, barriers, benefits, and disadvantages) are described in greater detail in subsequent chapters. However, Tables 1 to 4 provide an overview of each set.

The four sets of e-commerce aspects were presented as a series of statements and respondents were asked to rate each statement on a five point Likert scale. Each relevant question in the survey related to e-commerce criteria (Chapter IV), barriers (Chapter V), benefits (Chapter VI), and disadvantages (Chapter VII) is shown in the corresponding chapter.

*Table 1. Fourteen e-commerce adoption criteria*

| 1 | Demand and/or pressure from customers. |
|---|---|
| 2 | Pressure from competition. |
| 3 | Demand and/or pressure from suppliers. |
| 4 | To reduce costs. |
| 5 | To improve customer service. |
| 6 | To shorten lead time/reduce stock levels. |
| 7 | To increase sales. |
| 8 | To improve internal efficiency. |
| 9 | To strengthen relations with business partners. |
| 10 | The possibility of reaching new customers/markets. |
| 11 | To improve our competitiveness. |
| 12 | We were offered external support to adopt e-commerce. |
| 13 | To improve our marketing. |
| 14 | To improve control. |

*Table 2. Ten e-commerce adoption barriers*

| 1 | E-commerce is not suited to our products/services. |
|---|---|
| 2 | E-commerce is not suited to our way of doing business. |
| 3 | E-commerce is not suited to the ways our clients do business. |
| 4 | E-commerce does not offer any advantages to our organisation. |
| 5 | We do not have the technical knowledge in the organisation to implement e-commerce. |
| 6 | E-commerce is too complicated to implement. |
| 7 | E-commerce is not secure. |
| 8 | The financial investment required to implement e-commerce is too high. |
| 9 | We do not have time to implement e-commerce. |
| 10 | It is difficult to choose the most suitable e-commerce standard with so many different options available. |

*Table 3. Ten e-commerce adoption benefits*

| 1 | E-commerce reduced our administration costs. |
|---|---|
| 2 | E-commerce reduced our production costs. |
| 3 | E-commerce reduced our lead time. |
| 4 | E-commerce reduced our stock levels. |
| 5 | E-commerce lead to increased sales. |
| 6 | E-commerce increased our internal efficiency. |
| 7 | E-commerce improved our relations with business partners. |
| 8 | E-commerce gave us access to new customers and markets. |
| 9 | E-commerce improved our competitiveness. |
| 10 | E-commerce improved the quality of information in our organisation. |

*Table 4. Seven e-commerce adoption disadvantages*

| 1 | E-commerce deteriorated our relations with business partners. |
|---|---|
| 2 | E-commerce increased our costs. |
| 3 | E-commerce increased the computer maintenance required. |
| 4 | E-commerce doubled the amount of work. |
| 5 | E-commerce reduced the flexibility of the business processes. |
| 6 | E-commerce raised security concerns. |
| 7 | E-commerce made us increasingly dependent on this technology. |

# Pilot Study

A series of six interviews with SMEs was carried out in the Illawarra area. Three of the SMEs had adopted e-commerce, and three had not. The purpose of the interviews was to determine whether the four sets of adoption factors (Tables 1 to 4) were applicable to those SMEs and whether they were complete. The interviews were open-ended. For those that had adopted e-commerce, the criteria for adoption, benefits from having adopted and disadvantages for having adopted were asked. For those that had not adopted e-commerce, the interview sought reasons for non-adoption. The interviews took approximately 45 minutes and were taped for later analysis. The result of the case studies showed that all the criteria, barriers, benefits, and disadvantages were identified by at least one SME owner/manager and that no additional criteria, barriers, benefits, or disadvantages were nominated by a majority of the SME owners/managers. Results of the interviews were that all of the adoption factors were applicable and that no additional adoption factors needed to be added.

# Statistical Analysis

The design of the questions and the range of answers were deliberate to allow the use of chi-square, two-tailed t-tests, linear regressions, correlations, and factor analysis.

A formula for sample size was used:

$$E = z_{\alpha/2} \, \sigma/\sqrt{n}$$

or:

$$n = (z_{\alpha/2} \, \sigma/E)^2$$

$\sigma$ was determined to be 2.01.

A 99.9% degree of confidence was considered. The margin of error was 1. The minimum sample size was 37 (rounded up). The minimum sample size for 95% degree of confidence was 21 (rounded up). The two sample sizes were determined to be adequate. A series of Levene tests was carried out to determine homogeneity of variance. The Levene's tests provided a significance of <.001 for all questions being examined, indicating that data was sufficiently robust to apply t-tests, linear regressions and chi-square tests.

A number of analyses were performed on the data. These are considered separately. It should be noted that all statistical analyses are performed with the underlying assumption that the data was normally distributed.

A series of chi-square tests:

$$f(x) = e^{-x/2} \frac{x^{v/2-1}}{2^{v/2}\lceil(v/2)}$$

$$\lceil(a) = \int_{0}^{\infty} t^{a-1}\,e^{-t}\,dt$$

were carried out to determine whether the business characteristics were associated with the adoption of e-commerce and the decision to become an SME alliance member. Chi-Square is a statistical technique that can determine whether the groupings of cases on one variable are related to the groupings of cases on another variable. As this was the requirement for some of the research goals stated above, a chi-square technique was used.

A series of two-tailed t-tests:

$$t = \frac{\mu - x}{SD/\sqrt{n}}$$

were carried out to determine the answers to other research goals. Student's t-test are a statistical test used to test equality of means from two variables having normal distributions and equal variances; a critical value from the t-distribution As the distributions were considered to be normally distributed and the equality of the means was examined, a t-test was applied.

A series of linear regressions:

$$y = mx + b$$

**where**

$$m = \frac{n\sum(xy) - \sum x\sum y}{n\sum(x^2) - (\sum x)^2}$$

$$b = \frac{\sum y - m \sum x}{n}$$

were also carried out for several analyses. Linear regression is a method of estimating the conditional expected value of one variable y given the values of some other variable or variables x. For the data gathered in this study, the association of factors was considered linear in nature. For goals 3, 5, 7, 9, the aim was to estimate the value of one variable, given a set of independent variables.

Finally, a series of correlations and factor analyses:

$$r = \frac{N \sum XY - (\sum X)(\sum Y)}{\sqrt{\left(N \sum X^2 - (\sum X)^2\right)\left(N \sum Y^2 - (\sum Y)^2\right)}}$$

$$r_{ab.g} = (r_{ab} - r_{ag} r_{bg})/\text{sqrt}[(1 - r_{ag}^2)(1 - r_{bg}^2)]$$
$$\text{KMO} = (\Sigma\Sigma \, r_{ij}^2) \, / \, (\Sigma\Sigma \, r_{ij}^2 + (\Sigma\Sigma \, a_{ij}^2)$$

were carried out to identify groupings of barriers, criteria, benefits, and disadvantages of e-commerce. Factor analysis is a statistical technique for reducing large data sets to the smallest number of "factors" required to "explain" the pattern of relationships in the data. An examination of the list of criteria, barriers, benefits, and disadvantages are each a large set of data. The aim of factor analysis is to attempt to reduce these to a smaller "explainable" set of relationships.

# Conclusion

This chapter has provided an overview of the methodology employed in the study including the sampling, data collection methods, and statistical analyses performed on the data. The locations selected for the study were also described and the similarities between them highlighted. The following chapter will provide a general overview of the survey findings, including the response rates from each location and a profile of the respondents.

# References

Achrol, R. S., & Kotler, P. (1999). Marketing in the network economy. *Journal of Marketing, 63*, 146-163.

Blackburn, R., & Athayde, R. (2000). Making the connection: The effectiveness of Internet training in small businesses. *Education and Training, 42*(4/5).

Bunker, D. J., & MacGregor, R. C. (2000). Successful generation of information technology (IT) requirements for small/medium enterprises (SME's)—Cases from Regional Australia. In *Proceedings of SMEs in a Global Economy*, Wollongong, Australia (pp. 72-84).

Carter, S. (2000). Improving the numbers and performance of women-owned businesses: Some implications for training and advisory services. *Education & Training, 42*(4/5), 326-333.

CIA. (2006). *The World Factbook*. Retrieved from www.cia.gov/cia/publications/factbook

de Heer, W. (1999). International response trends: Results of an international survey. *Journal of Official Statistics, 15*(2), 129-142.

Donckels, R., & Lambrecht, J. (1997). The network position of small businesses: An explanatory model. *Journal of Small Business Management, 35*(2), 13-28.

Fallon, M., & Moran, P. (2000). Information communications technology (ICT) and manufacturing SMEs. In *Proceedings of the 2000 Small Business and Enterprise Development Conference*, University of Manchester (pp. 100-109).

Fusilier, M., & Durlabhji, S. (2003). No downturn here: Tracking e-business programs in higher education. *Decision Sciences, 1*(1), 73-98.

Hawkins, P., & Winter, J. (1996). The self-reliant graduate and the SME. *Education and Training, 38*(4), 3-9.

Hawkins, P., Winter, J., & Hunter, J. (1995). *Skills for graduates in the 21st Century*. Report Commissioned from the Whiteway Research, University of Cambridge, Association of Graduate Recruiters, Cambridge.

Internetworldstats. (2006). *Internet world stats: U.S.A. ge and population statistics*. Retrieved from www.internetworldstats.com/top25.htm

Karagozoglu, N., & Lindell, M. (2004). Electronic commerce strategy, operations, and performance in small and medium-sized enterprises. *Journal of Small Business and Enterprise Development, 11*(3), 290-301.

Karlstad Municipality. (2006). *Municipal facts*. Retrieved from www.karlstad.se/eng/ facts.shtml

Korper, S., & Ellis, J. (2001). *The e-commerce book*. San Diego: Academic Press.

MacGregor, R. C., & Bunker, D. J. (1996). The effect of priorities introduced during computer acquisition on continuing success with IT in small business environments. *Information Resource Management Association International Conference*, Washington (pp. 271-277).

MacGregor, R. C., Bunker, D. J., & Waugh, P. (1998). Electronic commerce and small/medium enterprises (SME's) in Australia: An electronic data interchange (EDI) pilot study. In *Proceedings of the 11ᵗʰ International Bled Electronic Commerce Conference*, Slovenia.

Martin, L. M., & Matlay, H. (2001). "Blanket" approaches to promoting ICT in small firms: Some lessons from the DTI ladder adoption model in the UK. *Internet Research: Electronic Networking Applications and Policy, 11*(5), 399-410.

Matlay, H. (2000). Training in the small business sector of the British Economy. In S. Carter & D. Jones (Eds.), *Enterprise and small business: Principles, policy, and practice.* London: Addison Wesley Longman.

Mitra, J., & Matlay, H. (2004, February). Entrepreneurial and vocational education and training: Lessons from eastern and central Europe. *Industry and Higher Education, 53.*

Poon, S., & Swatman, P. (1997). The Internet for small businesses: An enabling infrastructure. *Proceedings of the 5ᵗʰ Internet Society Conference* (pp. 221-231).

Quayle, M. (2002). E-commerce: The challenge for UK SMEs in the 21ˢᵗ Century. *International Journal of Operations and Production Management, 22*(10), 1148-1161.

Raymond, L. (2001). Determinants of Web site implementation in small business. *Internet Research: Electronic Network Applications and Policy, 11*(5), 411-422.

Rosa, P., Hamilton, D., Carter, S., & Bums, H. (1994). The impact of gender on small business management: Preliminary findings of a British study. *International Small Business Journal, 12*(3), 25-32.

Savin, J., & Silberg, D. (2000). There's more to e-business than point and click. *Journal of Business Strategy, 21*(5), 11-18.

Sonfield, M., Lussier, R., Corman, J., & McKinney, M. (2001). Gender comparisons in strategic decision-making: An empirical analysis of the entrepreneurial strategy matrix. *Journal of Small Business Management, 39*(2), 165-173.

Stauber, A. (2000). *A survey of the incorporation of electronic commerce in Tasmanian small and medium sized enterprises.* Tasmanian Electronic Commerce Centre, 37pp.

Sweden.se. (2006). *The official gateway to Sweden.* Retrieved from www.sweden.se

Tetteh, E., & Burn, J. (2001). Global strategies for SME-business: Applying the SMALL framework. *Logistics Information Management, 14*(1-2), 171-180.

## Chapter III

# Profile of SMEs in Sweden, Australia, and the USA:
## Associations Between Various Business Characteristics

Despite their size, SMEs are increasingly turning to global markets. This development has been enabled by the advent of electronic commerce technology, which provides SMEs with a platform to engage in international marketing, sales, and distribution through electronic channels. The benefits of e-commerce to the SME sector have been highlighted previously, however, it is important to reiterate the opportunities afforded by implementing e-commerce, which allows SMEs to enter foreign markets.

There have been numerous studies examining various facets of e-commerce adoption by SMEs. Many of these studies will be detailed in subsequent chapters; however, a criticism of some of these studies is their apparent "homogeneous approach" to the SME sector. Martin and Matlay (2001, p. 400) suggest that these studies do not "... *encompass the impact of key factors such as business size, sector, ethnicity, gender, human and financial resources, customer base, or levels of internationalisation.*"

The implications of this homogenous approach are serious in light of the drives to promote e-commerce adoption by SMEs. Culkin and Smith (2000, p. 145) support this view and argue that many previous studies are based on a "*[...] naïve, over-simplistic understanding of the motivations of those in the small business sector, [which] means that [the] interventions are inevitably blunt instruments destined to fail given the limited understanding shown of the complexity of the small business market.*" Neglecting to take into account the differences between SMEs in relation to organisational and industry factors will result in ineffective programs and strategies and limited success in increasing the rate of e-commerce adoption. As the results in this book will show, these differences have a substantial impact on the use of e-commerce by SMEs.

By way of answering some of these early criticisms and as a preface to the more detailed results in subsequent chapters, this chapter will present some general findings from our study to set the context for the research. To begin with, a profile of the survey respondents will be provided. The chapter will then examine whether any of the business characteristics such as business age (length of time in operation), business size (defined in terms of the number of employees), business sector, gender of the CEO, educational level of the CEO, level of IT skill within the business, the existence or non-existence of an enterprise-wide business system, product planning, market focus, strategic alliance membership, use of business-to-business (B2B), or business-to-customer (B2C) e-commerce are associated with the adoption of e-commerce by SMEs in our sample consisting of organisations from Sweden, Australia, and the U.S. In doing this, we will also consider the levels of e-commerce adoption in each of the three locations.

The purpose of this chapter is to provide an overview of the scope of our study and background information about the respondents. However, in addition to a simple summary, which indicates the number and percentage of respondents in different categories, we aim to delve deeper and analyse the effects of belonging to a particular category of respondents on e-commerce adoption. The results of this analysis will demonstrate any associations between different business characteristics and e-commerce use in a particular category of SMEs.

# Survey Instrument

As indicated in the previous chapter, a survey instrument was developed and administered in the three locations. This chapter will present the results from the first set of survey questions concerning the business characteristics described in the previous chapter and summarised in Table 1 for convenience. Table 1 lists the business characteristics examined and the range of responses associated with each characteristic.

In addition to the previous characteristics, respondents were also asked whether they had adopted and were using e-commerce in their day-to-day business activities.

As indicated in the previous chapter, three regional locations were chosen: Varmland (Sweden), Illawarra (Australia), and Salt Lake City (Utah, USA). All three locations met the specified guidelines and each location had personnel who could assist with the distribution and collection of the survey instrument. A total of 1170 surveys were distributed by mail in four towns in Varmland (Sweden): Karlstad, Filipstad, Saffle, and Arvika. A total of 250 surveys were administered by telephone in Wollongong and its suburbs (in the Illawarra region) and a total of 150 surveys were administered by telephone in the Utah region. The results of the data collection are presented next.

*Table 1. Business characteristics used in survey*

| Business Characteristics | Acceptable Range of Responses |
|---|---|
| Business age. | Less than 1 year<br>1 to 2 years<br>3 to 5 years<br>6 to 10 years<br>11 to 20 years<br>More than 20 years |
| Business size. | Sole proprietorship (0 employees)<br>1 to 9 employees<br>10 to 19 employees<br>20 to 49 employees<br>50 to 199 employees<br>200 or more employees |
| Business sector. | Industrial<br>Service<br>Retail<br>Finance<br>Other |
| Market focus. | Local<br>Regional<br>National<br>International |
| Level of IT skill. | None<br>Low<br>Average<br>Advanced<br>Expert |
| Gender of CEO. | Female<br>Male |
| Education level of CEO. | No formal education<br>Trade/matriculation<br>University qualification |
| Alliance membership. | Yes<br>No |
| Existence of an enterprise-wide system. | Yes<br>No |
| Product planning. | Yes<br>No |
| Type of e-commerce. | Business-to-business (B2B)<br>Business-to-customer (B2C) |

# Response Rates

Responses were obtained from 313 SMEs in Sweden, giving a response rate of 26.8%. This is consistent with de Heer's (1999) finding about declining survey response rates in Scandinavia. The total number of e-commerce adopters was 183, representing 58.5% of the responses. Responses were obtained from 160 SMEs in Australia giving a higher response rate of 64%, which is consistent with phone surveys (Frazer & Lawley, 2000). In Australia the total number of adopters was 25, representing 15.6% of the responses. Responses were obtained from 116 SME organisations in the U.S. giving a response rate of 75.3%. The total number adopters was 63, representing 54.3% of the responses. Table 2 shows a summary of the response rates, while Figure 1 provides the same information graphically.

*Table 2. Summary of survey response rates*

| Location | Total Adminis-tered | Responses | Response Rate | E-Commerce Adopters | E-Commerce Adopters (%) |
|---|---|---|---|---|---|
| Sweden | 1170 | 313 | 26.8% | 183 | 58.5% |
| Austra-lia | 250 | 160 | 64% | 25 | 15.6% |
| USA | 150 | 116 | 75.3% | 63 | 54.3% |

*Figure 1. Comparison of survey response rates*

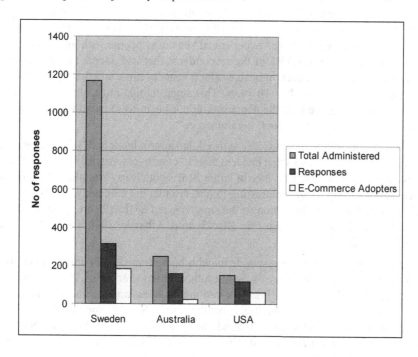

Despite each of the three locations satisfying conditions for classification as regional, the uptake of e-commerce is vastly different from location to location. While 58.5% of the regional Swedish SMEs surveyed had adopted e-commerce, 54.3% of the regional U.S. organisations had done likewise, and only 15.6% of the Australian businesses had done so. A number of explanations are possible. One explanation is that there is a deliberate "push" by some governments to develop professional and voluntary organisations and courses to "ease SMEs into e-commerce." This is supported by a number of recent studies (see for example Barry, Berg, & Chandler, 2003). A second explanation is supported by studies carried out in UK, U.S., and Australia, which found that there is a willingness by SMEs in the U.S. and UK to seek alternative approaches to marketing and technology. This was not found in Australia. We will discuss some of the reasons for this in subsequent chapters.

We will now profile each of the respondent locations separately and highlight differences between the three groups at the end of the chapter.

## Profile of Respondents in Sweden

The lowest response rate was encountered in Sweden where less than 30% of the sample size completed the survey. This can be partially attributed to the survey method used, which involved mailing the questionnaire to SME owners. Table 3 provides a detailed picture of the individuals who returned their completed questionnaire.

Table 3 provides a number of interesting findings about the profile of the Swedish respondents. In relation to the *length of time in business*, 62% of all the organisations surveyed indicated that they had been in business for more than 10 years (refer to Figure 2). This would tend to suggest that the respondents were "experienced" business people with long established procedures and practices. Over 95% of the respondents that had adopted e-commerce in their day-to-day activities had been in business for 3 years or more and the majority (63%) had been operational for more than 10 years. This suggests that most of the respondents had had sufficient experience with the demands of their business to make valid judgments on the decisions to adopt (or not adopt) e-commerce.

In contrast, the results for the *business size* showed that approximately 59% of the Swedish respondents were from businesses that had less than 10 employees. Again, this suggests that e-commerce adoption is not the province of larger SMEs but clearly "permeates" across all sizes of the sample group. It was interesting to observe that the percentage (85%) of non-adopters was significantly higher amongst the smaller sized SMEs (20 employees or less). This is in accord with earlier findings (see Blackburn & Athayde, 2000; Fallon & Moran, 2000; Matlay, 2000).

Sixty-five percent of the Swedish respondents who had adopted e-commerce were from the industrial or service *business sectors*. Some authors (Meikle & Willis, 2002; Riquelme, 2002) have suggested that at the SME level e-commerce is less applicable to the industrial sector. The data in Table 3 shows that this is not the case in Sweden and that SMEs across all sectors have adopted e-commerce. It should be noted that the low figure for SMEs in the finance sector was not a function of adoption, but a function of the small number of respondents from that sector.

*Table 3. Profile of Swedish respondents*

| Business Char-acteristics | Acceptable Range of Responses | No. of Responses (Adopters) | % | No. of Responses (Non-Adopters) | % | Total | Total (%) |
|---|---|---|---|---|---|---|---|
| **Business age.** | Less than 1 year | 1 | 0.5 | 3 | 2.3 | 4 | 1.3 |
| | 1 to 2 years | 7 | 3.8 | 6 | 4.6 | 13 | 4.2 |
| | 3 to 5 years | 25 | 13.7 | 15 | 11.5 | 40 | 12.8 |
| | 6 to 10 years | 35 | 19.1 | 25 | 19.2 | 60 | 19.2 |
| | 11 to 20 years | 42 | 23 | 31 | 23.8 | 73 | 23.3 |
| | More than 20 years | 73 | 39.9 | 48 | 36.9 | 121 | 38.7 |
| | Missing | 0 | 0 | 2 | 1.5 | 2 | 0.6 |
| **Business size.** | Sole proprietorship | 15 | 8.2 | 26 | 20 | 41 | 13.1 |
| | 1 to 9 employees | 77 | 42.1 | 67 | 51.5 | 144 | 46 |
| | 10 to 19 employees | 30 | 16.4 | 18 | 13.8 | 48 | 15.3 |
| | 20 to 49 employees | 30 | 16.4 | 10 | 7.7 | 40 | 12.8 |
| | 50 to 199 employees | 25 | 13.7 | 4 | 3.1 | 29 | 9.3 |
| | 200 or more employees | 6 | 3.3 | 2 | 1.5 | 8 | 2.6 |
| | Missing | 0 | 0 | 3 | 2.3 | 3 | 1 |
| **Business sector.** | Industrial | 54 | 29.5 | 25 | 19.2 | 79 | 25.2 |
| | Service | 65 | 35.5 | 49 | 37.7 | 114 | 36.4 |
| | Retail | 33 | 18 | 24 | 18.5 | 57 | 18.2 |
| | Finance | 9 | 4.9 | 0 | 0 | 9 | 2.9 |
| | Other | 22 | 12 | 31 | 23.8 | 53 | 16.9 |
| | Missing | 0 | 0 | 1 | 0.8 | 1 | 0.3 |
| **Alliance mem-bership.** | Yes | 61 | 33.3 | 63 | 48.5 | 124 | 39.6 |
| | No | 115 | 62.8 | 62 | 47.7 | 177 | 56.5 |
| | Missing | 7 | 3.8 | 5 | 3.8 | 12 | 3.8 |
| **Existence of enterprise-wide system.** | Yes | 122 | 66.7 | 58 | 44.6 | 180 | 57.5 |
| | No | 58 | 31.7 | 71 | 54.6 | 129 | 41.2 |
| | Missing | 3 | 1.6 | 1 | 0.8 | 4 | 1.3 |
| **Product plan-ning.** | Yes | 50 | 27.3 | 15 | 11.5 | 65 | 20.8 |
| | No | 133 | 72.7 | 114 | 87.7 | 247 | 78.9 |
| | Missing | 0 | 0 | 1 | 0.8 | 1 | 0.3 |
| **Gender of CEO.** | Female | 19 | 10.4 | 17 | 13.1 | 36 | 11.5 |
| | Male | 160 | 87.4 | 109 | 83.8 | 269 | 85.9 |
| | Missing | 4 | 2.2 | 4 | 3.1 | 8 | 2.6 |
| **Level of CEO education.** | No formal education | 17 | 9.3 | 20 | 15.4 | 37 | 11.8 |
| | Trade/matriculation | 62 | 33.9 | 56 | 43.1 | 118 | 37.7 |
| | University qualification | 91 | 49.7 | 47 | 36.2 | 138 | 44.1 |
| | Missing | 13 | 7.1 | 7 | 5.4 | 20 | 6.4 |

*continued on following page*

*Table 3. Continued*

| Business Char-acteristics | Acceptable Range of Responses | No. of Responses (Adopters) | % | No. of Responses (Non-Adopters) | % | Total | Total (%) |
|---|---|---|---|---|---|---|---|
| **Level of IT skill.** | None | 2 | 1.1 | 5 | 3.8 | 7 | 2.2 |
| | Low | 14 | 7.7 | 34 | 26.2 | 48 | 15.3 |
| | Average | 102 | 55.7 | 75 | 57.7 | 177 | 56.5 |
| | Advanced | 45 | 24.6 | 14 | 10.8 | 59 | 18.8 |
| | Expert | 20 | 10.9 | 1 | 0.8 | 21 | 6.7 |
| | Missing | 0 | 0 | 1 | 0.8 | 1 | 0.3 |
| **Market focus.** | Local | 74 | 40.4 | 75 | 57.7 | 149 | 47.6 |
| | Regional | 17 | 9.3 | 11 | 8.5 | 28 | 8.9 |
| | National | 69 | 37.7 | 27 | 20.8 | 96 | 30.7 |
| | International | 23 | 12.6 | 16 | 12.3 | 39 | 12.5 |
| | Missing | 0 | 0 | 1 | 0.8 | 1 | 0.3 |
| **E-commerce type.** | B2B | 144 | 78.7 | | | | |
| | B2C | 39 | 21.3 | | | | |
| | Missing | 0 | 0 | | | | |

*Figure 2. Length of time in business (Swedish respondents)*

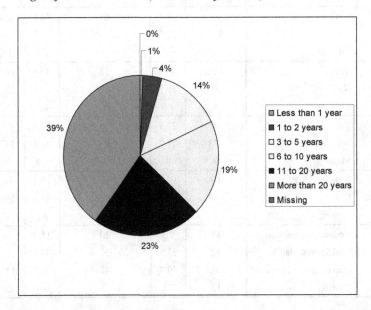

*Figure 3. Strategic alliance membership (Swedish e-commerce adopters)*

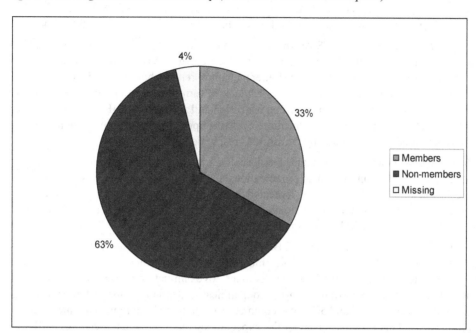

Previous research (Dennis, 2000; Marchewka & Towell, 2000) has stressed the potential importance of *strategic alliance membership* for the SME sector, particularly in an Internet environment. An examination of Figure 3 shows that only 33.3% of the respondents that had adopted e-commerce were members of any form of strategic alliance, while the non-adopters were equivocal regarding membership of an alliance. This implies that, despite the benefits of pooling resources and knowledge through alliances, SMEs see e-commerce as a competitive advantage and, subsequently, as a competitive strategy.

The existence of an *enterprise-wide information system* plays a role in e-commerce implementation. This appears to be supported by the Swedish respondents. Almost 70% of the e-commerce adopters had such a system in place, in contrast to 45% of non-adopters. The existence of an organizational system implies a strategic view of technology as a competitive tool, rather than a support function. This view is applied to e-commerce technology by extension.

A number of authors have stressed the need to develop some form of proactive *product planning* as a necessary first and vital step in the use of e-commerce in order to align products and services with an e-commerce strategy. In the Swedish sample, only 21% of the respondents indicated that they have undertaken and completed any form of product planning. This is particularly interesting if we include the findings for B2B/B2C respondents. While over 78% of the respondents indicated that their major business dealings were through B2B e-commerce, only 27% of adopters had undertaken any form of product planning.

Despite all attempts to randomly select respondents, the data shows that overwhelmingly, owners and managers of SMEs in regional Sweden are males (86%). There are two explanations for this: either the role of females in owning and managing SMEs in regional Sweden is not widespread, or males were more likely to respond to the questionnaire than females. The impact of *gender* on e-commerce adoption will be addressed in detail later in the book.

The *level of education* of the SME owners/managers shows that the majority (over 80%) have some form of qualification and only a small percentage have no formal education. This may appear to be incongruent with the belief that entrepreneurs have higher levels of practical business experience to compensate for a lack of formal education; however, previous studies have shown correlations between education and successful SME operations (Sage, 1993). The finding in relation to education levels is important as it indicates that the results throughout this book are made by "informed" respondents.

The availability or access to adequate IT skills is considered to be a prerequisite for successful e-commerce implementation in all organizations. In the Swedish sample, it is interesting to note that only 17.5% of respondents indicated that they had lower than average *IT skills*. This figure rose to 30% for female owner/managers and dropped to 9% for male owner/managers, suggesting that female SME owners perceived their IT skills to be inadequate.

It is widely accepted (see for example, BarNir & Smith, 2002; Blackburn et al., 2000; Schindehutte & Morris, 2001) that one of the "motivators" for e-commerce adoption is the need to reach customers beyond the local environment. An examination of our results in Sweden shows that more than 50% of the sample group indicated that their major customer base was beyond the local market, and 50% of e-commerce adopters had a national and international *market focus*. This is consistent with the expectations that e-commerce enables SMEs to target wider geographical areas and implies the need for using e-commerce technology to manage this focus. However, the non-adopter responses are indicative of the presence of

*Figure 4. Level of IT skill in the organisation (Swedish respondents)*

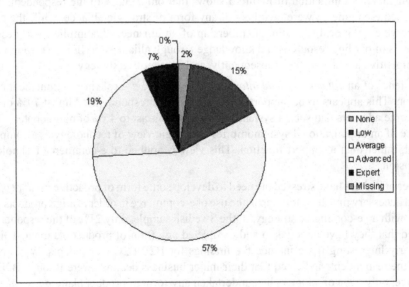

e-commerce barriers since 33% of respondents in this group had a national or international focus, yet they had not implemented e-commerce technology. The majority (58%) had a local market focus.

Finally, the Swedish sample shows that a higher percentage of e-commerce adopters (almost 80%) are engaged in B2B e-commerce. This is consistent with the finding that only 18% of the e-commerce adopters were in the retail sector selling directly to customers.

# Associations Between Business Characteristics in Sweden

By way of fully examining the profile of the Swedish respondents, a series of chi-square tests was applied to determine whether there was any association between the business characteristics. Several characteristics were found to be significantly associated. These are

*Table 4. Summary of associations between business characteristics (Sweden)*

| Business characteristic | Associated with... | Table | p value |
|---|---|---|---|
| **Length of time in business (business age).** | Number of employees (business size). | 3.5 | <.001 |
| | Business sector. | 3.6 | <.001 |
| | Alliance membership. | 3.7 | <.001 |
| **Number of employees (business size).** | Business sector. | 3.8 | <.001 |
| | Alliance membership. | 3.9 | <.005 |
| | Gender of CEO. | 3.10 | <.005 |
| | Level of CEO education. | 3.11 | <.005 |
| | Enterprise-wide system. | 3.12 | <.001 |
| | Product planning. | 3.13 | <.001 |
| | Level of IT skill. | 3.14 | <.001 |
| | Market focus. | 3.15 | <.001 |
| **Business sector.** | Level of CEO education. | 3.16 | <.001 |
| | Enterprise-wide system. | 3.17 | <.001 |
| | Product planning. | 3.18 | <.001 |
| | Level of IT skill. | 3.19 | <.005 |
| | Market focus. | 3.20 | <.001 |
| **Alliance membership.** | Level of CEO education. | 3.21 | <.05 |
| | Enterprise-wide system. | 3.22 | <.001 |
| **Gender of CEO.** | Level of CEO education. | 3.23 | <.05 |
| | Level of IT skill. | 3.24 | <.05 |
| | Market focus. | 3.25 | <.05 |
| **Level of CEO education.** | Level of IT skill. | 3.26 | <.001 |
| | Market focus. | 3.27 | <.001 |

summarized in Table 4, which also indicates the corresponding tables showing the associations and the relevant p value.

As can be seen from Table 4, the number of employees (or business size) is significantly associated with a wide range of other business characteristics. Each of the associations is shown and described in the tables next.

Table 5 shows that the larger SMEs are more likely to have been in business longer than the smaller ones. While 65.5% of SMEs with 50 to 199 employees are over 20 years old, only 22% of SMEs with 0 to 9 employees have been in business the same length of time. The data here suggests that regional Swedish SMEs appear to be "buoyant" and that long-term businesses have been able to maintain higher staff levels. This is consistent with the economic development of Sweden and indicates that the decisions about e-commerce adoption are being made in the context of a mature and viable economic market.

Table 6 provides the data for the association between business age and sector. It shows that in the regional Swedish sample, the industrial and finance respondents have been in

*Table 5. Association between business age and business size*

| Size | Sole owner | 1 to 9 employees | 10 to 19 employees | 20 to 49 employees | 50 to 199 employees | >200 employees |
|---|---|---|---|---|---|---|
| **Age** | | | | | | |
| **Less than 1 year** | 0 | 3 | 0 | 0 | 0 | 1 |
| **1 to 2 years** | 5 | 7 | 0 | 1 | 0 | 0 |
| **3 to 5 years** | 6 | 26 | 2 | 2 | 3 | 0 |
| **6 to 10 years** | 12 | 32 | 4 | 10 | 2 | 0 |
| **10 to 20 years** | 8 | 45 | 8 | 7 | 5 | 0 |
| **More than 20 years** | 10 | 31 | 34 | 20 | 19 | 7 |
| **TOTAL 310** | 41 | 144 | 48 | 40 | 29 | 8 |

*Note: 3 missing; p<.001*

*Table 6. Association between business age and business sector*

| Sector | Industrial | Service | Retail | Finance | Other |
|---|---|---|---|---|---|
| **Age** | | | | | |
| **Less than 1 year** | 1 | 1 | 1 | 0 | 1 |
| **1 to 2 years** | 1 | 7 | 4 | 0 | 1 |
| **3 to 5 years** | 8 | 18 | 11 | 0 | 3 |
| **6 to 10 years** | 11 | 27 | 7 | 0 | 15 |
| **10 to 20 years** | 13 | 34 | 11 | 0 | 15 |
| **More than 20 years** | 45 | 27 | 23 | 9 | 17 |
| **TOTAL 311** | 79 | 114 | 57 | 9 | 52 |

*Note: 2 missing; p<.001*

business longer than those respondents that indicated that they are retail or service sector organisations. Finance sector SMEs appear to demonstrate high levels of stability, although it should be noted that the sample size is quite small in this sector.

Table 7 shows that while younger SMEs are equivocal regarding membership of a strategic alliance, more of the older organisations have chosen to remain outside of such structures. 44% of SMEs, which were not part of an alliance were more than 20 years old. This suggests that older businesses are perhaps more "traditional" in their approach, preferring to remain outside any commitments to other businesses. A number of European studies (Dennis, 2000; Drakopolou-Dodd, Jack, & Anderson, 2002) have noted similar findings, adding the reluctance of older more established businesses to share their "hard fought for knowledge" with younger, less established businesses.

Conventional wisdom would suggest that SMEs involved in industrial production and manufacturing (grouped in this study under the industrial sector) would tend to be larger than those whose major function is service or retail. The findings shown in Table 8 support

*Table 7. Association between business age and membership of an alliance*

| Alliance Membership | Yes | No |
|---|---|---|
| Age | | |
| Less than 1 year | 1 | 3 |
| 1 to 2 years | 6 | 7 |
| 3 to 5 years | 18 | 22 |
| 6 to 10 years | 24 | 33 |
| 10 to 20 years | 34 | 34 |
| More than 20 years | 37 | 78 |
| TOTAL 301 | 124 | 177 |

*Note: 12 missing; p<.001*

*Table 8. Association between business size and business sector*

| Sector | Industrial | Service | Retail | Finance | Other |
|---|---|---|---|---|---|
| Size | | | | | |
| Sole owner | 5 | 19 | 12 | 0 | 5 |
| 1 to 9 employees | 21 | 61 | 26 | 3 | 33 |
| 10 to 19 employees | 11 | 18 | 13 | 2 | 4 |
| 20 to 49 employees | 18 | 9 | 4 | 1 | 8 |
| 50 to 199 employees | 18 | 7 | 1 | 2 | 1 |
| More than 200 employees | 6 | 0 | 0 | 1 | 1 |
| TOTAL 310 | 79 | 114 | 56 | 9 | 52 |

*Note: 3 missing; p<.001*

this. Retail and serviced-based SMEs in regional Sweden tend to be smaller than industrial organizations. Indeed, while almost 70% of both service and retail respondents have less than ten employees, less than 33% of the industrial respondents had the same number.

A number of studies (Gibb, 1993; MacGregor & Vrazalic, 2006; Ozcan, 1995) have suggested that strategic alliances lead to increased technical knowledge, market penetration opportunities, business efficiency, and legitimacy. As expected, Table 9 shows that it is the smaller organizations (i.e., having fewer employees) that are more likely to seek out membership of some form of strategic alliance. While 24% of the SMEs with more than 20 employees were members of a business strategic alliance, 51% of those with staff numbers under ten had sought out membership. This supports a number of earlier studies (Achrol & Kotler, 1999; Dean, Holmes, & Smith, 1997).

There are a number of interesting findings in the literature that compare various facets of gender differences in the ownership/management of SMEs. These facets include comparisons of ownership/management statistics and reasons for moving into the SME sector, finance availability, and networking. The primary motivation for moving into the SME sector is the

*Table 9. Association between business size and membership of an alliance*

| Alliance Membership | Yes | No |
|---|---|---|
| Size | | |
| Sole owner | 25 | 15 |
| 1 to 9 employees | 67 | 72 |
| 10 to 19 employees | 13 | 33 |
| 20 to 49 employees | 10 | 29 |
| 50 to 199 employees | 8 | 20 |
| More than 200 employees | 0 | 8 |
| TOTAL 300 | 123 | 177 |

*Note: 13 missing; p<.005*

*Table 10. Association between business size and gender of CEO*

| Gender of CEO | Male | Female |
|---|---|---|
| Size | | |
| Sole owner | 27 | 12 |
| 1 to 9 employees | 125 | 15 |
| 10 to 19 employees | 43 | 5 |
| 20 to 49 employees | 39 | 1 |
| 50 to 199 employees | 28 | 1 |
| More than 200 employees | 6 | 1 |
| TOTAL 304 | 269 | 35 |

*Note: 9 missing; p<.005*

desire to become self-employed. Studies by Nillson (1997), Brush and Hisrich (1999), and Sandberg (2003) have shown that the growth in self-employed females was significantly higher than for males. Table 10 supports these studies by indicating that female respondents in Sweden tended to have smaller staff levels than male counterparts. While more than 40% of the male owners/managers employed more than ten staff members, only 23% of females did so. This suggests that micro businesses in regional Sweden are predominantly owned by women.

Table 11 shows that for all categories of business size there were more formally educated CEOs than CEOs without formal education. However, in the sole proprietorship category, 27.5% of SME owners did not have any formal qualifications.

Several studies (Jeffcoate, Chappell, & Feindt, 2002; Tetteh & Burn, 2001) have suggested that smaller SMEs often work in a haphazard, reactive manner as compared to larger SMEs. These findings appear to be supported by the current findings in relation to enterprise-wide systems. Table 12 shows that larger organisations are more likely to develop and use some form of enterprise-wide business system than are smaller ones. Indeed while 86% of the

*Table 11. Association between business size and level of CEO education*

| Level of CEO Education | No Formal Education | Formal Education |
|---|---|---|
| **Size** | | |
| **Sole owner** | 11 | 29 |
| **1 to 9 employees** | 18 | 116 |
| **10 to 19 employees** | 5 | 43 |
| **20 to 49 employees** | 2 | 34 |
| **50 to 199 employees** | 1 | 28 |
| **More than 200 employees** | 0 | 6 |
| **TOTAL 293** | 37 | 256 |

*Note: 20 missing; p<.005*

*Table 12. Association between business size and existence of an enterprise wide system*

| Enterprise-Wide System | Yes | No |
|---|---|---|
| **Size** | | |
| **Sole owner** | 15 | 26 |
| **1 to 9 employees** | 66 | 78 |
| **10 to 19 employees** | 33 | 15 |
| **20 to 49 employees** | 33 | 7 |
| **50 to 199 employees** | 24 | 4 |
| **More than 200 employees** | 8 | 0 |
| **TOTAL 309** | 179 | 130 |

*Note: 4 missing: p<.001*

respondent businesses with 20 or more employees had developed an enterprise-wide business system, only 37% of the respondents that were sole owners had done likewise.

Similarly, Tetteh et al. (2001) and Jeffcoate et al. (2002) found that smaller SMEs are less capable of engaging in systematic product planning, when compared to larger SMEs. These findings appear to be supported in Table 13.

Table 13 shows that it is predominately the larger organisations (i.e., those with more than 50 employees) that had developed any form of product planning. Indeed while more than 80% of the respondents with over 50 employees had developed some form of product planning, only 7% of the respondents with less than 10 staff members had engaged product planning. Although this may reflect on the planning skills of smaller businesses, it is also potentially a manifestation of the amount of time available for planning. Micro businesses tend to have less time to engage in planning than their larger counterparts.

Previous studies (Culkin et al., 2000; Fallon et al., 2000) have concluded that larger SMEs are inherently more complex, resulting in a deeper understanding of IT as well as the wider marketplace. An examination of Table 14 shows a slightly different story in the Swedish

*Table 13. Association between business size and product planning*

| Product Planning | Yes | No |
|---|---|---|
| **Size** | | |
| **Sole owner** | 3 | 38 |
| **1 to 9 employees** | 10 | 134 |
| **10 to 19 employees** | 4 | 44 |
| **20 to 49 employees** | 18 | 22 |
| **50 to 199 employees** | 24 | 5 |
| **More than 200 employees** | 6 | 2 |
| **TOTAL 310** | 59 | 245 |

*Note: 3 missing; p<.001*

*Table 14. Association between business size and level of IT skill*

| Level of IT Skill | None | Low | Average | High | Expert |
|---|---|---|---|---|---|
| **Size** | | | | | |
| **Sole owner** | 6 | 8 | 23 | 3 | 1 |
| **1 to 9 employees** | 1 | 26 | 82 | 23 | 12 |
| **10 to 19 employees** | 0 | 8 | 27 | 11 | 2 |
| **20 to 49 employees** | 0 | 3 | 19 | 13 | 5 |
| **50 to 199 employees** | 0 | 1 | 21 | 6 | 1 |
| **More than 200 employees** | 0 | 0 | 5 | 3 | 0 |
| **TOTAL 310** | 7 | 46 | 177 | 59 | 21 |

*Note: 3 missing; p<.001*

sample. While almost 30% of the SMEs with 1 to 49 employees rate their IT skill levels as high or expert, only 24% of the 50 to 199 employee group had similar ratings. The advent and proliferation of the Internet appears to have "leveled the playing field" in relation to IT skills.

As expected, Table 15 indicates that smaller organisations tend to devote their attention to local and regional markets, while larger ones tend to focus on national and international markets. This is despite the early predictions that smaller businesses could and would focus their attention on the global marketplace. However SMEs with 1 to 9 employees had a higher than expected number of respondents whose focus was the national or international marketplace (approximately 43%).

An examination of Table 16 shows that there are a number of differences in the education level between the various business sectors in the Swedish sample. Conventional wisdom would suggest that the greatest concentration of CEOs without formal educational training would probably be in the retail sector. Indeed, while 9% of the CEOs in industrial SMEs and 11% of the CEOs in service-based organisations had no formal training, 16% of the retail CEOs did not have some form of formal education.

*Table 15. Association between business size and market focus*

| Market Focus | Local | Regional | National | International |
|---|---|---|---|---|
| **Size** | | | | |
| **Sole owner** | 28 | 5 | 7 | 1 |
| **1 to 9 employees** | 71 | 11 | 45 | 17 |
| **10 to 19 employees** | 25 | 7 | 13 | 3 |
| **20 to 49 employees** | 14 | 2 | 14 | 10 |
| **50 to 199 employees** | 6 | 3 | 16 | 4 |
| **More than 200 employees** | 3 | 0 | 1 | 4 |
| **TOTAL 310** | 147 | 28 | 96 | 39 |

*Note: 3 missing; p<.001*

*Table 16. Association between business sector and level of CEO education*

| Level of CEO Education | No Formal Education | Formal Education |
|---|---|---|
| **Sector** | | |
| **Industrial** | 7 | 68 |
| **Service** | 12 | 96 |
| **Retail** | 9 | 46 |
| **Finance** | 0 | 8 |
| **Other** | 9 | 38 |
| **TOTAL 293** | 37 | 256 |

*Note: 20 missing; p<.001*

The data in Table 17 indicates that it is the service sector that is less likely to develop and use any form of enterprise-wide business system in their organization, while a high portion of the industrial SMEs (82%) would. This result may be a function of the wording of the particular question; however, a study by Lawson, Alcock, Cooper, and Burgess (2003) suggest that very often service-based SMEs "plug" some form of Internet access to their existing business strategies. They add that modification to those strategies rarely occurs as the non-Internet functions remain the core of the business. This is particularly the case with professional SMEs (see for example MacGregor, Hyland, Harvie, & Lee, 2006) where the Internet is seen as a resource through which information can be gathered.

Table 18 shows that with the exception of the industrial sector, less than 20% of all other respondents have undertaken any form of product planning. The results in this table are not unexpected for the service sector respondents. However, it is interesting to note that while the majority of respondents from the retail sector indicated that they operated in a B2B manner, less than 2% had undertaken any form of planning with regards the products that they are dispersing. Porter (2001) and Tetteh et al. (2001) have concluded that failure to address factors such as core products, dispersal logistics, and value chains will often result in duplication of effort, less than expected benefits, and failure to gain reasonable market penetration. While the current study did not address these issues, the results in Table 18

*Table 17. Association between business sector and existence of an enterprise wide system*

| Enterprise-Wide System | Yes | No |
|---|---|---|
| Business Sector | | |
| Industrial | 65 | 14 |
| Service | 48 | 66 |
| Retail | 39 | 18 |
| Finance | 3 | 6 |
| Other | 25 | 25 |
| TOTAL 309 | 180 | 129 |

*Note: 4 missing; p<.001*

*Table 18. Association between business sector and product planning*

| Product Planning | Yes | No |
|---|---|---|
| Business Sector | | |
| Industrial | 42 | 37 |
| Service | 12 | 102 |
| Retail | 1 | 56 |
| Finance | 1 | 8 |
| Other | 9 | 44 |
| TOTAL 312 | 65 | 247 |

*Note: 1 missing; p<.001*

might lead to the conclusion that lack of product planning may lead to similar results for Swedish regional SMEs.

An examination of Table 19 indicates that 62% of those SMEs that rated their IT skills as being expert were operating in the service sector. Interestingly, the service sector also had the highest perception of low levels of IT skills within the organization (33%) compared to SMEs in other sectors. That having been said, the results show that the larger proportion of respondents had sufficient knowledge of IT to respond to issues addressed in later chapters.

In Table 20, 43% of the respondents operated outside the regional area of their business location. This would suggest that solid levels of geographic market expansion had occurred. Only 18% of industrial SMEs operated locally or regionally, compared to 54% of retail SMEs and 89% of finance SMEs, which had a local focus. Very few service sector SMEs (3.5%) engaged internationally. In fact, the majority of SMEs operating locally and regionally were service sector SMEs, while the majority of those operating nationally or internationally were industrial organisations. As might be expected, the finance sector did not engage in national or international trade. This is probably owing to country-specific finance and investment regulations.

*Table 19. Association between business sector and level of IT skill*

| Level of IT Skill | None | Low | Average | High | Expert |
|---|---|---|---|---|---|
| **Business Sector** | | | | | |
| **Industrial** | 2 | 9 | 50 | 15 | 3 |
| **Service** | 1 | 16 | 66 | 18 | 13 |
| **Retail** | 2 | 14 | 25 | 14 | 2 |
| **Finance** | 0 | 0 | 8 | 1 | 0 |
| **Other** | 2 | 9 | 28 | 11 | 3 |
| **TOTAL 312** | 7 | 48 | 177 | 59 | 21 |

*Note: 1 missing; p<.005*

*Table 20. Association between business sector and market focus*

| Market Focus | Local | Regional | National | International |
|---|---|---|---|---|
| **Business Sector** | | | | |
| **Industrial** | 12 | 2 | 40 | 25 |
| **Service** | 62 | 18 | 30 | 4 |
| **Retail** | 31 | 4 | 18 | 4 |
| **Finance** | 8 | 1 | 0 | 0 |
| **Other** | 36 | 3 | 8 | 6 |
| **TOTAL 312** | 149 | 28 | 96 | 39 |

*Note: 1 missing; p<.001*

Table 21 indicates that more than 88% of CEOs in SMEs that belonged to an alliance had formal education. This is comparable to 87% of CEOs in SMEs that were not members of an alliance, implying that educated CEOs were just as likely to enter into an alliance as those that had no formal training. Interestingly, more than 60% of CEOs without a formal education did not align themselves with other SMEs to compensate for the lack of qualifications and formal knowledge.

Table 22 provides an unexpected result. While member respondents were equivocal regarding the development and use of enterprise-wide business systems, overwhelmingly (68%), non-member respondents had developed some form of enterprise-wide business system.

While 9% of female CEOs (as shown in Table 23) did not have any form of formal education, this figure grew to 13% for male respondents. However, it should be noted that the sample size for female respondents was much smaller.

*Table 21. Association between membership of an alliance and level of CEO education*

| Alliance Membership Level of CEO Education | Yes | No |
|---|---|---|
| No Formal Education | 14 | 23 |
| Formal Education | 104 | 152 |
| TOTAL 293 | 118 | 175 |

*Note: 20 missing; p<.05*

*Table 22. Association between membership of an alliance and existence of an enterprise-wide system*

| Alliance Membership Enterprise-Wide System | Yes | No |
|---|---|---|
| Yes | 57 | 123 |
| No | 67 | 54 |
| TOTAL 301 | 124 | 177 |

*Note: 12 missing; p<.001*

*Table 23. Association between gender of CEO and level of CEO education*

| Gender of CEO Level of CEO Education | Male | Female |
|---|---|---|
| No Formal Education | 34 | 3 |
| Formal Education | 223 | 31 |
| TOTAL 291 | 257 | 34 |

*Note: 22 missing; p<.05*

An examination of Table 24 shows that the 27% of SMEs with a male CEO had a perception of higher IT expertise. In contrast, only 14% of SMEs with a female CEO rated their IT skills as highly. This tends to support previous findings that males are earlier adopters of technology.

The data in Table 25 points to a substantial difference in the level of national and international market focus between those SMEs with a male CEO and those with a female CEO. Twenty-five percent of those respondents that had a female CEO indicated that they had a national or international market focus. By comparison, 46% of those that had a male CEO had a national or international market focus.

Where gender is concerned, male SME owners/managers were more likely to rate the level of IT skill in their organization as being higher and were more likely to have a national or international focus which is consistent with e-commerce. Female CEOs showed the opposite tendencies.

*Table 24. Association between gender of CEO and IT skill level*

| Gender of CEO | Male | Female |
|---|---|---|
| Level of IT Skill | | |
| None | 5 | 2 |
| Low | 39 | 8 |
| Average | 152 | 21 |
| Advanced | 54 | 4 |
| Expert | 19 | 1 |
| TOTAL 305 | 269 | 36 |

Note: 8 missing; p<.05

*Table 25. Association between gender of CEO and market focus*

| Gender of CEO | Male | Female |
|---|---|---|
| Market Focus | | |
| Local | 123 | 23 |
| Regional | 22 | 4 |
| National | 88 | 7 |
| International | 36 | 2 |
| TOTAL 305 | 269 | 36 |

Note: 8 missing; p<.05

Table 26 shows that 27% of the CEOs with a formal education rated their IT skills as high or expert, while only 14% of the CEOs without formal training did so.

Finally, Table 27 provides the details of the association between the level of education of the CEO and the market focus of the organisation. The data in this table suggests that it is the SMEs whose CEO does not have a formal education are focusing more on the local marketplace (73%). However, CEOs with a formal education are equally likely to focus on the local market (44%) as they are on the national/international market (46%).

This section highlighted the associations between business characteristics in Swedish regional SMEs and showed strong associations between a number of characteristics. The following section will examine the association between the same characteristics and e-commerce adoption.

*Table 26. Association between level of CEO education and level of IT skill*

| Level of CEO Education | No Formal Education | Formal Education |
|---|---|---|
| Level of IT Skill | | |
| None | 5 | 2 |
| Low | 10 | 36 |
| Average | 17 | 149 |
| High | 4 | 51 |
| Expert | 1 | 18 |
| TOTAL 293 | 37 | 256 |

*Note: 20 missing; p<.001*

*Table 27. Association between level of CEO education and market focus*

| Level of CEO Education | No Formal Education | Formal Education |
|---|---|---|
| Market Focus | | |
| Local | 27 | 113 |
| Regional | 2 | 24 |
| National | 6 | 83 |
| International | 2 | 36 |
| TOTAL 293 | 37 | 256 |

*Note: 20 missing; p<.001*

# Associations Between Business Characteristics and E-Commerce Adoption in Sweden

A series of chi-square tests were applied to determine whether there was any association between business characteristics and e-commerce adoption. The results indicated strong associations with several different characteristics. These are summarized in Table 28, which also indicates the corresponding tables showing the associations and the relevant p value.

As can be seen from Table 28, e-commerce adoption is significantly associated with a wide range of other business characteristics. Each of the associations is shown and described in the tables next.

*Table 28. Summary of associations between business characteristics and e-commerce adoption*

| E-commerce adoption is associated with... | Table | p value |
|---|---|---|
| Number of employees (business size) | 3.29 | <.001 |
| Business sector | 3.30 | <.001 |
| Alliance membership | 3.31 | <.005 |
| Existence of an enterprise-wide system | 3.32 | <.001 |
| Product planning | 3.33 | <.001 |
| Level of IT skill | 3.34 | <.001 |
| Market focus | 3.35 | <.001 |

*Table 29. Association between business size and adoption of e-commerce*

| Business Size | E-commerce Adopters | Non-Adopters |
|---|---|---|
| 0 employees | 15 | 26 |
| 1-9 employees | 77 | 67 |
| 10-19 employees | 30 | 18 |
| 20-49 employees | 30 | 10 |
| 50-199 employees | 25 | 4 |
| More than 200 employees | 6 | 2 |
| TOTAL 310 | 183 | 127 |

*Note: 3 missing; p<.001*

A number of studies (Donckels & Lambrecht, 1997; Kai-Uwe Brock, 2000) have shown that adoption of e-commerce may be affected by the age of the business. These studies suggest that the very "young" SMEs (i.e., less than 3 years in business) and the very "old" ones (i.e., more than 20 years in business) are less likely to adopt e-commerce than those businesses in between. The results from the Swedish study do not support these earlier findings.

Table 29 shows that 50% of the adopters were SMEs that employed less than 10 people (i.e., micro businesses). At the same time, 73% of the non-adopters were in the same category. Of the SMEs with more than 20 employees, 77% have adopted e-commerce. This supports the earlier findings (Blackburn et al., 2000; Fallon et al., 2000; Hawkins & Winter, 1996; Hyland & Matlay, 1997).

A number of early studies (Blackburn et al., 2000; Matlay, 2000; Riquelme, 2002; Schindehutte et al., 2001) suggested that the service industries were more likely to adopt e-commerce than any of the other sectors. An examination of Table 30 supports these findings partially. Indeed, in Sweden, the industrial and service sectors appear to be the more likely groups to adopt e-commerce. However, the same can be said about non-adopters. Sixty-two of the SMEs surveyed in the industrial and service sectors had adopted e-commerce.

A number of government as well as academic articles (Dean et al., 1997; Marchewka et al., 2000) stress the need to develop and become members of a business strategic alliance as a first step to adopting e-commerce. The data shown in Table 31 shows that approximately 40% of the respondents had become members of a strategic alliance. This does not support

Table 30. Association between business sector and adoption of e-commerce

| Business Sector | E-Commerce Adopters | Non-Adopters |
|---|---|---|
| Industrial | 54 | 25 |
| Service | 65 | 49 |
| Retail | 33 | 24 |
| Finance | 9 | 0 |
| Other | 22 | 31 |
| TOTAL 312 | 183 | 129 |

Note: 1 missing; p<.001

Table 31. Association between alliance membership and adoption of e-commerce

| Alliance Membership | E-Commerce Adopters | Non-Adopters |
|---|---|---|
| Yes | 61 | 63 |
| No | 115 | 62 |
| TOTAL 301 | 176 | 125 |

Note: 12 missing; p<.005

previous findings, at least for the regional SMEs in Sweden. One proposition is that regional SMEs find it more difficult to develop strategic alliances because of distance concerns. This conclusion is supported by studies carried out by Dennis (2000) and Drakopolou-Dodd et al. (2002).

Previous research (Bunker & MacGregor, 2000; Tetteh et al., 2001) found that quite often SMEs did not develop any form of enterprise-wide business system prior to, or in some case after the adoption of e-commerce. These studies suggest that e-commerce used without an enterprise-wide system failed to live up to expectations and very often left the SME with severe disadvantages in their operation. An examination of Table 32 shows that 68% of the respondents that had introduced an enterprise-wide business system had adopted e-commerce. The data also shows that 53% of those businesses that had not developed an enterprise-wide business system had also not introduced e-commerce. While the level of success has not been tested, the results in Table 32 would tend to support the earlier findings of Tetteh et al. (2001) and Bunker et al. (2000).

Table 33 provides details of the association between product planning and e-commerce adoption. Again, a number of studies (Bunker et al., 2000; Schindehutte et al., 2001; Tetteh et al., 2001) have suggested that product planning is an essential element of successful e-commerce use. An examination of Table 33 shows that 77% of those respondents that had developed product plans had also adopted e-commerce; however, the majority of the adopters (73%) had not developed product-planning strategies. This would tend to make the results of the earlier studies questionable at best.

*Table 32. Association between existence of an enterprise-wide system and adoption of e-commerce*

| Existence of Enterprise-Wide system | E-Commerce Adopters | Non-Adopters |
|---|---|---|
| Yes | 122 | 58 |
| No | 58 | 71 |
| TOTAL 309 | 180 | 129 |

*Note: 4 missing; p<.001*

*Table 33. Association between the product planning and adoption of e-commerce*

| Product Planning | E-Commerce Adopters | Non-Adopters |
|---|---|---|
| Yes | 50 | 15 |
| No | 133 | 114 |
| T O T A L 312 | 183 | 129 |

*Note: 1 missing; p<.001*

A number of studies (O'Donnell, Gilmore, Cummins, & Carson, 2001; Tetteh et al., 2001) have concluded that greater exposure to computing technology normally leads to more willingness to adopt and use e-commerce. The data in Table 34 appears to support these findings. While over 80% of the high and expert respondents had adopted e-commerce, only 29% of the low/none group had adopted e-commerce. This would tend to support the earlier findings. Perhaps worthy of note is the fact that 20% of the respondent SMEs that had a high or expert IT skill set had not adopted e-commerce. One explanation may be that those respondents had analysed their own particular businesses and had validly concluded that e-commerce was not a viable option.

One noticeable finding shown in Table 35 is that 41% of internationally focused SMEs did not use e-commerce, while 72% of nationally focused SMEs were using e-commerce. This figure reduces to 50% for the locally focused respondents. Previous research (BarNir et al., 2001; Blackburn et al., 2000; Schindehutte et al., 2001) has concluded that nationally and internationally focused businesses are more likely to adopt e-commerce than local or regionally focused businesses. Despite the lower than expected numbers for the internationally focused SMEs, this is supported in the data in Table 35. However, more importantly the number of SMEs operating at a local level that had adopted e-commerce is almost the same as that of SMEs, which are not using e-commerce.

*Table 34. Association between the level of IT skill and adoption of e-commerce*

| Level of IT Skill | E-Commerce Adopters | Non-Adopters |
|---|---|---|
| None | 2 | 5 |
| Low | 14 | 34 |
| Average | 102 | 75 |
| High | 45 | 14 |
| Expert | 20 | 1 |
| TOTAL 312 | 183 | 129 |

*Note: 1 missing; p<.001*

*Table 35. Association between market focus and adoption of e-commerce*

| Market Focus | E-Commerce Adopters | Non-Adopters |
|---|---|---|
| Local | 74 | 75 |
| Regional | 17 | 11 |
| National | 69 | 27 |
| International | 23 | 16 |
| TOTAL 312 | 183 | 129 |

*Note: 1 missing; p<.001*

# Summary of Swedish Findings

Overall, the majority of the Swedish respondents were SMEs that had been in business for more than 10 years but employed less than 20 employees. They operate mainly in the local and national, industrial and service sectors, and tend not enter into strategic alliances with other businesses. The majority has an enterprise-wide system but do not engage in product planning. Their CEOs are predominantly male and well educated and they have access to advanced IT skills in their organization.

By comparison, the respondents who had adopted e-commerce were in business for more than 10 years, but employed between 10 and 20 staff members. They were local and national in their market focus and they operated mainly in the industrial and service sectors. The majority was not members of an alliance, but had an enterprise-wide system in their organization. They did not engage in product planning. Their CEOs are males with formal qualifications. The level of IT expertise in adopters was rated as being high and they engaged mainly in B2B e-commerce.

E-commerce non-adopters were similar in profile to the overall sample; however, they were equally split in terms of alliance membership and tended to have lower levels of IT knowledge in the organization. These findings are summarized at a glance in Table 36.

The results appear to suggest that Swedish regional SMEs, which are more likely to adopt e-commerce:

*Table 36. Comparison of Swedish respondents*

| Business Characteristics | Overall Sample | E-Commerce Adopters | Non-Adopters |
|---|---|---|---|
| **Business age.** | More than 10 years | More than 10 years | More than 10 years |
| **Business size.** | Less than 20 employees | Between 10 to 20 employees | Less than 20 employees |
| **Business sector.** | Industrial & service | Industrial & service | Industrial & service |
| **Alliance membership.** | No | No | Almost equal |
| **Existence of enterprise-wide system.** | Yes | Yes | No |
| **Product planning.** | No | No | No |
| **Gender of CEO.** | Male | Male | Male |
| **Level of CEO education.** | Formal education | Formal education | Formal education |
| **Level of IT skill.** | Average to Advanced | Average to Advanced | Low to Average |
| **Market focus.** | Local & national | Local & nationals | Local & national |
| **E-commerce type.** | N/A | B2B | N/A |

- Have between 10 and 20 employees
- Operate in the industrial or service sectors
- Do not belong to a strategic alliance
- Have enterprise-wide systems
- Do not engage in product planning
- Have advanced levels of IT skills in their organization
- Operate at a local and national level

We will now examine the Australian respondents in the same level of detail.

# Profile of Respondents in Australia

The response rate in Australia was significantly higher than in Sweden owing to the telephone survey method used. Table 37 provides a detailed picture of the individuals who participated in the Australian study.

Table 37 indicates some differences in the respondents' profile when compared to the Swedish data. One important observation that needs to be made is the lower than expected level of adoption of e-commerce in the Australian sample group. While the Swedish sample had a 58.5% adoption rate, the Australian sample shows only 15.6%. This needs to be kept in mind for some of the other findings presented later in this chapter and in subsequent chapters

*Table 37. Profile of Australian respondents*

| Business Char-acteristics | Acceptable Range of Responses | No of Responses (Adopters) | % | No of Responses (Non-Adopters) | % | Total | Total (%) |
|---|---|---|---|---|---|---|---|
| Business age. | Less than 1 year | 0 | 0 | 0 | 0 | 0 | 0 |
| | 1 to 2 years | 5 | 20 | 18 | 13.3 | 23 | 14.4 |
| | 3 to 5 years | 6 | 24 | 33 | 24.4 | 39 | 24.4 |
| | 6 to 10 years | 8 | 32 | 47 | 34.8 | 55 | 34.4 |
| | 11 to 20 years | 5 | 20 | 34 | 25.2 | 39 | 24.4 |
| | More than 20 years | 1 | 4 | 3 | 2.2 | 4 | 2.5 |
| Business size. | Sole proprietorship | 3 | 12 | 27 | 20 | 30 | 18.8 |
| | 1 to 9 employees | 22 | 88 | 90 | 66.7 | 112 | 70 |
| | 10 to 19 employees | 0 | 0 | 9 | 6.7 | 9 | 5.6 |
| | 20 to 49 employees | 0 | 0 | 8 | 5.9 | 8 | 5 |
| | 50 to 199 employees | 0 | 0 | 0 | 0 | 0 | 0 |
| | 200 or more employees | 0 | 0 | 1 | 0.7 | 1 | 0.6 |

*continued on following page*

*Table 37. Continued*

| Business Characteristics | Acceptable Range of Responses | No of Responses (Adopters) | % | No of Responses (Non-Adopters) | % | Total | Total (%) |
|---|---|---|---|---|---|---|---|
| Business sector. | Industrial | 1 | 4 | 11 | 8.1 | 12 | 7.5 |
| | Service | 8 | 32 | 35 | 25.9 | 43 | 26.9 |
| | Retail | 16 | 64 | 89 | 65.9 | 105 | 65.6 |
| | Finance | 0 | 0 | 0 | 0 | 0 | 0 |
| | Other | 0 | 0 | 0 | 0 | 0 | 0 |
| Alliance member. | Yes | 10 | 40 | 34 | 25.2 | 44 | 27.5 |
| | No | 15 | 60 | 101 | 74.8 | 116 | 72.5 |
| Gender of CEO. | Female | 7 | 28 | 51 | 37.8 | 58 | 36.3 |
| | Male | 18 | 72 | 84 | 62.2 | 102 | 63.7 |
| Level of CEO education. | No formal education | 5 | 20 | 27 | 20 | 32 | 20 |
| | Trade/matriculation | 11 | 44 | 73 | 54.1 | 84 | 52.5 |
| | University qualification | 9 | 36 | 35 | 25.9 | 44 | 27.5 |
| Level of IT skill. | None | 16 | 64 | 94 | 69.6 | 110 | 68.8 |
| | Low | 3 | 12 | 7 | 5.2 | 10 | 6.3 |
| | Average | 4 | 16 | 20 | 14.8 | 24 | 15 |
| | Advanced | 0 | 0 | 5 | 3.7 | 5 | 3.1 |
| | Expert | 2 | 8 | 9 | 6.7 | 11 | 6.9 |
| Market focus. | Local | 3 | 12 | 41 | 30.4 | 44 | 27.5 |
| | Regional | 19 | 76 | 88 | 65.2 | 107 | 66.9 |
| | National | 2 | 8 | 6 | 4.4 | 8 | 5 |
| | International | 1 | 4 | 0 | 0 | 1 | 0.6 |
| E-commerce type. | B2B | 5 | 20 | | | | |
| | B2C | 20 | 80 | | | | |

In relation to the *length of time in business*, only 27% of the respondents had been in business for more than 10 years. However, the data does suggest that the respondents were "experienced" business people with long established procedures and practices as there were few young (less than 2 years old) SMEs in the sample.

An examination of the Swedish responses (see Table 3) shows that 40% of the respondent SMEs had more than 10 employees. By comparison, the Australian data shows that only 11% of the respondent businesses had more than 10 employees (refer to Figure 5). The *business size* of the respondents in the Australian sample was much smaller than in Sweden. It is interesting to note that no business with employee numbers above 10 had adopted e-commerce. This is at odds with previous studies (Fallon et al., 2000; Hawkins et al., 1996; Matlay, 2000).

*Figure 5. Number of employees (Australian respondents)*

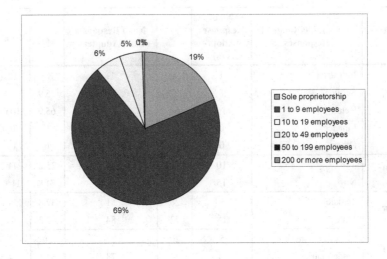

Also by contrast, most of the respondents in Australia, which had adopted e-commerce operated in the service or retail *business sectors*, suggested a more service-based economy. The large majority were retailers. In Sweden, a large number of respondents were industrial SMEs. The Australian findings are more consistent with the studies by Riquelme (2002) and Meikle et al. (2002).

The number of SMEs who were not *members of an alliance* was also higher with 72.5% of Australian respondents not belonging to any alliances, in contrast to 57% for the Swedish respondents. This suggests that Australian SMEs in regional areas were either reluctant to pool resources with competitors or simply did not have the opportunity to do so.

The number of female CEOs in the Australian sample was higher than in Sweden, with more than 36% (compared to 12% in Sweden). Clearly, the levels of SME participation by females are higher in Australia and the *gender* distribution is somewhat more evenly spread.

The *level of CEOs education* was comparable to that of Sweden, with 80% of SME owner/managers having some formal qualification. This percentage was only marginally higher in Sweden.

The results of the *level of IT skill* in the organisation are consistent with the low e-commerce adoption rate. Almost 70% of Australian respondents indicated that there was no IT skill in their organization (refer to Figure 6). This is in contrast to the Swedish sample where 2% had the same response. The e-commerce adopters had similar low levels of IT skills, which indicates that e-commerce implementation may have been outsourced.

The Swedish data showed that 43% of respondent businesses were trading either nationally or internationally. An examination of the Australian data shows that only 6% of respondent businesses were trading at a national or international level. Once again, this predominantly local *market focus* is consistent with the low e-commerce adoption rate in Australia.

*Figure 6. Level of IT skill (Australian respondents)*

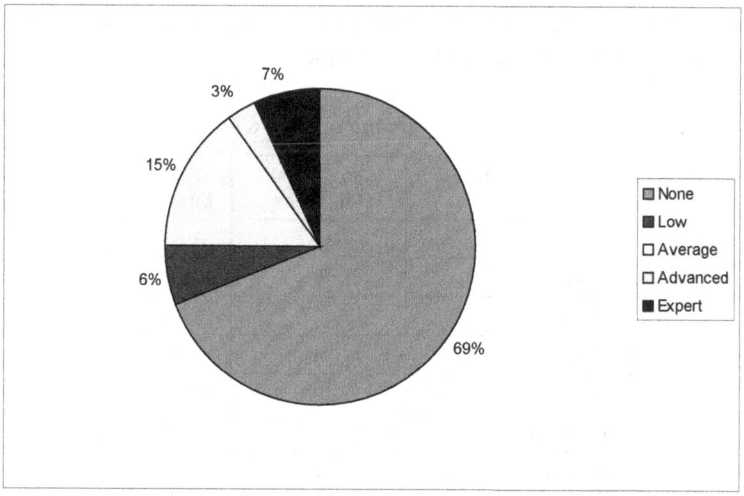

Another major difference between the Swedish and the Australian respondents can be found in the *type of e-commerce* implemented by the adopters. While 80% of the adopter SMEs in Sweden used B2B e-commerce, in Australia the situation is reverse, with a large majority engaging in B2C c-commerce.

# Associations Between Business Characteristics in Australia

Similarly, to the Swedish respondents, a series of chi-square tests was applied to the Australian sample to determine whether there was any association between the business characteristics. In contrast to Sweden where a large number of business characteristics were associated (refer to Table 4), in Australia only three characteristics showed associations with other business traits. These are summarized in Table 38, which also indicates the corresponding table number showing the associations and the relevant p value.

Each of the three associations is shown and described in Table 39.

*Table 38. Summary of associations between business characteristics (Australia)*

| Business characteristic | Associated with... | Table | p value |
|---|---|---|---|
| **Length of time in business (business age).** | Level of CEO education | 3.39 | p<.05 |
| **Level of CEO education.** | Market focus | 3.40 | p<.01 |
| **Business sector.** | Market focus | 3.41 | p<.001 |

Table 39 shows that the majority of SMEs whose CEO has no formal education are between 6 and 20 years old. By comparison, there is a "more even spread" with those SMEs whose owner/manager has some type of formal education, although 30% of the SMEs with a formally educated CEO were between 3 to 5 years old.

*Table 39. Association between business age and level of CEO education*

| Level of CEO Education | No Formal Education | Formal Education |
|---|---|---|
| Age | | |
| Less than 1 year | 0 | 0 |
| 1 to 2 years | 2 | 21 |
| 3 to 5 years | 4 | 35 |
| 6 to 10 years | 14 | 41 |
| 10 to 20 years | 11 | 28 |
| More than 20 years | 1 | 3 |
| TOTAL 160 | 32 | 118 |

Note: p<.05

*Table 40. Association between level of CEO education and market focus*

| Level of CEO Education | No Formal Education | Formal Education |
|---|---|---|
| Market Focus | | |
| Local | 9 | 35 |
| Regional | 20 | 87 |
| National | 3 | 5 |
| International | 0 | 1 |
| TOTAL 160 | 32 | 128 |

Note: p<.001

*Table 41. Association between business sector and market focus*

| Business Sector | Industrial | Service | Retail | Finance | Other |
|---|---|---|---|---|---|
| Market Focus | | | | | |
| Local | 1 | 4 | 39 | 0 | 0 |
| Regional | 11 | 36 | 60 | 0 | 0 |
| National | 0 | 3 | 5 | 0 | 0 |
| International | 0 | 0 | 1 | 0 | 0 |
| TOTAL 160 | 12 | 43 | 105 | 0 | 0 |

Note: p<.01

Table 40 indicates that the majority of CEOs (62.5%) without any formal education could be found in SMEs with a regional focus. By comparison, 68% of CEOs with formal training ran SMEs with a regional focus and only 4% had a national focus. This number increases to 9% for SMEs whose CEO had no formal education. These findings differ from Sweden where CEOs with no educational qualifications, as well as those who had undergone formal training, had a predominantly local focus.

Of interest in Table 41 is the fact that most of the SMEs have a local or regional focus across all of the sectors. Eighty-four percent of the service SMEs had a regional focus, and 100% of the industrial SMEs were operating locally or regionally. This dropped to 94% for retail SMEs. The majority of local SMEs were to be found in the retail sector.

# Associations Between Business Characteristics and E-Commerce Adoption in Australia

Unlike Sweden where seven business characteristics were found to be associated with e-commerce adoption (refer to Table 28), in Australia, none of the business characteristic were found to have an association. This is contrary to previous research by various authors. Blackburn et al. (2000), Schindehutte et al. (2001) and Donckels et al. (1997) have shown that adoption of e-commerce may be affected by the age of the business. The results from the Australian sample do not show any statistically significant associations between business age and adoption of e-commerce. Other studies (Blackburn et al., 2000; Fallon et al., 2000; Hawkins et al., 1996; Hyland et al., 1997) have concluded that business size is associated with adoption of e-commerce by SMEs. This was not found in the Australian data, either. Research by Schindehutte et al. (2001), Matlay (2000), Blackburn et al. (2000), and Riquelme (2002) have suggested that e-commerce adoption appears to be business sector specific. No statistically significant association was found between the business sector and adoption of e-commerce in the Australian sample. A number of studies (O'Donnell et al., 2001; Tetteh et al., 2001) have concluded that greater exposure to computing technology normally leads to more willingness to adopt and use e-commerce. This was not in evidence in the Australian sample. Other studies (BarNir et al., 2001; Blackburn et al., 2000: Schindehutte et al., 2001) have concluded that nationally and internationally focused businesses are more likely to adopt e-commerce than local or regionally focused businesses. Again, this was not in evidence in the Australian data.

# Summary of Australian Findings

Overall, the majority of Australian respondents were SMEs, which had been in business between 3 to 20 years, and had less than 10 employees. They operated predominantly in the retail (and service) sectors and were not members of any alliances. Most of the SMEs had a male CEO who had formal qualifications. However, the majority had low levels of IT

*Table 42. Comparison of Australian respondents*

| Business Characteristics | Overall Sample | E-Commerce Adopters | Non-Adopters |
|---|---|---|---|
| Business age. | 3 to 20 years | 3 to 20 years | 3 to 20 years |
| Business size. | Less than 10 employees | Less than 10 employees | Less than 10 employees |
| Business sector. | Service & retail | Service & retail | Service & retail |
| Alliance membership. | No | Somewhat even | No |
| Gender of CEO. | Male | Male | Male |
| Level of CEO education. | Formal education | Formal education | Formal education |
| Level of IT skill. | Low to none | Low to none | Low to none |
| Market focus. | Local & regional | Local | Local & regional |
| E-commerce type. | N/A | B2C | N/A |

skills in the organization and focused primarily on the regional (and local) markets. These findings from the whole sample are mirrored in the e-commerce adopters and non-adopters samples, with only minor differences. Slightly more adopters appeared to be members of an alliance (the split between adopters and non-adopters was 40%:60%) and tended to be owned by males. However, a very large portion of the adopters had a regional focus, which may seem unusual, but since the respondents are mainly retailers and service providers, it is less surprising. These findings are summarized at a glance in Table 42.

The results appear to suggest that Australian regional SMEs, which are more likely to adopt e-commerce:

- Have been in business anywhere between 3 to 20 years
- Are micro businesses (less than 10 employees)
- Operate in the retail sector
- Are more likely to belong to an alliance than their Swedish counterparts
- Have a male CEO who has formal qualifications
- Have low levels of IT skills in the organization
- Have a regional (and local) focus
- Use B2C e-commerce

We will now examine the U.S. respondents in the same level of detail.

## Profile of Respondents in the USA

The response rate in the U.S. was also significantly higher than in Sweden owing to the telephone survey method used. Table 43 provides a detailed picture of the individuals who

*Table 43. Profile of USA respondents*

| Business Character-istics | Acceptable Range of Responses | No of Responses (Adopters) | % | No of Responses (Non-Adopters) | % | Total | Total (%) |
|---|---|---|---|---|---|---|---|
| Business age. | Less than 1 year | 1 | 1.6 | 0 | 0 | 1 | 0.9 |
| | 1 to 2 years | 1 | 1.6 | 0 | 0 | 1 | 0.9 |
| | 3 to 5 years | 2 | 3.2 | 1 | 1.9 | 3 | 2.6 |
| | 6 to 10 years | 3 | 4.8 | 7 | 13.2 | 10 | 8.6 |
| | 11 to 20 years | 20 | 31.7 | 19 | 35.8 | 39 | 33.6 |
| | More than 20 years | 36 | 57.1 | 26 | 49.1 | 62 | 53.4 |
| Business size. | Sole proprietorship | 0 | 0 | 3 | 5.7 | 3 | 2.6 |
| | 1 to 9 employees | 24 | 38.1 | 23 | 43.4 | 47 | 40.5 |
| | 10 to 19 employees | 18 | 28.6 | 10 | 18.9 | 28 | 24.1 |
| | 20 to 49 employees | 17 | 27 | 13 | 24.5 | 30 | 25.9 |
| | 50 to 199 employees | 3 | 4.8 | 1 | 1.9 | 4 | 3.4 |
| | 200 or more employees | 1 | 1.6 | 3 | 5.7 | 4 | 3.4 |
| Business sec-tor. | Industrial | 21 | 33.3 | 27 | 50.9 | 48 | 41.4 |
| | Service | 13 | 20.6 | 4 | 7.5 | 17 | 14.7 |
| | Retail | 23 | 36.5 | 11 | 20.8 | 34 | 29.3 |
| | Finance | 0 | 0 | 0 | 0 | 0 | 0 |
| | Other | 5 | 7.9 | 8 | 15.1 | 13 | 11.2 |
| | Missing | 1 | 1.6 | 3 | 5.7 | 4 | 3.4 |
| Alliance member. | Yes | 19 | 30.2 | 6 | 11.3 | 25 | 21.6 |
| | No | 42 | 66.7 | 45 | 84.9 | 87 | 75 |
| | Missing | 2 | 3.2 | 2 | 3.8 | 4 | 3.4 |
| Gender of CEO. | Female | 9 | 14.3 | 8 | 15.1 | 17 | 14.7 |
| | Male | 49 | 77.8 | 40 | 75.5 | 89 | 76.7 |
| | Missing | 5 | 7.9 | 5 | 9.4 | 10 | 8.6 |
| Market fo-cus. | Local | 14 | 22.2 | 12 | 22.6 | 26 | 22.4 |
| | Regional | 21 | 33.3 | 26 | 49.1 | 47 | 40.5 |
| | National | 24 | 38.1 | 5 | 9.4 | 29 | 25 |
| | International | 2 | 3.2 | 7 | 13.2 | 9 | 7.8 |
| | Missing | 2 | 3.2 | 3 | 5.7 | 5 | 4.3 |
| Dedicated IT person. | Yes | 51 | 81 | 14 | 26.4 | 65 | 56 |
| | No | 12 | 19 | 36 | 67.9 | 48 | 41.4 |
| | Missing | 0 | 0 | 3 | 5.7 | 3 | 2.6 |

*Figure 7. Number of employees (USA respondents)*

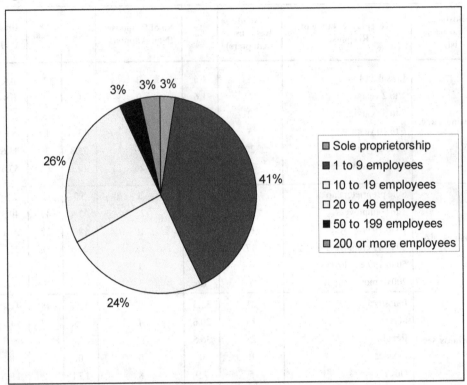

participated in the U.S. study.

The profile of the U.S. respondents indicates that the majority (87%) had been operating for more than 10 years. The *business age* of the SMEs in the USA was comparative to that of the Swedish respondents. Unlike the Australian sample, where the spread was more even across the different categories, in the U.S. the majority of the e-commerce adopters and non-adopters were mature organizations.

With regard to the *business size*, 65% of the respondents had less than 20 employees, which once again, was comparable to the Swedish group. Although the majority of the non-adopters fell into this category, a substantial number (25%) of the adopters had between 20 and 49 employees. Surprisingly, less than 5% of the larger sized SMEs (50 to 199 employees) had introduced e-commerce. The results of business size are shown in Figure 7.

Unlike Sweden, where industrial and service *sector* SMEs made up a large portion of the respondents and Australia, where service and retail organizations prevailed, in the U.S. it was the industrial and retail businesses that constituted almost three quarters of the sample. This number was somewhat diluted in the e-commerce adopters group, where service sector SMEs made up more than 20% of the respondents.

*Figure 8. Strategic alliance membership (USA respondents)*

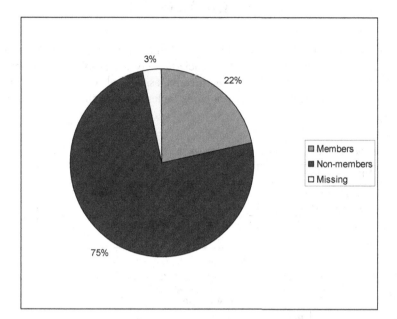

The U.S. SMEs were in agreement with their Australian counterparts in relation to *strategic alliance membership*: 75% of the U.S. respondents did not belong to an alliance, compared to 72.5% of Australian businesses. The contrast with the Swedish results is distinct because almost 40% of SMEs in Sweden were members of an alliance, which would suggest that U.S. and Australian organizations were more reluctant to engage in partnerships. This is shown in Figure 8.

We see comparable responses in relation to the *gender of the CEO*. Almost 77% are male in the U.S., 64% in Australia, and 86% in Sweden. Although the rate of participation by women is the highest in the Australian sample, it is still less than 50%.

Finally, U.S. SMEs tend to have a predominantly regional and national *market focus*, with 66% belonging to these two categories. The number of SMEs with an international focus is only 8%. This is compared to 12.5% in Sweden, but still significantly higher than in Australia, where only 0.6% of the respondents were doing business internationally. It should be noted that in the U.S. sample, almost 72% of non-adopters were operating locally and regionally, compared to 56% of e-commerce adopters.

In the U.S. study, we also asked whether there was a dedicated individual in the organization who was responsible for providing IT support. The contrast in the response to this question between the adopters and non-adopters was stark. While 81% of the adopters said they had a *dedicated IT support person*, only 26.4% of non-adopters said the same. This suggests that e-commerce requires dedicated IT support, a resource that most SMEs do not have, particularly in the early stages of their development.

# Associations Between Business Characteristics
# in the USA

By way of fully examining the profile of the U.S. respondents, a series of chi-square tests was applied to determine whether there was any association between the business characteristics. Several characteristics were found to be significantly associated. These are summarized in Table 44, which also indicates the corresponding tables showing the associations and the relevant p value.

*Table 44. Summary of associations between business characteristics (USA)*

| Business characteristic | Associated with... | Table | p value |
|---|---|---|---|
| Number of employees (business size). | Alliance membership | 3.46 | P<.05 |
| Gender of CEO. | Length of time in business (business age) | 3.47 | p<.005 |

*Table 45. Association between membership of an alliance and business size*

| Membership | Yes | No |
|---|---|---|
| **Business Size** | | |
| Sole owner | 0 | 3 |
| 1 to 9 employees | 4 | 43 |
| 10 to 19 employees | 9 | 17 |
| 20 to 49 employees | 11 | 18 |
| 50 to 199 employees | 0 | 4 |
| More than 200 employees | 1 | 2 |
| TOTAL 112 | 25 | 87 |

*Note: 4 missing; p<.05*

*Table 46. Association between gender of CEO and business age*

| Gender of the CEO | Male | Female |
|---|---|---|
| **Business Age** | | |
| Less than 1 year | 1 | 0 |
| 1 to 2 years | 1 | 0 |
| 3 to 5 years | 2 | 1 |
| 6 to 10 years | 8 | 2 |
| 10 to 20 years | 29 | 7 |
| More than 20 years | 48 | 7 |
| TOTAL 106 | 89 | 17 |

*Note: 10 missing; p<.005*

As can be seen from Table 44, the number of employees (or business size) is significantly associated with alliance membership.

An examination of Table 45 shows that while membership of an alliance remains relatively small, it is the "middle sized" SMEs (10 to 49 employees) in the U.S. that are more likely to seek out membership rather than the very small or the larger ones. This is in contrast to Sweden, where smaller SMEs tend to form or join alliances. Almost 50% of those SMEs that were not members of an alliance had between 1 and 9 employees.

Table 46 provides details about the association between business age and the gender of the CEO. It indicates similarities between male and female owned SMEs. The majority of SMEs with a male CEO are more than 10 years old (87%), and a similar result can be seen for the female owned SMEs.

# Associations Between Business Characteristics and E-Commerce Adoption in the USA

The results from the U.S. study do not show any statistically significant associations between business age, business size, business sector, or market focus and adoption of e-commerce. However, we did find an association between alliance membership and e-commerce use. This is shown in Table 47.

Table 47 shows that 31% of e-commerce adopters in the U.S. sample were members of some form of business alliance. By comparison, only 11.8% of non-adopters were members of an alliance. This is similar to Sweden, where almost 35% of the adopters were alliance members.

*Table 47. Association between membership of an alliance and adoption of e-commerce*

| Membership of a Alliance | E-Commerce Adopters | Non-adopters |
|---|---|---|
| Yes | 19 | 6 |
| No | 42 | 45 |
| TOTAL 112 | 61 | 51 |

*Note: 4 missing; p<.05*

*Table 48. Association between a dedicated IT person and adoption of e-commerce*

| Dedicated Person within the Organisation for IT | E-Commerce Adopters | Non-adopters |
|---|---|---|
| Yes | 51 | 14 |
| No | 12 | 36 |
| TOTAL 113 | 63 | 50 |

*3 missing; p<.001*

In the Swedish and Australian studies, respondents were asked to rate the level of IT skill in their organisation. On advice from experts, this question was altered in the U.S. study. Instead, we asked if there was a dedicated person responsible for IT in the organisation. This result was statistically analysed using a chi-square technique against adoption/non-adoption of e-commerce. Table 48 provides the results of the analysis and shows one more associations.

An examination of Table 48 shows that 81% of respondents that had adopted e-commerce had a dedicated person looking after their IT. The data shows that 68% of respondents that did not have a dedicated person looking after their IT also had not adopted e-commerce.

# Summary of USA Findings

Overall, the majority of U.S. respondents were SMEs that had been in business for more than a decade and employed less than 20 employees, which puts them in the small business category. Over 70% were housed in the industrial and retail sectors and the majority did not belong to any alliances. Almost 80% had male CEOs and the majority were focused on the regional and national markets.

The e-commerce adopters were similar to the overall sample, with the exception of the business size characteristic, which showed a more even spread between SMEs in the 1 to 9, 10 to 19, and 20 to 49 employees categories. This is in contrast to the non-adopters, which showed some distinct differences in that more than 50% were in the industrial sector and up to 85% did not belong to an alliance (compared to 67% for adopters). The non-adopters also had a local and regional focus, as opposed to a regional and national focus by adopters. These findings are summarized at a glance in Table 49.

*Table 49. Comparison of USA respondents*

| Business Characteristics | Overall Sample | E-Commerce Adopters | Non-Adopters |
|---|---|---|---|
| Business age. | More than 10 years | More than 10 years | More than 10 years |
| Business size. | 1 to 19 employees | 1 to 19 employees | 1 to 19 employees |
| Business sector. | Industrial & retail | Industrial & retail | Mainly industrial |
| Alliance membership. | No | No | No |
| Gender of CEO. | Male | Male | Male |
| Market focus. | Regional & national | Regional & national | Local & regional |
| Dedicated IT person. | Yes | Yes | No |

The results appear to suggest that U.S. regional SMEs, which are more likely to adopt e-commerce:

- Have less than 20 employees
- Are older (in business for more than 10 years)
- Operate in the industrial and retail sectors
- Do not belong to a strategic alliance
- Have a male CEO
- Operate at a regional and national level
- Have a dedicated IT support person

# A Comparison of Sweden, Australia, and the USA

Perhaps most notable in comparing the adoption of e-commerce across the three locations is the difference in the level of adoption and use in the three locations. While over 50% of respondents in Sweden and U.S. (58.5% Sweden, 54.3% U.S.) had adopted e-commerce, only 15.6% had adopted e-commerce in Australia. While the level of adoption in Sweden and the U.S. mirrors the Internet penetration rate in households in these two countries (according to the OECD statistics), the adoption rate in Australia lags significantly behind. Despite having an Internet penetration rate of over 50%, e-commerce adoption in regional areas stands at less than 20%.

Comparing the profile of e-commerce adopters and non-adopters across the three locations (Tables 50 and 51) shows a series of differences for which there are several explanations. Clearly, despite the economic similarities between the three countries, the circumstances associated with particular locations do have some bearing on the use of e-commerce. Other

*Table 50. Comparison of e-commerce adopters in Sweden, Australia, and USA*

| Business Characteristics | Sweden | Australia | USA |
|---|---|---|---|
| **Business age.** | More than 10 years | 3 to 20 years | More than 10 years |
| **Business size.** | Between 10 to 20 employees | Less than 10 employees | 1 to 19 employees |
| **Business sector.** | Industrial & service | Service & retail | Industrial & retail |
| **Alliance membership.** | No | Somewhat even | No |
| **Gender of CEO.** | Male | Male | Male |
| **Market focus.** | Local & nationals | Local | Regional & national |

*Table 51. Comparison of non-adopters in Sweden, Australia, and USA*

| Business Characteristics | Sweden | Australia | USA |
|---|---|---|---|
| **Business age.** | More than 10 years | 3 to 20 years | More than 10 years |
| **Business size.** | Less than 20 employees | Less than 10 employees | 1 to 19 employees |
| **Business sector.** | Industrial & service | Service & retail | Mainly industrial |
| **Alliance membership.** | Almost equal | No | No |
| **Gender of CEO.** | Male | Male | Male |
| **Market focus.** | Local & national | Local & regional | Local & regional |

*Table 52. Comparison of SMEs surveyed in Sweden, Australia, and USA*

| Business Characteristics | Sweden | Australia | USA |
|---|---|---|---|
| **Business age.** | More than 10 years | 3 to 20 years | More than 10 years |
| **Business size.** | Less than 20 employees | Less than 10 employees | 1 to 19 employees |
| **Business sector.** | Industrial & service | Service & retail | Industrial & retail |
| **Alliance membership.** | No | No | No |
| **Gender of CEO.** | Male | Male | Male |
| **Market focus.** | Local & regional | Local & regional | Regional & national |

possibilities include differences in the regulatory environment in which the SMEs operate, as well as their customer base and support available for implementing e-commerce. We will explore some of these issues in later chapters as we examine e-commerce adoption (and non-adoption) in more detail.

Several parallels can be drawn between e-commerce adopters in the three locations. In Sweden, Australia, and the U.S. SMEs, which are using e-commerce are usually owned by men, well established (i.e., operating for at least 3 years), fall into the small business category (i.e., less than 20 employees), and shy away from alliances. There are few similarities between the business sectors and the market focus of these SMEs, except that all of them predominantly operate within their national boundaries.

Even more striking are the similarities between the adopters and non-adopters because Table 51 shows that non-adopters also tend to be well-established small businesses that are owned by males and do not enter into alliances with other SMEs. Although their market focus is mainly local and regional, they operate in all of the different sectors. We will examine the adopters and non-adopters in subsequent chapters when we look at the barriers to e-commerce adoption and the driving forces behind this technology. This will shed some light on the profiles we have extracted in this chapter.

Table 52 provides the profile of our overall samples in the three locations and can be used as the context to the subsequent chapters.

# Conclusion

A comparison of the findings from Sweden, Australia, and the U.S. suggests that the regional SME sector is far from homogeneous, despite similarities of location. The data clearly shows that not only are the levels of e-commerce adoption different from location to location, but the business characteristics associated with that adoption show few similarities in the three studies. Indeed, it may be argued that some of the findings are totally contradictory both to previous studies as well as to the findings from other locations used in the study. Further investigation is required to understand the reasons behind this and we will attempt to do this in subsequent chapters.

# References

Achrol, R. S., & Kotler, P. (1999). Marketing in the network economy. *Journal of Marketing, 63*, 146-163.

BarNir, A., & Smith, K. A. (2002). Interfirm alliances in the small business: The role of social networks. *Journal of Small Business Management, 40*(3), 219-232.

Barry, J., Berg, E., & Chandler, J. (2003). Managing intellectual labour in Sweden and England. *Cross Cultural Management, 10*(3), 3-22.

Blackburn, R., & Athayde, R. (2000). Making the connection: The effectiveness of Internet training in small businesses. *Education and Training, 42*(4/5).

Brush, C. G., & Hisrich, R. (1999). Women owned businesses: Why do they matter? In Z. Acs (Ed.), *Are small firms important? Their role and impact*. Boston: Kluwer Academic Publishers.

Bunker, D. J., & MacGregor, R. C. (2000). Successful generation of information technology (IT) requirements for small/medium enterprises (SME's)—Cases from Regional Australia. In *Proceedings of SMEs in a Global Economy*, Wollongong, Australia (pp. 72-84).

Culkin, N., & Smith, D. (2000). An emotional business: A guide to understanding the motivations of small business decision takers. *Qualitative Market Research: An International Journal, 3*(3), 145-157.

de Heer, W. (1999). International response trends: Results of an international survey. *Journal of Official Statistics, 15*(2), 129-142.

Dean, J., Holmes, S., & Smith, S. (1997). Understanding business networks: Evidence from manufacturing and service sectors in Australia. *Journal of Small Business Management, 35*(1), 79-84.

Dennis, C. (2000). Networking for marketing advantage. *Management Decision, 38*(4), 287-292.

Donckels, R., & Lambrecht, J. (1997). The network position of small businesses: An explanatory model. *Journal of Small Business Management, 35*(2), 13-28.

Drakopolou-Dodd, S., Jack, S., & Anderson, A. R. (2002). Scottish entrepreneurial networks in the international context. *International Small Business Journal, 20*(2), 213-219.

Fallon, M., & Moran, P. (2000). Information communications technology (ICT) and manufacturing SMEs. In *Proceedings of the 2000 Small Business and Enterprise Development Conference*, University of Manchester (pp. 100-109).

Frazer, L., & Lawley, M. (2000). *Questionnaire design and administration*. Brisbane: John Wiley & Sons.

Gibb, A. (1993). Small business development in Central and Eastern Europe—Opportunity for a rethink. *Journal of Business Venturing, 8,* 461-486.

Hawkins, P., & Winter, J. (1996). The self reliant graduate and the SME. *Education and Training, 38*(4), 3-9.

Hyland, T., & Matlay, H. (1997). Small businesses, training needs, and VET provisions. *Journal of Education and Work, 10*(2).

Jeffcoate, J., Chappell, C., & Feindt, S. (2002). Best practice in SME adoption of e-commerce. *Benchmarking: An International Journal, 9*(2), 122-132.

Kai-Uwe Brock, J. (2000). Information and technology in the small firm. In S. Carter & Jones-Evans (Eds.), *Enterprise and the small business* (pp. 384-408). Prentice Hall.

Lawson, R., Alcock, C., Cooper, J., & Burgess, L. (2003). Factors affecting the adoption of electronic commerce technologies by SMEs: An Australian study. *Journal of Small Business and Enterprise Development, 11*(2), 265-276.

MacGregor, R., & Vrazalic, L. (2006). The effect of small business clusters in prioritising barriers to e-commerce adoption in regional SMEs. *Journal of New Business Ideas and Trends, 4*(1).

MacGregor, R., Hyland, P., Harvie, C., & Lee, B. C. (2006). Benefits derived from ICT adoption in regional medical practices: Perceptual differences between male and female general practitioners. To appear in *International Journal of Health Informatics and Information Systems*.

Marchewka, J. T., & Towell, E. R. (2000). A comparison of structure and strategy in electronic commerce. *Information Technology and People, 13*(2), 137-149.

Martin, L. M., & Matlay, H. (2001). "Blanket" approaches to promoting ICT in small firms: Some lessons from the DTI ladder adoption model in the UK. *Internet Research: Electronic Networking Applications and Policy, 11*(5), 399-410.

Matlay, H. (2000). Training in the small business sector of the British Economy. In S. Carter & D. Jones (Eds.), *Enterprise and small business: Principles, policy, and practice*. London: Addison Wesley Longman.

Meikle, F., & Willis, D. (2002). A pilot study of regional differences: Ecommerce development in UK SMEs. *In Proceedings of the Information Resources Management Association 2002 Conference*, Seattle. Idea Group Publishing.

Nillson, P. (1997). Business counselling services directed towards female entrepreneurs--some legitimacy dilemmas. *Entrepreneurship and Regional Development, 9*(3), 239-258.

O'Donnell, A., Gilmore, A., Cummins, D., & Carson, D. (2001). The network construct in entrepreneurship research: A review and critique. *Management Decision, 39*(9), 749-760.

Ozcan, G. (1995). Small business networks and local ties in Turkey. *Entrepreneurship and Regional Development, 7*, 265-282.

Porter, M. (2001, March). Strategy and the Internet. *Harvard Business Review*, 63-78.

Riquelme, H. (2002). Commercial Internet adoption in China: Comparing the experience of small, medium, and large business. *Internet Research: Electronic Networking Applications and Policy, 12*(3), 276-286.

Sage, G. (1993). Entrepreneurship as an economic development strategy. *Economic Development Review, 11*(2), 66-67.

Sandberg, K. W. (2003). An exploratory study of women in micro enterprises: Gender related difficulties. *Journal of Small Business and Enterprise Development, 10*(4), 408-417.

Schindehutte, M., & Morris, M. H. (2001). Understanding strategic adaptation in small firms. *International Journal of Entrepreneurial Behaviour and Research, 7*(3), 84-107.

Tetteh, E., & Burn, J. (2001). Global strategies for SME-business: Applying the SMALL framework. *Logistics Information Management, 14*(1-2), 171-180.

**Chapter IV**

# Criteria for the Adoption of E-Commerce:
## Why Do SMEs Decide to Implement E-Commerce?

Most commentators, and indeed substantial research efforts, have focused on four connected but different areas of e-commerce adoption. These are the reasons for adoption (criteria), the reasons for non-adoption (barriers), the positive outcomes of adoption (benefits), and the negative aspects of adoption (disadvantages). The next four chapters will be devoted to these four areas of e-commerce adoption. Each chapter will provide a detailed analysis of a particular area in each of the three different locations. This will be followed by a comparison of the results to highlight any similarities and differences. It should be noted this book presents the outcomes of an empirical study and, subsequently, it provides statistical analyses on the data collected. While the academic reader will find these of particular interest, the business reader is directed to the business implications sections and the conclusion and may use the tables with statistical results as a reference point.

We will begin with the reasons or drivers leading to e-commerce adoption. We have termed these "e-commerce adoption criteria."

# Background

In its earliest inception, e-commerce was seen as a "pot of gold" for SMEs trying to compete with their larger counterparts on a worldwide stage. E-commerce potentially gave SMEs a cost effective way of reaching customers globally and thus competing on par with large organisations. Indeed, many governments recognised this potential and created funding schemes and initiatives to facilitate e-commerce adoption by smaller firms.

As with previous technologies, the SME sector, as a whole, was slow to adopt e-commerce (Magnusson, 2001; Poon & Swatman, 1997; Van Akkeren & Cavaye, 1999). According to the National Research Council (2000), only 25% of SMEs had a Web site in mid-1999. Of those that did have a Web site, the revenue they generated via business-to-customer (B2C) e-commerce was negligible (Wall Street Journal, August 17, 1999 *cited in* National Research Council, 2000; Ruth, 2000). Similar findings were reported in Australia with only 22% of SMEs using the Internet for e-commerce (Telstra, 1999).

The results of the latest Sensis® e-Business Report (2006) show increases in the use of e-commerce in Australia. With 90% of SMEs having Internet connectivity and 48% having a Web site, 47% are taking orders online. This growth reflects an increase in the confidence of SMEs with regards to e-commerce benefits. The large number of adopters (57%), which had already recovered their e-commerce investment, is a clear indicator of this. It should be noted, however, that almost 40% of the SMEs surveyed reported that they would not use e-commerce at all. (The reasons for this are explored in subsequent chapters.)

An early study (MacGregor & Bunker, 1996) showed that the major driving force for most SMEs adopting e-commerce was pressure by larger trading partners or suppliers to do so. Since then there have been many studies investigating the criteria or driving forces that have led SMEs to adopt e-commerce. These studies (see for example, Eid, 2005; Power & Sohal, 2002; PriceWaterhouseCoopers, 1999; Reimenschneider & Mykytyn, 2000) have found that pressure from customers was also an important adoption criterion. Raisch (2001) also cites pressure from competitors as the reason behind SMEs' decision to implement e-commerce. The increasing levels of competition have driven SMEs to seek competitive advantages through innovative technology. Clearly, in the early days of e-commerce, SMEs were reluctant adopters "pushed" into e-commerce adoption by external pressures from suppliers, customers, business partners, and competitors. This is understandable considering the lack of resources available to SMEs. The dilemma faced by most SMEs was whether the benefits of e-commerce outweighed the costs associated with adopting an e-commerce strategy and implementing the technology.

In one of the first studies of e-commerce adoption drivers, with a sample size consisting of 146 SMEs, Poon et al. (1997) derived a list of five drivers or criteria for e-commerce adoption based on data collected from the respondents. These include new modes of direct or indirect marketing, strengthening of relationships with business partners, the ability to reach new customers, improvements to customer services and the reduction of communication costs. Other studies have derived similar criteria. Poon et al.'s (1997) study highlighted the business benefits of e-commerce, which SMEs were considering in their decision to adopt e-commerce. SMEs were quick to recognise that, aside from external motivators, e-commerce would result in internal advantages by way of organisational improvements and additional revenues.

Lawrence (1997), in an examination of Tasmanian SMEs noted that improved marketing and the ability to reach new customers were the most common incentives for adopting and using e-commerce. This is, without a doubt, the most widely recognised and cited reason for e-commerce adoption because sales and marketing are the "public" side of e-commerce technology and SMEs view the use of the Internet as an opportunity to increase awareness about their products and services without any of the physical limitations associated with doing so, and at very low cost. This in turn would lead to new customers and the possibility of entering new geographical markets as well as new market segments.

Other studies have shown various internal reasons that have lead to e-commerce adoption. Abell and Lim (1996) found that reduction in communication costs, improvements in customer services, improvements in lead time, and improvements in sales were the major criteria for e-commerce adoption and use by SMEs in New Zealand. It is interesting that these findings highlight business efficiency as a major driving force for e-commerce adoption and emphasise e-commerce as a business strategy, rather than simply a technology solution. Increasing costs have always been a major concern for SMEs and e-commerce appeared to be a means to reduce both tangible and intangible costs by removing layers between the organisation and its customers, and integrating front-end with back-end systems.

Auger and Gallaugher (1997) also noted that improvements in customer service in addition to better internal control of the business were strong criteria for e-commerce adoption in SMEs. The perception that e-commerce would provide more effective organisational controls and an easier means of controlling operations was a somewhat surprising finding, however, it was also noted in studies carried out by Reimenschneider et al. (2000), Poon and Joseph (2001) and Domke-Damonte and Levsen (2002). The desire for better internal controls was symptomatic of the organisational business and IT integration that e-commerce underscored. By creating a system that would seamlessly integrate the customer interface with the business functions, SMEs saw an opportunity to develop more efficient management and planning structures.

Previous research examining e-commerce adoption drivers clearly shows a linear progression from external pressures to adopt, to internal efficiencies as the main reason for doing so. Initially, SMEs found their reasons to adopt e-commerce outside the organisation, however, over time, as Internet penetration grew and the benefits of doing business online became apparent, SMEs began to view e-commerce as a strategic tool for business expansion and for streamlining operations. For brevity and convenience, e-commerce adoption criteria identified in previous research studies are summarised in Table 1.

It is clear from previous research that e-commerce was viewed by SMEs as somewhat of a panacea that would lead to better financial performance, increased competitiveness, and efficient operations. We will discuss to what extent the adoption criteria were realised through actual e-commerce benefits in a later chapter. We will now examine some of the research related to e-commerce adoption in specific categories of SMEs.

*Table 1. E-commerce adoption criteria: A summary of previous research*

| Adoption Criteria | Reported by |
|---|---|
| Demand/pressure from customers. | Grandon & Pearson (2004)<br>Power et al. (2002)<br>Cragg, Mehrtens, & Mills (2001)<br>Reimenschneider et al. (2000)<br>PriceWaterhouseCoopers (1999) |
| Pressure from suppliers. | Grandon et al. (2004)<br>Raymond (2001)<br>Cragg et al. (2001)<br>Reimenschneider et al. (2000)<br>Lawrence (1997)<br>MacGregor et al. (1996) |
| Pressure from competitors. | Grandon et al. (2004)<br>Eid (2005)<br>Daniel, Wilson, & Myers (2002)<br>Cragg et al. (2001)<br>Raisch (2001)<br>Sadowski et al. (2002)<br>Poon & Strom (1997) |
| Reduction of costs. | Eid (2005)<br>Raisch (2001)<br>Auger et al. (1997)<br>Abell et al. (1996) |
| Increased sales. | Lee (2001)<br>Phan (2001)<br>Abell et al. (1996) |
| Improvements to customer services. | Power et al. (2002)<br>Daniel et al. (2002)<br>Auger et al. (1997)<br>Abell et al. (1996)<br>Senn (1996) |
| Improvements to lead time. | Power et al. (2002)<br>Reimenschneider et al. (2000)<br>Abell et al. (1996) |
| Improvements to internal efficiency. | Kaynak, Tatoglu, & Kula (2005)<br>Porter (2001) |
| Stronger relations with business partners. | Raymond (2001)<br>Evans & Wurster (1997)<br>Poon et al. (1997) |

*continued on following page*

*Table 1. Continued*

| Adoption Criteria | Reported by |
|---|---|
| Ability to reach new customers/markets. | Fillis, Johansson, & Wagner (2004)<br>Power et al. (2002)<br>Reimenschneider et al. (2000)<br>Poon et al. (1997) |
| Improved competitiveness. | Raymond (2001)<br>Turban, Lee, King, & Chung (2000)<br>Chapman, James-Moore, Szczygiel, & Thompson (2000)<br>Reimenschneider et al. (2000) |
| Availability of external technical support. | Abell et al. (1996) |
| Improved marketing. | Power et al. (2002)<br>Reimenschneider et al. (2000)<br>Poon et al. (1997)<br>Lawrence (1997) |
| Improved control. | Domke-Damonte et al. (2002)<br>Poon et al. (2001)<br>Reimenschneider et al. (2000)<br>Auger et al. (1997) |

# E-Commerce Adoption Criteria and Business Characteristics

Hawkins and Winter (1996) and Hyland and Matlay (1997) have noted that because SMEs are diverse in terms of business size, sector, target market, and other factors, it is not possible to generalise across the SME population. Several studies have been carried out to determine which business characteristics affect the adoption of e-commerce technology by SMEs. The studies have shown a range of differences in e-commerce adoption depending on the business size, sector, gender of the CEO, and other factors.

Fallon and Moran (2000) and van Beveren et al. (2002) found significant links between the business size (defined in terms of the number of employees) of the SME and the level of Internet adoption. The results of these studies indicated that businesses with fewer than ten employees were less likely to adopt e-commerce technology, when compared to their larger counterparts. Daniel et al. (2002) claim that as SMEs increase in size, they require different channels to communicate with their customers, leading to e-commerce implementation. They also found that SMEs, which had been in business for longer were less likely to use e-commerce.

Martin and Matlay (2001) showed that the business sector was also significantly associated with e-commerce adoption. They also found that micro-sized service organisations were more likely to adopt e-commerce than manufacturing businesses. Riquelme (2002) confirmed this in a study of 75 Chinese SMEs, which found that those involved in the service industry tended to adopt e-commerce far more readily than their manufacturing counterparts. Blackburn and Athayde (2000) identified not only business size and business sector but also the level of international marketing as a business characteristic associated with adoption of e-commerce technology.

As with the pre-e-commerce adoption of IT, research (O'Donnell, Gilmore, Cummins, & Carson, 2001; Tetteh & Burn, 2001) has found that successful e-commerce adoption is associated with both the level of IT skill within the SME as well as with the development (prior to e-commerce adoption) of organisational-wide information systems. These studies support earlier findings on EDI adoption (Iacovou, Benbasat, & Dexter, 1995; MacGregor, Bunker, & Waugh, 1998; Turban, 2000).

In a study of 102 SMEs, Mazzarol, Volery, Doss, and Thein (1999) concluded that the gender of the CEO was significantly associated with the level of adoption of e-commerce, while the age and level of education of the CEO did not show any significant association. This study is supported by the findings of Venkatash and Morris (2000).

The previous research in this area appears to suggest that certain characteristics of an SME will have an effect on the e-commerce adoption process, which implies an effect on the reasons for implementing e-commerce in the first place. From these previous studies, we can draw a preliminary conclusion that e-commerce drivers or criteria are specific to certain categories

*Table 2. Business characteristics affecting the adoption of e-commerce by SMEs*

| Business Characteristics | Reported by |
|---|---|
| Business size. | van Beveren et al. (2002) |
| | Fallon et al. (2000) |
| | Blackburn et al. (2000) |
| | Martin et al. (2001) |
| | Hawkins et al. (1996) |
| Business age. | MacGregor, Vrazalic, Carlsson, Bunker, & Magnusson (2002) |
| | Daniel et al. (2002) |
| | Kai-Uwe Brock (2000) |
| | Donckels & Lambrecht (1997) |
| Business sector. | Bodorick, Dhaliwal, & Jutla (2002) |
| | MacGregor et al. (2002) |
| | BarNir & Smith (2002) |
| | Schindehutte & Morris (2001) |
| | Matlay (2000) |
| | Blackburn et al. (2000) |
| Market focus. | BarNir et al. (2002) |
| | Schindehutte et al. (2001) |
| | Blackburn et al. (2000) |
| Level of IT skill in the organization. | Tetteh et al. (2001) |
| | O'Donnell et al. (2001) |

of SMEs depending on their size, business sector, level of IT skill in the organisation, and gender of the CEO. One of the aims of this chapter is to determine whether this holds true. For convenience, the studies previously discussed are summarized in Table 2.

# Research Questions

Based on the outcomes of previous studies, we set out to answer several questions about e-commerce adoption criteria in our study. Specifically, we wanted to find out:

1.   Do any of the business characteristics listed previously (in Table 2) affect how SMEs perceive e-commerce adoption criteria?

2.   Are there any underlying factors or groupings of e-commerce adoption criteria in each of the three locations (Sweden, Australia, and the USA) which would serve to explain the key reasons behind SMEs' decisions to use e-commerce?

3.   Are there any differences in how e-commerce adoption criteria are perceived across the three locations (Sweden, Australia, and the USA)?

In the first part of this chapter, our intention was to isolate specific business characteristics, which affected the reasons why SMEs adopted e-commerce. For example, did the size of an SME have any effect on its decision to adopt e-commerce as a cost-cutting strategy? Or did belonging to the retail sector have any effect on SMEs adopting e-commerce to increase sales? To answer these questions, a series of linear regressions was carried out to determine whether business characteristics (such as the age and size of the business, business sector, gender of the CEO, educational level of the CEO, level of IT skill within the business, the existence of an enterprise-wide system, product planning, membership of a strategic alliance, market focus, or type of e-commerce) had any effects on the perception of adoption criteria. Linear regression was chosen over other techniques because it allows for interaction of the business characteristics which other techniques fail to do.

The second question was concerned with grouping e-commerce drivers or criteria in order to provide a clearer explanation of the reasons why SMEs were choosing to implement e-commerce in specific locations. Rather than dealing with a multitude of explanations, the answer to this question provides a "bigger picture" of the key issues that need to be addressed by government organisations in developing strategies to promote e-commerce adoption. For example, could the drivers in Australia be attributed to two main groups--generating revenue and increasing business efficiency? Having this insight allows us to target SMEs in a particular region with specific strategies to implement e-commerce in such a way that will see these drivers materialise into benefits. To provide data for the second question a series of correlations and factor analyses was undertaken.

The final part of this chapter provides a comparison between the three locations and determines what differences exist between Sweden, Australia, and the USA in relation to e-commerce adoption drivers or criteria. This question will be addressed in the Discussion section of this chapter.

# Methodology

Fourteen of the most commonly occurring criteria for e-commerce adoption were identified from the literature. A series of six in depth interviews with regional SMEs were undertaken to determine whether the criteria were applicable and complete. All identified criteria were found to be applicable.

Based on the six in-depth interviews, a survey instrument was developed to collect data about e-commerce adoption criteria (amongst other things). Respondents who had adopted e-commerce were asked to rate the importance of each criterion to their decision to adopt e-commerce (as shown in Figure 1) using a standard 5 point Likert scale with 1 meaning very unimportant and 5 meaning very important. The Likert scale responses were assumed to posses the characteristics of an interval measurement scale for data analysis purposes.

*Figure 1. Question about criteria (drivers) to e-commerce adoption used in survey*

This question relates to the reasons why your organisation decided to implement e-commerce. Below is a list of statements indicating possible reasons. Based on your opinion, please rank each statement on a scale of 1 to 5 to indicate how important this reason was to your decision to implement e-commerce, as follows:

1 = the reason was very unimportant to your decision to use e-commerce

2 = the reason was unimportant to your decision to use e-commerce

3 = the reason was neither unimportant nor important to your decision to use e-commerce

4 = the reason was important to your decision to use e-commerce

5 = the reason was very important to your decision to use e-commerce

| | Our organisation adopted e-commerce because of: | Rating | | | | |
|---|---|---|---|---|---|---|
| C1 | Demand and/or pressure from customers. | 1 | 2 | 3 | 4 | 5 |
| C2 | Pressure from competition. | 1 | 2 | 3 | 4 | 5 |
| C3 | Demand and/or pressure from suppliers. | 1 | 2 | 3 | 4 | 5 |
| C4 | To reduce costs. | 1 | 2 | 3 | 4 | 5 |
| C5 | To improve customer service. | 1 | 2 | 3 | 4 | 5 |
| C6 | To shorten lead time/reduce stock levels. | 1 | 2 | 3 | 4 | 5 |
| C7 | To increase sales. | 1 | 2 | 3 | 4 | 5 |
| C8 | To improve internal efficiency. | 1 | 2 | 3 | 4 | 5 |
| C9 | To strengthen relations with business partners. | 1 | 2 | 3 | 4 | 5 |
| C10 | The possibility of reaching new customers/markets. | 1 | 2 | 3 | 4 | 5 |
| C11 | To improve our competitiveness. | 1 | 2 | 3 | 4 | 5 |
| C12 | We were offered external support to adopt e-commerce. | 1 | 2 | 3 | 4 | 5 |
| C13 | To improve our marketing. | 1 | 2 | 3 | 4 | 5 |
| C14 | To improve control. | 1 | 2 | 3 | 4 | 5 |

Chapter II provides a detailed account of how the data was collected and the total responses received for each of the three locations. The following sections will provide the results of the statistical analysis for each location in order to answer the three questions about e-commerce adoption criteria stated previously.

The rest of this chapter is structured as follows. First, we will examine the associations between different business characteristics and e-commerce adoption criteria in Sweden. Then we will present the results of a factor analysis, which will group the e-commerce adoption criteria indicated by the Swedish respondents. This process will be repeated for Australia and then for the U.S. sample. The final part of the chapter will discuss and compare the findings, and present the business implications of the results.

# Business Characteristics and E-Commerce Adoption Criteria in Swedish SMEs

The first question was concerned with the effect of business characteristics on the fourteen e-commerce adoption criteria listed in Figure 1. We found a number of statistically significant associations in the Swedish sample between business size and various e-commerce adoption criteria. These are summarized in Table 3, which also indicates the corresponding tables showing the associations and the relevant p value.

As can be seen from Table 3, the number of employees (or business size) is significantly associated with a wide range of the reasons why SMEs are adopting e-commerce. This is an important finding because it indicates that the size of the business does have an effect on the motives for using e-commerce. Equally interesting is the finding that none of the other business characteristics (excluding market focus and the type of e-commerce) have any statistically significant effect on the majority of e-commerce adoption criteria. Thus, at least in the regional Swedish situation, decisions to adopt e-commerce are not affected

*Table 3. Summary of associations between e-commerce adoption criteria and business characteristics (Sweden)*

| E-commerce adoption criteria | Correlated with... | Table | p value |
|---|---|---|---|
| Demand and/or pressure from customers. | Business size | 4.4 | .000 |
| Pressure from competition. | Business size | 4.5 | .017 |
| Demand and/or pressure from suppliers. | Market focus | 4.6 | .020 |
| Reduced costs. | Business size | 4.7 | .005 |
| Improved customer service. | Business size | 4.8 | .016 |
| Improved internal efficiency. | Business size<br>Type of e-commerce (B2B/B2C) | 4.9 | .041<br>.001 |
| External support to adopt e-commerce. | Business size | 4.10 | .001 |
| Improved control. | Business size<br>Type of e-commerce (B2B/B2C) | 4.11 | .011<br>.021 |

by particular sectors, market foci, membership of a strategic alliance, or any of the other business characteristics. The lack of association is a valuable insight both for businesses as well as government agencies as it suggests that the strategies adopted for one category of SMEs appear to be equally applicable to others.

We will examine and comment on each of the associations in turn next.

A number of authors (Blackburn et al., 2000; Fallon et al., 2000; Hyland et al., 1997; Matlay, 2000) have suggested that the larger the business size, in terms of employee numbers, the more likely the business will move to adopt e-commerce. The data in Table 4 shows that business size is significantly associated with the adoption criterion "Demand and/or pressure from customers" in the Swedish context. It appears that SMEs with more employees assign a higher importance to demand and pressure from customers in their decision to adopt e-commerce, compared to SMEs with fewer employees.

Similarly, there is a statistically significant association between business size and the perceived level of importance attributed to pressure from competitors as a reason for e-commerce adoption. The data in Table 5 shows once again that larger SMEs are more likely to consider pressure from competition as being important.

An examination of Table 6 shows that the Beta value for market focus is both statistically significant and negative. This suggests that local and regional SMEs in Sweden are more likely to assign a higher level of importance on pressure from suppliers as an e-commerce adoption criterion than those SMEs that are trading at a national or international level. This is contrary to earlier findings of Blackburn et al. (2000), Schindehutte et al. (2001), and BarNir et al. (2002). Previous studies (Raymond, 2001) have also suggested that pressure

*Table 4. Regression table for demand/pressure from customers*

| Dependant Variable Demand/Pressure from Customers | | |
|---|---|---|
| | **Beta** | **p value** |
| Business Size | .367 | .000 |
| R Squared | .166 | |
| Adjusted R squared | .133 | |
| p value for the complete regression table | .000 | |

*Table 5. Regression table for pressure from competitors*

| Dependant Variable Pressure from Competitors | | |
|---|---|---|
| | **Beta** | **p value** |
| Business Size | .210 | .017 |
| R Squared | .090 | |
| Adjusted R squared | .053 | |
| p value for the complete regression table | .020 | |

from suppliers is a strong driver for SMEs in a particular sector; however, the data from Sweden does not support these results as there is no association between suppliers and business sector.

Previous research (Blackburn et al., 2000; Fallon et al., 2000; Hyland et al., 1997; Matlay, 2000) has suggested that the number of employees in an SME may affect the need to keep costs to a minimum. The data in Table 7 supports these earlier contentions. The results indicate that larger SMEs are more likely to perceive cost reductions as an important adoption criterion. This is consistent with the higher cost of running an SME and SME owners' desire to minimize costs through e-commerce adoption.

Table 8 provides the regression for the "improved customer service" criterion. As can be seen, there is a statistically significant association (at the .05) level between improvements to customer services and business size. The data suggest that the larger the SME, the more likely they are concerned with improving customer services through e-commerce. Since larger organisations tend to have more customers, this finding was not unexpected.

An examination of Table 9 highlights some interesting results. As can be seen, two business characteristics (type of e-commerce and business size) are statistically significantly associated with the criterion "improved internal efficiency." Business size has a Beta value of .290. This suggests that for the Swedish respondents, the larger the business size in terms of employee numbers, the more importance is placed on the need for improvements to internal efficiency. The type of e-commerce, on the other had, has a negative Beta value (-.172). This suggests that B2C businesses are less likely than B2B businesses to consider improvements to internal efficiency as an important criterion. There are a number of possible

*Table 6. Regression table for pressure from suppliers*

| Dependant Variable Pressure from Suppliers | | |
|---|---|---|
| | Beta | p value |
| Market Focus | -.199 | .020 |
| R Squared | .093 | |
| Adjusted R squared | .057 | |
| p value for the complete regression table | .015 | |

*Table 7. Regression table for reduced costs*

| Dependant Variable Reduced Costs | | |
|---|---|---|
| | Beta | p value |
| Business Size | .281 | .001 |
| R Squared | .107 | |
| Adjusted R squared | .071 | |
| p value for the complete regression table | .005 | |

reasons for this. Traditionally, B2B businesses, with the inherent pressures placed on them by other business partners, have required a detailed development of logistics, supply chain management, and warehousing functions. As such, they would tend to be far more efficient in terms of their internal functions than perhaps some B2C organisations.

Conventional wisdom would suggest that SMEs with fewer employees would place a higher level of importance on being able to gain outside assistance to develop their e-commerce systems. The results, however, show that it is the larger SMEs that rate the importance of this criterion higher.

As with Table 9, the data in Table 11 shows that two business characteristics (type of e-commerce and business size) are significantly associated with the criterion "improved control." Business size has a Beta value of .222. This suggests that for the Swedish respondents the larger the business size in terms of employee numbers, the more importance is placed on the need for improvements in control as a reason for adopting e-commerce. The type of e-commerce, on the other hand, has a negative Beta value. This suggests that B2C businesses are less likely than B2B businesses to consider improvement in control as an important criterion.

Based on the previous results we can conclude that regional SMEs in Sweden with more employees place a higher importance on the following reasons for adopting e-commerce: pressure from customers and competitors, reducing costs, improving customer service, internal efficiency and control, and access to external support. By comparison, SMEs with a local or regional focus are more likely to be concerned with pressure from suppliers. Finally, businesses that engage in B2C e-commerce are less likely to emphasise improve-

*Table 8. Regression table for improved customer service*

| Dependant Variable Improved Customer Service | | |
|---|---|---|
| | Beta | p value |
| Business Size | .209 | .016 |
| R Squared | .097 | |
| Adjusted R squared | .061 | |
| p value for the complete regression table | .012 | |

*Table 9. Regression table for improved internal efficiency*

| Dependant Variable Improved Internal Efficiency | | |
|---|---|---|
| | Beta | p value |
| Type of e-commerce (B2B/B2C) | -.172 | .041 |
| Business Size | .290 | .001 |
| R Squared | .120 | |
| Adjusted R squared | .085 | |
| p value for the complete regression table | .002 | |

ments to internal efficiency or control as reasons for adopting e-commerce than their B2B counterparts.

Although there were no associations between the other business characteristics and e-commerce adoption criteria, this is not to say that their importance as criteria is lower. Instead, it suggests that the different categories of SMEs place the same level of importance on the e-commerce drivers.

We will now take a closer look at the groupings of e-commerce adoption criteria in the Swedish context with the purpose of answering our second question: Are there any underlying factors or groupings of e-commerce adoption criteria, which would serve to explain the key reasons behind SMEs' decisions to use e-commerce?

# Groupings of E-Commerce Adoption Criteria in Sweden

To answer our second question, a combination of correlations and factor analysis was applied to the data. The results of this analysis are shown in the tables next and discussed at the end of this section.

Table 12 provides the correlation matrix of the importance ratings for e-commerce adoption criteria. All correlations significant at the .001 level are shown in bold.

Table 10. Regression table for external support

| Dependant Variable External Support | | |
|---|---|---|
| | Beta | p value |
| Business Size | .301 | .001 |
| R Squared | .084 | |
| Adjusted R squared | .047 | |
| p value for the complete regression table | .030 | |

Table 11. Regression table for improved control

| Dependant Variable Improved control | | |
|---|---|---|
| | Beta | p value |
| Business Size | .222 | .011 |
| B2B/B2C | -.198 | .021 |
| R Squared | .084 | |
| Adjusted R squared | .048 | |
| p value for the complete regression table | .029 | |

*Table 12. Adoption criteria correlation matrix (Sweden)*

| | Demand and/or pressure from customers. | Demand and/or pressure from suppliers. | To reduce costs. | To improve customer service. | To shorten lead time/reduce stock levels. | To increase sales. | To improve internal efficiency. | To strengthen relations with business partners. | The possibility of reaching new customers/markets. | To improve our competitiveness. | We were offered external support to adopt e-commerce. | To improve our marketing. | To improve control. |
|---|---|---|---|---|---|---|---|---|---|---|---|---|---|
| Pressure from competition. | .644 | | | | | | | | | | | | |
| Demand and/or pressure from suppliers. | .335 | .466 | | | | | | | | | | | |
| To reduce costs. | .456 | .513 | .594 | | | | | | | | | | |
| To improve customer service. | .517 | .539 | .429 | .726 | | | | | | | | | |
| To shorten lead time/reduce stock levels. | .319 | .408 | .578 | .666 | .541 | | | | | | | | |
| To increase sales. | .377 | .411 | .423 | .590 | .657 | .521 | | | | | | | |
| To improve internal efficiency. | .354 | .415 | .401 | .643 | .615 | .550 | .517 | | | | | | |
| To strengthen relations with business partners. | .503 | .501 | .528 | .564 | .704 | .567 | .570 | .544 | | | | | |
| The possibility of reaching new customers/markets. | .397 | .443 | .406 | .466 | .681 | .469 | .738 | .461 | .628 | | | | |
| To improve our competitiveness. | .481 | .635 | .488 | .602 | .711 | .569 | .673 | .590 | .756 | .752 | | | |
| We were offered external support to adopt e-commerce. | .251** | .347 | .465 | .400 | .283 | .446 | .373 | .307 | .414 | .300 | .409 | | |
| To improve our marketing. | .392 | .436 | .385 | .410 | .622 | .384 | .682 | .454 | .547 | .829 | .675 | .341 | |
| To improve control. | .383 | .449 | .507 | .653 | .579 | .626 | .520 | .552 | .551 | .529 | .622 | .489 | .444 |

*Note:* * significant at 0.05 level    ** significant at 0.01 level

The findings in Table 12 suggested the use of factor analysis to investigate any separate underlying factors and to reduce the redundancy of certain criteria indicated in the correlation matrices. The results of the Kaiser-Meyer-Olkin MSA (.911) and Bartlett's test for Sphericity ($\chi 2 = 1820$, $p = .000$) indicated that the data set satisfied the assumptions for factorability. Principle components analysis was chosen as the method of extraction in order to account for maximum variance in the data using a minimum number of factors. A two factor solution was extracted for Sweden with Eigenvalues 7.767 and 1.204. The two factors accounted for 64.079% of the variance. Table 13 shows the variance.

The resulting components were rotated using the Varimax procedure and a simple structure was achieved as shown in the rotated component matrix (see Table 14).

*Table 13. Total variance explained: Adoption criteria (Sweden)*

| Component | Eigenvalue | % Variance | Cumulative % |
|---|---|---|---|
| 1 | 7.767 | 55.482 | 55.482 |
| 2 | 1.204 | 8.596 | 64.079 |

*Table 14. Rotated component matrix: Adoption criteria (Sweden)*

| Criteria | Component 1: Marketing and Partnerships | Component 2: Internal Operations |
|---|---|---|
| Demand and/or pressure from customers. | .498 | |
| Pressure from competition. | .490 | .483 |
| Demand and/or pressure from suppliers. | | .748 |
| To reduce costs. | | .750 |
| To improve customer service. | .740 | |
| To shorten lead time/reduce stock levels. | | .766 |
| To increase sales. | .755 | |
| To improve internal efficiency. | | .553 |
| To strengthen relations with business partners. | .632 | |
| The possibility of reaching new customers/markets. | .892 | |
| To improve our competitiveness. | .762 | |
| We were offered external support to adopt e-commerce. | | .675 |
| To improve our marketing. | .866 | |
| To improve control. | | .704 |

As can be seen in Table 14, the Swedish respondents grouped adoption criteria based on two factors. We have termed these two factors "marketing and partnerships" and "internal operations." The adoption criteria associated with improvements to sales, marketing, and relationships with customers (customer service) held the higher priority from respondents. This indicates that external activities related to increasing the customer base and using online marketing channels were a priority for Swedish SMEs when it came to making a decision about adopting e-commerce.

Another set of criteria, which loaded on to the internal operations factor was related mainly to aspects and functions inside the organisation such as cost reductions, inventory levels, IT resources, and control. Interestingly, the demand/pressure from suppliers' criterion also loaded onto this factor, which is consistent with the desire for reduced stock and improved lead time ratings. Pressure from competitors, on the other hand, loaded almost equally onto both factors. Of interest, also, is the fact that demand/pressure from suppliers and reduced costs have been mapped to the internal operations component rather than the marketing and market focus component. Clearly, respondents saw that these two issues required internal functions and were achievable through e-commerce.

These results are an important first step in consolidating our understanding of the reasons that motivate SMEs to adopt e-commerce because they indicate that correlations between the criteria exist and 14 of the most common criteria can be grouped in relation to two main factors. This reduces the fragmentation associated with having a large number of e-commerce adoption criteria and allows a more targeted approach for government programs and initiatives. It is a powerful explanatory tool because it reduces the "noise" in the data. The rotated component matrix also enables the prediction of the scores of each individual criterion based on the score of the two factors, and vice versa, for an SME. This has implications for research into e-commerce criteria. Instead of accounting for fourteen different criteria, the drivers for e-commerce adoption can be explained as a result of one of two things: e-commerce either assists with the sales and marketing side of the business or it results in more streamlined internal operations. This is summarised in Figure 2.

*Figure 2. E-commerce adoption criteria groupings in Sweden*

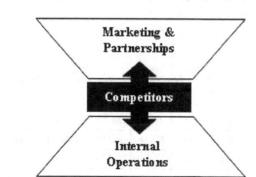

We undertook an extended analysis to determine whether the groupings previously identified differed for categories of SMEs depending on their business size, market focus, and type of e-commerce. These three characteristics were previously found to be associated with e-commerce drivers. The Swedish respondents were sub-divided and the same factor analysis was applied to each category of SMEs.

## Business Size

Four categories of SMEs had sufficient data to apply factor analysis. The results of the Kaiser-Meyer-Olkin MSA (.908 for 1-9 employees, .820 for 10-19 employees, .639 for 20-49 employees, .760 for 50-199 employees) and Bartlett's test for Sphericity ($\chi2 = 923$ p = .000 for 1-9 employees, $\chi2 = 308$ p = .000 for 10-19 employees, $\chi2 = 223$ p = .000 for 20-49 employees and $\chi2 = 268$ p = .000 for 50-199 employees) ) indicated that the data set satisfied the assumptions for factorability. Principle components analysis was chosen as the method of extraction in order to account for maximum variance in the data using a minimum number of factors. A two factor solution with Eigenvalues 8.674 and 1.112 was chosen for the 1-9 employee group. This accounted for 69.900% of the variance. A four factor solution with Eigenvalues 7.378, 1.885, 1.103, and 1.048 was chosen for the 10-19 employee group. This accounted for 81.525% of the variance. A four factor solution with Eigenvalues 5.057, 1.956, 1.861, and 1.339 was chosen for the 20-49 employee group. This accounted for 72.945% of the variance. A three factor solution with Eigenvalues 7.551, 1.564, and 1.136 was chosen for the 50-199 employee group. This accounted for 73.23% of the variance. These results can be seen in Table 15.

The resulting components were rotated using the Varimax procedure and a simple structure was achieved as shown in the rotated component matrices (Tables 16 to 19).

The analysis contains some interesting findings across the different size categories of SMEs. Although the smallest SMEs (i.e., with under 10 employees) grouped criteria based on marketing issues and internal operations, they considered the former to be of more importance. This is unsurprising considering that the single most important priority of a small SME is to grow the business through sales and marketing. The larger SMEs were in agreement with the smallest sized organisations, except in relation to the availability of external IT support,

*Table 15. Total variation explained: Adoption criteria and business size (Sweden)*

| Comp | Eigenvalue | | | | % Variance | | | | Cumulative % | | | |
|---|---|---|---|---|---|---|---|---|---|---|---|---|
| Size | 1-9 | 10-19 | 20-49 | 50-199 | 1-9 | 10-19 | 20-49 | 50-199 | 1-9 | 10-19 | 20-49 | 50-199 |
| 1 | 8.674 | 7.378 | 5.057 | 7.551 | 61.959 | 52.700 | 36.121 | 53.935 | 61.959 | 52.700 | 36.121 | 53.935 |
| 2 | 1.112 | 1.885 | 1.956 | 1.564 | 7.941 | 13.465 | 13.970 | 11.173 | 69.900 | 66.166 | 50.091 | 65.108 |
| 3 | | 1.103 | 1.861 | 1.136 | | 7.877 | 13.292 | 8.115 | | 74.073 | 63.383 | 73.223 |
| 4 | | 1.048 | 1.339 | | | 7.482 | 9.562 | | | 81.525 | 72.945 | |

which they isolated as a separate factor. Increasing competitiveness also featured highly amongst the larger SMEs.

In contrast to these two categories of SMEs, the middle categories (between 10 and 50 employees) grouped criteria based on four factors. While the loading of criteria was similar for both of these categories, the priorities differed between the two. For both categories the marketing factor had the highest priority, however, for the 10-19 employee group market forces was the second most important factor, while for the 20-49 group, internal efficiency was the second most important factor. This would suggest that smaller businesses feel that they are under more pressure by customers, competition, and suppliers to adopt e-commerce, while larger SMEs were concerned with maintaining efficient operations as the organisation grew. SMEs with 50-199 employees, and their inherently more complex business systems, see e-commerce adoption and use as a mechanism whereby some of that complexity can be simplified.

The overall results clearly show that priorities of criteria where e-commerce adoption is concerned appear to move from a strong marketing perspective for small SMEs to a stronger concern for internal functions for the larger SMEs. Clearly, a single perspective for SMEs fails to adequately address the priorities of the business. While smaller businesses are intent on enhancing their marketing, larger businesses are looking to the technology to enhance and "correct" internal problems within the business. Government agencies ignoring these differences would, at best, produce a simplistic model that services only a sub-section of the entire SME spectrum.

*Table 16. Rotated component matrix (1-9 employees): Adoption criteria (Sweden)*

| Criteria | Component 1: Marketing & Partnerships | Component 2: Internal Operations |
|---|---|---|
| Demand and/or pressure from customers. | .644 | |
| Pressure from competition. | .592 | |
| Demand and/or pressure from suppliers. | | .569 |
| To reduce costs. | | .710 |
| To improve customer service. | .793 | |
| To shorten lead time/reduce stock levels. | | .710 |
| To increase sales. | .786 | |
| To improve internal efficiency. | | .577 |
| To strengthen relations with business partners. | .702 | |
| The possibility of reaching new customers/markets. | .887 | |
| To improve our competitiveness. | .748 | |
| We were offered external support to adopt e-commerce. | | .783 |
| To improve our marketing. | .888 | |
| To improve control. | | .762 |

*Table 17. Rotated component matrix (10-19 employees): Adoption criteria (Sweden)*

| Criteria | Component 1: Marketing | Component 2: Market Forces | Component 3: Cost Efficiency | Component 4: Relationships |
|---|---|---|---|---|
| Demand and/or pressure from customers. | | .771 | | |
| Pressure from competition. | | .882 | | |
| Demand and/or pressure from suppliers. | | | | .764 |
| To reduce costs. | | | .643 | |
| To improve customer service. | .829 | | | |
| To shorten lead time/reduce stock levels. | | | .880 | |
| To increase sales. | .707 | | .412 | |
| To improve internal efficiency. | .796 | | .284 | |
| To strengthen relations with business partners. | .563 | | | .618 |
| The possibility of reaching new customers/markets. | .882 | | | |
| To improve our competitiveness. | .831 | | | |
| We were offered external support to adopt e-commerce. | .241 | | | .767 |
| To improve our marketing. | .903 | | | .167 |
| To improve control. | | | .522 | |

# Market Focus

Three categories of SMEs had sufficient data to apply factor analysis. The results of the Kaiser-Meyer-Olkin MSA (.883 for local, .855 for national, and .772 for international) and Bartlett's test of Sphericity ($\chi 2$ = 789 p=.000 for local, $\chi 2$ = 650 p=.000 for national, and $\chi 2$ = 314 p=.000 for international) indicated that the data set satisfied the assumptions for factorability. Principle components analysis was chosen as the method of extraction in order to account for maximum variance in the data using a minimum number of factors. A three factor solution with Eigenvalues 7.796, 1.467, and 1.098 was chosen for local respondents. This accounted for 74.009% of the variance. A two factor solution with Eigenvalues 7.152 and 1.667 was chosen for the national respondents. This accounted for 62.996% of the variance. A three factor solution with Eigenvalues 8.650, 1.482, and 1.289 was chosen for the international respondents. This accounted for 81.580% of the variance. These can be seen in Table 20.

The resulting components were rotated using the Varimax procedure and a simple structure was achieved as shown in the rotated component matrices (Tables 21 to 23).

*Table 18. Rotated component matrix (20-49 employees): Adoption criteria (Sweden)*

| Criteria | Component 1: Marketing | Component 2: Internal Efficiency | Component 3: Relationships | Component 4: Market Forces |
|---|---|---|---|---|
| Demand and/or pressure from customers. | | | | .729 |
| Pressure from competition. | | | | .836 |
| Demand and/or pressure from suppliers. | | | .705 | |
| To reduce costs. | | .847 | | |
| To improve customer service. | | .352 | | |
| To shorten lead time/reduce stock levels. | | .670 | | |
| To increase sales. | .625 | | | |
| To improve internal efficiency. | | .625 | | |
| To strengthen relations with business partners. | .607 | | | |
| The possibility of reaching new customers/markets. | .812 | | | |
| To improve our competitiveness. | .758 | | | |
| We were offered external support to adopt e-commerce. | | | .832 | |
| To improve our marketing. | .799 | | | |
| To improve control. | | .726 | | |

The previous results highlight several issues. Firstly, while the respondents with a national focus considered that there were only two groupings of criteria, both the local respondents and the international respondents loaded the criteria on to three groupings. Secondly, while the local respondents considered marketing and market forces to be separate factors to internal efficiency, the national respondents grouped market forces with internal efficiency and the internationals grouped marketing criteria with internal efficiency. Most importantly, however, in all three sets of data, internal efficiency was rated the highest priority.

A closer examination of the loadings of the individual criteria shows a number of differences. Local respondents considered improvements to customer service an internal efficiency criterion, while the national respondents loaded this criterion almost equally onto both factors, and the international respondents loaded it almost equally onto the efficiency and market forces factors. The criterion related to the availability of external support was loaded onto the internal efficiency factor by the local respondents, and was equally loaded across all factors by the national and international respondents.

*Table 19. Rotated component matrix (50-199 employees): Adoption criteria (Sweden)*

| Criteria | Component 1: Internal Operations | Component 2: Competitiveness | Component 3: External Support |
|---|---|---|---|
| Demand and/or pressure from customers. | | .750 | |
| Pressure from competition. | | .897 | |
| Demand and/or pressure from suppliers. | .624 | | |
| To reduce costs. | .871 | | |
| To improve customer service. | .828 | | |
| To shorten lead time/reduce stock levels. | .762 | | |
| To increase sales. | .479 | | |
| To improve internal efficiency. | .657 | | |
| To strengthen relations with business partners. | | .695 | |
| The possibility of reaching new customers/markets. | | .742 | |
| To improve our competitiveness. | | .852 | |
| We were offered external support to adopt e-commerce. | | .115 | .827 |
| To improve our marketing. | | .658 | |
| To improve control | .666 | | |

*Table 20. Total variation explained: Adoption criteria and market focus (Sweden)*

| Comp | Eigenvalue | | | % Variance | | | Cumulative % | | |
|---|---|---|---|---|---|---|---|---|---|
| Focus | Local | National | International | Local | National | International | Local | National | International |
| 1 | 7.796 | 7.152 | 8.650 | 55.685 | 51.087 | 61.788 | 55.685 | 51.087 | 61.788 |
| 2 | 1.467 | 1.667 | 1.482 | 10.479 | 11.908 | 10.585 | 66.164 | 62.996 | 72.373 |
| 3 | 1.098 | | 1.289 | 7.845 | | 9.207 | 74.009 | | 81.580 |

*Table 21. Rotated component matrix (local market focus): Adoption criteria (Sweden)*

| Criteria | Component 1: Internal Efficiency | Component 2: Marketing | Component 3: Market Forces |
|---|---|---|---|
| Demand and/or pressure from customers. | | | .846 |
| Pressure from competition. | | | .809 |
| Demand and/or pressure from suppliers | .708 | | |
| To reduce costs. | .693 | | |
| To improve customer service. | | .564 | |
| To shorten lead time/reduce stock levels. | .759 | | |
| To increase sales. | | .760 | |
| To improve internal efficiency. | .615 | | |
| To strengthen relations with business partners. | .700 | | |
| The possibility of reaching new customers/markets. | | .913 | |
| To improve our competitiveness. | | .712 | |
| We were offered external support to adopt e-commerce. | .723 | | |
| To improve our marketing. | | .848 | |
| To improve control. | .731 | | |

*Table 22. Rotated component matrix (national market focus): Adoption criteria (Sweden)*

| Criteria | Component 1: Internal & External Efficiency | Component 2: Sales & Marketing |
|---|---|---|
| Demand and/or pressure from customers. | .673 | |
| Pressure from competition. | .664 | |
| Demand and/or pressure from suppliers. | .570 | |
| To reduce costs. | .855 | |
| To improve customer service. | | .610 |
| To shorten lead time/reduce stock levels. | .805 | |
| To increase sales. | | .832 |
| To improve internal efficiency. | .625 | |
| To strengthen relations with business partners. | | .612 |
| The possibility of reaching new customers/markets. | | .888 |
| To improve our competitiveness. | | .648 |
| We were offered external support to adopt e-commerce. | .483 | |
| To improve our marketing. | | .896 |
| To improve control. | .809 | |

*Table 23. Rotated component matrix (international market focus): Adoption criteria (Sweden)*

| Criteria | Component 1: Efficiency | Component 2: Market Forces | Component 3: Support & Control |
|---|---|---|---|
| Demand and/or pressure from customers. | | .928 | |
| Pressure from competition. | | .905 | |
| Demand and/or pressure from suppliers. | | | .559 |
| To reduce costs. | .851 | | |
| To improve customer service. | .693 | | |
| To shorten lead time/reduce stock levels. | .717 | | |
| To increase sales. | .771 | | |
| To improve internal efficiency. | .868 | | |
| To strengthen relations with business partners. | | .739 | |
| The possibility of reaching new customers/markets. | .597 | | |
| To improve our competitiveness. | | .658 | |
| We were offered external support to adopt e-commerce. | | .069 | .903 |
| To improve our marketing. | .569 | | |
| To improve control. | | | .763 |

# Type of E-Commerce

Finally, the responses were subdivided between those SMEs that indicated they were B2B businesses and those that catered to customers directly (B2C).

The results of the Kaiser-Meyer-Olkin MSA (.900 for B2B and .862 for B2C) and Bartlett's test for Sphericity ($\chi2$ = 1302 p=.000 for B2B and $\chi2$ = 559 p=.000 for B2C) indicated that the data set satisfied the assumptions for factorability. Principle components analysis was chosen as the method of extraction in order to account for maximum variance in the data using a minimum number of factors. A three factor solution with Eigenvalues 7.282, 1.274, and 1.092 was extracted for the B2B respondents. This accounted for 68.913% of the variance. A two factor solution with Eigenvalues 9.156 and 1.333 was extracted for the B2C respondents. This accounted for 74.921% of the variance. These can be seen in Table 24.

The resulting components were rotated using the Varimax procedure and a simple structure was achieved as shown in the rotated component matrices (Tables 25 and 26).

Apart from the differences in the number of factors between B2B and B2C organisations, B2B respondents clearly delineated each of the criteria into one of three specific factors. In the case of B2C respondents, several factors loaded almost equally onto both factors. Tables 25 and 26 also indicate that B2B businesses consider pressure from customers and pressure from competition to be a very low priority (Eigenvalue 1.092, % var. 7.804) and to be essentially different to the overall marketing strategies of the business. This would suggest that the regional Swedish respondents who are engaged in B2B have a stable and ongoing relationship with their current business customers.

*Table 24. Total variation explained: Adoption criteria and type of e-commerce (Sweden)*

| Component | Eigenvalues | | % Variation | | Cumulative % | |
|---|---|---|---|---|---|---|
| Type of EC | B2B | B2C | B2B | B2C | B2B | B2C |
| 1 | 7.282 | 9.156 | 52.011 | 65.397 | 52.011 | 65.397 |
| 2 | 1.274 | 1.333 | 9.098 | 9.524 | 61.109 | 74.921 |
| 3 | 1.092 | | 7.804 | | 68.913 | |

*Table 25. Rotated component matrix (B2B): Adoption criteria (Sweden)*

| Criteria | Component 1: Marketing | Component 2: Internal Operations | Component 3: Market Forces |
|---|---|---|---|
| Demand and/or pressure from customers. | | | .839 |
| Pressure from competition. | | | .782 |
| Demand and/or pressure from suppliers. | | .667 | |
| To reduce costs. | | .759 | |
| To improve customer service. | .693 | | |
| To shorten lead time/reduce stock levels. | | .768 | |
| To increase sales. | .752 | | |
| To improve internal efficiency. | | .629 | |
| To strengthen relations with business partners. | .591 | | |
| The possibility of reaching new customers/ markets. | .871 | | |
| To improve our competitiveness. | .714 | | |
| We were offered external support to adopt e-commerce. | | .483 | |
| To improve our marketing. | .851 | | |
| To improve control. | | .732 | |

*Table 26. Rotated component matrix (B2C): Adoption criteria (Sweden)*

| Criteria | Component 1: Market Forces & Marketing | Component 2: Internal Business |
|---|---|---|
| Demand and/or pressure from customers. | .811 | |
| Pressure from competition. | .810 | |
| Demand and/or pressure from suppliers. | | .702 |
| To reduce costs. | | .670 |
| To improve customer service. | .764 | |
| To shorten lead time/reduce stock levels. | | .887 |
| To increase sales. | .687 | |
| To improve internal efficiency. | .618 | .545 |
| To strengthen relations with business partners. | | .767 |
| The possibility of reaching new customers/markets. | .860 | |
| To improve our competitiveness. | .706 | |
| We were offered external support to adopt e-commerce. | | .872 |
| To improve our marketing. | .777 | |
| To improve control. | | .728 |

Again, for both researchers and government agencies, these findings show that a single approach fails to delineate fundamental differences between those businesses that are primarily B2B and those that are primarily B2C. Clearly, while marketing is the most important reason for both groups, there is far less competitive or customer pressure for the B2B businesses.

# Summary: E-Commerce Adoption Criteria in Swedish SMEs

The results of the Swedish study show an interesting trend in relation to the size of the business (as defined by the number of employees) and e-commerce adoption, with larger SMEs more likely to implement e-commerce due to pressure from external stakeholders (suppliers and competitors) and internal efficiencies. SMEs with a local or regional focus also indicate a higher likelihood of succumbing to pressure from suppliers than their national or international counterparts.

The results also indicate clear differences in the ratings assigned to various adoption criteria by SMEs in different categories. Smaller and larger SMEs grouped e-commerce drivers differently, as did SMEs with different market foci and types of e-commerce used. However, for the most part, these groupings are related to market forces and internal operational issues. The results from Sweden will be revisited at the end of the chapter and compared to the other locations. We now turn to SMEs located in Australia.

# Business Characteristics and E-Commerce Adoption Criteria in Australia

Following the same analysis pattern as that of Sweden, our first question was concerned with the effects of different business characteristics on how the fourteen e-commerce adoption criteria listed in Figure 1 were perceived by SMEs. Although we found a number of statistically significant associations in the Swedish sample, only one criterion (Pressure from competition) showed any statistically significant association with any of the business characteristics in the Australian study. This is shown in Table 27. The lack of additional associations suggests that all of the other adoption criteria are equally important to different categories of SMEs.

The previous table indicates that there is a weak but statistically significant association between pressure from competitors and belonging to a business strategic alliance. The data shows that non-members are more likely to place a higher level of importance on this criterion than member respondents. One possible explanation is that membership of a business strategic alliance reduces the need to deal with pressure from competition due to "power in numbers."

If we compare this result to the Swedish findings, we see that pressure from competition was associated with business size, and not membership of a strategic alliance. One argument for the lack of association with business size is the fact that the Australian study had a large number of respondents in the 1-9 employee range, compared to Sweden, which had a wider range of business sizes. The results, however, remain somewhat enigmatic as the Australian study showed far fewer members of any form of alliance than did the Swedish responses.

We now proceed with answering our second question: Are there any underlying factors or groupings of e-commerce adoption criteria, which would serve to explain the key reasons behind SMEs' decisions to use e-commerce?

*Table 27. Regression table for pressure from competitors*

| Dependant Variable Pressure from competitors | | |
|---|---|---|
| | **Beta** | **p value** |
| Strategic Alliance Membership | .473 | .041 |
| R Squared | .696 | |
| Adjusted R squared | .438 | |
| p value for the complete regression table | .046 | |

# Groupings of E-Commerce Adoption Criteria in Australia

To answer our second question, a combination of correlations and factor analysis was applied to the data. The results of this analysis are shown in the tables next and discussed at the end of this section.

Table 28 provides the correlation matrix of the importance ratings for e-commerce adoption criteria. All correlations significant at the .001 level are shown in bold.

These findings suggested the use of factor analysis to investigate any separate underlying factors and to reduce the redundancy of certain criteria indicated in the correlation matrix. The results of the Kaiser-Meyer-Olkin MSA (.751) and Bartlett's test for Sphericity ($\chi2 = 250$, $p = .000$) indicated that the data set satisfied the assumptions for factorability. Principle components analysis was chosen as the method of extraction in order to account for maximum variance in the data using a minimum number of factors. A three factor solution was extracted with Eigenvalues 7.154, 1.585, and 1.101. The three factors accounted for 70.280% of the variance. Table 29 shows the variance.

The resulting components were rotated using the Varimax procedure and a simple structure was achieved as shown in the rotated component matrix (see Table 30).

As can be seen in Table 30, respondents loaded the criteria onto three factors: internal operations, marketing & relationships, and competition & markets. The data shows that the highest priority (Eigenvalue 7.154, % var. 51.098%) was on the internal operations factor. The second priority (Eigenvalue 1.585, % var. 11.321%) was assigned to the criteria under marketing and relationships, while the least level of priority (Eigenvalue 1.101, % var. 7.861%) was given to the component we have termed competition and markets. The groupings found in the Australian sample are shown in Figure 3.

In comparison to the findings in Sweden (Table 14), which showed that only two factors were in evidence and that by far the highest priority was on marketing and partnerships, the Australian respondents have split marketing into two components, which are independent and uncorrelated as an orthogonal rotation method was applied. The marketing and relationships component contains three of the adoption criteria, while the second component contains five

*Figure 3. E-commerce adoption criteria groupings in Australia*

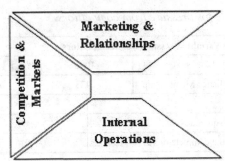

*Table 28. Adoption criteria correlation matrix (Australia)*

| | Demand and/or pressure from customers. | Demand and/or pressure from suppliers. | To reduce costs. | To improve customer service. | To shorten lead time/reduce stock levels. | To increase sales. | To improve internal efficiency. | To strengthen relations with business partners. | The possibility of reaching new customers/markets. | To improve our competitiveness. | We were offered external support to adopt e-commerce. | To improve our marketing. | To improve control. |
|---|---|---|---|---|---|---|---|---|---|---|---|---|---|
| Pressure from competition. | .497* | | | | | | | | | | | | |
| Demand and/or pressure from suppliers. | .516** | .408* | | | | | | | | | | | |
| To reduce costs. | .384 | .074 | .437* | | | | | | | | | | |
| To improve customer service. | .476* | .203 | .224 | .313 | | | | | | | | | |
| To shorten lead time/reduce stock levels. | .506* | .322 | .455* | .431* | .402* | | | | | | | | |
| To increase sales. | .666 | .517** | .434* | .466* | .600** | .584** | | | | | | | |
| To improve internal efficiency. | .432* | .336 | .432* | .426* | .578** | .595** | .781 | | | | | | |
| To strengthen relations with business partners. | .334 | .097 | .128 | -.039 | .318 | .012 | .326 | .162 | | | | | |
| The possibility of reaching new customers/markets. | .602** | .593** | .239 | .238 | .494* | .519** | .833 | .642** | .193 | | | | |
| To improve our competitiveness. | .568** | .619** | .442* | .356 | .574** | .486* | .893 | .752 | .321 | .895 | | | |
| We were offered external support to adopt e-commerce. | .434* | .373 | -.066 | .178 | .447* | .238 | .427* | .193 | .447* | .438* | .386 | | |
| To improve our marketing. | .576** | .267 | .196 | .434* | .598** | .423* | .667 | .470* | .297 | .780 | .736 | .461* | |
| To improve control. | .598** | .353 | .497* | .360 | .657 | .617** | .711 | .789 | .247 | .644** | .751 | .141 | .617** |

*Note: * significant at 0.05 level    ** significant at 0.01 level*

*Table 29. Total variance explained: Adoption criteria (Australia)*

| Component | Eigenvalue | % Variance | Cumulative % |
|-----------|-----------|-----------|--------------|
| 1 | 7.154 | 51.098 | 51.098 |
| 2 | 1.585 | 11.321 | 62.419 |
| 3 | 1.101 | 7.861 | 70.280 |

*Table 30. Rotated component matrix: Adoption criteria (Australia)*

| Criteria | Component 1: Internal Operations | Component 2: Marketing & Relationships | Component 3: Competition & Markets |
|----------|------|------|------|
| Demand and/or pressure from customers. | | | .499 |
| Pressure from competition. | | | .928 |
| Demand and/or pressure from suppliers | .557 | | .491 |
| To reduce costs. | .748 | | |
| To improve customer service. | .602 | | |
| To shorten lead time/reduce stock levels. | .698 | | |
| To increase sales. | .656 | | |
| To improve internal efficiency. | .773 | | |
| To strengthen relations with business partners. | | .690 | |
| The possibility of reaching new customers/markets. | | | .587 |
| To improve our competitiveness. | .575 | | .583 |
| We were offered external support to adopt e-commerce. | | .798 | |
| To improve our marketing. | .565 | .611 | |
| To improve control. | .782 | | |

criteria. Other differences between the two include the location of several criteria (increased sales, improved customer service, and external support). While the Swedish SMEs placed increased sales and improved customer service into the marketing and partnerships factor and external support into the internal operations factor, the Australians have reversed these, placing increased sales and improved customer service into the internal operations factor and external support into the marketing and relationships factor. Above all, the results clearly show that neither the grouping of criteria nor their priority can be considered universal, but must be examined for each region separately.

Due to the small number of e-commerce adopters in Australia, it was not possible to split up the data further and conduct additional statistical analyses.

# Summary: E-Commerce Adoption Criteria in Australian SMEs

The results in the Australian context show that SMEs adopt e-commerce for three main reasons: improvements to their internal business processes, marketing benefits and outcomes, and competition. However, the results also show that becoming a member of a strategic alliance diminished the effects of competition. SMEs, which are members of strategic alliances, were less likely to succumb to pressure from competition and adopt e-commerce. This highlights one of the key benefits for participating in strategic relationships with other businesses. A detailed discussion of the relationship between e-commerce and strategic alliances will be presented later. We now turn to SMEs located in the USA.

# Business Characteristics and E-Commerce Adoption Criteria in the USA

The first question was concerned with the effect of business characteristics on how the fourteen e-commerce adoption criteria listed in Figure 1 were perceived. We found three statistically significant associations in the U.S. sample between the business age and various e-commerce adoption criteria. These are summarized in Table 31, which also indicates the corresponding tables showing the associations and the relevant p value.

Clearly the length of time an SME has been in business has an effect on several reasons for adopting e-commerce, including pressure from suppliers, marketing improvements, and better internal control. However, in regional U.S. SMEs, the decision to adopt e-commerce does not appear to be affected by other characteristics such as the business sector, gender of the CEO, and so forth. This lack of association suggests that the adoption criteria are viewed as being equally important by SMEs operating in different sectors, having CEOs of opposite genders, and so forth. We will now examine and comment on each of the associations in turn next.

Table 32 indicates that older businesses assign a higher level of importance to pressure from suppliers than younger businesses. This could be due to the fact that older businesses often tend to have well established relationships with suppliers and are keen to maintain these, while younger businesses do not have such loyalties in place.

The age of the business was also found to be significantly associated with the improved marketing criterion (Table 33). Again, the data suggest that the older businesses place a higher level of importance on this criterion than do the younger businesses. This could be attributed to younger SMEs' concern with setting up their basic operations, rather than focusing on developing electronic marketing channels through e-commerce. More established SMEs would logically tend to focus on market expansion and alternative marketing channels.

Finally, the criterion related to improved control was found to be associated with two business characteristics: business age and business size (Table 34). Older and larger SMEs were found to be more likely to assign a higher importance rating on this criterion than the smaller or younger ones. Once again, this can be attributed to the higher maturity level of SMEs that have been in business for longer periods and the desire to introduce an innovative technology into the organisation to improve the internal control processes.

We will now take a closer look at the groupings of e-commerce adoption criteria in the U.S. context with the purpose of answering our second question: Are there any underlying factors or groupings of e-commerce adoption criteria, which would serve to explain the key reasons behind SMEs' decisions to use e-commerce?

*Table 31. Summary of associations between e-commerce adoption criteria and business characteristics (USA)*

| E-commerce adoption criteria | Correlated with... | Table | p value |
|---|---|---|---|
| Demand and/or pressure from suppliers. | Business age | 4.32 | .001 |
| Improved marketing. | Business age | 4.33 | .006 |
| Improved control. | Business age | 4.34 | .033 |
|  | Business size |  | .030 |

*Table 32. Regression table for pressure from suppliers*

| Dependant Variable Pressure from Suppliers | | |
|---|---|---|
|  | Beta | p value |
| Business Age | .433 | .001 |
| R Squared | | .195 |
| Adjusted R squared | | .149 |
| p value for the complete regression table | | .010 |

# Groupings of E-Commerce Adoption Criteria in the USA

To answer our second question, a combination of correlations and factor analysis was applied to the data. The results of this analysis are shown in the tables next and discussed at the end of this section.

Table 35 provides the correlation matrix of the importance ratings for e-commerce adoption criteria. All correlations significant at the .001 level are shown in bold.

The results of the Kaiser-Meyer-Olkin MSA (.652) and Bartlett's test for Sphericity ($\chi2 = 283$, p=.000) indicated that the data set satisfied the assumptions for factorability. Principle components analysis was chosen as the method of extraction in order to account for maximum variance in the data using a minimum number of factors. A four factor solution was extracted with Eigenvalues 4.352, 2.150, 1.272, and 1.118. The four factors accounted for 63.517% of the variance. This was supported by the Scree plots. Table 36 shows the variance.

The resulting components were rotated using the Varimax procedure and a simple structure was achieved as shown in the rotated component matrix (see Table 37).

SMEs in the U.S. showed somewhat similar groupings to their Australian counterparts, with the exception of the fourth component (customer service). However, a comparison of the U.S. findings with both the Swedish and Australian findings shows a substantial number of differences between the three locations.

*Table 33. Regression table for improved marketing*

| Dependant Variable Improved marketing | | |
|---|---|---|
| | Beta | p value |
| Business age | .364 | .006 |
| R Squared | | .186 |
| Adjusted R squared | | .139 |
| p value for the complete regression table | | .013 |

*Table 34. Regression table for improved control*

| Dependant Variable Improved control | | |
|---|---|---|
| | Beta | p value |
| Business size | .286 | .033 |
| Business age | .291 | .030 |
| R Squared | | .159 |
| Adjusted R squared | | .108 |
| p value for the complete regression table | | .033 |

Firstly, and most obviously, is that where the Swedish respondents mapped all 14 criteria to only two factors, the Australians mapped them to three factors and the U.S. respondents mapped them to four factors. The highest priority in the U.S. sample was assigned to internal operations (Eigenvalue 4.432, % var. 31.082). This factor had six adoption criteria mapped onto it. It was also the highest priority for the Australian respondents, but was the lower of the two factors in the Swedish study. The second highest priority for the U.S. study was marketing (Eigenvalue 2.150, % var. 15.360%). This factor had four criteria loading onto it and did not really match any factor from the other two studies. A third factor termed "cost and competitiveness" (Eigenvalue 1.272, % var. 9.085%) had three criteria mapped to it in the U.S. study. Improved customer service, which was mapped to marketing and market forces by the Swedish respondents and onto the internal operations factor by the Australians, was mapped onto its own unique and uncorrelated factor in the U.S. study. It had the lowest priority (Eigenvalue 1.118, % var. 7.989%). Again, the results clearly show that neither the grouping of criteria nor their priority can be considered universal, but must be examined for each location separately. A summary of the U.S. groupings can be seen in Figure 4.

Due to the low number of adopters in the U.S. sample, there was insufficient data to perform factor analyses by subdividing the data further.

# Summary: E-Commerce Adoption Criteria in USA SMEs

The results indicate that older SMEs based in the U.S. rated several adoption criteria as more important than newer ones. These include pressure from suppliers, improved marketing, and improved control. This is consistent with the operations and development of well-established SMEs, which often have long-term relationships with suppliers and are concerned with internal efficiency rather than survival and breaking even, as is the case with newer SMEs. The results also show that there are four overarching reasons that lead to e-commerce adoption by U.S. respondents. These include better internal operations, improved marketing, reduced cost and increased competitiveness, and improved customer services.

We will now compare and discuss the key findings across the three locations.

# Comparison of Results: A Discussion

The e-commerce adoption criteria part of our study shows an interesting pattern of results across the three locations. While similarities do exist, the differences are more pronounced, particularly where the effects of business characteristics are concerned and despite the economic and technological development similarities between the three countries.

In Sweden, business size was found to be associated with a number of adoption criteria, including pressure from external stakeholders (competitors and customers), cost reductions, improved customer services and internal efficiency, availability of external support,

*Table 35. Adoption Criteria Correlation Matrix (USA)*

| | Demand and/or pressure from customers. | Demand and/or pressure from suppliers. | To reduce costs. | To improve customer service. | To shorten lead time/reduce stock levels. | To increase sales. | To improve internal efficiency. | To strengthen relations with business partners. | The possibility of reaching new customers/markets. | To improve our competitiveness. | We were offered external support to adopt e-commerce. | To improve our marketing. | To improve control. |
|---|---|---|---|---|---|---|---|---|---|---|---|---|---|
| Pressure from competition. | .221 | | | | | | | | | | | | |
| Demand and/or pressure from suppliers. | .146 | .365** | | | | | | | | | | | |
| To reduce costs. | .134 | .533 | .339** | | | | | | | | | | |
| To improve customer service. | .044 | .031 | .160 | .065 | | | | | | | | | |
| To shorten lead time/reduce stock levels. | .099 | .389** | .230 | .127 | .180 | | | | | | | | |
| To increase sales. | .232 | .552 | .454 | .154 | .135 | .710 | | | | | | | |
| To improve internal efficiency. | .305* | .320* | .294* | .247 | .040 | .259 | .510 | | | | | | |
| To strengthen relations with business partners. | .276* | .493 | .325* | .396** | -.034 | .594 | .576 | .501 | | | | | |
| The possibility of reaching new customers/markets. | .230 | .561 | .378** | .223 | .161 | .561 | .810 | .438** | .655 | | | | |
| To improve our competitiveness. | .049 | .621 | .223 | .293* | .002 | .443** | .524 | .330* | .546 | .677 | | | |
| We were offered external support to adopt e-commerce. | .260 | -.084 | .015 | -.035 | .194 | .017 | -.044 | .016 | -.061 | -.045 | -.043 | | |
| To improve our marketing. | .052 | .072 | .253 | .047 | .091 | .072 | .023 | .257 | -.028 | -.067 | -.068 | .369* | |
| To improve control. | .154 | -.067 | .098 | .055 | .204 | -.122 | -.067 | .132 | -.152 | -.115 | -.110 | .307* | .557 |

*Note:  * significant at 0.05 level     ** significant at 0.01 level*

*Table 36. Total variance explained: Adoption criteria (USA)*

| Component | Eigenvalue | % Variance | Cumulative % |
|-----------|-----------|-----------|--------------|
| 1 | 4.432 | 31.082 | 31.082 |
| 2 | 2.150 | 15.360 | 46.443 |
| 3 | 1.272 | 9.085 | 55.528 |
| 4 | 1.118 | 7.989 | 63.517 |

*Table 37. Rotated component matrix: Adoption criteria (USA)*

| Criteria | Component 1: Internal Operations | Component 2: Marketing | Component 3: Cost & Competitiveness | Component 4: Customer Service |
|----------|----------------------------------|------------------------|--------------------------------------|-------------------------------|
| Demand and/or pressure from customers. | | .497 | | |
| Pressure from competition. | | | .635 | |
| Demand and/or pressure from suppliers. | | | .497 | |
| To reduce costs. | | | .883 | |
| To improve customer service. | | | | .775 |
| To shorten lead time/reduce stock levels. | .799 | | | |
| To increase sales. | .855 | | | |
| To improve internal efficiency. | .500 | | | |
| To strengthen relations with business partners. | .736 | | | |
| The possibility of reaching new customers/markets. | .865 | | | |
| To improve our competitiveness. | .646 | | | |
| We were offered external support to adopt e-commerce. | | .644 | | |
| To improve our marketing. | | .750 | | |
| To improve control. | | .754 | | |

*Figure 4. E-commerce adoption criteria groupings in the USA*

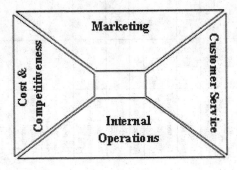

and improvements to control. This tends to support the findings of Hawkins, Winter, and Hunter (1995), Hyland et al. (1997), Fallon et al. (2000), Matlay (2000), and Blackburn et al. (2000). Two criteria (improved internal efficiency and improved control) were positively affected by business size and negatively affected by decisions concerning B2B/B2C. Indeed, the data suggests that those respondents who indicated that they were B2C businesses felt that improved internal efficiency and improved control were far less important than their B2B counterparts. Of particular interest was the finding that showed a negative association between market focus and pressure from suppliers. This appears to be contrary to the findings of Poon et al. (1997), Lawrence (1997), Power et al. (2002), and Reimenschneider et al. (2000) who suggested that it was the SMEs with a national or international that would be more concerned with pressure from suppliers.

In contrast to the Swedish respondents, for the Australian SMEs, only one criterion (pressure from competition) showed a statistically significant association with membership/non-membership of a business strategic alliance. Indeed, the data shows that those businesses that were not part of a business strategic alliance considered this criterion more important than those that were members. This is not an unexpected result since previous studies have shown that strategic alliance membership dissipates the effects of competition. Much of the discussion of strategic alliances will be presented in Chapter VIII.

In the U.S., the business characteristic that showed an association with three adoption criteria (pressure from suppliers, improved marketing, and improved control) was the age of the business with older businesses more likely to be concerned with these criteria than newer ones. The data from the U.S. supports the earlier findings (Donckels et al., 1997; Kai-Uwe-Brock, 2000; MacGregor et al., 2002) and suggests different strategies for promoting e-commerce adoption in older and newer SMEs.

What is perhaps most notable across the three locations is that despite all three being similar in terms of infrastructure, OECD, and World Bank ratings, there is no uniformity or agreement from any of the findings of the linear regressions. Adoption criteria in Swedish SMEs were associated with predominantly with the business size, while in the U.S. business age was the dominant characteristic. This implies the use of customised approaches in each of the three locations to promote e-commerce adoption. In Sweden, SMEs of different sizes are likely to respond differently to certain e-commerce drivers, while in the U.S., these differences would be manifested through the length of time the SME had been in operation. Table 38 provides a summary and comparison of the answers to the first question posed at the outset of this chapter. The category of SMEs that assigns a higher importance to a particular criterion is indicated in the columns.

Certain authors (Martin et al., 2001) have noted that, among other things, the location an SME does have a bearing on the decision-making process when it comes to the adoption of e-commerce. The results of our study would appear to confirm previous research since they show that the groupings of e-commerce adoption criteria differ widely between Sweden, Australia, and the U.S.

In Sweden, two factors (groupings) were derived and termed "marketing and partnerships" and "internal operations." In Australia, three factors, termed "internal operations," "marketing and relationships," and "competition and markets" were found to exist. Finally, in the U.S., there were four factors: "internal operations," "marketing," "costs and competitiveness," and "customer service." The loading of the criteria on each of the different groupings is

*Table 38. Association between business characteristics and e-commerce adoption criteria: A comparison*

| Adoption Criteria | Higher rating by... | | |
|---|---|---|---|
| | Sweden | Australia | USA |
| Demand and/or pressure from customers. | Larger SMEs | | |
| Pressure from competition. | Larger SMEs | SMEs not members of an alliance | |
| Demand and/or pressure from suppliers. | Local & regional SMEs | | Older SMEs |
| Reduced costs. | Larger SMEs | | |
| Improved customer service. | Larger SMEs | | |
| Improved internal efficiency. | Larger SMEs B2B SMEs | | |
| External support to adopt e-commerce. | Larger SMEs | | |
| Improved marketing. | | | Older SMEs |
| Improved control. | Larger SMEs B2B SMEs | | Older SMEs Larger SMEs |

summarised in Table 39. The groupings, which are underlined and shown in bold are those to which the SMEs in that particular location assigned the highest priority.

While Australian and U.S. SMEs were predominantly concerned about adopting e-commerce to improve internal operations, Swedish SMEs were keen to use e-commerce for marketing and partnership building purposes. Although there are similarities in the nature of the groupings, a closer examination reveals many differences. For example, adopting e-commerce to improve competitiveness was seen as a marketing driver by Swedish SMEs. In contrast, this criterion was attributed to improving internal operations by Australian and U.S. SMEs, implying that competitiveness could be achieved through internal means, rather than externally. Another difference relates to the presence of the fourth factor (customer service) in the U.S. group. This is seen as a distinct and separate factor by U.S. SMEs.

# E-Commerce Adoption Criteria: Implications

As already indicated, there have been a number of criticisms levelled at government-developed programs and methodologies aimed at assisting SMEs to adopt e-commerce (see for example MacGregor, 2004; Martin et al., 2001). Foremost in these criticisms has been that most governments, and most methodologies developed by governments, view the SME

*Table 39. Loading of adoption criteria on different factors (groupings): A comparison*

| Criteria | SWEDEN 1 Marketing & Partnerships | SWEDEN 2 Internal Operations | AUSTRALIA 1 Internal Operations | AUSTRALIA 2 Marketing & Relationships | AUSTRALIA 3 Competition & Markets | USA 1 Internal Operations | USA 2 Marketing | USA 3 Cost & Competitiveness | USA 4 Customer Service |
|---|---|---|---|---|---|---|---|---|---|
| Demand and/or pressure from customers. | ✓ | | | | ✓ | | ✓ | | |
| Pressure from competition. | ✓ | ✓ | | | ✓ | | | ✓ | |
| Demand and/or pressure from suppliers. | | ✓ | ✓ | | ✓ | | | ✓ | |
| To reduce costs. | | ✓ | ✓ | | | | | ✓ | |
| To improve customer service. | ✓ | | ✓ | | | | | | ✓ |
| To shorten lead time/reduce stock levels. | | ✓ | ✓ | | | ✓ | | | |
| To increase sales. | ✓ | | ✓ | | | ✓ | | | |
| To improve internal efficiency. | | ✓ | ✓ | | | ✓ | | | |
| To strengthen relations with business partners. | ✓ | | | ✓ | | ✓ | | | |
| The possibility of reaching new customers/markets. | ✓ | | | | ✓ | ✓ | | | |
| To improve our competitiveness. | ✓ | | ✓ | | ✓ | ✓ | | | |
| We were offered external support to adopt e-commerce. | ✓ | | | ✓ | | | ✓ | | |
| To improve our marketing. | ✓ | | ✓ | ✓ | | | ✓ | | |
| To improve control. | | ✓ | ✓ | | | | ✓ | | |

sector as being largely homogeneous. This research shows that in regard to regional SMEs in developed nations, this is not the case. While three locations were deliberately chosen for their apparent similarity, not only was the uptake of e-commerce different, but the groupings of reasons for that uptake differed as well. Therefore, prior to developing e-commerce awareness and support programs for SMEs, it is important to understand e-commerce drivers in a specific location. Any programs or methodologies developed to promote e-commerce adoption must be tailored based on the specific needs in each location. Indeed, this applies equally to e-commerce solution providers who must target their products and the benefits of their products to specific categories of SMEs. The findings presented in this chapter can assist both government organisations and e-commerce solution providers with this.

# E-Commerce Adoption Criteria: Key Findings

## Sweden

- Business size is associated with a number of e-commerce adoption criteria. SMEs with more employees assign a higher level of importance to the following criteria: demand and/or pressure from customers, pressure from competition, cost reductions, improved customer services, improved internal efficiency, availability of external support, and improved control.

- Local and regional SMEs perceive pressure from suppliers as a more important e-commerce adoption criterion than those SMEs that are trading at a national or international level.

- B2C businesses are less likely than B2B businesses to consider improvements to internal efficiency and improvements to control as important criteria.

- Swedish respondents grouped adoption criteria based on two factors: improving marketing and business partnerships and improving internal operations.

- Differences in the groupings exist depending on the size of the SMEs, the market focus, and whether the business had adopted B2C or B2B e-commerce.

## Australia

- SMEs, which are not members of a strategic alliance, are more likely to place a higher level of importance on pressure of competition as an adoption criterion than member respondents.

- Australian SMEs adopted e-commerce for three overarching reasons: improving internal operations, improving marketing and business relationships, and dealing with competition and markets forces.

## USA

- Older SMEs assign a higher level of importance to pressure from suppliers, improved marketing, and improvements to control than younger businesses as adoption criteria.

- U.S.-based SMEs adopted e-commerce for four overarching reasons: improving internal operations, better marketing, reducing costs and increasing competitiveness, and improving customer service.

# References

Abell, W., & Lim, L. (1996). Business use of the Internet in New Zealand: An exploratory study. In *Proceedings of AUSWeb 96*. Retrieved from http//www.scu.edu.au/sponsored/ausweb96

Auger, P., & Gallaugher, J. M. (1997). Factors affecting adoption of an Internet-based sales presence for small businesses. *The Information Society, 13*(1), 55-74.

BarNir, A., & Smith, K. A. (2002). Interfirm alliances in the small business: The role of social networks. *Journal of Small Business Management, 40*(3), 219-232.

Blackburn, R., & Athayde, R. (2000). Making the connection: The effectiveness of Internet training in small businesses. *Education and Training, 42*(4/5).

Bodorick, P., Dhaliwal, J., & Jutla, D. (2002). Supporting the e-business readiness of small and medium-sized enterprises: Approaches and metrics. *Internet Research: Electronic Networking Applications and Policy, 12*(2), 139-164.

Chapman, P., James-Moore, M., Szczygiel, M., & Thompson, D. (2000). Building Internet capabilities in SMEs. *Logistics Information Management, 13*(6), 353-360.

Cragg, P., Mehrtens, J., & Mills, A. (2001). A model of Internet adoption by SMEs. *Information and Management, 39*, 165-176.

Daniel, E. M., Wilson, H., & Myers, A. (2002). Adoption of e-commerce by SMEs in the UK: Towards a stage model. *International Small Business Journal, 20*(3), 253-270.

Domke-Damonte, D., & Levsen, V. B. (2002, summer). The effect of Internet usage on cooperation and performance in small hotels. *SAM Advanced Management Journal*, 31-38.

Donckels, R., & Lambrecht, J. (1997). The network position of small businesses: An explanatory model. *Journal of Small Business Management, 35*(2), 13-28.

Eid, R. (2005). International Internet marketing: A triangulation study of drivers and barriers in the business-to-business context in the United Kingdom. *Market Intelligence & Planning, 23*(3), 266-280.

Evans, P. B., & Wurster, T. S. (1997, September-October). Strategy and the new economics of information. *Harvard Business Review*, 70-82.

Fallon, M., & Moran, P. (2000). Information communications technology (ICT) and manufacturing SMEs. In *Proceedings of the 2000 Small Business and Enterprise Development Conference* (pp. 100-109), University of Manchester.

Fillis, I., Johansson, U., & Wagner, B. (2004). A qualitative investigation of smaller firm e-business development. *Journal of Small Business & Enterprise Development, 11*(3), 349-361.

Grandon, E. E., & Pearson, J. M. (2004). Electronic commerce adoption: An empirical study of small and medium U.S. businesses. *Information and Management, 42*(1), 197-216.

Hawkins, P., & Winter, J. (1996). The self-reliant graduate and the SME. *Education and Training, 38*(4), 3-9.

Hawkins, P., Winter, J., & Hunter, J. (1995). *Skills for graduates in the 21st Century*. Report Commissioned from the Whiteway Research, University of Cambridge, Association of Graduate Recruiters, Cambridge.

Hyland, T., & Matlay, H. (1997). Small businesses, training needs, and VET provisions. *Journal of Education and Work, 10*(2).

Iacovou, C. L., Benbasat, I., & Dexter, A. S. (1995). Electronic data interchange and small organisations: Adoption and impact of technology. *MIS Quarterly, 19*(4), 465-485.

Kai-Uwe Brock, J. (2000). Information and technology in the small firm. In S. Carter & Jones-Evans (Eds.), *Enterprise and the small business* (pp. 384-408). Prentice Hall.

Kaynak, E., Tatoglu, E., & Kula, V. (2005). An analysis of the factors affecting the adoption of electronic commerce by SMEs: Evidence from an emerging market. *International Marketing Review, 22*(6), 623-640.

Lawrence, K. L. (1997). Factors inhibiting the utilisation of electronic commerce facilities in Tasmanian small-to-medium sized enterprises. In *Proceedings of the 8th Australasian Conference on Information Systems* (pp. 587-597).

Lee, C. S. (2001). An analytical framework for evaluating e-commerce business models and strategies. *Internet Research: Electronic Network Applications and Policy, 11*(4), 349-359.

Lee, J., & Runge, J. (2001). Adoption of information technology in small business: testing drivers of adoption for entrepreneurs. *Journal of Computer Information Systems, 42*(1), 44-57.

MacGregor, R. C. (2004). The role of formal networks in the ongoing use of electronic commerce technology in regional small business. *Journal of Electronic Commerce in Organisations, 2*(1), 1-14.

MacGregor, R. C., & Bunker, D. J. (1996). The effect of priorities introduced during computer acquisition on continuing success with IT in small business environments. In *Proceedings of the Information Resource Management Association International Conference*, Washington (pp. 271-277).

MacGregor, R. C., Bunker, D. J., & Waugh, P. (1998). Electronic commerce and small/medium enterprises (SME's) in Australia: An electronic data interchange (EDI) pilot study. In *Proceedings of the 11th International Bled Electronic Commerce Conference*, Slovenia.

MacGregor, R. C., Vrazalic, L., Carlsson, S., Bunker, D. J. & Magnusson, M. (2002). The impact of business size and business type on small business investment in electronic commerce: A study of Swedish small businesses. *Australian Journal of Information Systems*, *9*(2), 31-39.

Magnusson, M. (2001) E-commerce in small businesses: Focusing on adoption and implementation, *Proceedings of the 1st Nordic Workshop on Electronic Commerce*, Halmstad, Sweden, May 28-29

Martin, L. M., & Matlay, H. (2001). "Blanket" approaches to promoting ICT in small firms: Some lessons from the DTI ladder adoption model in the UK. *Internet Research: Electronic Networking Applications and Policy*, *11*(5), 399-410.

Matlay, H. (2000). Training in the small business sector of the British economy. In S. Carter & D. Jones (Eds.), *Enterprise and small business: Principles, policy, and practice*. London: Addison Wesley Longman.

Mazzarol, T., Volery, T., Doss, N., & Thein, V. (1999). Factors influencing small business start-ups. *International Journal of Entrepreneurial Behaviour and Research*, *5*(2), 48-63.

O'Donnell, A., Gilmore, A., Cummins, D., & Carson, D. (2001). The network construct in entrepreneurship research: A review and critique. *Management Decision*, *39*(9), 749-760.

Phan, D. D. (2001, fall). E-business management strategies: A business-to-business case study. *Information Systems Management*, 61-69.

Poon, S., & Joseph, M. (2001). A preliminary study of product nature and electronic commerce. *Marketing Intelligence & Planning*, *19*(7), 493-499.

Poon, S., & Strom, J. (1997). Small business use of the Internet: Some realities. In *Proceedings of the Association for Information Systems Americas Conference*, Indianapolis, IN.

Poon, S., & Swatman, P. (1997). The Internet for small businesses: An enabling infrastructure. In *Proceedings of the 5th Internet Society Conference* (pp. 221-231).

Power, D. J., & Sohal, A. S. (2002). Implementation and usage of electronic commerce in managing the supply chain: A comparative study of ten Australian companies. *Benchmarking: An International Journal*, *9*(2), 190-208.

PriceWaterhouseCoopers. (1999). *SME Electronic Commerce Study Final Report*, 37pp.

Raisch, W. D. (2001). *The e-marketplace: Strategies for success in B2B*. New York: McGraw-Hill.

Raymond, L. (2001). Determinants of Web site implementation in small business. *Internet Research: Electronic Network Applications and Policy*, *11*(5), 411-422.

Reimenschneider, C. K., & Mykytyn, P. P. Jr. (2000). What small business executives have learned about managing information technology. *Information & Management*, *37*, 257-267.

Riquelme, H. (2002). Commercial Internet adoption in China: Comparing the experience of small, medium, and large business. *Internet Research: Electronic Networking Applications and Policy*, *12*(3), 276-286.

Ruth, J. P. S. (2000). So far small biz only dabbling in e-commerce. *Business News New Jersey, 13*(23), 24.

Sadowski, B. M., Maitland, C. and van Dongen, J. (2002) Strategic use of the Internet by small- and medium-sized companies: an exploratory study. *Information Economics and Policy, 14*(1), 75-93.

Schindehutte, M., & Morris, M. H. (2001). Understanding strategic adaptation in small firms. *International Journal of Entrepreneurial Behaviour and Research, 7*(3), 84-107.

Senn, J. A. (1996). Capitalisation on electronic commerce. *Information Systems Management.* Summer.

*Sensis® e-Business Report.* (2006). Retrieved September 12, 2006, from www.about.sensis. com.au/resources/sebr.php

Telstra (1999) *Small Business Index: Characteristics of Home Based Small Businesses.* Retrieved June 3, 2005 from http://www.sensis.com.au/Internet/small_business/ypbi/ smeiypbisr_018.pdf

Tetteh, E., & Burn, J. (2001). Global strategies for SME-business: Applying the SMALL framework. *Logistics Information Management, 14*(1-2), 171-180.

Turban, E., Lee, J., King, D., & Chung, H. (2000). *Electronic commerce: A managerial perspective.* NJ: Prentice Hall.

Van Akkeren, J., & Cavaye, A. L. M. (1999). Factors affecting entry-level Internet technology adoption by small business in Australia: An empirical study. In *Proceedings of the 10th Australasian Conference on Information Systems*, Wellington, New Zealand.

Van Beveren, J., & Thomson, H. (2002). The use of electronic commerce by SMEs in Victoria, Australia. *Journal of Small Business Management, 40*(3), 250-253.

Venkatash, V., & Morris, M. G. (2000). Why don't men ever stop to ask for directions? Gender, social influence, and their role in technology acceptance and usage behavior. *MIS Quarterly, 24*(1).

## Chapter V

# Barriers to E-Commerce Adoption:
## Why are SMEs Staying Away from E-Commerce?

Despite government support and the exponential growth of e-commerce, it is mainly the larger businesses that have reaped the benefits of this technology (Riquelme, 2002). In contrast, the rate of e-commerce adoption in the SME sector has remained relatively low (Ihlström, Magnusson, Scupola, & Tuunainen, 2003; Poon & Swatman, 1999; Van Akkeren & Cavaye, 1999). This sluggish pace of e-commerce diffusion into SMEs has been attributed to various barriers or impediments that are faced by these organisations. A number of different e-commerce adoption barriers have been documented in research studies. Some of these include the high costs associated with e-commerce, lack of technical resources and expertise to implement e-commerce, the complexity of e-commerce technology, and concerns about e-commerce security. Regardless of the type of barriers cited by SME owners as impediments to e-commerce implementation, it is important to develop strategies to overcome these obstacles. The first step in this process involves developing a deeper understanding of the barriers faced by SMEs, which is the main objective of this chapter.

# Background

Although many studies have investigated the reasons why SMEs are reluctant to use e-commerce, the key concern that has arisen repeatedly in every study is security. Without a doubt, concern about security is the most commonly cited barrier to e-commerce adoption. SMEs perceive any technology that supports doing business online as being high risk due to the increase in online security breaches and incidents in recent years. A number of early studies in the U.S. and Greece (Hadjimonolis, 1999; Purao & Campbell, 1998) showed that the apparent lack of security of e-commerce was a major stumbling block for many SMEs. More recent studies (Oxley & Yeung, 2001; Reimenschneider & McKinney, 2001; Vrazalic, Stern, MacGregor, Carlsson, & Magnusson, 2003) have shown that security still dominates the e-commerce landscape as an area of concern. The latest Sensis® e-Business report (2006) found that 49% of online businesses in Australia are worried about people being able to hack into their computer systems.

However, although important, security is not the only barrier faced by SMEs. Another key barrier is related to the limited resources available to SMEs. In their study of 27 SME manufacturing firms, Cragg and King (1993) identified the lack of financial and managerial resources, and inadequate levels of technical expertise as the major inhibitors of IT growth. These three factors were also identified by Welsh and White (1981) as being symptomatic of the SME sector. Purao et al. (1998) identified the lack of technical know how, and Ratnasingham (2000) highlighted prohibitive set up costs as strong disincentives to many SME owners/managers. Since SMEs are inherently under-resourced due to their small size, limited expertise, and poor access to funds, it is to be expected that resource limitations would deter SME owners from investing money, time, and effort into implementing a technology that has no proven track record in the SME sector.

Purao et al. (1998), who conducted a series of interviews with SME owners, found that another major barrier was a failure to see any advantages in using e-commerce. This was also reported by Bakos and Brynjolfsson (2000). Abell and Lim (1996), Tambini (1999), and Eid, Trueman, and Ahmed (2002) all found many SME owners felt that e-commerce did not suit either their day-to-day business procedures or the product mix offered by their business. This barrier seemed to transcend borders. In a cross-cultural study of SMEs in Hong Kong and Finland, Farhoomand, Tuunainen, and Yee (2000) found that both cultures reported a failure to see how e-commerce fit the current mode of business practices as a major obstacle to e-commerce adoption. This is an interesting barrier because it implies that SMEs are considering e-commerce in the context of their business strategy, rather than simply as a technology that must be implemented to keep up with competitors. Although security is constantly emphasised as the key barrier, the unsuitability of e-commerce to the organisation is a precluding barrier.

Studies by Bakos et al. (2000), Sawhney and Zabin (2002), and Mehrtens, Cragg, and Mills (2001) showed that there was still a reluctance among SME owners to adjust their businesses to the requirements and demands placed on it by e-commerce participation. Implementing e-commerce is not a simple and straightforward process requiring the installation of hardware and software. Instead, it is a complex and time-consuming activity that may involve a complete re-design of the business strategy and an integration of organisational systems at multiple levels. It is understandable that SMEs are disinclined to embark on (or manager) this type of business transformation.

If e-commerce is considered to be an innovation in the context of SMEs (where diffusion has been slow), several types of barriers to innovation exist, which apply to e-commerce. These barriers have been summarised by Hadjimanolis (1999) in a study of innovation in Cypriot SMEs. The two basic categories are external and internal barriers. External barriers include supply barriers (difficulties in obtaining technical knowledge, financial support, and raw materials), demand barriers (related to customers' needs, their risk perceptions, and market limitations), and environmental barriers (government regulations and policies). Internal barriers are split into resource barriers (lack of internal resources such as funds, time, expertise, etc.) and human nature barriers (management attitudes, resistance to change). Previous studies discussed have shown that the barriers to innovation identified by Hadjimanolis (1999) are applicable to the implementation of e-commerce in SMEs.

Lawrence (1997) defined three broad categories of e-commerce barriers. These were termed company, personal, and industry barriers. Company barriers included a low level of technology use within the business, limited availability of financial and technical resources, organisational resistance to change, and lack of perceived return on investment. Barriers categorised as personal included lack of information on e-commerce, management preferring conventional approaches to business practices, and an inability to see the advantages of using e-commerce. Industry barriers included some respondents believing that the industry, as a whole was not ready for e-commerce technology.

Based on the previous discussion, we can conclude that the main reasons why SMEs have been slow to use e-commerce are related to security, lack of resources, and incompatibility. We have summarised some of the literature in the field of e-commerce barriers in Table 1. The main purpose of our chapter is to determine to what extent our findings in regional SMEs in Sweden, Australia, and the U.S. agree or disagree with this previous research.

Similarly to e-commerce adoption criteria, previous research has shown that business characteristics such as size can have an impact on e-commerce barriers (see for example Timmers, 1999). Hawkins and Winter (1996), Fallon and Moran (2000), Blackburn and Athayde (2000), and Matlay (2000) found that smaller SMEs were less likely to adopt e-commerce, in part because of the lack of technical expertise and also because, in many cases, the approach to business did not easily allow for e-commerce adoption. Apart from the business size, the age of the business appeared to be relevant to e-commerce adoption. Kai-Uwe Brock (2000) and Donckels and Lambrecht (1997) argued that older SMEs (more than 20 years in business) were less likely to adopt e-commerce because they and their customers were too set in their ways to make alterations to suit an e-commerce strategy. Similarly, very young businesses (those in business for less than 2 years) were often insufficiently organised to really contemplate e-commerce.

Previous studies (BarNir & Smith, 2002; Schindehutte & Morris, 2001) also found that organisations whose focus was outside the local marketplace were less likely to perceive barriers to e-commerce when compared to those whose business was primarily in the local arena. Other business characteristics that have been shown to be associated with e-commerce adoption barriers include IT skill levels (Tetteh & Burn, 2001), the gender of the CEO (MacGregor, Hyland, Harvie, & Lee, 2006; Sandberg, 2003), and membership of strategic alliances (MacGregor & Vrazalic, 2006).

*Table 1. E-commerce adoption barriers: A summary of previous research*

| Adoption Barriers | Reported by |
|---|---|
| E-commerce is not deemed to be suited to the products/services offered by the SME. | Eid et al. (2002)<br>Kendall & Kendall (2001)<br>Tambini (1999)<br>Abell et al. (1996) |
| E-commerce is not suited to the way the organisation does business. | Sawhney et al. (2002)<br>Bakos et al. (2000)<br>Farhoomand et al. (2000)<br>Abell et al. (1996)<br>Mehrtens et al. (2001)<br>Poon & Swatman (1997)<br>Lawrence (1997)<br>Iacovou et al. (1995) |
| E-commerce is not suited to the way the organisation's clients/ customers. | Bakos et al. (2000)<br>Abell et al. (1996) |
| E-commerce does not provide any business advantages. | Lee & Runge (2001)<br>Chau & Hui (2001)<br>Purao et al. (1998)<br>Lawrence (1997) |
| Lack of technical skills and IT knowledge in the organisation. | Stansfield & Grant (2003)<br>Darch & Lucas (2002)<br>Mirchandani & Motwani (2001)<br>Farhoomand et al. (2000)<br>Purao et al. (1998) |
| Concern about security of e-commerce. | Oxley et al. (2001)<br>Reimenschneider et al. (2001)<br>Purao et al. (1998)<br>Aldridge, White, & Forcht (1997) |
| High cost of e-commerce implementation. | Darch et al. (2002)<br>Bodorick, Dhaliwal, & Jutla (2002)<br>Reimenschneider et al. (2001)<br>Ratnasingham (2000)<br>Purao et al. (1998)<br>Lawrence (1997) |
| E-commerce is too complex to implement. | Quayle (2002)<br>Timmers (1999) |
| Unsure about which e-commerce technology (hardware/software) to choose. | Bodorick et al. (2002)<br>Dongen, Maitland, & Sadowski (2002)<br>Farhoomand et al. (2000)<br>Purao et al. (1998) |

*continued on following page*

*Table 1. Continued*

| Adoption Barriers | Reported by |
|---|---|
| Lack of e-commerce standards. | Stockdale & Standing (2004) |
| | Tuunainen (1999) |
| Lack of time to implement e-commerce. | Darch et al. (2002) |
| | Walczuch, Van Braven, & Lundgren (2000) |
| | Van Akkeren et al. (1999) |
| | Lawrence (1997) |

# Research Questions

Based on the outcomes of previous studies, we set out to answer several questions about e-commerce adoption barriers in our study. Specifically, we wanted to find out:

1.  Are there any business characteristics (e.g., size, length of time in business, sector, market focus, etc.) that affect how SMEs perceive e-commerce adoption barriers?

2.  Are there any underlying factors or groupings of e-commerce adoption barriers in each of the three locations (Sweden, Australia, and the U.S.) which would serve to explain the key reasons behind SMEs' reluctance to use e-commerce?

3.  Are there any differences in how e-commerce barriers are perceived across the three locations (Sweden, Australia, and the U.S.)?

In the first part of this chapter, our intention was to isolate specific business characteristics, which influence barriers to e-commerce adoption in SMEs. For example, what effect does business size have on the decision not to use e-commerce due to security concerns? Does the gender of the CEO affect the lack of IT skills barrier? To answer these questions, a series of linear regressions was carried out to determine whether business characteristics (such as the age and size of the business, business sector, gender of the CEO, educational level of the CEO, level of IT skill within the business, the existence of an enterprise wide system, product planning, membership of a strategic alliance, or market focus) had any effects on the perception of adoption barriers. Linear regression was chosen over other techniques because it allows for interaction of the business characteristics which other techniques fail to do.

The second question was concerned with grouping e-commerce barriers or obstacles in order to provide a clearer explanation of the reasons why SMEs were avoiding e-commerce in specific locations. Rather than dealing with a multitude of explanations, the answer to this question provides a "bigger picture" of the key issues that need to be addressed by government organisations in developing strategies to promote e-commerce adoption. For example, could the barriers in Sweden be attributed to two main groups—lack of resources and unsuitability of e-commerce? Having this insight allows us to target SMEs with specific strategies to overcome certain barriers that they face. To provide data for the second question a series of correlations and factor analyses was undertaken.

The final part of this chapter provides a comparison between the three locations and determines what differences exist between Sweden, Australia, and the U.S. in relation to e-commerce adoption barriers. This question will be addressed in the Discussion section of this chapter.

# Methodology

Ten of the most commonly occurring barriers to e-commerce adoption were identified from the literature. A series of six in-depth interviews with regional SMEs were undertaken to determine whether the barriers were applicable and complete. All identified barriers were found to be applicable.

*Figure 1. Question about barriers to e-commerce adoption used in survey*

This question relates to the reasons why your organisation is not be using e-commerce. Below is a list of statements indicating possible reasons. Based on your opinion, please rank each statement on a scale of 1 to 5 to indicate how important it was to your decision NOT to use e-commerce, as follows:

1 = the reason was very unimportant to your decision not to use e-commerce

2 = the reason was unimportant to your decision not to use e-commerce

3 = the reason was neither unimportant nor important to your decision not to use e-commerce

4 = the reason was important to your decision not to use e-commerce

5 = the reason was very important to your decision not to use e-commerce

| | Our organisation does not use e-commerce because: | Rating |
|---|---|---|
| B1 | It is not suited to our products/services. | 1 2 3 4 5 |
| B2 | It is not suited to our way of doing business. | 1 2 3 4 5 |
| B3 | It is not suited to the ways our clients do business. | 1 2 3 4 5 |
| B4 | It does not offer any advantages to our organisation. | 1 2 3 4 5 |
| B5 | We do not have the technical knowledge in the organisation to implement e-commerce. | 1 2 3 4 5 |
| B6 | It is too complicated to implement. | 1 2 3 4 5 |
| B7 | It is not secure. | 1 2 3 4 5 |
| B8 | The financial investment required to implement e-commerce is too high. | 1 2 3 4 5 |
| B9 | We do not have time to implement e-commerce. | 1 2 3 4 5 |
| B10 | It is difficult to choose the most suitable e-commerce standard with so many different options available. | 1 2 3 4 5 |

Based on the findings of the six in-depth interviews, a survey instrument was developed to collect data about e-commerce adoption barriers (amongst other things). Respondents who had not adopted e-commerce were asked to rate the importance of each barrier to their decision to not adopt e-commerce (as shown in Figure 1) using a standard 5 point Likert scale with 1 meaning very unimportant and 5 meaning very important. The Likert scale responses were assumed to posses the characteristics of an interval measurement scale for data analysis purposes.

Chapter II provides a detailed account of how the data was collected and the total responses received for each of the three locations. The following sections will provide the results of the statistical analysis for each location in order to answer the three questions about e-commerce barriers stated previously.

The rest of this chapter is structured as follows. First, we will examine the associations between different business characteristics and e-commerce adoption barriers in Sweden. Then we will present the results of a factor analysis, which will group the e-commerce adoption barriers indicated by the Swedish respondents. This process will be repeated for Australia and then for the U.S. sample. The final part of the chapter will discuss and compare the findings, and present the business implications of the results.

# Business Characteristics and E-Commerce Adoption Barriers in Sweden

The first question was concerned with the effect of business characteristics on how the ten e-commerce adoption barriers listed in Figure 1 were perceived. There were no statistically significant regressions for any of the barriers in the Swedish sample. It would appear that business characteristics do not have any association with e-commerce barriers in regional SMEs in Sweden. Therefore, barriers to e-commerce adoption are not affected by the SME operating in a particular sector, being of a specific size or having a female CEO. The lack of association is a valuable insight both for businesses as well as government agencies as it suggests that the strategies adopted to overcome e-commerce barriers for one category of SMEs appear to be equally applicable to others.

# Groupings of E-Commerce Adoption Barriers in Sweden

To answer our second question, a combination of correlations and factor analysis was applied to the data. The results of this analysis are shown in the tables next and discussed at the end of this section.

Table 2 provides the correlation matrix of the importance ratings for e-commerce adoption barriers. All correlations significant at the .001 level are shown in bold.

*Table 2. Adoption barriers correlation matrix (Sweden)*

|  | E-commerce is not suited to our products/services. | E-commerce is not suited to our way of doing business. | E-commerce is not suited to the ways our clients do business. | E-commerce does not offer any advantages to our organisation. |
|---|---|---|---|---|
| E-commerce is not suited to our way of doing business. | .746 | | | |
| E-commerce is not suited to the ways our clients do business. | .462 | .530 | | |
| E-commerce does not offer any advantages to our organisation. | .482 | .547 | .280 | |
| We do not have the technical knowledge in the organisation to implement e-commerce. | -.030 | .054 | -.097 | 0.249* |
| E-commerce is too complicated to implement. | -.009 | .059 | .065 | .106 |
| E-commerce is not secure. | 0.184* | 0.303** | .098 | 0.249* |
| The financial investment required to implement e-commerce is too high. | -0.51 | -.138 | .092 | -.104 |
| We do not have time to implement e-commerce. | -0.245* | -0.261** | -.056 | -0.195* |
| It is difficult to choose the most suitable e-commerce standard with so many different options available. | -.056 | -.005 | -.033 | .062 |

*Note: * significant at 0.05 level    ** significant at 0.01 level*

For the Swedish respondents, the first four barriers seem to all correlate with each other, but show weak or no correlations with the last set of barriers. Similarly, it appears that correlations exist between the last five barriers in the correlation matrix. Therefore, two distinct groupings of results can be identified in the correlation matrix. In the first grouping, there is a strong positive correlation between the barriers "e-commerce is not suited to our products/services" and "e-commerce is not suited to our way of doing business" (Pearson's r = .747, p < .000). These two barriers also show moderately strong positive correlations with the barriers "e-commerce is not suited to the ways our clients do business" and "e-commerce does not offer any advantages to our organisation." In the second grouping, the barriers relating to the investment, time, number of options, complexity and security aspects of e-commerce adoption generally show moderately strong positive correlations with each other.

The findings in Table 2 suggested the use of factor analysis to investigate any separate underlying factors and to reduce the redundancy of certain barriers indicated in the correlation matrices. The results of Kaiser-Meyer-Olkin MSA (.735) and Bartlett's Test of Sphericity ($\chi^2$ = 343, p = .000 for Sweden) indicated that the data set satisfied the assumptions for factorability. Principle components analysis was chosen as the method of extraction in order to account for maximum variance in the data using a minimum number of factors. A two-factor solution was extracted with Eigenvalues of 3.252 and 2.745. This was supported by an inspection of the Scree Plots. The two factors accounted for 59.973% of the total variance. Table 3 shows the variance.

*Table 2. Continued*

| We do not have the technical knowledge in the organisation to implement e-commerce. | E-commerce is too complicated to implement. | E-commerce is not secure. | The financial investment required to implement e-commerce is too high. | We do not have time to implement e-commerce. |
|---|---|---|---|---|
|  |  |  |  |  |
|  |  |  |  |  |
|  |  |  |  |  |
|  |  |  |  |  |
| .544 |  |  |  |  |
| 0.277* | .516 |  |  |  |
| .445 | .481 | 0.217* |  |  |
| .432 | .587 | .174 | .448 |  |
| .514 | .579 | .334 | .494 | .532 |

The resulting components were rotated using the Varimax procedure and a simple structure was achieved as shown in the rotated component matrix (see Table 4).

As can be seen in Table 4, the Swedish respondents grouped adoption barriers based on two factors. We have termed these two factors "too difficult" and "unsuitable." The adoption barriers associated with difficulties in implementing e-commerce such as lack of technical expertise, having to make difficult choices, obtaining financing and finding time held the higher priority from respondents. This suggests that Swedish SMEs were more reluctant to adopt e-commerce due to the complexities involved in the implementation process.

Another set of barriers, which loaded on to the unsuitability factor, was related to the lack of compatibility between e-commerce and the SMEs way of doing business, its customers, and its products/services. SMEs such as local grocery stores might fit in this category because they are unlikely to benefit from doing business online. Security concerns loaded almost equally onto both factors, although more so toward the "too difficult" factor.

These results are an important first step in consolidating our understanding of the reasons that hinder SMEs in e-commerce adoption because they indicate that correlations between the barriers exist and ten of the most common barriers can be grouped in relation to two main factors. This reduces the fragmentation associated with having a large number of e-commerce adoption barriers and allows a more targeted approach for government programs and initiatives. It is a powerful explanatory tool because it reduces the "noise" in the data.

*Table 3. Total variance explained: Adoption barriers (Sweden)*

| Component | Eigenvalue | % Variance | Cumulative % |
|-----------|-----------|-----------|-------------|
| 1 | 3.252 | 32.520 | 32.520 |
| 2 | 2.745 | 27.453 | 59.973 |

*Table 4. Rotated component matrix: Adoption barriers (Sweden)*

| Barrier | Component 1: *Too Difficult* | Component 2: *Unsuitable* |
|---------|------------------------------|---------------------------|
| E-commerce is not suited to our products/services. | | .844 |
| E-commerce is not suited to our way of doing business. | | .909 |
| E-commerce is not suited to the ways our clients do business. | | .643 |
| E-commerce does not offer any advantages to our organisation. | | .731 |
| We do not have the technical knowledge in the organisation to implement e-commerce. | .743 | |
| E-commerce is too complicated to implement. | .852 | |
| E-commerce is not secure. | .525 | |
| The financial investment required to implement e-commerce is too high. | .703 | |
| We do not have time to implement e-commerce. | .742 | |
| It is difficult to choose the most suitable e-commerce standard with so many different options available. | .800 | |

*Figure 2. E-commerce adoption barrier groupings in Sweden*

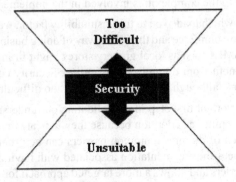

The rotated component matrix also enables the prediction of the scores of each individual barrier based on the score of the two factors, and vice versa, for an SME. This has implications for research into e-commerce barriers. Instead of accounting for 10 different barriers, the obstacles to e-commerce adoption can be explained as a result of one of two things: SMEs either find e-commerce to difficult to implement or they believe it is unsuitable for their organisation. This is summarised in Figure 2.

We undertook an extended analysis to determine whether the groupings previously identified differed for categories of SMEs depending on various business characteristics. Although there was insufficient data to examine all of the business characteristics, we did find differences in groupings when the SMEs were sub-divided by the gender of the CEO and his or her education level. The differences in gender will be discussed in Chapter IX.

# Education Level of the CEO

The data was split based on the education level of the CEO. The results of the Kaiser-Meyer-Olkin MSA (.796 for no-formal-education, .871 for formal-education) and Bartlett's Test for Sphericity ($\chi2 = 328$ p=.000 for no-formal-education, $\chi2 = 969$ p=.000 for formal-education) indicated that the data set satisfied the assumptions for factorability. Principle components analysis was chosen as the method of extraction in order to account for maximum variance in the data using a minimum number of factors. A two factor solution was extracted with Eigenvalues 6.314 and 1.980 for respondents whose CEO had no formal education. This accounted for 82.944% of the variance. A two factor solution was extracted with Eigenvalues 5.909 and 1.761 for respondents whose CEO did have some form of formal education. This accounted for 76.698% of the variance. The results can be seen in Table 5.

The resulting components were rotated using the Varimax procedure and a simple structure was achieved as shown in the rotated component matrix (see Table 6).

An examination of Table 6 shows that there are no differences between the groupings or factors between the respondents that had formally educated CEOs and those without any formal qualifications. Both groups assigned the same level of priority to each of the two factors. This is a somewhat surprising finding because conventional wisdom would suggest that educated individuals would make better informed decisions and have better developed skills and knowledge. Therefore, they would be more likely to assign a lower priority to the "too difficult" factor and a higher priority to the "suitability" factor. The results indicate that this was not the case in Sweden.

*Table 5. Total variation explained: Adoption barriers & education level of CEO (Sweden)*

| Comp | Eigenvalue | | % Variance | | Cumulative % | |
|---|---|---|---|---|---|---|
| Education Level | No Formal Education | Formal Education | No Formal Education | Formal Education | No Formal Education | Formal Education |
| 1 | 6.314 | 5.909 | 63.139% | 59.088% | 63.139% | 59.088% |
| 2 | 1.980 | 1.761 | 19.805% | 17.610% | 82.944% | 76.698% |

*Table 6. Rotated component matrix: Adoption barriers & education level of CEO (Sweden)*

| Barrier | No Formal Education | | Formal Education | |
| --- | --- | --- | --- | --- |
| | Component 1: Too Difficult | Component 2: Unsuitable | Component 1: Too Difficult | Component 2: Unsuitable |
| E-commerce is not suited to our products/services. | | .906 | | .917 |
| E-commerce is not suited to our way of doing business. | | .939 | | .910 |
| E-commerce is not suited to the ways our clients do business. | | .884 | | .923 |
| E-commerce does not offer any advantages to our organisation. | | .864 | | .831 |
| We do not have the technical knowledge in the organisation to implement e-commerce. | .761 | | .818 | |
| E-commerce is too complicated to implement. | .925 | | .865 | |
| E-commerce is not secure. | .740 | | .841 | |
| The financial investment required to implement e-commerce is too high. | .883 | | .752 | |
| We do not have time to implement e-commerce. | .858 | | .776 | |
| It is difficult to choose the most suitable e-commerce standard with so many different options available. | .909 | | .724 | |

# Summary: Adoption Barriers in Swedish SMEs

The results of the Swedish study indicate that decisions not to adopt e-commerce are not influenced by any of the business characteristics such as size, age, sector, gender of the CEO, etc. This implies that the same strategies to promote e-commerce adoption may work in different settings. We did find, however, that SMEs in Sweden grouped e-commerce barriers depending on the difficulties associated with introducing this technology and its suitability to the business. SMEs are concerned about the extent to which e-commerce is aligned with the way they do business, or with the way their clients do business as well as the products/services they sell. Clearly, SMEs believe that not all types of businesses and products/services lend themselves to e-commerce strategies. The results from Sweden will be revisited at the end of the chapter and compared to the other locations. We now turn to SMEs located in Australia.

# Business Characteristics and E-Commerce Adoption Barriers in Australia

Following the same analysis pattern as that of Sweden, our first question was concerned with the effects of different business characteristics on how the 10 e-commerce adoption barriers listed in Figure 1 were perceived by SMEs. Although we did not find any statistically significant associations in the Swedish sample, we found associations between five of the ten barriers and various business characteristics in the Australian sample. These are summarized in Table 7, which also indicates the corresponding tables showing the associations and the relevant p value.

As can be seen from Table 7, the gender of the CEO is significantly associated with several of the reasons why SMEs are not adopting e-commerce. This is an important finding because it indicates that the CEO's gender does have an effect on the obstacles to using e-commerce. Equally interesting is the finding that three other business characteristics (market focus, educational level of the CEO, and business sector) have statistically significant effects some of the e-commerce barriers. We will examine and comment on each of the associations in turn below.

*Table 7. Summary of associations between e-commerce adoption barriers and business characteristics (Australia)*

| E-Commerce adoption barriers | Correlated with... | Table | p value |
|---|---|---|---|
| E-commerce is not suited to our products/services. | Gender of CEO | 5.10 | .003 |
| E-commerce is not suited to our way of doing business. | Gender of CEO Market focus | 5.11 | .025<br>.017 |
| E-commerce does not offer any advantages to our organization. | Gender of CEO | 5.12 | .034 |
| We do not have the technical knowledge in the organisation to implement e-commerce. | Education level of CEO Market focus | 5.13 | .020<br>.041 |
| E-commerce is too complicated to implement. | Business sector | 5.14 | .018 |

*Table 8. Regression table for e-commerce is not suited to our products/services*

| Dependant Variable E-commerce is not suited to our products/services | | |
|---|---|---|
| | Beta | p value |
| Gender of CEO | .261 | .003 |
| R Squared | | .173 |
| Adjusted R squared | | .099 |
| p value for the complete regression table | | .012 |

An examination of Table 8 shows that the gender of the CEO affected how the barrier "e-commerce is not suited to our products/services" was perceived. The results show that males felt more strongly regarding the importance of this barrier than the female CEOs. Previous research (Carter, 2000; MacGregor et al., 2006; Sandberg, 2003) has shown that females tend to be far more hesitant about e-commerce adoption and the use of technology in business. The results in Table 8, while supporting these gender differences, show that it is the male owner/managers that are more hesitant with this barrier. One possible reason for these differences is the involvement of educational institutions with SMEs. If, as suggested by Boter and Lundstrom (2005), SMEs are being re-educated about e-commerce, previous gender-based fears may have been dispelled.

Table 9 shows that two business characteristics (gender of the CEO and market focus) had a statistically significant effect on another suitability barrier—this one related to the way the SME does business. Again, the data shows that males are more likely to rate this barrier as being more important than females. This is an interesting finding, suggesting perhaps, that males are less concerned about technical issues and more aware about aligning the business with the technology. The data also shows a negative Beta value for market focus. This suggests that businesses that have a national or international market focus place a lower level of importance on this barrier than those businesses that are trading at a local or regional level. One of the reasons for this could be that SMEs operating at a local level do not require online sales and marketing channels as much as those operating at broader levels due to the geographical proximity and ease of access to their customer base. The results also highlight one of the attractions of e-commerce, which lies in giving SMEs the ability to "tap into" the global market.

*Table 9. Regression table for e-commerce is not suited to our way of doing business*

| Dependant Variable E-commerce is not suited to our way of doing business | | |
|---|---|---|
| | Beta | p value |
| Gender of the CEO | .195 | .025 |
| Market Focus | -.212 | .017 |
| R Squared | | .181 |
| Adjusted R squared | | .107 |
| p value for the complete regression table | | .009 |

*Table 10. Regression table for e-commerce does not offer any advantages to our organization*

| Dependant Variable E-commerce does not offer any advantages to our organisation | | |
|---|---|---|
| | Beta | p value |
| Gender of the CEO | .182 | .034 |
| R Squared | | .179 |
| Adjusted R squared | | .105 |
| p value for the complete regression table | | .009 |

The gender of the CEO is associated with another barrier related to the lack of benefits that e-commerce brings. As with the previous two barriers, males seem more concerned with the importance of this barrier than females. Once again this may be attributed to lesser technical concerns and more business concerns by make CEO's.

The importance of the barrier "We do not have the technical knowledge in the organisation to implement e-commerce" was associated with two business characteristics: the educational level of the CEO and market focus. The data shows that both the level of education of the CEO and market focus gave rise to negative Beta values (-.219 and -.175 respectively). As with earlier barriers, this suggests that SMEs focusing on a "wider" market are likely to place a lesser level of importance on this barrier than those whose market focus is either local or regional. The negative Beta value for level of education of the CEO suggests that organisations whose owner/manager does not have any formal education are more likely to place a greater importance on this barrier. This is not an unexpected result. However, it is unexpected to find that there is no association between this barrier and the low level of IT skill in Australian SMEs.

An examination of the data in Table 12 shows that a single business characteristic, business sector, has an effect on the barrier related to e-commerce complexity. Retail and service respondents are more likely to place a higher level of importance on this barrier than the industrial respondents. This may be a function of the actual requirements of any e-commerce development or it may be indicative of the expertise within the SME sector.

Based on the previous results we can conclude that regional SMEs in Australia with male CEOs place a higher importance on the following e-commerce adoption barriers: suitability of e-commerce in relation to the organisations products/services and operations, and lack

*Table 11. Regression table for we do not have the technical knowledge in the organisation to implement e-commerce*

| Dependant Variable We do not have the technical knowledge in the organisation to implement e-commerce | | |
|---|---|---|
| | Beta | p value |
| Education level of CEO | -.219 | .020 |
| Market Focus | -.175 | .041 |
| R Squared | | .221 |
| Adjusted R squared | | .151 |
| p value for the complete regression table | | .001 |

*Table 12. Regression table for e-commerce is too complicated to implement*

| Dependant Variable E-commerce is too complicated to implement | | |
|---|---|---|
| | Beta | p value |
| Business Sector | .222 | .018 |
| R Squared | | .148 |
| Adjusted R squared | | .072 |
| p value for the complete regression table | | .040 |

of benefits from e-commerce implementation. SMEs with a local or regional focus, on the other hand, are more likely to be concerned about the incompatibility of e-commerce with the organisation's way of doing business and the lack of technical expertise. We also found that formally educated CEOs were assigned a lower rating to the lack of technical knowledge barrier. Finally, our results suggest that retail and service sector respondents find the complexity of e-commerce to be an important obstacle.

Although there were no associations between the other business characteristics and e-commerce adoption barriers, this is not to say that their importance as barriers is lower. Instead, it suggests that the different categories of SMEs place the same level of importance on the e-commerce obstacles.

We will now take a closer look at the groupings of e-commerce adoption barriers in the Australian context with the purpose of answering our second question: Are there any underlying factors or groupings of e-commerce adoption barriers, which would serve to explain the key reasons behind SMEs' decisions not to use e-commerce?

*Table 13. Adoption barriers correlation matrix (Australia)*

|  | E-commerce is not suited to our products/ services. | E-commerce is not suited to our way of doing business. | E-commerce is not suited to the ways our clients do business. | E-commerce does not offer any advantages to our organisation. |
|---|---|---|---|---|
| E-commerce is not suited to our way of doing business. | .747 | | | |
| E-commerce is not suited to the ways our clients do business. | .435 | .804 | | |
| E-commerce does not offer any advantages to our organisation. | .654 | .647 | .413 | |
| We do not have the technical knowledge in the organisation to implement e-commerce. | .213* | .221** | .206* | .255** |
| E-commerce is too complicated to implement. | .039 | .105 | .155 | .177** |
| E-commerce is not secure. | -.047 | .027 | .101 | .156 |
| The financial investment required to implement e-commerce is too high. | .119 | .140 | .024 | .201* |
| We do not have time to implement e-commerce. | .011 | .033 | .106 | .142 |
| It is difficult to choose the most suitable e-commerce standard with so many different options available. | .035 | .075 | -.047 | .174* |

*Note: * significant at 0.05 level     ** significant at 0.01 level*

# Groupings of E-Commerce Adoption Barriers in Australia

To answer our second question, a combination of correlations and factor analysis was applied to the data. The results of this analysis are shown in the tables next and discussed at the end of this section.

Table 13 provides the correlation matrix of the importance ratings for e-commerce adoption barriers. All correlations significant at the .001 level are shown in bold.

As with the Swedish results, the first four barriers seem to all correlate with each other, but show weak or no correlations with the last set of barriers. Correlations also exist between the last five barriers in the correlation matrix. These findings suggested the use of factor analysis to investigate any separate underlying factors and to reduce the redundancy of certain barriers indicated in the correlation matrices. The results of Kaiser-Meyer-Olkin MSA (.905) and Bartlett's Test of Sphericity ($\chi^2 = 1395.670$, $p = .000$) indicated that the data set satisfied the assumptions for factorability. Principle components analysis was chosen as the method of extraction in order to account for maximum variance in the data using a minimum number of factors. A

*Table 13. Continued*

| We do not have the technical knowledge in the organisation to implement e-commerce. | E-commerce is too complicated to implement. | E-commerce is not secure. | The financial investment required to implement e-commerce is too high. | We do not have time to implement e-commerce. |
|---|---|---|---|---|
| | | | | |
| | | | | |
| | | | | |
| .708 | | | | |
| .441 | .554 | | | |
| .525 | .537 | .357 | | |
| .420 | .510 | .299 | .556 | |
| .415 | .484 | .366 | .407 | .603 |

two-factor solution was extracted with Eigenvalues of 4.212 and 3.586. This was supported by an inspection of the Scree Plots. The two factors accounted for 77.977% of the total variance. Table 14 shows the variance.

The resulting components were rotated using the Varimax procedure and a simple structure was achieved as shown in the rotated component matrix (see Table 15).

*Table 14. Total variance explained: Adoption barriers (Australia)*

| Component | Eigenvalue | % Variance | Cumulative % |
|-----------|-----------|-----------|--------------|
| 1 | 4.212 | 42.116 | 42.116 |
| 2 | 3.586 | 35.860 | 77.977 |

*Table 15. Rotated component matrix: Adoption barriers (Australia)*

| Barrier | Component 1: *Too Difficult* | Component 2: *Unsuitable* |
|---------|------------------------------|---------------------------|
| E-commerce is not suited to our products/services. | | .917 |
| E-commerce is not suited to our way of doing business. | | .912 |
| E-commerce is not suited to the ways our clients do business. | | .909 |
| E-commerce does not offer any advantages to our organisation. | | .837 |
| We do not have the technical knowledge in the organisation to implement e-commerce. | .787 | |
| E-commerce is too complicated to implement. | .869 | |
| E-commerce is not secure. | .767 | |
| The financial investment required to implement e-commerce is too high. | .795 | |
| We do not have time to implement e-commerce. | .813 | |
| It is difficult to choose the most suitable e-commerce standard with so many different options available. | .802 | |

*Figure 3. E-commerce adoption barrier groupings in Australia*

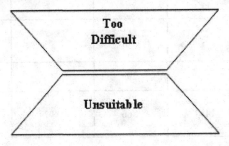

Table 15 shows very similar results to those found in the Swedish sample. Like their European counterparts, the regional SMEs in Australia grouped adoption barriers based on two factors: "too difficult" and "unsuitable." Respondents in both locations also assigned the same order of priority to the two groupings, with difficulties being singled out as more important than compatibility. However, in the Australian study, the security barrier was more clearly aligned with the difficulties associated with e-commerce. It is interesting that Australian SMEs perceive this to be the case since the latest study by Sensis® (2006) reports that security is the major concern when it comes to e-commerce. The groupings found in the Australian sample are shown in Figure 3.

## Summary: Adoption Barriers in Australian SMEs

The results in the Australian context show that SMEs are reluctant to adopt e-commerce for the same two reasons as their Swedish counterparts; the difficulties associated with implementing e-commerce and the incompatibility of e-commerce with organisational operations. However, the results also show that the gender of the CEO is associated with several e-commerce barriers, with males being more concerned about suitability issues than females. The gender findings are of particular interest and indicative of the general research, which shows that males are less concerned with technical issues in e-commerce implementation. Of additional interest is the fact that we found no associations between the security barrier and business characteristics such as the low level of IT skill. We now turn to SMEs located in the U.S.

## Business Characteristics and E-Commerce Adoption Barriers in the USA

The first question was concerned with the effect of business characteristics on how the 10 e-commerce adoption barriers listed in Figure 1 were perceived. We found three statistically significant associations in the U.S. sample between the business size and various e-commerce adoption barriers. These are summarized in Table 16, which also indicates the corresponding tables showing the associations and the relevant p value.

Unlike the Australian SMEs, where gender of the CEO was associated with a number of e-commerce barriers, in the U.S. context, business size had an influence. This is shown in tables 17 to 19.

An examination of Tables 17 to 19 shows that in all three cases, the Beta value was in the negative range. This suggests that it is the smaller SMEs that have placed a higher level of importance on each of these barriers compared to the larger ones. In all cases the p-value for the characteristic is highly statistically significant suggesting that there is a substantial difference in the rating of importance of these barriers between the two groups. In light of the barriers involved in these associations (complexity, security, and cost) it is not surprising that these would be rated as more important by SMEs with fewer employees, and by extension, fewer resources and expertise.

We will now take a closer look at the groupings of e-commerce adoption barriers in the U.S. context with the purpose of answering our second question: Are there any underlying factors or groupings of e-commerce adoption barriers, which would serve to explain the key reasons behind SMEs' decisions not to use e-commerce?

*Table 16. Summary of associations between e-commerce adoption barriers and business characteristics (USA)*

| E-Commerce adoption barriers | Correlated with... | Table | p value |
|---|---|---|---|
| E-commerce is too complicated to implement. | Business size | 5.19 | .003 |
| E-commerce is not secure. | Business size | 5.20 | .004 |
| The financial investment required to implement e-commerce is too high. | Business size | 5.21 | .006 |

*Table 17. Regression table for e-commerce is too complicated to implement*

| Dependant Variable E-commerce is too complicated to implement | | |
|---|---|---|
| | Beta | p value |
| Business Size | -.433 | .003 |
| R Squared | .221 | |
| Adjusted R squared | .164 | |
| p value for the complete regression table | .016 | |

*Table 18. Regression table for e-commerce is not secure*

| Dependant Variable E-commerce is not secure | | |
|---|---|---|
| | Beta | p value |
| Business Size | -.438 | .004 |
| R Squared | .221 | |
| Adjusted R squared | .163 | |
| p value for the complete regression table | .018 | |

*Table 19. Regression table for the financial investment required to implement e-commerce is too high*

| Dependant Variable The financial investment required to implement e-commerce is too high | | |
|---|---|---|
| | Beta | p value |
| Business Size | -.420 | .006 |
| R Squared | .176 | |
| Adjusted R squared | .115 | |
| p value for the complete regression table | .046 | |

# Groupings of E-Commerce Adoption Barriers in the USA

To answer our second question, a combination of correlations and factor analysis was applied to the data. The results of this analysis are shown in the tables next and discussed at the end of this section.

Table 20 provides the correlation matrix of the importance ratings for e-commerce adoption barriers. All correlations significant at the .001 level are shown in bold.

These findings suggested the use of factor analysis to investigate any separate underlying factors and to reduce the redundancy of certain barriers indicated in the correlation matrices. The results of Kaiser-Meyer-Olkin MSA (.530) and Bartlett's Test of Sphericity ($\chi^2$ = 355.044, $p$ = .000) indicated that the data set satisfied the assumptions for factorability. Principle components analysis was chosen as the method of extraction in order to account for maximum variance in the data using a minimum number of factors. A three factor solution was extracted with Eigenvalues of 4.624, 2.435, and 1.419. This was supported by an inspection of the Scree Plots. The three factors accounted for 70.646% of the total variance in the U.S. sample. Table 21 shows the variance.

The resulting components were rotated using the Varimax procedure and a simple structure was achieved as shown in the rotated component matrix (see Table 22).

Although we can draw parallels between the Swedish, Australian, and U.S. results where e-commerce difficulties and suitability are concerned, Table 22 shows that in the U.S. study, a third factor termed "cost & security" was extracted. Two barriers (high investment and security) loaded onto this factor, which suggests that funding and security are a separate and distinct concern for the U.S. SMEs. The groupings found in the U.S. sample are shown in Figure 4. Once again, it has become apparent that the results for all three locations differ providing further evidence of the heterogeneity of the SME sector.

*Figure 4. E-commerce adoption barriers groupings in the USA*

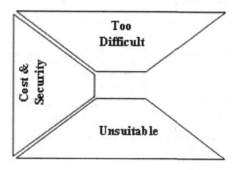

# Summary: E-Commerce Adoption Barriers in USA SMEs

Based on the findings in the previous sections, it can be seen that smaller SMEs based in the U.S. rated several adoption barriers as more important than larger organisations. This is inherent to the lack of resources available to small SMEs and suggests that they require additional support and funding through government and other schemes in order to introduce e-commerce. The results also show that there are three overarching obstacles to e-commerce implementation including difficulties associated with the technology, unsuitability of e-commerce and cost and security concerns.

We will now compare and discuss the key findings across the three locations.

*Table 20. Adoption barriers correlation matrix (USA)*

|  | E-commerce is not suited to our products/ser-vices. | E-commerce is not suited to our way of doing business. | E-commerce is not suited to the ways our clients do business. | E-commerce does not offer any advantages to our organisa-tion. |
|---|---|---|---|---|
| E-commerce is not suited to our way of doing business. | .415** |  |  |  |
| E-commerce is not suited to the ways our clients do business. | .437** | .586 |  |  |
| E-commerce does not offer any advantages to our organisation. | .642 | .355* | .344* |  |
| We do not have the technical knowledge in the organisation to implement e-commerce. | -.023 | .218 | .115 | -.061 |
| E-commerce is too complicated to implement. | .067 | .079 | .034 | .079 |
| E-commerce is not secure. | .119 | .454** | -.073 | .114 |
| The financial investment required to implement e-commerce is too high. | .089 | .193 | .017 | .001 |
| We do not have time to implement e-commerce. | .123 | .099 | .179 | .142 |
| It is difficult to choose the most suitable e-commerce standard with so many different options available. | .095 | .156 | .148 | .200 |

*Note: * significant at 0.05 level    ** significant at 0.01 level*

# Comparison of Results: A Discussion

Perhaps the most interesting result of our research into e-commerce barriers is related to the low adoption rate in Australia, when compared to Sweden or the U.S. This would suggest that the barriers are more prominent in Australian regional areas and this requires particular attention in order to isolate or lessen the impact of the obstacles, which prevent these SMEs from using e-commerce. While some similarities can be observed between the three locations in relation to e-commerce barriers, for the most part the findings are indicative of disparities.

After examining the associations between e-commerce barriers and business characteristics in the three locations, we can conclude that there are important differences in the effects of characteristics such as the gender of the CEO and the business size in Australia and the U.S. respectively. In the Australian context, SMEs with a male CEO were more likely to

*Table 20. Continued*

| We do not have the technical knowledge in the organisation to implement e-commerce. | E-commerce is too complicated to implement. | E-commerce is not secure. | The financial investment required to implement e-commerce is too high. | We do not have time to implement e-commerce. |
|---|---|---|---|---|
| | | | | |
| | | | | |
| | | | | |
| | | | | |
| .679 | | | | |
| .371* | .383** | | | |
| .426** | .338* | .344* | | |
| .762 | .811 | .259 | .245 | |
| .614 | .873 | .498 | .361* | .686 |

*Table 21. Total variance explained: Adoption barriers (USA)*

| Component | Eigenvalue | % Variance | Cumulative % |
|-----------|-----------|-----------|--------------|
| 1 | 4.624 | 38.530 | 38.530 |
| 2 | 2.435 | 20.290 | 58.820 |
| 3 | 1.419 | 11.826 | 70.646 |

*Table 22. Rotated component matrix: Adoption barriers (USA)*

| Barrier | Component 1: Too Difficult | Component 2: Un-suitable | Component 3: Cost & Security |
|---------|---------------------------|--------------------------|------------------------------|
| E-commerce is not suited to our products/services. | | .721 | |
| E-commerce is not suited to our way of doing business. | | .563 | |
| E-commerce is not suited to the ways our clients do business. | | .694 | |
| E-commerce does not offer any advantages to our organisation. | | .689 | |
| We do not have the technical knowledge in the organisation to implement e-commerce. | .840 | | |
| E-commerce is too complicated to implement. | .850 | | |
| E-commerce is not secure. | | | .580 |
| The financial investment required to implement e-commerce is too high. | | | .580 |
| We do not have time to implement e-commerce. | .840 | | |
| It is difficult to choose the most suitable e-commerce standard with so many different options available. | .840 | | |

emphasise certain barriers than female CEOs. As we will show later (in Chapter IX), male owners/managers tend to be more concerned about technical issues associated with e-commerce implementation. In the U.S. study, the size of the business was associated with several barriers including security, cost, and the complexity of e-commerce. This is in line with the findings of previous research (Blackburn et al., 2000; Fallon et al., 2000; Hawkins et al., 1996; Matlay, 2000), which showed that smaller SMEs suffered from a lack of technical expertise and were less e-commerce friendly, which raised barriers to e-commerce adop-

*Table 23. Association between business characteristics and e-commerce adoption barriers: A comparison*

| Adoption Barriers | Higher rating by... | | |
|---|---|---|---|
| | Sweden | Australia | USA |
| E-commerce is not suited to our products/services. | None | Male CEOs | |
| E-commerce is not suited to our way of doing business. | | Male CEOs<br><br>Local & regional SMEs | |
| E-commerce does not offer any advantages to our organization. | | Male CEOs | |
| We do not have the technical knowledge in the organisation to implement e-commerce. | | CEOs with no formal education<br><br>Local & regional SMEs | |
| E-commerce is too complicated to implement. | | Retail & service sector SMEs | Smaller SMEs |
| E-commerce is not secure. | | | Smaller SMEs |
| The financial investment required to implement e-commerce is too high. | | | Smaller SMEs |

tion. This implies that smaller sized organisations in the U.S. require financial and technical support with implementing e-commerce.

There were no significant associations found in Sweden, which suggests that different SMEs do not place a specific emphasis on any single barrier in particular. A number of reports examining the involvement of government and educational institutions with SMEs in Sweden (Boter et al., 2005; Johansson, 2003; Kjellberg, Soderstrom, & Svensson, 1998; Klofsten, 2000) suggested that, unlike many Western economies, there is a strong "push" by the Swedish government for entrepreneurship in SMEs as well as an involvement by educational institutions with assisting SMEs to adopt innovative technologies. It would seem that this involvement of business, government, and education has resulted in breaking down business characteristic-based barriers to e-commerce. This in no way suggests that barriers have necessarily reduced. It does, however, show that where particular sections of the SME community might have been more susceptible to barriers, this no longer exists.

Once again, we can see large differences in the way barriers are influenced by business characteristics across the three locations, despite the similarities between them (refer to Table 23).

In answering our second question, we found that, for the most part, SMEs are reluctant to adopt e-commerce due to its unsuitability or the difficulties involved with implementation. These appeared to the overarching reasons in Australia and Sweden. While they also exist in the U.S. context, SMEs there were also concerned with the high investment required and security issues. Where both the Swedish and Australian SMEs considered security to be a technical problem and cost to be an internal problem, the U.S. respondents saw these two

154 MacGregor & Vrazalic

*Table 24. Loading of adoption barriers on different factors (groupings): A comparison*

| Barriers | SWEDEN 1 Too Difficult | SWEDEN 2 Unsuitable | AUSTRALIA 1 Too Difficult | AUSTRALIA 2 Unsuitable | USA 1 Too Difficult | USA 2 Unsuitable | USA 3 Cost & Security |
|---|---|---|---|---|---|---|---|
| E-commerce is not suited to our products/services. | | ✓ | | ✓ | | ✓ | |
| E-commerce is not suited to our way of doing business. | | ✓ | | ✓ | | ✓ | |
| E-commerce is not suited to the ways our clients do business. | | ✓ | | ✓ | | ✓ | |
| E-commerce does not offer any advantages to our organisation. | | ✓ | | ✓ | | ✓ | |
| We do not have the technical knowledge in the organisation to implement e-commerce. | ✓ | | ✓ | | ✓ | | |
| E-commerce is too complicated to implement. | ✓ | | ✓ | | ✓ | | |
| E-commerce is not secure. | ✓ | | ✓ | | | | ✓ |
| The financial investment required to implement e-commerce is too high. | ✓ | | ✓ | | | | ✓ |
| We do not have time to implement e-commerce. | ✓ | | ✓ | | ✓ | | |
| It is difficult to choose the most suitable e-commerce standard with so many different options available. | ✓ | | ✓ | | ✓ | | |

barriers as being aligned and an entirely different class of barrier to deal with. These findings are consistent with previous studies, which have identified similar barriers and point to the lack of resources inherent in SMEs as a potential cause of low e-commerce uptake in this sector.

Once again, we have been able to reduce and group the ten most common barriers to e-commerce adoption in relation to two or three main factors. Whereas previous research has identified various barriers, this study has shown that certain barriers are correlated and can be logically grouped. This makes it simpler not only to explain, but also predict barriers to e-commerce adoption in SMEs. Table 24 summarises the loadings of each e-commerce barrier on the resulting factors.

# E-Commerce Adoption Barriers: Implications

Our results have contributed toward reducing the fragmentation associated with having a large number of e-commerce adoption barriers and providing a more concise understanding of the obstacles that SMEs face. When taken into account together with the adoption criteria, it becomes even more evident that tailored or customised government support programs and e-commerce solutions are necessary to promote the adoption of this technology. Whereas, in the past government organisations have spent millions of dollars to facilitate e-commerce technology use in SMEs, this research indicates that the funding should be more explicitly targeted toward potential adopters in the form of technical expertise and financial assistance to purchase the required components. It also indicates a strong need for awareness programs to highlight the advantages of e-commerce and persuade SME owners of the benefits that e-commerce can bring to the organization. SMEs clearly fall into two categories in relation to e-commerce: potential adopters and non-adopters. The non-adopters do not perceive e-commerce as being suited to their organisation at all. This may include SMEs such as a corner shop selling basic groceries. Government initiatives should therefore be targeted more toward potential adopters and offer them support in two key areas: technical expertise and financial assistance, if e-commerce is to be implemented successfully. In the following chapter, we will examine the benefits of doing so.

# E-Commerce Adoption Barriers: Key Findings

## Sweden

- Swedish respondents grouped e-commerce barriers based on two factors: unsuitability of the technology and difficulties associated with implementation.
- None of the business characteristics were found to have any effect on e-commerce barriers in Sweden.

# Australia

- SMEs with male CEOs rated several e-commerce barriers as being more important. These included barriers related to the suitability and benefits of e-commerce.

- SMEs with a national or international market focus assign a lower level of importance to the barrier "E-commerce doesn't fit the way our business works" than those businesses that are trading at a local or regional level.

- Retail and service businesses are more likely to place a higher level of importance on e-commerce complexity as a barrier than the industrial respondents.

- Australian SMEs rejected e-commerce for two overarching reasons: the difficulties associated with implementing e-commerce and the perception that e-commerce is unsuitable to the organisation. This was found to be virtually identical to Sweden.

# USA

- SMEs with fewer employees are more likely to rate security, cost, and complexity as important e-commerce barriers.

- Unlike Sweden and Australia, U.S. SMEs rejected e-commerce for three overarching reasons: the difficulties associated with implementing e-commerce, the perception that e-commerce is unsuitable to the organisation, and cost and security issues as a separate concern all together.

# References

Abell, W., & Lim, L. (1996). Business use of the Internet in New Zealand: An exploratory study. In *Proceedings of AUSWeb 96*. Retrieved from http//www.scu.edu.au/sponsored/ausweb96

Aldridge, A., White, M., & Forcht, K. (1997). Security considerations of doing business via the Internet: Cautions to be considered. *Internet Research-Electronic Networking Applications and Policy, 7*(1), 9-15.

Bakos, Y., & Brynjolfsson, E. (2000). Bundling and competition on the Internet. *Marketing Science, 19*(1), 63-82.

BarNir, A., & Smith, K. A. (2002). Interfirm alliances in the small business: The role of social networks. *Journal of Small Business Management, 40*(3), 219-232.

Blackburn, R., & Athayde, R. (2000). Making the connection: The effectiveness of Internet training in small businesses. *Education and Training, 42*(4/5).

Bodorick, P., Dhaliwal, J., & Jutla, D. (2002). Supporting the e-business readiness of small and medium-sized enterprises: Approaches and metrics. *Internet Research: Electronic Networking Applications and Policy, 12*(2), 139-164.

Boter, H., & Lundstrom, A. (2005). SME perspectives on business supplier services. *Journal of Small Business and Entrepreneurial Development, 12*(2), 244-258.

Carter, S. (2000). Improving the numbers and performance of women-owned businesses: Some implications for training and advisory services. *Education & Training, 42*(4/5), 326-333.

Chau, P. Y. K., & Hui, K. L (2001). Determinants of small business EDI adoption: An empirical investigation. *Journal of Organisational Computing and Electronic Commerce, 11*(4), 229-252.

Cragg, P. B., & King, M. (1993). Small firm computing: Motivators and inhibitors. *MIS Quarterly, 17*(1), 47-60.

Darch, H., & Lucas, T. (2002). Training as an e-commerce enabler. *Journal of Workplace Learning, 14*(4), 148-155.

Donckels, R., & Lambrecht, J. (1997). The network position of small businesses: An explanatory model. *Journal of Small Business Management, 35*(2), 13-28.

Dongen, J., Maitland, C., & Sadowski, B. (2002). Strategic use of the Internet by small- and medium-sized companies: An exploratory study. *Information Economics & Policy, 14*, 75-93.

Eid, R., Trueman, M., & Ahmed, A. M. (2002). A cross-industry review of B2B critical success factors. *Internet Research: Electronic Networking Applications and Policy, 12*(2), 110-123.

Fallon, M., & Moran, P. (2000). Information communications technology (ICT) and manufacturing SMEs. In *Proceedings of the 2000 Small Business and Enterprise Development Conference*, University of Manchester (pp. 100-109).

Farhoomand, A. F., Tuunainen, V. K., & Yee, L. W. (2000). Barriers to global electronic commerce: A cross-country study of Hong Kong and Finland. *Journal of Organisational Computing and Electronic Commerce, 10*(1), 23-48.

Hadjimanolis, A. (1999). Barriers to innovation for SMEs in a small less developed country (Cyprus). *Technovation, 19*(9), 561-570.

Hawkins, P., & Winter, J. (1996). The self-reliant graduate and the SME. *Education and Training, 38*(4), 3-9.

Iacovou, C. L., Benbasat, I., & Dexter, A. S. (1995). Electronic data interchange and small organisations: Adoption and impact of technology. *MIS Quarterly, 19*(4), 465-485.

Ihlström, C., Magnusson, M., Scupola, A., & Tuunainen, V. K. (2003). SME barriers to electronic commerce adoption: Nothing changes—Everything is new. In G. Gingrich (Ed.), *Managing IT in government, business, & communities* (pp. 147-163). Hershey, PA: Idea Group Publishing.

Johansson, U. (2003). *Regional development in Sweden: October 2003*. Svenska Kommunförbundet. Retrieved December 14, 2003, from http://www.lf.svekom.se/tru/RSO/Regional_ development_in_Sweden.pdf

Kai-Uwe Brock, J. (2000). Information and technology in the small firm. In S. Carter & Jones-Evans (Eds.), *Enterprise and the small business* (pp. 384-408). Prentice Hall.

Kendall, J. E., & Kendall, K. E. (2001). A paradoxically peaceful coexistence between commerce and ecommerce. *Journal of Information Technology, Theory, and Application*, *3*(4), 1-6.

Kjellberg, Y., Soderstrom, M., & Svensson, L. (1998). Training and development in the Swedish context: Structural change and a new paradigm. *Journal of European Industrial Training, 22*(4/5), 205-216.

Klofsten, M. (2000). Training entrepreneurship at universities: A Swedish case. *Journal of European Industrial Training, 24*(6), 337-344.

Lawrence, K. L. (1997). Factors inhibiting the utilisation of electronic commerce facilities in Tasmanian small-to-medium sized enterprises. In *Proceedings of the 8th Australasian Conference on Information Systems* (pp. 587-597).

Lee J. & Runge J. (2001) Adoption of Information Technology in Small Business: Testing Drivers of Adoption for Entrepreneurs. *Journal of Computer Information Systems, 42*(1), 44 - 57.

MacGregor, R., & Vrazalic, L. (2006). The effect of small business clusters in prioritising barriers to e-commerce adoption in regional SMEs. Journal of New Business *Ideas and Trends, 4*(1).

MacGregor, R., Hyland, P., Harvie, C., & Lee, B. C. (2006). Benefits derived from ICT adoption in regional medical practices: Perceptual differences between male and female general practitioners, to appear in *International Journal of Health Informatics and Information Systems*.

Matlay. H. (2000). Training in the small business sector of the British economy. In S. Carter & D. Jones (Eds.), *Enterprise and small business: Principles, policy, and practice*. London: Addison Wesley Longman.

Mehrtens, J., Cragg, P. B., & Mills, A. M. (2001). A model of Internet adoption by SMEs. *Information and Management, 39*, 165-176.

Mirchandani, D. A., & Motwani, J. (2001). Understanding small business electronic commerce adoption: An empirical analysis. *Journal of Computer Information Systems, 41*(3), 70-73.

Oxley, J. E., & Yeung, B. (2001). E-commerce readiness: Institutional environment and international competitiveness. *Journal of International Business Studies, 32*(4), 705-723.

Poon, S., & Swatman, P. (1999). An exploratory study of small business Internet commerce issues. *Information and Management, 35*(1), 9-18.

Poon, S., & Swatman, P. (1997). The Internet for small businesses: An enabling infrastructure. In *Proceedings of the 5th Internet Society Conference* (pp. 221-231).

Purao, S., & Campbell, B. (1998). Critical concerns for small business electronic commerce: Some reflections based on interviews of small business owners. In *Proceedings of the Association for Information Systems Americas Conference*, Baltimore (pp. 325-327).

Quayle, M. (2002). E-commerce: The challenge for UK SMEs in the Twenty-First Century. *International Journal of Operations and Production Management, 22*(10), 1148-1161.

Ratnasingham, P. (2000). The influence of power on trading partners in electronic commerce. *Internet Research, 10*(1), 56-62.

Reimenschneider, C. K., & McKinney, V. R. (2001). Assessing beliefs in small business adopters and non-adopters of Web-based e-commerce. *Journal of Computer Information Systems, 42*(2), 101-107.

Riquelme, H. (2002). Commercial Internet adoption in China: Comparing the experience of small, medium, and large business. *Internet Research: Electronic Networking Applications and Policy, 12*(3), 276-286.

Sandberg, K. W. (2003). An exploratory study of women in micro enterprises: Gender related difficulties. *Journal of Small Business and Enterprise Development, 10*(4), 408-417.

Sawhney, M., & Zabin, J. (2002). Managing and measuring relational equity in the network economy. *Journal of the Academy of Marketing Science, 30*(4), 313-332.

Schindehutte, M., & Morris, M. H. (2001). Understanding strategic adaptation in small firms. *International Journal of Entrepreneurial Behaviour and Research, 7*(3), 84-107.

*Sensis® e-Business Report.* (2006). Retrieved September 12, 2006, from www.about.sensis.com.au/resources/sebr.php

Stansfield, M., & Grant, K. (2003). An investigation into the use of electronic commerce among small- to medium-sized enterprises. *Journal of Electronic Commerce Research, 4*(1), 15-33.

Stockdale, R., & Standing, C. (2004). Benefits and barriers of electronic marketplace participation: An SME perspective. *Journal of Enterprise Information Management, 17*(4), 301-311.

Tambini, A. M. (1999). E-shoppers demand e-service. *Discount Store News, 11*(38).

Tetteh, E., & Burn, J. (2001). Global strategies for SME-business: Applying the SMALL framework. *Logistics Information Management, 14*(1-2), 171-180.

Timmers, P. (1999). *Electronic commerce: Strategies and models for business-to-business trading.* Chichester: John Wiley.

Tuunainen, V. K. (1999). Opportunities of effective integration of EDI for small businesses in the automotive industry. *Information & Management, 36*(6), 361-375.

Van Akkeren, J., & Cavaye, A. L. M. (1999). Factors Affecting entry-level Internet technology adoption by small business in Australia: An empirical study. In *Proceedings of the 10th Australasian Conference on Information Systems*, Wellington, New Zealand.

Vrazalic, L., Stern, D., MacGregor, R., Carlsson, S., & Magnusson, M. (2003). Barriers to e-commerce adoption in SMEs: Underlying factors from a Swedish study. In *Proceedings of the Australian Conference on Information Systems (ACIS)*, Perth.

Walczuch, R., Van Braven, G., & Lundgren, H. (2000). Internet adoption barriers for small firms in the Netherlands. *European Management Journal, 18*(5), 561-572.

Welsh, J. A., & White, J. F. (1981). A small business is not a little big business. *Harvard Business Review*, July.

Chapter VI

# Benefits of E-Commerce Adoption:
## What Can SMEs Expect to Gain from E-Commerce Adoption?

The previous two chapters were concerned with the drivers or criteria leading to e-commerce adoption, and the barriers or obstacles faced by SMEs in e-commerce adoption. Both the criteria and barriers reflect pre-e-commerce adoption issues. The criteria are related to positive expectations to be realised post e-commerce adoption, while the barriers are related to negative perceptions and other constraints, which hinder e-commerce adoption. This chapter is concerned with the benefits or advantages experienced by SMEs, *following* e-commerce adoption. Unfortunately, this chapter does not contain data from the U.S., as there were insufficient responses to the e-commerce benefit question in the U.S. sample group. As with previous chapters, we will begin by providing an overview of the relevant background literature, which has examined the benefits of e-commerce.

# Background

Most e-commerce benefits fall into the "intangible" category and are often not realised by SMEs at the time of adoption (MacGregor, 2004). Instead, these benefits are reaped post e-commerce implementation and do not necessarily match the initial drivers that actually lead to e-commerce adoption (the relationship between expected e-commerce criteria and actual e-commerce benefits will be explored in a subsequent chapter). The latest Sensis® e-Business report (2006) found that approximately 57% of SMEs were able to recover their investment in e-commerce technology, but 16% were not expecting to recover it at all. Of those that had recovered their investment, most reported their return had been less than 5%. This may suggest that the benefits of e-commerce adoption in the Australian context are trivial compared to the amount of time, effort, and funding required to implement e-commerce. However, this refers to the measurable benefits only. The main incentives for using e-commerce lie in the intangible advantages.

A number of studies have examined both the tangible and intangible e-commerce benefits achieved by SMEs. Studies by Abell and Lim (1996), Poon and Swatman (1997), and Quayle (2002) found that the tangible benefits (such as reduced administration costs, reduced production costs, reduced lead time, and increased sales) derived from e-commerce were marginal in terms of direct earnings in the short term, contrary to the expectations of SME owners/managers, and that at best these may be more fruitful in the longer term. This is supported in a recent article by Vrazalic, Bunker, MacGregor, Carlsson, and Magnusson (2002), as well as the Sensis® e-Business report (2006).

The same studies found that the intangible benefits (such as improvements in the quality of information, improved internal control of the business, and improved relations with business partners) were of far greater value to SMEs. The benefits from the customer relationship point of view were even more pronounced. While Poon et al. (1997) showed that e-commerce led to an improved relationship with customers, other studies found that SMEs benefited in their ability to reach new customers and new markets through the use of e-commerce (Quayle, 2002; Ritchie & Brindley, 2001; Sparkes & Thomas, 2001; Vescovi, 2000).

Another tangible benefit of e-commerce was related to the functions performed by the SME. Woerndl, Powell, and Vidgen (2005) found that many SMEs had expanded their activities beyond those performed prior to adoption. Stockdale and Standing's (2004) research also showed improvements in internal efficiencies as one of the benefits. This included changes in production methods and costs, enhanced levels of communications, and reduced transaction costs. Brunn, Jensen, and Skovgaard (2002) highlighted the flexibility in administration and communication that e-commerce brought. Apart from the benefits associated with reaching new customers and sales revenues, e-commerce benefited SMEs internally by lowering costs and improving the quality of communication and information inside the business.

The benefits of e-commerce reported in most studies are in alignment with the very reasons why SMEs are adopting e-commerce in the first place (i.e., e-commerce criteria). One of the questions that arises is whether e-commerce lives up to expectations? In other words, do the e-commerce drivers materialised into the benefits we have previously discussed. We will examine this in a subsequent chapter. For the purposes of this chapter, the benefits of e-commerce adoption identified in previous research studies are summarised in Table 1.

*Table 1. E-commerce benefits: A summary of previous research*

| E-Commerce Benefits | Reported by |
| --- | --- |
| Lower administration costs. | Quayle (2002)<br>Brunn et al. (2002)<br>Poon et al. (1997)<br>Abell et al. (1996) |
| Lower production costs. | Stockdale et al. (2004)<br>Quayle (2002)<br>Poon et al. (1997)<br>Abell et al. (1996) |
| Reduced lead time/stock levels. | Quayle (2002)<br>Poon et al. (1997)<br>Abell et al. (1996) |
| Increased sales. | Abell et al. (1996) |
| Increased internal efficiency. | Mustaffa & Beaumont (2004)<br>Tetteh & Burn (2001)<br>MacGregor, Bunker, & Waugh (1998) |
| Improved relations with business partners. | Hurwitz (2000)<br>Poon et al. (1997) |
| Access to new customers and markets. | Quayle (2002)<br>Ritchie et al. (2001)<br>Raymond (2001)<br>Sparkes et al. (2001)<br>Vescovi (2000)<br>Poon et al. (1997)<br>Abell et al. (1996) |
| Improved competitiveness. | Woerndl et al. (2005)<br>Vescovi (2000) |
| Improved quality of information. | Stockdale et al. (2004)<br>Quayle (2002)<br>Poon et al. (1997)<br>Abell et al. (1996) |

Some research (Fariselli, Oughton, Picory, & Sugden, 1999; Goode, 2002) has suggested that many SME owner/managers view e-commerce benefits as "one size fits all." In other words, the expectation is that most of the previously mentioned e-commerce benefits will be observed in any type of SME that implements the technology. This is one of the issues we will address in this chapter.

# Research Questions

Based on the outcomes of previous studies, we set out to answer several questions about e-commerce adoption benefits in our study. Specifically, we wanted to find out:

1.   Are there any business characteristics (e.g., size, length of time in business, sector, market focus, etc.) that affect how SMEs perceive e-commerce adoption benefits?

2.   Are there any underlying factors or groupings of e-commerce adoption benefits in each of the locations (Sweden and Australia), which would serve to explain the key advantages of e-commerce technology?

3.   Are there any differences in how e-commerce benefits are perceived across the locations (Sweden and Australia)?

In the first part of this chapter, our intention was to isolate specific business characteristics, which influence benefits of e-commerce adoption in SMEs. For example, what effect does the age of an SME have on reduced costs as a benefit of e-commerce? Does the education level of the CEO influence the ability to access new markets as an e-commerce benefit? To answer these questions, a series of linear regressions was carried out to determine whether business characteristics (such as the age and size of the business, business sector, gender of the CEO, educational level of the CEO, level of IT skill within the business, the existence of an enterprise-wide system, product planning, membership of a strategic alliance, market focus, or type of e-commerce) had any effects on e-commerce benefits. Linear regression was chosen over other techniques because it allows for interaction of the business characteristics, which other techniques fail to do.

The second question was concerned with grouping e-commerce benefits in order to provide a clearer explanation of the advantages that SMEs had experienced as a result of implementing e-commerce in each particular location. This provides a valuable tool in the campaign to increase e-commerce adoption levels in SMEs because incentive programs can focus on particular benefits that SMEs can expect to achieve as a result of using e-commerce. To provide data for the second question a series of correlations and factor analyses was undertaken.

The final part of this chapter provides a comparison between the two locations and determines what differences exist between Sweden and Australia in relation to e-commerce adoption benefits. This question will be addressed in the Discussion section of this chapter.

# Methodology

Ten of the most common benefits of e-commerce adoption were identified from the literature. A series of six in-depth interviews with regional SMEs were undertaken to determine whether the benefits were applicable and complete. All identified benefits were found to be applicable.

Based on the findings of the six in-depth interviews, a survey instrument was developed to collect data about e-commerce adoption benefits (amongst other things). Respondents who had adopted e-commerce were asked to rate how applicable each benefit achieved through e-commerce (as shown in Figure 1) was to their experience, using a standard 5 point Likert scale with 1 meaning highly inapplicable and 5 meaning highly applicable. The Likert scale responses were assumed to posses the characteristics of an interval measurement scale for data analysis purposes.

Chapter II provides a detailed account of how the data was collected and the total responses received for each of the three locations. The following sections will provide the results of the statistical analysis for Sweden and Australia in order to answer the three questions about e-commerce adoption benefits stated previously.

The rest of this chapter is structured as follows. First, we will examine the associations between different business characteristics and e-commerce adoption benefits in Sweden. Then we will present the results of a factor analysis, which will group the e-commerce adoption benefits indicated by the Swedish respondents. This process will be repeated for Australia. The final part of the chapter will discuss and compare the findings, and present the business implications of the results.

*Figure 1. Question about e-commerce benefits used in survey*

This question relates to the benefits experienced by your organisation following e-commerce adoption. Below is a list of statements indicating possible benefits your organisation may have experienced after implementing e-commerce. Please rank each of the statements on a scale of 1 to 5 to indicate to what extent each is applicable to your organisation, as follows:

1 = highly inapplicable to our organisation's experience

2 = inapplicable to our organisation's experience

3 = neither applicable nor inapplicable to our organisation's experience

4 = applicable to our organisation's experience

5 = highly applicable to our organisation's experience

| | E-commerce... | Rating | | | | |
|---|---|---|---|---|---|---|
| A1 | Reduced our administration costs. | 1 | 2 | 3 | 4 | 5 |
| A2 | Reduced our production costs. | 1 | 2 | 3 | 4 | 5 |
| A3 | Reduced our lead time. | 1 | 2 | 3 | 4 | 5 |
| A4 | Reduced our stock levels. | 1 | 2 | 3 | 4 | 5 |
| A5 | Lead to increased sales. | 1 | 2 | 3 | 4 | 5 |
| A6 | Increased our internal efficiency. | 1 | 2 | 3 | 4 | 5 |
| A7 | Improved our relations with business partners. | 1 | 2 | 3 | 4 | 5 |
| A8 | Gave us access to new customers and markets. | 1 | 2 | 3 | 4 | 5 |
| A9 | Improved our competitiveness. | 1 | 2 | 3 | 4 | 5 |
| A10 | Improved the quality of information in our organisation. | 1 | 2 | 3 | 4 | 5 |

*Table 2. Regression table for lower production costs*

| Dependant Variable Lower Production Costs | | |
|---|---|---|
| | Beta | p value |
| Business Size | .282 | .001 |
| Product Planning | .285 | .001 |
| R Squared | | .129 |
| Adjusted R squared | | .095 |
| p value for the complete regression table | | .001 |

# Business Characteristics and E-Commerce Benefits in Sweden

The first question was concerned with the effect of business characteristics on the 10 e-commerce adoption benefits listed in Figure 1. We found only one statistically significant association in the Swedish sample. The size of the business and the utilisation of product planning were associated with lower production costs as shown in Table 2.

Table 2 indicates that SMEs with more employees are more likely to have experienced lower production costs than those with fewer staff. The data also shows that SMEs that undertake product planning are more likely to rate this benefit as being applicable. Since none of the other business characteristics had any associations with any of the e-commerce benefits, we can assume that all of those e-commerce benefits were equally applicable in different categories of SMEs.

# Groupings of E-Commerce Benefits in Sweden

To answer our second question, a combination of correlations and factor analysis was applied to the data. The results of this analysis are shown in the tables next and discussed at the end of this section.

Table 3 provides the correlation matrix of the ratings for e-commerce adoption benefits. All correlations significant at the .001 level are shown in bold.

The findings in Table 3 suggested the use of factor analysis to investigate any separate underlying factors and to reduce the redundancy of certain benefits indicated in the correlation matrices. The results of Kaiser-Meyer-Olkin MSA (.798) and Bartlett's Test of Sphericity ($\chi^2 = 576$, p = .000) indicated that the data set satisfied the assumptions for factorability. Principle components analysis was chosen as the method of extraction in order to account for maximum variance in the data using a minimum number of factors. A three-factor solution was extracted with Eigenvalues of 4.083, 1.657, and 1.007, and was supported by an inspection of the Screen Plot. These three factors accounted for 67.476% of the total variance as shown in Table 4.

*Table 3. Adoption benefits correlation matrix (Sweden)*

| E-commerce… | Reduced our administration costs. | Reduced our production costs. | Reduced our lead time. | Reduced our stock levels. | Lead to increased sales. | Increased our internal efficiency. | Improved our relations with business partners. | Gave us access to new customers and markets. | Improved our competitiveness. |
|---|---|---|---|---|---|---|---|---|---|
| Reduced our production costs. | .259** | | | | | | | | |
| Reduced our lead time. | .619 | .251** | | | | | | | |
| Reduced our stock levels. | .343 | .099 | .412 | | | | | | |
| Lead to increased sales. | .274** | .239** | .439 | .506 | | | | | |
| Increased our internal efficiency. | .307 | .270** | .462 | .364 | .283** | | | | |
| Improved our relations with business partners. | .644 | .214** | .476 | .372 | .241** | .396 | | | |
| Gave us access to new customers and markets. | .298 | .166* | .359 | .364 | .355 | .457 | .365 | | |
| Improved our competitiveness. | .103 | .161* | .222** | .151 | .098 | .709 | .315 | .393 | |
| Improved the quality of information in our organisation. | .316 | .192* | .326 | .291 | .160 | .558 | .395 | .602 | .620 |

*Note: * significant at 0.05 level    ** significant at 0.01 level*

Table 4. Total variance explained: E-commerce benefits (Sweden)

| Component | Eigenvalue | % Variance | Cumulative % |
|---|---|---|---|
| 1 | 4.083 | 29.911 | 29.911 |
| 2 | 1.657 | 19.985 | 49.897 |
| 3 | 1.007 | 17.580 | 67.476 |

Table 5. Rotated component matrix: Adoption benefits (Sweden)

| Benefits | Component 1: Competitiveness | Component 2: Efficiency & Costs | Component 3: Inventory |
|---|---|---|---|
| Reduced our administration costs. | | .822 | |
| Reduced our production costs. | | .447 | |
| Reduced our lead time. | | | .788 |
| Reduced our stock levels. | | | .874 |
| Lead to increased sales. | .759 | | |
| Increased our internal efficiency. | | .820 | |
| Improved our relations with business partners. | .489 | | |
| Gave us access to new customers and markets. | .905 | | |
| Improved our competitiveness. | .742 | | |
| Improved the quality of information in our organisation. | .850 | | |

Figure 2. E-commerce adoption benefits groupings in Sweden

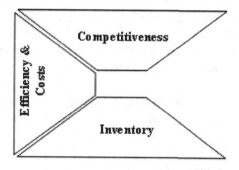

The resulting components were rotated using the Varimax procedure and a simple structure was achieved as shown in the rotated component matrix (see Table 5).

Table 4 indicates that we can group e-commerce benefits based on three factors. These three factors are independent and uncorrelated, as an orthogonal rotation procedure was used, and have been termed "competitiveness," "efficiency & cost," and "inventory." The five benefits that loaded on to the first factor are all related to better competitiveness in terms if sales and customers, as well as business partners. The improved quality of information in the organization is also a source of competitive advantage. It is interesting to note that sales and marketing have not emerged as a separate and distinct group of benefits. The second group of benefits is internal in nature and related to lower costs and more efficient operations due to e-commerce. The final grouping is related to inventory costs; however, it is viewed as a separate issue by the Swedish SMEs. Clearly, the reduction in stock levels and lead times is an important but distinct benefit from regional SMEs in Sweden.

For government organizations in Sweden aiming to promote e-commerce use in SMEs, this is an important result because it indicates where SMEs can expect to achieve benefits if they implement this new technology. Table 4 is a simple but powerful motivator in the campaign to convince SMEs that e-commerce adoption is worthwhile because it highlights the three main groups of benefits: improving competitiveness, reducing costs, and helping lower inventory. These results are shown in Figure 2.

We undertook an extended analysis to determine whether the groupings previously identified differed for categories of SMEs depending on their business size and whether they used any form of product planning. These two characteristics were previously found to be associated with e-commerce benefits. The Swedish respondents were sub-divided and the same factor analysis was applied to each category of SMEs.

# Business Size

Three categories of SMEs had sufficient data to apply factor analysis. The results of the Kaiser-Meyer-Olkin MSA (.927 for 1-9 employees, .739 for 10-19 employees and .811 for 20-49 employees) and Bartlett's test for Sphericity ($\chi^2 = 1027$ p=.000 for 1-9 employees, $\chi^2 = 270$ p=.000 for 10-19 employees and $\chi^2 = 388$ p=.000 for 20-49 employees) indicated that the data satisfied the assumptions for factorability. A two-factor solution with Eigenvalues 9.293 and 1.063 was extracted for the 1-9 employees group. These factors accounted for 73.969% of the variance. A four-factor solution with Eigenvalues 6.050, 2.253, 1.502, and 1.049 was extracted for the 10-19 employees group. These factors accounted for 77.535% of the variance. A two factor solution with Eigenvalues 8.694 and 1.568 was extracted for the 20-49 employees group. These factors accounted for 73.298% of the variance. The results can be seen in Table 6.

The resulting components were rotated using the Varimax procedure and a simple structure was achieved as shown in the rotated component matrices (Tables 7 to 9).

Table 6. Total variation explained: E-commerce benefits and business size (Sweden)

| Comp | Eigenvalue | | | % Variance | | | Cumulative % | | |
|---|---|---|---|---|---|---|---|---|---|
| Size | 1-9 | 10-19 | 20-49 | 1-9 | 10-19 | 20-49 | 1-9 | 10-19 | 20-49 |
| 1 | 9.293 | 6.050 | 8.694 | 66.379 | 43.213 | 62.100 | 66.379 | 43.213 | 62.100 |
| 2 | 1.063 | 2.253 | 1.568 | 7.590 | 16.095 | 11.199 | 73.969 | 59.308 | 73.298 |
| 3 | | 1.502 | | | 10.732 | | | 70.039 | |
| 4 | | 1.049 | | | 7.496 | | | 77.535 | |

*Table 7. Rotated component matrix (1-9 employees): E-commerce benefits (Sweden)*

| Benefits | Component 1 : Financial | Component 2: Competitiveness |
|---|---|---|
| Reduced our administration costs. | .810 | |
| Reduced our production costs. | .789 | |
| Reduced our lead time. | .867 | |
| Reduced our stock levels. | .805 | |
| Lead to increased sales. | .689 | |
| Increased our internal efficiency. | .592 | .644 |
| Improved our relations with business partners. | .666 | |
| Gave us access to new customers and markets. | .558 | .656 |
| Improved our competitiveness. | | .901 |
| Improved the quality of information in our organisation. | | .711 |

*Table 8. Rotated component matrix (10-19 employees): E-commerce benefits (Sweden)*

| Benefits | Component 1: Competitiveness | Component 2: Sales & Marketing | Component 3: Administration & Partnerships | Component 4: Production |
|---|---|---|---|---|
| Reduced our administration costs. | | | .708 | |
| Reduced our production costs. | | | | .867 |
| Reduced our lead time. | | | | .792 |
| Reduced our stock levels. | | | | .509 |
| Lead to increased sales. | | .837 | | |
| Increased our internal efficiency. | .742 | | | |
| Improved our relations with business partners. | | | .763 | |
| Gave us access to new customers and markets. | | .793 | | |
| Improved our competitiveness. | .935 | | | |
| Improved the quality of information in our organisation. | .655 | | | |

The previous tables indicate that SMEs with less than 10 employees and those with 20 to 49 employees were in agreement in relation grouping e-commerce benefits. Both categories of SMEs loaded the same benefits on to the same factors—financial benefits and improving competitiveness. Internal efficiency as a benefit loaded almost equally on both of these factors suggesting that this lead to both financial advantages, as well as increasing competitiveness.

In contrast to these two categories of SMEs, businesses, which employed between 10 and 19 staff members grouped benefits based on four factors. These SMEs ranked benefits related to competitiveness as being of a higher priority, and clearly included internal efficiency

*Table 9. Rotated component matrix (20-49 employees)—e-commerce benefits (Sweden)*

| Benefits | Component 1: Financial | Component 2: Competitiveness |
|---|---|---|
| Reduced our administration costs. | .757 | |
| Reduced our production costs. | .762 | |
| Reduced our lead time. | .847 | |
| Reduced our stock levels. | .779 | |
| Lead to increased sales. | .909 | |
| Increased our internal efficiency. | .594 | .551 |
| Improved our relations with business partners. | .803 | |
| Gave us access to new customers and markets. | | .819 |
| Improved our competitiveness. | | .876 |
| Improved the quality of information in our organisation. | | .826 |

improvements in this grouping (unlike in the other two categories where this benefit was not clearly grouped). This would suggest that financial considerations were not as relevant as they were to SMEs with less than 10 and those with more than 20 employees. Production issues and costs were also isolated by SMEs in this group as separate group of benefits, which was not found with the other categories.

Overall, the results do not show a "linear" pattern in how SMEs of different sizes experienced e-commerce benefits, although we can see clear parallels between the smallest SMEs those with more than 20 employees.

## Product Planning

The data for this analysis was subdivided into two categories: those SMEs, which engaged in product planning and those that did not. The results of the Kaiser-Meyer-Olkin MSA (.906 for respondents that used product planning, .936 for respondents that did not) and Bartlett's test for Sphericity ($\chi^2 = 658$ p=.000 for respondents that used product planning, $\chi^2= 1407$ p=.000 for respondents that did not) indicated that the data set satisfied the assumptions for factorability. Principle Components Analysis was chosen as the method of extraction in order to account for maximum variance in the data using a minimum number of factors. A two-factor solution was extracted for both sets of respondents with Eigenvalues of 8.838 and 1.386 for product planners and 8.789 and 1.046 for non-planners. These factors accounted for 73.027% of the variance for product planners and 70.255% for non-planners. The results can be seen in Table 10.

The resulting components were rotated using the Varimax procedure and a simple structure was achieved as shown in the rotated component matrices (Tables 11 and 12).

Unlike the entire respondent group (which produced a three factor solution), separate categories of SMEs produced two factor solutions. The two benefits related to inventory

*Table 10. Total variation explained: E-commerce benefits and product planning (Sweden)*

| Comp. | Eigenvalue | | % Variance | | Cumulative % | |
|---|---|---|---|---|---|---|
| Product Planning | Yes | No | Yes | No | Yes | No |
| 1 | 8.838 | 8.789 | 63.128 | 62.781 | 63.128 | 62.781 |
| 2 | 1.386 | 1.046 | 9.899 | 7.474 | 73.027 | 70.255 |

*Table 11. Rotated component matrix (product planners): E-commerce benefits (Sweden)*

| Benefits | Component 1 : Revenues & Costs | Component 2: Competitiveness |
|---|---|---|
| Reduced our administration costs. | .817 | |
| Reduced our production costs. | .755 | |
| Reduced our lead time. | .872 | |
| Reduced our stock levels. | .716 | |
| Lead to increased sales. | .861 | |
| Increased our internal efficiency. | | .715 |
| Improved our relations with business partners. | | .502 |
| Gave us access to new customers and markets. | | .610 |
| Improved our competitiveness. | .923 | |
| Improved the quality of information in our organisation. | .858 | |

*Table 12. Rotated component matrix (product non-planners): E-commerce benefits (Sweden)*

| Benefits | Component 1 : Revenues & Costs | Component 2: Competitiveness |
|---|---|---|
| Reduced our administration costs. | .846 | |
| Reduced our production costs. | .773 | |
| Reduced our lead time. | .741 | |
| Reduced our stock levels. | .778 | |
| Lead to increased sales. | .515 | |
| Increased our internal efficiency. | | .671 |
| Improved our relations with business partners. | .727 | |
| Gave us access to new customers and markets. | | .681 |
| Improved our competitiveness. | | .883 |
| Improved the quality of information in our organisation. | | .663 |

(Table 5) have been "re-absorbed" into the revenues & costs factor. When comparing those SMEs that engaged in product planning to those that didn't, one difference is noticeable. Whereas those that were planners grouped the benefits related to business partners with the competitiveness factor, the non-planners mapped this on to the revenues and costs factor. This suggests the SMEs, which used product planning, experienced improved relations with their business partners as a benefit of e-commerce, which gave them a competitive edge, particularly if the partner is a member of the SMEs' supply chain. By contrast, those that did not plan their products saw this benefit mainly as a cost saving/revenue generating factor. This implies that the relationship between the SME and its business partners was less integrated and that the SMEs saw this benefit simply as a method of reducing costs.

# Summary: E-Commerce Adoption Benefits in Swedish SMEs

The results of the Swedish study indicate that the size of an SME and whether it engages in product planning has some bearing on production costs as a benefit of e-commerce. It is the larger SMEs and those, which plan that, would appear to emphasise this benefit. However, overall, the benefits experienced by Swedish regional SMEs can be grouped into those that give them a competitive advantage, those that improve their efficiency (and reduce costs), and those that lower their inventory-related expenses. There was some disagreement about this when the data was split up based on the size of the business and whether the SME engaged in product planning, although the key benefits remain related to financial advantages and improved competitiveness. The results from Sweden will be revisited at the end of the chapter and compared to the Australian results. We now turn to SMEs located in Australia.

# Business Characteristics and E-Commerce Benefits in Australia

Once again, the first question was concerned with the effect of business characteristics on the 10 e-commerce benefits listed in Figure 1. There were no statistically significant associations between any of the benefits and any of the business characteristics for the Australian data. This implies that none of the business characteristics affect e-commerce benefits in Australian SMEs, specifically. Rather, they are all equally applicable. This differs from the Swedish results described previously.

We will now take a closer look at the groupings of e-commerce benefits in the Australian context with the purpose of answering our second question: Are there any underlying factors or groupings of e-commerce adoption benefits in Australian SMEs, which would serve to explain the key advantages of e-commerce technology?

*Table 13. Adoption benefits correlation matrix (Australia)*

| E-commerce… | Reduced our administration costs. | Reduced our production costs. | Reduced our lead time. | Reduced our stock levels. | Lead to increased sales. | Increased our internal efficiency. | Improved our relations with business partners. | Gave us access to new customers and markets. | Improved our competitiveness. |
|---|---|---|---|---|---|---|---|---|---|
| Reduced our production costs. | .361 | | | | | | | | |
| Reduced our lead time. | .340 | .490* | | | | | | | |
| Reduced our stock levels. | .127 | .559** | .167 | | | | | | |
| Lead to increased sales. | .120 | .493* | .213 | .662 | | | | | |
| Increased our internal efficiency. | .273 | .742 | .523** | .702 | .659 | | | | |
| Improved our relations with business partners. | .536** | .337 | .411* | .276 | .191 | .506** | | | |
| Gave us access to new customers and markets. | .108 | .033 | .114 | .341 | .274 | .219 | .055 | | |
| Improved our competitiveness. | .339 | .623** | .653 | .473* | .340 | .695 | .468* | .161 | |
| Improved the quality of information in our organisation. | .423* | .641** | .614** | .446* | .443* | .712 | .313 | .009 | .789 |

*Note: * significant at 0.05 level   ** significant at 0.01 level*

# Groupings of E-Commerce Adoption
# Benefits in Australia

To answer our second question, a combination of correlations and factor analysis was applied to the data. The results of this analysis are shown in the tables next and discussed at the end of this section.

Table 13 provides the correlation matrix of the ratings for e-commerce benefits. All correlations significant at the .001 level are shown in bold.

The results of the Kaiser-Meyer-Olkin MSA (.694) and Bartlett's test for Sphericity ($\chi^2 = 210$ p=.000) indicated that the data set satisfied the assumptions for factorability. Principle components analysis was chosen as the method of extraction in order to account for maximum variance in the data using a minimum number of factors. A three-factor solution was extracted with Eigenvalues 6.315, 1.648, and 1.223 and was supported by an inspection of the Scree plot. These factors accounted for 70.661% of the variance. Table 14 shows the variance.

The resulting components were rotated using the Varimax procedure and a simple structure was achieved as shown in the rotated component matrix (see Table 15).

The Australian data also resulted in a three-factor solution, however with some distinct differences compared to the Swedish data. The highest level of priority was assigned to the cost & competitiveness factor and a far lower level of priority was given to the other two factors. The results for the Australian respondents raise an interesting question. If the lowest level of applicability was assigned to the sales and marketing benefits, had the Australian SMEs not achieved any large perceptual increase in their customer and market levels after the introduction of e-commerce. A number of explanations are possible. One obvious answer is that the expectations regarding increased customers and markets were not forthcoming. The very low adoption rate of e-commerce in the Australian sample might suggest that indeed,

*Table 15. Rotated component matrix: E-commerce benefits (Australia)*

| Benefits | Component 1: Cost & Competitiveness | Component 2: Administration & Partnerships | Component 3: Sales & Marketing |
|---|---|---|---|
| Reduced our administration costs. | | .515 | |
| Reduced our production costs. | .746 | | |
| Reduced our lead time. | .717 | | |
| Reduced our stock levels. | | | .793 |
| Lead to increased sales. | | | .794 |
| Increased our internal efficiency. | .704 | | .529 |
| Improved our relations with business partners. | | .877 | |
| Gave us access to new customers and markets. | | | .612 |
| Improved our competitiveness. | .815 | | |
| Improved the quality of information in our organisation. | .862 | | |

*Figure 3. E-commerce adoption benefits groupings in Australia*

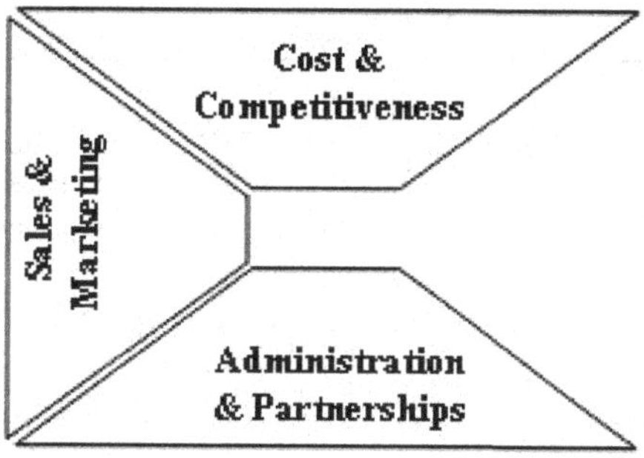

actual increases of customers, markets, and sales were quite small. The other explanation is that many of the Australian respondents did not have particularly efficient businesses prior to the adoption of e-commerce and that this change in business approach outweighed any other considerations. A third possibility is that while Australian SMEs had adopted the technology, they had not gained the necessary entrepreneurial skills to fully exploit the technology in order to gain larger market share. Again, if we consider the results in Chapter III (that show a large number of Australian respondents still trading at a local level), it would suggest that Australian respondents, unlike the Swedish SMEs are either unwilling or unknowing of how to fully exploit potential entry into the larger marketplace. Figure 3 provides a summary of the benefits in the Australian context.

# Summary: E-Commerce Benefits in Australian SMEs

The Australian SMEs did not show any associations between business characteristics and e-commerce benefits, implying that the benefits were experienced similarly across the range of SME categories. Although the Australian respondents also grouped the benefits based on three factors, these were different to the Swedish SMEs and included reduced costs/improved competitiveness, better administration/better business partnerships, and sales/marketing.

We will now compare and discuss the key findings across the two locations.

# Comparison of Results: A Discussion

Since we only found one association between business size/product planning and reduced production costs in Sweden, the main differences between Australian and Swedish SMEs are related to the derived factors or groupings of e-commerce benefits (summarized in Table 16 with highest priority factors underlined). While the Swedish respondents grouped the

*Table 16. Loading of adoption benefits on different factors (groupings): A comparison*

| Benefits | SWEDEN | | | AUSTRALIA | | |
|---|---|---|---|---|---|---|
| | 1: Competitiveness | 2: Efficiency & Costs | 3: Inventory | 1: Cost & Competitiveness | 2: Administration & Partnerships | 3: Sales & Marketing |
| Reduced our administration costs. | | ✓ | | | ✓ | |
| Reduced our production costs. | | ✓ | | ✓ | | |
| Reduced our lead time. | | | ✓ | ✓ | | |
| Reduced our stock levels. | | | ✓ | | | ✓ |
| Lead to increased sales. | ✓ | | | | | ✓ |
| Increased our internal efficiency. | | ✓ | | ✓ | | ✓ |
| Improved our relations with business partners. | ✓ | | | | ✓ | |
| Gave us access to new customers and markets. | ✓ | | | | | ✓ |
| Improved our competitiveness. | ✓ | | | ✓ | | |
| Improved the quality of information in our organisation. | ✓ | | | ✓ | | |

benefits they achieved through e-commerce adoption into competitive advantages, improved efficiency through reduced costs, and inventory improvements, Australian SMEs identified lower administration costs and promoted business partnerships as a separate group of benefits. Higher sales and new markets also emerged as a separate grouping by the Australian SMEs. This would suggest that Swedish SMEs experienced supply side benefits, while Australian-based organisations derived customer (or demand) side benefits from e-commerce. In both cases, however, it was the intangible benefits that SMEs ranked as being more relevant. This is in line with earlier findings, as discussed at the outset of this chapter, and directly relevant to programs and initiatives that are aimed at encouraging e-commerce adoption by SMEs.

The differences within the different sized businesses in Sweden are also of interest. The source of this can perhaps be traced to the growth stages of an SME. As it progresses through a critical and turbulent growth stage by doubling in size from 10 (or less) employees to 20, an SME experiences a higher administration burden. E-commerce may provide a source of relief by lowering administration costs at this stage. When the business reaches a critical mass of 20 employees or more, these issues tend to become resolved through established administration procedures.

# E-Commerce Benefits: Implications

This chapter has highlighted several differences between the benefits of e-commerce in SMEs located Sweden and Australia. Once again, the diversity of the SME sector is highlighted through these differences. The importance of the results presented here lies in how they are used by government organisations, as well as e-commerce solution providers, to promote e-commerce adoption by SMEs. If achievable benefits are a "selling point" to encourage SMEs to use e-commerce, then it is important to recognise what these benefits are. Failure to do so will result in broken promises in terms of what e-commerce can deliver to the SME sector.

In light of the findings reported in the previous chapter, which showed the SMEs, mainly raised concerns about the difficulties of implementing e-commerce and unsuitability of e-commerce to their organisation, the benefits emphasised in this chapter can act as a strong and convincing counter argument to demonstrate that e-commerce implementation does lead to important advantages that far outweigh the difficulties associated with it. However, it remains critically important to understand that these benefits are not uniform across locations, or indeed, across different categories of SMEs. Subsequently, it is not advisable to offer "one size fits all" solutions to SMEs, but rather more targeted approaches and programs are required. For example, in Australia, one of the benefits highlighted as a distinct advantage is an improved relationship with business partners. For SMEs seeking more integration with their business partners, this can be a compelling argument to adopt e-commerce.

Finally, the results in this chapter also show a divergence from the criteria or drivers leading to e-commerce adoption discussed previously (see Chapter IV). This raises questions about expected vs. actual benefits of e-commerce, which we will address in detail in a later chapter.

# E-Commerce Adoption Benefits: Key Findings

## Sweden

- SMEs with more employees and those that have undertaken product planning are more likely to have experienced lower production costs as an e-commerce benefit than those with fewer staff and those that have not.

- The benefits experienced by SMEs in Sweden can be summarised into three groups: competitive benefits, efficiency and cost benefits, and inventory benefits. However, these groupings do not necessarily hold for different categories of SMEs (e.g., SMEs with different number of employees).

# Australia

- None of the business characteristics were found to have any effect on e-commerce benefits in Australia.
- Australian SMEs experienced three overarching groups of benefits: costs & competitiveness benefits, administration & partnership benefits, and sales/marketing benefits.

# USA

- There was insufficient data to conduct a statistical analysis of the U.S. sample.

# References

Abell, W., & Lim, L. (1996). Business use of the Internet in New Zealand: An exploratory study. In *Proceedings of AUSWeb 96*. Retrieved from http//www.scu.edu.au/sponsored/ausweb96

Brunn, P., Jensen, M., & Skovgaard, J. (2002). E-marketplaces: Crafting a winning strategy. *European Management Journal, 20*(3), 286-298.

Fariselli, P., Oughton, C., Picory, C., & Sugden, R. (1999). Electronic commerce and the future for SMEs in a global market place: Networking and public policies. *Small Business Economics, 12*(3), 261-276.

Goode, S. (2002). Management attitudes towards the World Wide Web in Australian small business. *Information Systems Management, 19*(1), 45-48.

Hurwitz. (2000). *E-marketplaces: Issues, risks, and requirements for success*. White paper, Hurwitz Group Inc., Framingham, MA.

MacGregor, R. C. (2004). The role of formal networks in the ongoing use of electronic commerce technology in regional small business. *Journal of Electronic Commerce in Organisations, 2*(1), 1-14.

MacGregor, R. C., Bunker, D. J., & Waugh, P. (1998). Electronic commerce and small/medium enterprises (SME's) in Australia: An electronic data interchange (EDI) pilot study. In *Proceedings of the 11th International Bled Electronic Commerce Conference*, Slovenia.

Mustaffa, S., & Beaumont, N. (2004). The effect of electronic commerce on small Australian enterprises. *Technovation, 24*(2), 85-95.

Poon, S., & Swatman, P. (1997). The Internet for small businesses: An enabling infrastructure. In *Proceedings of the 5th Internet Society Conference* (pp. 221-231).

Quayle, M. (2002). E-commerce: The challenge for UK SMEs in the Twenty-First Century. *International Journal of Operations and Production Management, 22*(10), 1148-1161.

Raymond, L. (2001). Determinants of Web site implementation in small business. *Internet Research: Electronic Network Applications and Policy, 11*(5), 411-422.

Ritchie, R., & Brindley, C. (2000). Disintermediation, disintegration, and risk in the SME global supply chain. *Management Decision, 38*(8), 575-583.

*Sensis® e-Business Report*. (2006). Retrieved September 12, 2006, from www.about.sensis. com.au/resources/sebr.php

Sparkes, A., & Thomas, B. (2001). The use of the Internet as a critical success factor for the marketing of Welsh Agri-food SMEs in the Twenty First Century. *British Food Journal, 103*(4), 331-347.

Stockdale, R., & Standing, C. (2004). Benefits and barriers of electronic marketplace participation: An SME perspective. *Journal of Enterprise Information Management, 17*(4), 301-311.

Tetteh, E., & Burn, J. (2001). Global strategies for SME-business: Applying the SMALL framework. *Logistics Information Management, 14*(1-2), 171-180.

Vescovi, T. (2000). Internet communication: The Italian SME case. *Corporate Communications: An International Journal, 5*(2), 107-112.

Vrazalic, L., Bunker, D., MacGregor, R. C., Carlsson, S., & Magnusson, M. (2002). Electronic commerce and market focus: Some findings from a study of Swedish small to medium enterprises. *Australian Journal of Information Systems, 10*(1), 110-119.

Woerndl, M., Powell, P., & Vidgen, R. (2005). Netsourcing in SMEs: E-ticketing in art venues. *Electronic Markets, 15*(2), 119-127.

**Chapter VII**

# Disadvantages of E-Commerce Adoption:
## What Types of Problems do SMEs Face from E-Commerce?

Like any other technology, e-commerce has both positive and negative effects on the organisation. While the positive effects were discussed in the previous chapter as benefits experienced through e-commerce adoption, this chapter will focus on the negative effects or disadvantages associated with e-commerce. Like the previous chapter, this chapter does not contain data from the U.S., as there were insufficient responses to the questions concerned with disadvantages from the U.S. sample group. This is the final chapter, which concludes our examination of the four aspects of e-commerce in SMEs:

- Criteria (the reasons why SMEs are adopting e-commerce) – Chapter IV
- Barriers (the obstacles that prevent SMEs from using e-commerce) – Chapter V
- Benefits (the advantages experienced by SMEs as a result of implementing e-commerce) – Chapter VI
- Disadvantages (the problems encountered by SMEs following e-commerce adoption) – Chapter VII

Together, these four chapters provide a multi-faceted perspective of the key issues faced by SMEs in different locations in relation to e-commerce. In this chapter, we will examine the difficulties, which SMEs have reported following e-commerce adoption so that useful strategies and programs can be developed to provide support to SMEs and resolve these difficulties. We will begin with examining the literature in this area.

# Background

Unlike previous technological innovations, e-commerce brings with it changes to both procedures within the organisation as well as changes to the structure of the organisation itself. These changes include the way businesses interact, their approaches to marketing, products, and customers, and the way decisions are made and disseminated, particularly decisions concerning technology adoption and use. For SMEs, these changes can have both positive and negative effects. Lawrence (1997), Tetteh and Burn (2001), and Lee (2001) contend that e-commerce adoption fundamentally alters the internal procedures within an SME. Meanwhile, studies by Raymond (2001) and Ritchie and Brindley (2000) found that, while e-commerce adoption has eroded trading barriers for SMEs, this has often come at the price of altering or eliminating commercial relationships and exposing the business to external risks. Clearly, e-commerce adoption has brought about both internal and external changes to the organisation, some with adverse effects.

E-commerce inevitably brings with it changes in communication (Chellappa, Barua, & Whinston, 1996), the ways of doing business (Henning, 1998), the approach to marketing (Giaglis et al., 1999), as well as changes in day-to-day activities (Doukidis, Poulymenakou, Terpsidis, Themisticleous, & Miliotis, 1998). These changes are exacerbated in the SME sector as few organisations have an integrated implementation plan and, for the most part, they fail to understand the need for competitive strategies (Jeffcoate, Chappell, & Feindt, 2002). Introducing e-commerce into an SME is not simply a matter of installing the relevant hardware and software components. It involves a number of changes to the business itself and to the way business is done. If e-commerce implementation is not approached as a fundamental strategic change in the organisation, it is highly likely that SMEs will experience difficulties in managing the business following implementation. The research into this aspect of e-commerce has been limited with fewer studies examining e-commerce disadvantages than those looking at e-commerce drivers, benefits, and barriers.

A closer examination of some of the studies, which have examined e-commerce implementation, shows that the results are sometimes conflicting. Raymond (2001), in examining the removal of business intermediaries by e-commerce, noted a deterioration of relationships with business partners and customers. He termed this effect as "disintermediation." Stauber (2000) also noted the negative effect of e-commerce on SMEs. Specifically he found that many firms felt that there was a decline in contact with customers and in some cases managers felt that this had led to a loss of revenue.

By comparison, a study by Poon and Swatman (1997) found that e-commerce had led to an improved relationship with customers, but not with suppliers. In the same study, they reported that SME operators complained about e-commerce failing to meet expectations

*Table 1. E-commerce disadvantages: A summary of previous research*

| E-Commerce Benefits | Reported by |
|---|---|
| Deterioration of relations with business partners. | Raymond (2001)<br>Stauber (2000) |
| Higher costs. | Stauber (2000)<br>MacGregor et al. (1998) |
| Increased computer maintenance. | MacGregor et al. (1998) |
| Doubling of work in the organisation. | MacGregor et al. (1998) |
| Reduced the flexibility. | Lee (2001)<br>MacGregor et al. (1998)<br>Lawrence (1997) |
| Increased security risks. | Ritchie et al. (2001) |
| Monotonous work. | Healy & DeLuca (2000) |
| Dependence on e-commerce (non-e-commerce procedures having to be done through e-commerce formats). | Sparkes et al. (2001)<br>MacGregor et al. (1998)<br>Lawrence (1997) |

concerning marketing or sales, and failing to result in savings in terms of communications costs. In relation to costs, Stauber (2000) actually found that many organisations complained of increasing costs in their business dealings attributable to e-commerce use.

Lawrence (1997) showed that e-commerce, particularly (but not exclusively) EDI, resulted in reduced flexibility of work practices and heavier reliance on the technology. Her findings are supported in studies by MacGregor, Bunker, and Waugh (1998), Lee (2001), and Sparkes and Thomas (2001). MacGregor et al. (1998), in a study of 131 regional SMEs in Australia, found that many respondents complained that they were doubling their work effort, this, in part, being due to technology systems not being fully integrated into the existing business systems in the organisation. They also established that, not surprisingly, the technology had resulted in higher computer maintenance costs.

The disadvantages or difficulties encountered by SMEs following e-commerce adoption that have been identified in previous research studies are summarised in Table 1.

# Research Questions

Based on the outcomes of previous studies, we set out to answer several questions about e-commerce disadvantages in our study. Specifically, we wanted to find out:

1.   Do any business characteristics (e.g., size, length of time in business, sector, market focus, etc.) affect the difficulties associated with e-commerce?

2.  Are there any underlying factors or groupings of e-commerce disadvantages in each of the locations (Sweden and Australia), which would serve to explain the key problems faced by SMEs after the adopt e-commerce?

3.  Are there any differences in how e-commerce disadvantages are perceived across the two locations (Sweden and Australia)?

In the first part of this chapter, our intention was to isolate specific business characteristics, which affected the problems that SMEs encountered following e-commerce implementation. For example, did the gender of the CEO have any effect on increased costs as a difficulty experienced after e-commerce adoption? Or did having an international market focus have any influence on reduced flexibility in doing business? To answer these questions, a series of linear regressions was carried out to determine whether business characteristics (such as the age and size of the business, business sector, gender of the CEO, educational level of the CEO, level of IT skill within the business, the existence of an enterprise-wide system, product planning, membership of a strategic alliance, market focus, or type of e-commerce) had any effects on e-commerce disadvantages. Linear regression was chosen over other techniques because it allows for interaction of the business characteristics, which other techniques fail to do.

The second question was concerned with grouping e-commerce disadvantages in order to provide a clearer explanation of the key problems SMEs were having to deal with post implementation. Rather than dealing with a multitude of explanations, the answer to this question provides a "bigger picture" of the key issues that need to be addressed by government organisations in developing strategies to support SMEs and provide post-implementation assistance. For example, could the drivers in Sweden be attributed to two main groups—increasing costs and poorer relationships? Having this insight allows us to develop targeted support programs to assist SMEs. To provide data for the second question a series of correlations and factor analyses was undertaken.

The final part of this chapter provides a comparison between the two locations and determines what differences exist between Sweden and Australia in relation to e-commerce disadvantages. This question will be addressed in the Discussion section of this chapter.

# Methodology

Seven of the most common e-commerce disadvantages were identified from the literature. A series of six in-depth interviews with regional SMEs were undertaken to determine whether the disadvantages were applicable and complete. All identified disadvantages were found to be applicable.

Based on the findings of the six in-depth interviews, a survey instrument was developed to collect data about e-commerce adoption disadvantages (amongst other things). Respondents who had adopted e-commerce were asked to rate how applicable each disadvantage experienced as a result of e-commerce (as shown in Figure 1) was to their experience, using

*Figure 1. Question about e-commerce disadvantages used in survey*

This question relates to the disadvantages experienced by your organisation following e-commerce adoption. Below is a list of statements indicating possible disadvantages your organisation may have experienced after implementing e-commerce. Please rank each of the statements on a scale of 1 to 5 to indicate to what extent each is applicable to your organisation, as follows:

1 = highly inapplicable to our organisation's experience

2 = inapplicable to our organisation's experience

3 = neither applicable nor inapplicable to our organisation's experience

4 = applicable to our organisation's experience

5 = highly applicable to our organisation's experience

| | Implementing e-commerce in the organisation... | Rating | | | | |
|---|---|---|---|---|---|---|
| D1 | Deteriorated relations with our business partners. | 1 | 2 | 3 | 4 | 5 |
| D2 | Increased costs. | 1 | 2 | 3 | 4 | 5 |
| D3 | Increased the computer maintenance required. | 1 | 2 | 3 | 4 | 5 |
| D4 | Doubled the amount of work. | 1 | 2 | 3 | 4 | 5 |
| D5 | Reduced the flexibility of the business processes. | 1 | 2 | 3 | 4 | 5 |
| D6 | Raised security concerns. | 1 | 2 | 3 | 4 | 5 |
| D7 | Made us increasingly dependent on this technology. | 1 | 2 | 3 | 4 | 5 |

a standard 5 point Likert scale with 1 meaning highly inapplicable and 5 meaning highly applicable. The Likert scale responses were assumed to posses the characteristics of an interval measurement scale for data analysis purposes.

Chapter II provided a detailed account of how the data was collected and the total responses received for each of the three locations. The following sections will provide the results of the statistical analysis for Sweden and Australia in order to answer the three questions about e-commerce disadvantages stated previously.

The rest of this chapter is structured as follows. First, we will examine the associations between different business characteristics and e-commerce disadvantages in Sweden. Then we will present the results of a factor analysis, which will group the e-commerce disadvantages indicated by the Swedish respondents. This process will be repeated for Australia. The final part of the chapter will discuss and compare the findings and present the business implications of the results.

# Business Characteristics and E-Commerce Disadvantages in Sweden

The first question was concerned with the effect of business characteristics on the seven e-commerce disadvantages listed in Figure 1. We found only two statistically significant

*Table 2. Regression table for raised security concerns*

| Dependant Variable Raised security concerns | | |
|---|---|---|
| | Beta | p value |
| Business Size | .175 | .046 |
| Market Focus | -.193 | .024 |
| R Squared | | .081 |
| Adjusted R squared | | .044 |
| p value for the complete regression table | | .036 |

*Table 3. Regression table for dependence on e-commerce*

| Dependant Variable Dependence on e-commerce | | |
|---|---|---|
| | Beta | P value |
| Market focus | -.211 | .013 |
| R Squared | | .092 |
| Adjusted R squared | | .056 |
| p value for the complete regression table | | .016 |

associations in the Swedish sample. The size of the business and the market focus were associated with security concerns, and the market focus was associated with dependence on e-commerce as shown in Tables 7.2 and 7.3 respectively.

The data shows that the larger SMEs appear more concerned with this disadvantage than the smaller ones. The results also indicate a negative Beta value for market focus, suggesting that locally focussed SMEs are more concerned with matters of security than those that are focussed on national or international markets. It is interesting to note that despite the findings of recent studies (Boter & Lundstrom, 2005) showing Denmark and Sweden are more "business ready" for e-commerce than most other nations, that security is still considered a disadvantage by the Swedish respondents. It is also interesting to note that where conventional wisdom might suggest that businesses with a "wider" market or businesses that are on the "smaller end of the SME spectrum" who would find security more of a concern, it is those businesses that are trading locally and the larger SMEs that place more importance on security as a disadvantage.

Table 3 shows a similar result to the previous table, in that being dependent on e-commerce as a disadvantage has the SME's market focus associated with it. Again, the Beta value is negative suggesting that local and regionally focussed businesses are more likely to rate this disadvantage as being more applicable than organisations with a national or international market focus. A number of studies (Lawrence, 1997; Sparkes et al., 2001) have suggested that for those SMEs, which deal with customers face-to-face, e-commerce can, and often does, alter the mechanism of those dealings. They add that those organisations that traditionally dealt with most of their customers face-to-face see the changes brought about by e-commerce as a disadvantage. Assuming that most face-to-face dealings would occur at a local or regional level, the data in Table 3 supports those earlier findings.

Although there were no associations between the other business characteristics and e-commerce disadvantages, this is not to say that their importance as difficulties is lower. Instead, it suggests that the different categories of SMEs place the same level of importance on the problems they encountered with e-commerce adoption.

We will now take a closer look at the groupings of e-commerce disadvantages in the Swedish context with the purpose of answering our second question: Are there any underlying factors or groupings of e-commerce disadvantages in Sweden, which would serve to explain the key problems faced by SMEs after the adopt e-commerce?

## Groupings of E-Commerce Disadvantages in Sweden

To answer our second question, a combination of correlations and factor analysis was applied to the data. The results of this analysis are shown in the tables next and discussed at the end of this section.

Table 4 provides the correlation matrix of the importance ratings for e-commerce disadvantages. All correlations significant at the .001 level are shown in bold.

The results of Kaiser-Meyer-Olkin MSA (.879) and Bartlett's Test of Sphericity ($\chi^2 = 767.73$, $p = .000$) indicated that the data set satisfied the assumptions for factorability. Principle components analysis was chosen as the method of extraction in order to account for maximum variance in the data using a minimum number of factors. A two factor solution was extracted with Eigenvalues of 5.274 and 1.429 and was supported by the Scree plot. The two factors accounted for 60.935% of the variance. Table 5 shows the variance.

*Table 4. E-commerce disadvantages correlation matrix (Sweden)*

| E-Commerce... | Deteriorated relations with our business partners. | Increased costs. | Increased the computer maintenance required. | Doubled the amount of work. | Reduced the flexibility of the business processes. | Raised security concerns. |
|---|---|---|---|---|---|---|
| Increased costs. | .322 | | | | | |
| Increased the computer maintenance required. | .358 | .494 | | | | |
| Doubled the amount of work. | .319 | .340 | .416 | | | |
| Reduced the flexibility of the business processes. | .633 | .336 | .360 | .443 | | |
| Raised security concerns. | .453 | .343 | .394 | .401 | .578 | |
| Made us increasingly dependent on this technology. | .336 | .407 | .527 | .333 | .389 | .570 |

*Note: * significant at 0.05 level    ** significant at 0.01 level*

*Table 5. Total variance explained: E-commerce disadvantages (Sweden)*

| Component | Eigenvalue | % Variance | Cumulative % |
|---|---|---|---|
| 1 | 5.274 | 47.923 | 47.923 |
| 2 | 1.429 | 12.992 | 60.935 |

*Table 6. Rotated component matrix: E-commerce disadvantages (Sweden)*

| Disadvantage | Component 1: Resources | Component 2: Business Practices |
|---|---|---|
| Deteriorated relations with business partners. | | .731 |
| Increased costs. | .683 | |
| Increased the computer maintenance required. | .717 | |
| Doubled the amount of work. | | .523 |
| Reduced the flexibility of the business processes. | | .874 |
| Raised security concerns. | | .763 |
| Made us increasingly dependent on this technology. | .541 | |

*Figure 2. E-commerce disadvantage groupings in Sweden*

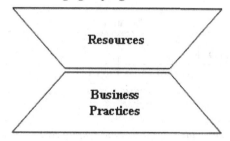

The resulting components were rotated using the Varimax procedure and a simple structure was achieved as shown in the rotated component matrix (see Table 6).

Table 6 indicates that SMEs in Sweden grouped e-commerce disadvantages based on two factors, which we have termed those related to "resources" and those related to "business practices." The former has been assigned a higher priority by the SMEs and includes problems related to costs, maintaining computer resources, and a dependence on e-commerce. The latter is not rated as highly by the respondents and includes difficulties that have affected business practices, including relationships with business partners, workloads, flexibility of business processes, and security concerns. These results suggest that SMEs in regional areas in Sweden require support and assistance such as the provision of IT support and access to business development managers to help SMEs plan their e-commerce strategy in order to avoid duplication of work and maintain the flexibility that is often associated with SMEs. The groupings found in the Swedish study are shown in Figure 2.

We undertook an extended analysis to determine whether the groupings previously identified differed for categories of SMEs depending on their business size and market focus. These two characteristics were previously found to be associated with e-commerce disadvantages. The Swedish respondents were sub-divided and the same factor analysis was applied to each category of SMEs.

# Business Size

Four categories of SMEs had sufficient data to apply factor analysis. The results of the Kaiser-Meyer-Olkin MSA (.921 for 1-9 employees, .821 for 10-19 employees, .834 for 20-49 employees, .761 for 50-199 employees) and Bartlett's test for Sphericity ($\chi^2 = 711$ p=.000 for 1-9 employees, $\chi^2 = 253$ p=.000 for 10-19 employees, $\chi^2 = 263$ p=.000 for 20-49 employees, $\chi^2 = 197$ p=.000 for 50-199 employees) indicated that the data set satisfied the assumptions for factorability. Principle components analysis was chosen as the method of extraction in order to account for maximum variance in the data using a minimum number of factors. A single factor solution with Eigenvalue 7.286 was chosen for the 1-9 employee group. This was supported by an inspection of the Scree plot and accounted for 66.239% of the variance. A two factor solution with Eigenvalues 6.646 and 1.453 was chosen for

*Table 7. Total variation explained: E-commerce disadvantages and business size (Sweden)*

| Comp | Eigenvalue | | | | % Variance | | | | Cumulative % | | | |
|---|---|---|---|---|---|---|---|---|---|---|---|---|
| Size | 1-9 | 10-19 | 20-49 | 50-199 | 1-9 | 10-19 | 20-49 | 50-199 | 1-9 | 10-19 | 20-49 | 50-199 |
| 1 | 7.286 | 6.646 | 7.006 | 6.458 | 66.239 | 60.415 | 63.691 | 58.705 | 66.239 | 60.415 | 63.691 | 58.705 |
| 2 | | 1.453 | 1.164 | 1.106 | | 13.210 | 10.579 | 10.055 | | 73.625 | 74.270 | 68.760 |

*Table 8. Rotated component matrix (one to nine employees): E-commerce disadvantages (Sweden)*

| Disadvantage | Component 1 |
|---|---|
| Deteriorated relations with business partners. | .737 |
| Increased costs. | .696 |
| Increased the computer maintenance required. | .691 |
| Doubled the amount of work. | .886 |
| Reduced the flexibility of the business processes. | .832 |
| Raised security concerns. | .886 |
| Made us increasingly dependent on this technology. | .854 |

*Table 9. Rotated component matrix (10-19 employees): E-commerce disadvantages (Sweden)*

| Disadvantage | Component 1: Business Practices | Component 2: Resources |
|---|---|---|
| Deteriorated relations with business partners. | .662 | |
| Increased costs. | | .760 |
| Increased the computer maintenance required. | | .792 |
| Doubled the amount of work. | | .726 |
| Reduced the flexibility of the business processes. | .790 | |
| Raised security concerns. | .929 | |
| Made us increasingly dependent on this technology. | .860 | |

*Table 10. Rotated component matrix (20-49 employees): E-commerce disadvantages (Sweden)*

| Disadvantage | Component 1: Business Practices | Component 2: Costs |
|---|---|---|
| Deteriorated relations with business partners. | .843 | |
| Increased costs. | | .799 |
| Increased the computer maintenance required. | .640 | .550 |
| Doubled the amount of work. | .784 | |
| Reduced the flexibility of the business processes. | .793 | |
| Raised security concerns. | .694 | |
| Made us increasingly dependent on this technology. | .675 | |

*Table 11. Rotated component matrix (50-199 employees): E-commerce disadvantages (Sweden)*

| Disadvantage | Component 1 |
|---|---|
| Deteriorated relations with business partners. | .696 |
| Increased costs. | .793 |
| Increased the computer maintenance required. | .680 |
| Doubled the amount of work. | .761 |
| Reduced the flexibility of the business processes. | .684 |
| Raised security concerns. | .809 |
| Made us increasingly dependent on this technology. | .798 |

the 10-19 employee group. This was also supported by an inspection of the Scree plot and accounted for 73.625% of the variance. A two factor solution with Eigenvalues 7.006 and 1.164 was chosen for the 20-49 employee group. This was supported by an inspection of the Scree plot and accounted for 74.270% of the variance. A two factor solution with Eigenvalues 6.458 and 1.106 was chosen for the 50-199 employee group. This was supported by an inspection of the Scree plot and accounted for 68.760% of the variance. The results can be seen in Table 7.

The resulting components were rotated using the Varimax procedure and a simple structure was achieved as shown in the rotated component matrices (Tables 8 to 11).

An examination of Tables 8 to 11 shows a number of interesting differences. Firstly, and most obviously is the fact that unlike the other business size categories, the 1-9 employee category and the 50 to 199 category considered that there was only a single factor underlying the disadvantages of e-commerce adoption. For the other two categories of respondents, both the 10-19 and the 20-49 categories considered the "business practices" factor to be of greater importance. The composition of this factor varies between the two categories. For the 10-19 employee category, four disadvantages were mapped to this factor. On the other hand, for the 20-49 employee category, six disadvantages loaded on to the same factor. Thus, while computer maintenance and workloads were considered disadvantages related to resources smaller SMEs, they were considered to be more organizational in nature by SMEs employing 20 to 49 staff members. These results show that very small and very large SMEs tend to view disadvantages very similarly, while those in between these two categories saw them very differently. The differences between the different categories provide yet another insight into the heterogeneous nature of SMEs where even slight increases in business size result in variations.

## Market Focus

Three categories of SMEs had sufficient data to apply factor analysis. The results of the Kaiser-Meyer-Olkin MSA (.903 for local, .895 for national and .815 for international) and Bartlett's test for Sphericity ($\chi^2 = 598$ p=.000 for local, $\chi^2 = 501$ p=.000 for national and $\chi^2 = 288$ p=.000 for international) indicated that the data set satisfied the assumptions for factorability. Principle components analysis was chosen as the method of extraction in order

*Table 12. Total variation explained: E-commerce disadvantages and market focus (Sweden)*

| Comp | Eigenvalue | | | % Variance | | | Cumulative % | | |
|---|---|---|---|---|---|---|---|---|---|
| Market Focus | Local | National | International | Local | National | International | Local | National | International |
| 1 | 6.693 | 6.580 | 7.837 | 66.066 | 59.821 | 71.242 | 66.066 | 59.821 | 71.242 |
| 2 | | 1.035 | | | 9.411 | | | 69.232 | |

*Table 13. Rotated component matrix (local): E-commerce disadvantages (Sweden)*

| Disadvantage | Component 1 |
|---|---|
| Deteriorated relations with business partners. | .711 |
| Increased costs. | .782 |
| Increased the computer maintenance required. | .827 |
| Doubled the amount of work. | .866 |
| Reduced the flexibility of the business processes. | .795 |
| Raised security concerns. | .812 |
| Made us increasingly dependent on this technology. | .780 |

*Table 14. Rotated component matrix (national): E-commerce disadvantages (Sweden)*

| Disadvantage | Component 1: Business Practices | Component 2: Resources |
|---|---|---|
| Deteriorated relations with business partners. | .801 | |
| Increased costs. | | .772 |
| Increased the computer maintenance required. | | .722 |
| Doubled the amount of work. | .568 | .643 |
| Reduced the flexibility of the business processes. | .597 | |
| Raised security concerns. | .754 | |
| Made us increasingly dependent on this technology. | .799 | |

*Table 15. Rotated component matrix (international): E-commerce disadvantages (Sweden)*

| Disadvantage | Component 1 |
|---|---|
| Deteriorated relations with business partners. | .864 |
| Increased costs. | .846 |
| Increased the computer maintenance required. | .491 |
| Doubled the amount of work. | .909 |
| Reduced the flexibility of the business processes. | .822 |
| Raised security concerns. | .903 |
| Made us increasingly dependent on this technology. | .873 |

to account for maximum variance in the data using a minimum number of factors. A single factor solution with Eigenvalue 6.937 was chosen for local respondents. This was supported by an inspection of the Scree plot and accounted for 63.066% of the variance. A two factor solution with Eigenvalues 6.580 and 1.035 was chosen for the national respondents. This was supported by an inspection of the Scree plot and accounted for 69.232% of the variance. A single factor solution with Eigenvalue 7.837 was chosen for international respondents. This was supported by an inspection of the Scree plot and accounted for 71.242% of the variance. Table 12 provides the details.

The resulting components were rotated using the Varimax procedure and a simple structure was achieved as shown in the rotated component matrices (Tables 13 to 15).

The findings show that both the local and international respondents felt that there was a single factor underlying the disadvantages. By comparison, the national respondents considered that there were two underlying factors. For nationally focussed respondents the most important grouping of disadvantages has been those related to business practices. One disadvantage (doubling of work) was loaded onto both factors. These results are important, particularly for government agencies involved and assisting SMEs to adopt e-commerce because they stress that there are clear differences between SMEs that are trading locally, nationally, and internationally. Both local and international businesses considered that there was no real distinction between the disadvantages associated with e-commerce adoption. Those that are trading at a national level saw costs and computer maintenance as a "lesser" problem to the reduction in flexibility, security issues, dependence on e-commerce, and deterioration of relations with business partners. Clearly, any single approach to e-commerce is inadequate to all market focus groups, suggesting that certain disadvantages would be rated higher than they actually were or would be overlooked completely.

## Summary: E-Commerce Disadvantages in Swedish SMEs

In response to our first question, we found that business size and market focus mattered in the Swedish context. Indeed, larger and locally focused SMEs were affected by security issues, while a dependence on e-commerce was more likely to be experienced by the locally focused organisations. In relation to the groupings of e-commerce disadvantages, the Swedish respondents clearly clustered these according to resources problems and difficulties in their business practices. This was somewhat different for different categories of SMEs (based on the size and the market focus of the business); however, the key issues were centred around the pressures on resources and the changes in business practices. We now turn to SMEs located in Australia.

# Business Characteristics and E-Commerce Disadvantages in Australia

Once again, our first question was concerned with the effect of business characteristics on the seven e-commerce disadvantages listed in Figure 1. There were no statistically significant associations between any of the disadvantages and any of the business characteristics for the Australian data. One possibility for the lack of associations in the Australian study is the small number of adopters. An examination of the data in Chapter III shows that most of these came from the 1-9 employee group, most were B2C businesses and most were trading locally. Thus, the lack of association may be simply a function of the data collected. However, it may also imply that none of the business characteristics affect e-commerce disadvantages in Australian SMEs, specifically. Rather, they are all equally applicable. This differs from the Swedish results, described previously.

We will now take a closer look at the groupings of e-commerce disadvantages in the Australian context with the purpose of answering our second question: Are there any underlying factors or groupings of e-commerce disadvantages in Australian SMEs which would serve to explain the key problems faced by SMEs after the adopt e-commerce?

*Table 16. E-commerce disadvantages correlation matrix (Australia)*

| E-Commerce... | Deteriorated relations with our business partners. | Increased costs. | Increased the computer maintenance required. | Doubled the amount of work. | Reduced the flexibility of the business processes. | Raised security concerns. |
|---|---|---|---|---|---|---|
| Increased costs. | .208 | | | | | |
| Increased the computer maintenance required. | .278 | .804 | | | | |
| Doubled the amount of work. | .060 | .470* | .383 | | | |
| Reduced the flexibility of the business processes. | .274 | .853 | .837 | .502* | | |
| Raised security concerns. | -.070 | .362 | .455* | .037 | .389 | |
| Made us increasingly dependent on this technology. | .100 | .297 | .393 | .256 | .382 | .544** |

*Note: * significant at 0.05 level    ** significant at 0.01 level*

*Table 17. Total variance explained: E-commerce disadvantages (Australia)*

| Component | Eigenvalue | % Variance | Cumulative % |
|---|---|---|---|
| 1 | 4.898 | 37.678 | 37.678 |
| 2 | 2.501 | 19.238 | 56.916 |
| 3 | 1.344 | 10.340 | 67.255 |
| 4 | 1.009 | 7.759 | 75.015 |

*Table 18. Rotated component matrix: E-commerce disadvantages (Australia)*

| Disadvantage | Component 1: Resources & Flexibility | Component 2: Security | Component 3: Workloads | Component 4: Relationships |
|---|---|---|---|---|
| Deteriorated relations with business partners. | | | | .796 |
| Increased costs. | .906 | | | |
| Increased the computer maintenance required. | .911 | | | |
| Doubled the amount of work. | | | .704 | |
| Reduced the flexibility of the business processes. | .869 | | | |
| Raised security concerns. | | .558 | | |
| Made us increasingly dependent on this technology. | | | .603 | |

# Groupings of E-Commerce Disadvantages in Australia

To answer our second question, a combination of correlations and factor analysis was applied to the data. The results of this analysis are shown in the tables next and discussed at the end of this section.

Table 16 provides the correlation matrix of the importance ratings for e-commerce disadvantages. All correlations significant at the .001 level are shown in bold.

The results of the Kaiser-Meyer-Olkin MSA (.663) and Bartlett's test for Sphericity ($\chi^2 =$ 174, p = .000) indicated that the data set satisfied the assumptions for factorability. Principle components analysis was chosen as the method of extraction in order to account for maximum variance in the data using a minimum number of factors. A four factor solution was chosen with Eigenvalues 4.898, 2.501, 1.344, and 1.009. This was supported by an inspection of the Scree plot and accounted for 75.015% of the variance. These are shown in Table 17.

*Figure 3. E-commerce disadvantage groupings in Australia*

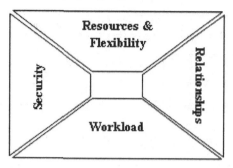

The resulting components were rotated using the Varimax procedure and a simple structure was achieved as shown in the rotated component matrix (see Table 18).

Unlike their Swedish counterparts, regional SMEs in Australia indicated four distinct groups of e-commerce disadvantages. The first, and most important group, was related to increased pressure on resources and reduced flexibility in the way the SME operated. This was rated as the most relevant factor by the Australian SMEs. The second factor was related to security concerns, and SMEs believed that e-commerce increased security risks. This is in alignment with what was reported in Chapter V where security issues were found to be a significant barrier to e-commerce adoption in Australia. The third group of disadvantages was related to workload matters, including duplication of work coupled with a dependence on e-commerce, which made it difficult for SMEs to address the issue without re-structuring their entire e-commerce strategy. The final, and least relevant factor, was related to the relationships with business partners. This was seen as a distinct disadvantage by the Australian SMEs, whereas the Swedish businesses grouped this together with other organisational problems brought about by e-commerce.

# Summary: E-Commerce Disadvantages in Australian SMEs

In the Australian context, there were no business characteristics, which showed any impact on the disadvantages experienced by SMEs after e-commerce adoption. In other words, the size or age of the business bore no influence on whether the organisation experienced increased workloads as a result of e-commerce. This suggests that Australian SMEs rated e-commerce disadvantages equally across all of the different categories. However, they did group these disadvantages into four overarching groups including problems associated with resources, workloads, security, and relationships. This implies that different types of support are required by SMEs in Australia to assist with the post-implementation phase of development.

We will now compare and discuss the key findings across the two locations.

*Table 19. Association between business characteristics and e-commerce disadvantages: A comparison*

| E-Commerce Disadvantages | Higher rating by... | |
|---|---|---|
| | Sweden | Australia |
| Raised security concerns. | Larger & local SMEs | |
| Made us increasingly dependent on this technology. | Local SMEs | None |

*Table 20. Loading of e-commerce disadvantages on different factors (groupings): A comparison*

| Disadvantages | SWEDEN | | AUSTRALIA | | | |
|---|---|---|---|---|---|---|
| | 1 Resources | 2 Business Pressures | 1 Resources & Flexibility | 2 Security | 2 Workloads | 2 Relationships |
| Deteriorated relations with business partners. | | ✓ | | | | ✓ |
| Increased costs. | ✓ | | ✓ | | | |
| Increased the computer maintenance required. | ✓ | | ✓ | | | |
| Doubled the amount of work. | | ✓ | | | ✓ | |
| Reduced the flexibility of the business processes. | | ✓ | ✓ | | | |
| Raised security concerns. | | ✓ | | ✓ | | |
| Made us increasingly dependent on this technology. | ✓ | | | | ✓ | |

# Comparison of Results: A Discussion

Once again, we see diverging patterns in the respondents' perceptions, this time in relation to e-commerce disadvantages. In Swedish SMEs, business size and market focus were found to be associated with security disadvantages (see Table 19). SMEs with more employees and a local market focus were likely to experience greater security risks, while locally focused organisations also had higher dependence on e-commerce. This is at odds with earlier findings (see Blackburn & Athayde, 2000; Fallon & Moran, 2000; Hawkins, Winter, J. & Hunter et al., 1995; Hawkins & Winter, 1996; Hyland & Matlay, 1997; Matlay, 2000). By contrast, the Australian SMEs showed no associations between business characteristics and e-commerce disadvantages. It appears that, overall, business characteristics have a greater effect on the Swedish sample in relation to e-commerce adoption. This needs to be explored further through quantitative and qualitative research.

A comparison of the findings also shows that whereas the Swedish respondents grouped their disadvantages under two factors, there was almost no grouping of disadvantages by the Australian respondents, resulting in four factors for seven disadvantages (see Table 20). Regardless of these differences, the main disadvantages were related to resourcing pressures and constraints, as well as changes to the way business is done. This is largely consistent with previous research (Lee, 2001; Stauber, 2000; Tetteh et al., 2001). Those factors to which the SMEs assigned the highest priority have been underlined in Table 20. It is clear that disadvantages related to costs and IT support (computer maintenance) are common to both the Swedish and the Australian respondents in terms of priority. This result highlights an important support element that SMEs require post-implementation.

While no attempt was made to examine sub-groups for the Australian responses, the data shows that for the Swedish respondents, groupings and priorities vary both with differing business sizes as well as different market focuses. Organisations employing between 1 to 9 and between 50 to 100 employees, and locally and internationally focused SMEs all grouped disadvantages under one factor. This is highly unusual and once again can perhaps be attributed to the stages of SME development, as discussed in the previous chapter.

## E-Commerce Disadvantages: Implications

The findings presented in this chapter serve as a realistic picture of what SMEs can expect when they implement e-commerce in the organisation. Any attempt to promote e-commerce adoption must refer to these disadvantages and ensure that there are support strategies in place to assist SMEs with managing and controlling the different problems that arise as a result of e-commerce use. The findings also serve as a somber reminder that e-commerce, like any other technology, is not a panacea and brings its own set of issues that SMEs must be prepared to deal with. In order to facilitate this, it is important that e-commerce is introduced into the organization using a planned and strategic method in the first place. This will help avoid some of the issues raised in this chapter, especially if appropriate resources are organized and business processes are re-engineered to align with an e-commerce approach. This will reduce the impact of the problems raised in this chapter and ensure that e-commerce is successfully implemented.

## E-Commerce Adoption Disadvantages: Key Findings

### Sweden

*   SMEs with more employees and those that have a local focus are more likely to rate security as an e-commerce disadvantage. Locally focussed SMEs are also likely to rate dependence on e-commerce as being more relevant to their situation.

- The disadvantages experienced by SMEs in Sweden can be reduced to two factors: resource pressures and alterations to business practices. However, when the data is split further based on business size and market focus, the results differ between very small or very large SMEs. Similarly those organisations with a local or international focus differ from businesses with a national focus.

## Australia

- None of the business characteristics were found to have any effect on e-commerce disadvantages in Australia.
- Australian SMEs experienced four groups of disadvantages: resource pressures/lower flexibility, security, increased workloads, and deteriorating relationships with business partners.

## USA

- There was insufficient data to conduct a statistical analysis of the U.S. sample.

# References

Blackburn, R., & Athayde, R. (2000). Making the connection: The effectiveness of Internet training in small businesses. *Education and Training, 42*(4/5).

Boter, H., & Lundstrom, A. (2005). SME perspectives on business supplier services. *Journal of Small Business and Entrepreneurial Development, 12*(2), 244-258.

Chellappa, R., Barua, A., & Whinston, A. (1996). Looking beyond internal corporate Web servers. In R. Kalakota & A. Whinston (Eds.), *Readings in electronic commerce* (pp. 311-321), Reading: Addison Wesley.

Doukidis, G., Poulymenakou, A., Terpsidis, I., Themisticleous, M., & Miliotis, P. (1998). *The impact of the development of electronic commerce on the employment situation in European commerce.* Report published by Athens University.

Fallon, M., & Moran, P. (2000). Information communications technology (ICT) and manufacturing SMEs. In *Proceedings of the 2000 Small Business and Enterprise Development Conference*, University of Manchester (pp. 100-109).

Giaglas G., Klein S. & O'Keefe R. (1999) Disintermediation, Reintermediation, or Cybermediation? The Future of Intermediaries in Electronic Marketplaces. *12th Bled Electronic Commerce Conference*, Bled, Slovenia, (pp 389 – 407).

Hawkins, P., & Winter, J. (1996). The self-reliant graduate and the SME. *Education and Training, 38*(4), 3-9.

Hawkins, P., Winter, J., & Hunter, J. (1995). *Skills for graduates in the 21ˢᵗ century*. Report Commissioned from the Whiteway Research, University of Cambridge, Association of Graduate Recruiters, Cambridge.

Healy, J., & DeLuca, J. M. (2000). Electronic commerce: Beyond the Euphoria. *Journal of Health Information Management*, Summer.

Henning, K. (1998). *The digital enterprise. how digitisation is redefining business*. New York: Random House Business Books.

Hyland, T., & Matlay, H. (1997). Small businesses, training needs, and VET Provisions. *Journal of Education and Work, 10*(2).

Jeffcoate, J., Chappell, C., & Feindt, S. (2002). Best practice in SME adoption of e-commerce. *Benchmarking: An International Journal, 9*(2), 122-132.

Lawrence, K. L. (1997). Factors inhibiting the utilisation of electronic commerce facilities in Tasmanian small-to-medium sized enterprises. In *Proceedings of the 8ᵗʰ Australasian Conference on Information Systems* (pp. 587-597).

Lee, C. S. (2001). An analytical framework for evaluating e-commerce business models and strategies. *Internet Research: Electronic Network Applications and Policy, 11*(4), 349-359.

MacGregor, R. C., Bunker, D. J., & Waugh, P. (1998). Electronic commerce and small/medium enterprises (SME's) in Australia: An electronic data interchange (EDI) pilot study. In *Proceedings of the 11ᵗʰ International Bled Electronic Commerce Conference*, Slovenia.

Matlay. H. (2000). Training in the small business sector of the British economy. In S. Carter & D. Jones (Eds.), *Enterprise and small business: Principles, policy, and practice*. London: Addison Wesley Longman.

Poon, S., & Swatman, P. (1997). The Internet for small businesses: An enabling infrastructure. In *Proceedings of the 5ᵗʰ Internet Society Conference* (pp. 221-231).

Raymond, L. (2001). Determinants of Web site implementation in small business. *Internet Research: Electronic Network Applications and Policy, 11*(5), 411-422.

Ritchie, R., & Brindley, C. (2000). Disintermediation, disintegration, and risk in the SME global supply chain. *Management Decision, 38*(8), 575-583

Sparkes, A., & Thomas, B. (2001). The use of the Internet as a critical success factor for the marketing of Welsh Agri-food SMEs in the Twenty First Century. *British Food Journal, 103*(4), 331-347.

Stauber, A. (2000). *A survey of the incorporation of electronic commerce in Tasmanian small and medium sized enterprises*. Tasmanian Electronic Commerce Centre, 37pp.

Tetteh, E., & Burn, J. (2001). Global strategies for SME-business: Applying the SMALL framework. *Logistics Information Management, 14*(1-2), 171-180.

**Chapter VIII**

# Strategic Alliances and E-Commerce Adoption:
## Does Partnering with Other SMEs Affect E-Commerce Adoption?

In the previous four chapters, we examined four different aspects of e-commerce adoption in some detail. The drivers, barriers, benefits, and disadvantages of e-commerce adoption were analysed across the three locations with mixed results, indicating that the SME sector is far from homogeneous. In the subsequent three chapters, we will study the effects of three business characteristics on e-commerce adoption, namely whether the SME belongs to a strategic alliance, the gender of the CEO, and the education level of the CEO. Our research has found a number of interactions between these characteristics and e-commerce adoption, and we will now examine these in detail, beginning with strategic alliance membership.

## Background

In the late 1990s, a number of Western governments (see Blair, 2000; European Commission, 2000), realising that e-commerce might be a mechanism whereby SMEs might gain a larger share of the marketplace, thus increasing employment and reducing trade deficits, developed a variety of initiatives to encourage SMEs to become "wired to the marketplace." These initiatives consisted of a series of step-wise strategies through which an SME might move in order to achieve e-commerce adoption and use. Together with these steps were a set of benefits deemed achievable through the adoption of e-commerce. In most cases, these government initiatives were prefaced with the view that SMEs should cluster or form strategic alliances such that they may pool resources and knowledge in order to compete with larger businesses in the marketplace.

However, the development of strategic alliances has been criticised in the literature because it failed to adequately consider the effects of various business characteristics on the formation of alliances or networks. Indeed, the view that SMEs, which belonged to alliances would be able to compete with large businesses is based on the incorrect assumption that SMEs are really "small large businesses," which is clearly not the case. Under such models, business characteristics such as business size, business age, business sector, geographic location, and level of internationalisation are simply removed and replaced by the simplistic notion that all SMEs are intent on gaining a proportion of the global market share. Furthermore, such an approach fails to take into account substantial research (Hadjimonolis, 1999; Lawrence, 1997; MacGregor & Bunker, 1996; Quayle, 2002; Westhead & Storey, 1996; Walczuch, Van Braven, & Lundgren, 2000), which suggests that many SMEs have little desire to reach a wider marketplace either alone or in some form of an alliance. Thus, while strategic alliances might be a valuable source of technical or marketing information (see Copp & Ivy, 2001; Jarratt, 1998; O'Donnell, Gilmore, Cummins, & Carson, 2001; Tetteh & Burn, 2001), this does not presuppose that such alliances are part of any attempt to reach global markets or are part of the decision making process for the adoption of e-commerce.

The criticisms having been noted, we will now examine the nature and role of SME strategic alliances in e-commerce adoption.

# The Role of Strategic Alliances

It could be argued that by the very nature of business, all organisations relate to others and are thus part of some form of cluster or alliance arrangement. On the surface, these relationships may appear to be nothing more than exchanges of goods and payments but relationships with customers, suppliers, and competitors can never be simply described in terms of financial transactions. Dennis (2000) suggests that any dealing with other organisations must impinge on the decision making process even if these decisions only involve the strengthening or relaxing of the relationships themselves. Nalebuff and Brandenburg (1996) state that for a relationship to be truly an alliance it must be conscious, interdependent, and cooperating toward a predetermined set of goals.

Viewed then as "self designing" partnerships, Eccles and Crane (1998, *cited in* Dennis 2000), suggest that strategic alliances are a dynamic arrangement evolving and adjusting to accommodate changes in the business environment. Achrol and Kotler (1999) take this a step further by stating that strategic alliances:

*... are more adaptable and flexible because of loose coupling and openness to information. Environmental disturbances transfer imperfectly through loose coupled networks and tend to dissipate in intensity as they spread through the system.* (p. 147)

Thus, member organisations have interconnected linkages that allow more efficient movement toward predetermined objectives than would be the case if they operated as a single separate entity. By developing and organising functional components, strategic alliances/clusters provide a better mechanism to learn and adapt to changes in their environment.

In addition to providing much needed information, alliances often provide legitimacy to their members. For businesses that provide a service and whose products are intangible, company image and reputation becomes crucial since customers can rarely test or inspect the service before purchase. Cropper (1996) suggests that alliance or cluster membership very often supplies this image to potential customers.

The advent of e-commerce technology has given rise to a "new wave" of research examining the role of strategic alliances, particularly in SMEs. Much of this research has been prompted by the realisation that old hierarchical forms of organisation produced relationships, which are too tightly coupled (Marchewka & Towell, 2000), and do not fit an often turbulent marketplace (Overby & Min, 2000; Tikkanen, 1998).

There are many definitions of alliances in the literature. Dennis (2000) suggests that they:

*... are dynamic arrangement (sic) that are constantly evolving and adjusting in order to accommodate changes in the business environment. Member companies have interconnected linkages that allow them to move more efficiently toward set objectives than those operating as a separate entity.* (p. 287)

She adds that while all companies form relationships with suppliers, customers, and other partners, it is the extent of the closeness, interdependence, and consciousness of these relationships that determines whether they are truly part of an alliance. This definition implies that only those interorganisational links that have formal governance can be termed strategic alliances. By comparison, Yeung (1994) defines an alliance as:

*... an integrated and coordinated set of ongoing economic and non-economic relations embedded within, among and outside business firms.* (p. 476)

Thus for Yeung, an alliance is not only a structure but embodies processes between organisations. These processes may be formal economic processes or may be informal cooperative relationships, sharing expertise, and know-how. Indeed, Dahlstrand (1999) suggests that informal links may be conscious or unconscious mechanisms.

While recent studies (Keeble, Lawson, Moore, & Wilkinson, 1999; O'Donnell et al., 2001; Overby et al., 2001) stress the importance of informal interorganisational links, the definition of these links in SMEs varies widely. As this chapter has as its focus SME alliances with some implied form of governance (be they organisationally linked SMEs or firms who have made use of SME associations), the definition provided by Achrol et al. (1999) will be adopted, viz:

*... an independent coalition of task- or skill-specialised economic entities (independent firms or autonomous organisational units) that operates without hierarchical control but is embedded by dense lateral connections, mutuality, and reciprocity, in a shared value system that defines "membership" roles and responsibilities.* (p. 148)

As with the origin and definition of alliances, there are a number of differing taxonomies in the literature. These taxonomies are normally based on the structure, processes, or power of strategic alliances.

Veradarajan and Cunningham (1995) suggest that clusters or alliances can be subdivided into four groups based on *structure*, as follows:

1. **Functional alliances:** These link functional aspects of organisations that result in joint manufacturing, marketing, or product development. These tend to share knowledge, information, and resources.

2. **Intra-interorganisational alliances:** These are based on developing relationships either nationally or internationally. These share information.

3. **Intra-inter-industry alliances:** These are developed by building relationships through resource pooling. These share resources.

4. **Motivational alliances:** These take place through the sharing of marketing and technological know-how. These tend only to share knowledge.

Whereas Veradarajan et al. (1995) subdivided clusters or alliances in terms of structure, Johannisson, Ramirez-Pasillas, and Karlsson (2002) suggest that they can be subdivided into four groups based on *processes*. The four groups are:

1. **Resource-based**, where each firm controls their own unique resources which are combined to strategic advantage

2. **Industrial**, where firms are autonomous entities establishing their own unique market position

3. **Virtual organisations** with independent yet interdependent organisations striving for joint variety using advanced technology

4. **Industrial district** where small firms characterised by production type are organised for internal cooperation and external competition

Achrol et al. (1999) also suggested that clusters or alliances can be subdivided in terms of process. They provide the following four groups:

1.   **Internal:** Designed to reduce hierarchy and open firms to the environment
2.   **Vertical:** Clusters that maximise the productivity of serially dependent functions by creating partnerships among independent skill-specialised firms
3.   **Intermarket:** Clusters that seek to leverage horizontal synergies across industries
4.   **Opportunity:** Clusters that are organised around customer needs and market opportunities and are designed to seek the best solutions to them

Dennis (2000) considers *power* to be the most important factor upon which to classify alliances. She provides two classifications:

1.   **Dominated,** where a group of smaller companies is dominated by a single larger company
2.   **Equal partner,** where there is no governing partner and each relationship is based on reciprocal, preferential, mutually supportive actions

An obvious bi-product of different alliance or cluster taxonomies is the analysis of organisations, which form the various types. Golden and Dollinger (1993) in an exploration of business relationships concluded that "differences in strategic postures are associated with differences in the quality and type of intraorganisational relationships" (p. 52). This is particularly apparent in smaller organisations. Jarratt (1998) suggests that particular strategic postures lead organisations to adopt particular alliance forms. She suggested that there were four distinct categories of strategic posture, termed:

1.   **Defenders,** who were more likely to select conjugate relationships
2.   **Prospectors,** who were more likely to select confederate relationships
3.   **Analysers,** who were more likely to select agglomerate relationships
4.   **Reactors,** whose business relationships were unpredictable

Miles, Preece, and Baetz (1999) suggest that for SMEs, the decision to join an alliance comes from a perception of goals by the individual organisation. If the organisation sees itself as strong in its own right, an alliance may be seen as an option to increase that strength. The distribution of power moves in favour of the strong organisation allowing it to capitalise and influence weaker members without losing its own identity.

If, on the other hand, the organisation sees itself as weak, an alliance may be a necessity in order to survive and compete in the larger marketplace. For these organisations, the distribution of power works away from them leaving them in a weak position in exchange relationships.

This of course varies from alliance to alliance. In a small alliance (few participating organisations) there is more likely to be an asymmetric relationship between partners. As the size of the alliance increases, there are a greater number of potential partners providing a greater chance to benefit for all members.

Properly utilised, formal alliances can provide a number of advantages over stand-alone organisations. These include the sharing of financial risk (Jorde & Teece, 1989), technical knowledge (Marchewka et al., 2000), market penetration (Achrol et al., 1999), and internal efficiency (Datta, 1988).

Early studies of SME alliances (Gibb, 1993; Ozcan, 1995) concentrated on formal alliances, and concluded that few small firms were able to function without some form of inter-organisational relationship having been established (Golden et al., 1993). They added that these inter-organisational relationships were associated with successful strategic adaptation by SMEs, and the pooling of resources to achieve economies of scale (Dean, Holmes, & Smith, 1997).

In the 1990s, many SME alliances took a more semi-formal approach. Local or government agencies such as SME associations/clubs and chambers of commerce provided a formal umbrella in the form of advisory services that assisted in legal, financial, training, or technical advice. Individual members operated formally with the umbrella organisation but could interact informally with fellow members. Recent literature (Premaratne, 2001) suggests that informal or social linkages may provide a higher and more stable flow of information and resources in the SME environment.

## The Role of Alliances E-Commerce Adoption

As already mentioned, the advent of e-commerce has given rise to a number of research initiatives examining the role of SME strategic alliances or clusters in the adoption of e-commerce.

A study by Wheelen and Hunger (2002) found that membership of some form of alliance allowed businesses to concentrate on their distinctive competencies while gathering efficiencies from the other firms in the cluster, who, likewise, were concentrating their efforts in their own areas of expertise. They found this particularly applicable to the adoption and use of e-commerce. Cirillo (2000) and Terziovski (2003) found that membership of a strategic alliance allowed functions such as supply chain management and logistics to be managed more easily than stand-alone businesses, and the utilisation of e-commerce technology facilitates this.

A number of studies in the UK and Europe (Ciappei & Simoni, 2005; Daniel, Wilson, & Myers, 2002b; Daniel & Wilson, 2002a) have shown that greater success with e-commerce use appears to occur through membership of a strategic alliance. These results have been mirrored in the U.S. (Singh & Gilchrist, 2002), while a recent study comparing strategically aligned and stand-alone SMEs (MacGregor & Vrazalic, 2005) showed that while there were no significant differences in benefits enjoyed by both groups, membership of a strategic alliance appeared to "dampen" the problems incurred through e-commerce, compared to stand-alone businesses.

# Research Questions

Our aim in this chapter is to explore the issues related to strategic alliances and e-commerce in several ways. First, we will examine whether strategic alliance membership is associated with any business characteristics (such as business age, business size, business sector, gender of the CEO, educational level of the CEO, level of IT skill within the business, the existence of an enterprise-wide business system, product planning, market focus, or type of e-commerce). Our aim is to find out whether certain types of SMEs are more likely to seek out membership of a strategic alliance.

Secondly, the chapter aims to determine whether the importance assigned to e-commerce adoption criteria, e-commerce barriers, or e-commerce benefits or disadvantages differs between members of a strategic alliances and stand-alone businesses.

Thirdly, our aim is to determine whether the groupings and priorities of criteria for adoption, barriers to adoption, or e-commerce benefits and disadvantages differ between members of a strategic alliance and stand-alone businesses. Subsequently, the chapter is organised based on the following three questions:

1.  Are certain types of SMEs more likely to seek out membership of a strategic alliance?

2.  Are there any differences between stand alone SMEs and SMEs that are members of a strategic alliance in relation to e-commerce adoption criteria, barriers, benefits and disadvantages?

3.  Do the groupings of e-commerce adoption criteria, barriers, benefits and disadvantages differ between strategic alliance members and non-members?

# Methodology

Respondents in all three locations were asked to indicate whether they belonged to any form of alliance. Chapter III provided a summary of the responses to this question. These are replicated next for the benefit of the reader.

Table 1 shows that Sweden led the way in alliances between SMEs with the largest percentage (40%) of respondents who were in an alliance with other organisation coming from Sweden. By contrast, the U.S. had the lowest number of alliance members. However, interestingly, Sweden was also the only location where the number of alliance members who had not adopted e-commerce exceeded those that were using e-commerce.

A series of chi-square tests was then carried out to examine whether membership or non-membership of an alliance was associated with business characteristics (business age, business size, business sector, gender of the CEO, educational level of the CEO, level of IT skill within the business, the existence or non-existence of an enterprise-wide business system, product planning, market focus, or e-commerce type) in order to answer the first research question. This was followed by a series of two-tailed t-tests in order to answer

*Table 1. Summary of responses to alliance membership question*

| | | Sweden | | Australia | | USA | |
|---|---|---|---|---|---|---|---|
| | | **TOTAL RESPONDENTS** | | | | | |
| | | No of responses | % | No of responses | % | No of responses | % |
| | Yes | 124 | 39.6 | 44 | 27.5 | 25 | 21.6 |
| | No | 177 | 56.5 | 116 | 72.5 | 87 | 75 |
| | Missing | 12 | 3.8 | 0 | 0 | 4 | 3.4 |
| | | **E-COMMERCE ADOPTERS** | | | | | |
| | | No of responses | % | No of responses | % | No of responses | % |
| | Yes | 61 | 33.3 | 10 | 40 | 19 | 30.2 |
| | No | 115 | 62.8 | 15 | 60 | 42 | 66.7 |
| | Missing | 7 | 3.8 | 0 | 0 | 2 | 3.2 |
| | | **NON-ADOPTERS** | | | | | |
| | | No of responses | % | No of responses | % | No of responses | % |
| | Yes | 63 | 48.5 | 34 | 25.2 | 6 | 11.3 |
| | No | 62 | 47.7 | 101 | 74.8 | 45 | 84.9 |
| | Missing | 5 | 3.8 | 0 | 0 | 2 | 3.8 |

the second question, and finally factor analysis was applied to determine the answer to the third research question.

The rest of this chapter is structured as follows. First, we will examine the associations between different business characteristics and strategic alliance membership in all three locations. Then we will present the results of the two-tailed t-tests in each location and finally, the results of the factor analysis. The final part of the chapter will discuss and compare the findings, and present the business implications of the results.

# Business Characteristics and Strategic Alliance Membership

This section presents the results of the chi-square tests, which were applied to determine whether there were any associations between business characteristics and alliance membership. Since we have presented this information previously in Chapter III, the relevant tables will be replicated here and discussed together for each location. There were no associations found in the Australian sample.

# Sweden

There were four associations between various business characteristics and alliance membership in Sweden. In addition to this, we also found an association between e-commerce adoption and alliance membership in Sweden. These results are shown in Tables 2 to 6.

*Table 2. Association between business age and membership of an alliance*

| Alliance Membership | Yes | No |
|---|---|---|
| Age | | |
| Less than 1 year | 1 | 3 |
| 1 to 2 years | 6 | 7 |
| 3 to 5 years | 18 | 22 |
| 6 to 10 years | 24 | 33 |
| 10 to 20 years | 34 | 34 |
| More than 20 years | 37 | 78 |
| TOTAL 301 | 124 | 177 |

*Note: 12 missing; p<.001*

*Table 3. Association between business size and membership of an alliance*

| Alliance Membership | Yes | No |
|---|---|---|
| Size | | |
| Sole owner | 25 | 15 |
| 1 to 9 employees | 67 | 72 |
| 10 to 19 employees | 13 | 33 |
| 20 to 49 employees | 10 | 29 |
| 50 to 199 employees | 8 | 20 |
| More than 200 employees | 0 | 8 |
| TOTAL 300 | 123 | 177 |

*Note: 13 missing; p<.005*

*Table 4. Association between membership of an alliance and level of CEO education*

| Alliance Membership | Yes | No |
|---|---|---|
| Level of CEO Education | | |
| No Formal Education | 14 | 23 |
| Formal Education | 104 | 152 |
| TOTAL 293 | 118 | 175 |

*Note: 20 missing; p<.05*

*Table 5. Association between membership of an alliance and existence of an enterprise-wide system*

| Alliance Membership | Yes | No |
|---|---|---|
| Enterprise-Wide System | | |
| Yes | 57 | 123 |
| No | 67 | 54 |
| TOTAL 301 | 124 | 177 |

*Note: 12 missing; p<.001*

*Table 6. Association between alliance membership and adoption of e-commerce*

| Alliance Membership | E-Commerce Adopters | Non-Adopters |
|---|---|---|
| Yes | 61 | 63 |
| No | 115 | 62 |
| TOTAL 301 | 176 | 125 |

*Note: 12 missing; p<.005*

The previous results highlight the influence of four business characteristics, namely business age, size, level of CEO education, and existence of an enterprise-wide system on alliance membership. The tables indicate that older SMEs tend to shy away from entering into networks or alliances with other businesses. An explanation for this can perhaps be found in the stages of SME development, where more established SMEs consider themselves to be self-sufficient in terms of resources and are reluctant to share their expertise with the competition. In contrast, younger SMEs tend to seek out alliances in order to pool resources and fill functional gaps in the organisation. The data also shows that smaller SMEs are more likely to follow suit. Once again, it is the larger organisations, which do not stand to gain as much from alliances since they are better resourced. This supports a number of earlier studies (Achrol et al., 1999; Dean et al., 1997). There was a more ambiguous interaction between alliance membership and the level of the CEO's education. Both formally educated and unqualified CEO's were equally likely to enter into an alliance arrangement. Interestingly, it was the non-members that were more likely to have an enterprise-wide system in their organisation. One possibility for this, supported by the literature (Keeble et al., 1999; O'Donnell et al., 2001; Overby et al., 2001; Tikkanen, 1998) is that those respondents that did not have any form of enterprise-wide business system had sought membership of an alliance to gain the necessary experience and assistance in order to develop their business further.

Finally, we found an association between alliance membership and e-commerce adoption. However, while 50% of e-commerce non-adopters were members of an alliance, only 35% of the adopters had entered into this arrangement. Despite suggestions that becoming members of an alliance would promote e-commerce adoption, the results in Sweden indicate that this is not necessarily the case. One explanation is that regional SMEs find it more difficult to develop strategic alliances because of distance concerns. This conclusion is supported by studies carried out by Dennis (2000) and Drakopoulou-Dodd, Jack, and Anderson (2002).

## USA

One association was found between business size and alliance membership in the U.S. study. This is shown in Table 7.

Unlike Sweden where the smaller sized SMEs were benefiting from alliance membership, in the U.S. context it is the "middle sized" SMEs (10 to 49 employees) that are more likely to seek out membership. Once again, however, we see a reluctance by larger SMEs to pursue this arrangement.

We also found an association between alliance membership and e-commerce adoption in the U.S. This is shown in Table 8.

Although the number of e-commerce adopters who were alliance members in the U.S. was comparable to that of Sweden (31%), the findings for the non-adopters are in contrast to Sweden where 50% of non-adopters are alliance members. In the U.S., only 12% of those SMEs that had not adopted e-commerce joined an alliance. This would suggest that Swedish regional SMEs are more interested in partnering with their counterparts that SMEs in the U.S.

We now turn to examine whether there are any statistically significant differences between the alliance members and non-members in relation to e-commerce criteria, barriers, benefits, and disadvantages.

*Table 7. Association between membership of an alliance and business size*

| Membership | Yes | No |
|---|---|---|
| Business Size | | |
| Sole owner | 0 | 3 |
| 1 to 9 employees | 4 | 43 |
| 10 to 19 employees | 9 | 17 |
| 20 to 49 employees | 11 | 18 |
| 50 to 199 employees | 0 | 4 |
| More than 200 employees | 1 | 2 |
| TOTAL 112 | 25 | 87 |

*Note: 4 missing; p<.05*

*Table 8. Association between membership of an alliance and adoption of e-commerce*

| Membership of a Alliance | E-Commerce Adopters | Non-adopters |
|---|---|---|
| Yes | 19 | 6 |
| No | 42 | 45 |
| TOTAL 112 | 61 | 51 |

*Note: 4 missing; p<.05*

# Strategic Alliances and E-Commerce Adoption

Our second research question was concerned with the differences between alliance members and non-members in terms of their ratings of various e-commerce aspects. To find out if any such differences existed, the data was subdivided for each location into members and non-members. A series of two-tailed t-tests was then applied to the data to determine if there were any statistically significant differences in the ratings of e-commerce adoption criteria, barriers to adoption, benefits derived from e-commerce adoption, or disadvantages incurred through adoption of e-commerce. The results are discussed next.

## Sweden

Table 9 provides the results of the two-tailed t-tests for criteria to adopt e-commerce. The data shows that for the Swedish regional SME respondents, there were no statistically significant differences between member and non-member respondents for any criteria of

Table 9. Comparison of e-commerce adoption criteria (alliance members vs. non-members): Sweden

| Criteria | Mean Members | N Members | Mean Non-Members | N Non-Members | t value | Significance |
|---|---|---|---|---|---|---|
| Demand and/or pressure from customers. | 1.82 | 61 | 2.10 | 115 | 1.241 | .216 |
| Pressure from competition. | 2.10 | 61 | 2.34 | 115 | 1.011 | .313 |
| Demand and/or pressure from suppliers. | 1.61 | 61 | 1.71 | 115 | .522 | .602 |
| To reduce costs. | 3.03 | 61 | 3.00 | 115 | -.126 | .899 |
| To improve customer service. | 3.64 | 61 | 3.64 | 115 | .016 | .987 |
| To shorten lead time/reduce stock levels. | 2.44 | 61 | 2.59 | 115 | .549 | .584 |
| To increase sales. | 2.70 | 61 | 2.98 | 115 | 1.040 | .300 |
| To improve internal efficiency. | 3.38 | 61 | 3.71 | 115 | 1.316 | .191 |
| To strengthen relations with business partners. | 2.69 | 61 | 2.98 | 115 | 1.169 | .244 |
| The possibility of reaching new customers/markets. | 2.84 | 61 | 2.91 | 115 | .283 | .777 |
| To improve our competitiveness. | 2.97 | 61 | 3.42 | 115 | 1.587 | .115 |
| We were offered external support to adopt e-commerce. | 1.16 | 61 | 1.42 | 115 | 1.555 | .122 |
| To improve our marketing. | 2.72 | 61 | 3.01 | 115 | 1.027 | .306 |
| To improve control. | 2.25 | 61 | 2.72 | 115 | 1.884 | .061 |

adoption of e-commerce. In other words, both alliance members and stand-alone businesses viewed e-commerce adoption criteria in the same way.

A number of authors (Singh et al., 2002; Terziovski, 2003; Wheelen et al., 2002) have suggested that strategic alliances "shape" SMEs such that e-commerce adoption and use is made easier, and ultimately more successful. At first glance, the findings in Table 9 would tend to refute these earlier claims, however, it must be noted that in Sweden there is a conscious pro-active approach by the government to link SMEs to educational institutions with the express purpose of assisting in entrepreneurial activities including e-commerce adoption. It is argued that the lack of differences may be attributed to that intervention

Table 10 provides the data for the barriers to e-commerce adoption.

A number of previous studies (Cirillo, 2000; Daniel et al., 2002a; Terziovski, 2003) suggest that membership of an alliance reduces barriers to e-commerce adoption by providing the necessary organisational and technical expertise to the members. However, an examination of Table 10 shows that, when comparing the means, nine of the ten barriers are rated higher by member respondents than they are by non-members. One possible explanation is that through membership of a business alliance, respondents are better placed to fully appreciate e-commerce and the potential barriers to its adoption than stand-alone businesses.

Table 10 shows that two barriers ("E-commerce is not suited to our products/services" and "E-commerce does not offer any advantages to our organisation") showed a statistically

Table 10. Comparison of e-commerce adoption barriers (alliance members vs. non-members): Sweden

| Barriers | Mean Members | N Members | Mean Non-Members | N Non-Members | t value | Significance |
|---|---|---|---|---|---|---|
| E-commerce is not suited to our products/services. | 3.14 | 63 | 2.27 | 62 | -2.597 | .011 |
| E-commerce is not suited to our way of doing business. | 2.92 | 63 | 2.27 | 62 | -1.949 | .054 |
| E-commerce is not suited to the ways our clients do business. | 2.65 | 63 | 2.47 | 62 | .542 | .589 |
| E-commerce does not offer any advantages to our organisation. | 2.86 | 63 | 1.81 | 62 | -3.408 | .001 |
| We do not have the technical knowledge in the organisation to implement e-commerce. | 2.84 | 63 | 2.21 | 62 | -1.937 | .055 |
| E-commerce is too complicated to implement. | 2.11 | 63 | 1.77 | 62 | -1.169 | .245 |
| E-commerce is not secure. | 2.29 | 63 | 1.84 | 62 | -1.541 | .126 |
| The financial investment required to implement e-commerce is too high. | 2.38 | 63 | 2.05 | 62 | -1.069 | .287 |
| We do not have time to implement e-commerce. | 2.33 | 63 | 2.52 | 62 | .557 | .579 |
| It is difficult to choose the most suitable e-commerce standard with so many different options available. | 2.41 | 63 | 2.11 | 62 | -.907 | .366 |

significant difference in rating of importance between member respondents and non-member respondents, which suggest that alliance members and stand-alone SMEs have divergent views about these two barriers.

This is an important premise. Many authors, whether consciously or unconsciously, suggest that reduction of barriers is a positive result, while the opposite is negative. The wide range of businesses in any regional, or, indeed, metropolitan setting will always include those for whom e-commerce is not suitable. If membership of an alliance convinces some businesses that adoption of e-commerce is a retrograde step, this should not be seen as negative, but a positive affirmation that certain technologies do not suit certain businesses. Unfortunately, as Taylor & Murphy (2004) suggested, many advocates of e-commerce see that linking of businesses to the Internet is the only way to sustain economic growth. Clearly, for many businesses this may not be a positive step.

Table 11 provides the data for the benefits derived from e-commerce adoption and use.

A number of studies (Daniel et al., 2002a; Daniel et al., 2002b; Ciappei et al., 2005; Singh et al., 2002) have shown that SMEs that are part of some form of alliance benefit more from the adoption and use of e-commerce than those that stand-alone. An examination of Table 11 shows that for the regional Swedish SME respondents this appears not to be the case as there are no significant differences between members and non-members when it comes to e-commerce benefits. Again, this must be taken in the context of the government's actions in the regional SME sector. While many of these benefits may have been achieved by the respondents, they may have been achieved through educational means rather than through alliance membership.

Finally, Table 12 provides the data for disadvantages incurred through the adoption and use of e-commerce.

*Table 11. Comparison of e-commerce benefits (alliance members vs. non-members): Sweden*

| Benefits | Mean Members | N Members | Mean Non-Members | N Non-Members | t value | Significance |
|---|---|---|---|---|---|---|
| Reduced our administration costs. | 2.85 | 61 | 2.76 | 115 | -.384 | .701 |
| Reduced our production costs. | 2.64 | 61 | 2.80 | 115 | .300 | .765 |
| Reduced our lead time. | 2.15 | 61 | 2.11 | 115 | -.148 | .882 |
| Reduced our stock levels. | 2.82 | 61 | 2.75 | 115 | -.271 | .787 |
| Lead to increased sales. | 1.85 | 61 | 2.06 | 115 | .847 | .398 |
| Increased our internal efficiency. | 2.51 | 61 | 2.43 | 115 | -.341 | .733 |
| Improved our relations with business partners. | 2.57 | 61 | 2.87 | 115 | 1.208 | .229 |
| Gave us access to new customers and markets. | 2.56 | 61 | 2.50 | 115 | -.244 | .808 |
| Improved our competitiveness. | 2.67 | 61 | 2.95 | 115 | 1.106 | .270 |
| Improved the quality of information in our organisation. | 2.92 | 61 | 2.90 | 115 | -.082 | .934 |

*Table 12. Comparison of e-commerce disadvantages (alliance members vs. non-members): Sweden*

| Disadvantages | Mean Members | N Members | Mean Non-Members | N Non-Members | t value | Significance |
|---|---|---|---|---|---|---|
| Deteriorated relations with business partners. | 1.16 | 61 | 1.29 | 115 | .886 | .388 |
| Increased costs. | 1.59 | 61 | 1.98 | 115 | 1.917 | .057 |
| Increased the computer maintenance required. | 1.89 | 61 | 2.24 | 115 | 1.691 | .093 |
| Doubled the amount of work. | 1.59 | 61 | 1.94 | 115 | 1.863 | .064 |
| Reduced the flexibility of the business processes. | 1.44 | 61 | 1.83 | 115 | 2.152 | .033 |
| Raised security concerns. | 1.05 | 61 | 1.25 | 115 | 1.673 | .096 |
| Made us increasingly dependent on this technology. | 1.16 | 61 | 1.41 | 115 | 1.729 | .086 |

An examination of Table 12 shows that one disadvantage (reduced flexibility of work) showed a statistically significant difference between member and non-member respondents. While both sets of respondents rated the disadvantage as fairly unimportant, respondents that were not members of an alliance perceived this disadvantage as being more important than member respondents. A number of studies (Dennis, 2000; Overby et al., 2000) have suggested that membership in an alliance dissipates difficulties and disadvantages for their members. For the disadvantage of reduced flexibility of work, this appears to be the case.

## Summary of Findings: Sweden

Our results indicate that there are no differences between alliance members and non-members when it comes to e-commerce adoption criteria and benefits. This suggests that being a member of an alliance does not necessarily imply a different set of drivers would be applicable, or that a different set of benefits would be experienced. Subsequently, where advantages are concerned, being an alliance member does not necessarily mean more benefits from e-commerce.

There are however, differences between e-commerce barriers and disadvantages. Swedish SMEs, which were members of an alliance, rated two barriers as being more important than stand-alone organisations. These two barriers were related to the unsuitability of e-commerce to the business' products/services and to the lack of advantages from e-commerce, and were related more highly by alliance members than non-members.

Swedish businesses, which our alliance members did not experience fewer e-commerce disadvantages than their stand-alone counterparts, except in relation to the flexibility of work. Members assigned a slightly lower rating to reduced work flexibility than non-members, implying that e-commerce had not significantly decreased their ability to adapt to changes.

We now turn to the results of the Australian study, where the same statistical analysis has been applied.

# Australia

Table 13 provides the results of the two-tailed t-tests for e-commerce adoption criteria in the Australian context. Unlike the Swedish respondents, where no significant differences were found, in the Australian respondents' group there were statistically significant differences in the ratings of importance of four adoption criteria (pressure from competition, access to new customers and markets, improvements to competitiveness, and the availability of external support) between members of an alliance and non-members. In all cases, those that were not members of an alliance rated these higher in importance than those that were members. One possible explanation, supported by previous studies (Jorde et al., 1989; Marchewka et al., 2000) is that many of the criteria for e-commerce adoption had been achieved through

*Table 13. Comparison of e-commerce adoption criteria (alliance members vs. non-members): Australia*

| Criteria | Mean Members | N Members | Mean Non-Members | N Non-Members | t value | Significance |
|---|---|---|---|---|---|---|
| Demand and/or pressure from customers. | 1.90 | 10 | 3.20 | 15 | -1.983 | .059 |
| Pressure from competition. | 1.40 | 10 | 3.53 | 15 | -4.290 | .000 |
| Demand and/or pressure from suppliers. | 1.80 | 10 | 1.73 | 15 | .096 | .924 |
| To reduce costs. | 3.50 | 10 | 3.47 | 15 | .047 | .963 |
| To improve customer service. | 3.20 | 10 | 4.00 | 15 | -1.362 | .186 |
| To shorten lead time/reduce stock levels. | 2.10 | 10 | 2.93 | 15 | -1.255 | .223 |
| To increase sales. | 2.70 | 10 | 4.13 | 15 | -2.135 | .051 |
| To improve internal efficiency. | 3.20 | 10 | 4.13 | 15 | -1.352 | .205 |
| To strengthen relations with business partners. | 1.00 | 10 | 1.00 | 15 | 0 | 1.000 |
| The possibility of reaching new customers/markets. | 2.50 | 10 | 4.13 | 15 | -2.349 | .038 |
| To improve our competitiveness. | 2.60 | 10 | 4.20 | 15 | -2.238 | .048 |
| We were offered external support to adopt e-commerce. | 1.40 | 10 | 2.07 | 15 | -2.991 | .008 |
| To improve our marketing. | 2.90 | 10 | 3.73 | 15 | -1.310 | .203 |
| To improve control. | 2.80 | 10 | 3.73 | 15 | -1.415 | .182 |

*Table 14. Comparison of e-commerce adoption barriers (alliance members vs. non-members): Australia*

| Barriers | Mean Members | N Members | Mean Non-Members | N Non-Members | t value | Significance |
|---|---|---|---|---|---|---|
| E-commerce is not suited to our products/services. | 3.01 | 34 | 3.03 | 101 | -.069 | .945 |
| E-commerce is not suited to our way of doing business. | 3.19 | 34 | 3.22 | 101 | -.119 | .905 |
| E-commerce is not suited to the ways our clients do business. | 3.42 | 34 | 3.07 | 101 | 1.252 | .212 |
| E-commerce does not offer any advantages to our organisation. | 2.74 | 34 | 3.11 | 101 | -1.694 | .091 |
| We do not have the technical knowledge in the organisation to implement e-commerce. | 3.04 | 34 | 3.08 | 101 | -.178 | .859 |
| E-commerce is too complicated to implement. | 2.71 | 34 | 2.94 | 101 | -1.048 | .296 |
| E-commerce is not secure. | 2.55 | 34 | 2.71 | 101 | -.793 | .429 |
| The financial investment required to implement e-commerce is too high. | 2.51 | 34 | 3.07 | 101 | -2.666 | .008 |
| We do not have time to implement e-commerce. | 2.86 | 34 | 3.06 | 101 | -.735 | .563 |
| It is difficult to choose the most suitable e-commerce standard with so many different options available. | 2.51 | 34 | 2.77 | 101 | -.842 | .401 |

membership of the alliance. This, however, raises the question as to why other criteria failed to show any statistically significant differences.

While not significant, 12 of the 14 criteria examined showed a higher level of importance amongst non-member respondents. Those that did not show this difference (reduced costs and stronger relations with business partners) were almost identically rated by both groups. The criterion related to stronger relations with partners has been rated "universally" as not very important (1). This very clearly shows that, at least for the Australian adopters of e-commerce, there is a unanimous desire to remain totally independent of any other business. This does, however, raise the question as to why at least some respondents had decided to become members of an alliance.

Table 14 provides the data for barriers to e-commerce adoption.

The results show that the perception of importance of one barrier (high investment), showed a statistically significant difference between respondents that were members of an alliance and respondents that were not. The data shows that non-member respondents felt that this was a more important barrier than member respondents. Again, one possible explanation

*Table 15. Comparison of e-commerce benefits (alliance members vs. non-members): Australia*

| Benefits | Mean Members | N Members | Mean Non-Members | N Non-Members | t value | Significance |
|---|---|---|---|---|---|---|
| Reduced our administration costs. | 3.30 | 10 | 3.13 | 15 | .257 | .799 |
| Reduced our production costs. | 1.50 | 10 | 2.53 | 15 | -1.428 | .167 |
| Reduced our lead time. | 1.60 | 10 | 2.67 | 15 | -1.742 | .095 |
| Reduced our stock levels. | 2.10 | 10 | 2.47 | 15 | -.499 | .623 |
| Lead to increased sales. | 1.00 | 10 | 2.40 | 15 | -2.095 | .047 |
| Increased our internal efficiency. | 1.80 | 10 | 3.33 | 15 | -2.815 | .010 |
| Improved our relations with business partners. | 3.30 | 10 | 3.87 | 15 | -.963 | .346 |
| Gave us access to new customers and markets. | * | * | * | * | * | * |
| Improved our competitiveness. | 2.20 | 10 | 3.33 | 15 | -1.604 | .122 |
| Improved the quality of information in our organisation. | 2.50 | 10 | 3.80 | 15 | -2.100 | .047 |

*Note: * insufficient data*

is that membership reduces the importance of this barrier. This is in line with the findings of Jorde et al. (1989) and Marchewka et al. (2000). However, this raises the question as to why only one barrier showed any significant difference.

Table 15 provides the data for the benefits derived from e-commerce adoption and use.

Before examining the data in Table 15 in detail, a number of comments should be made. Firstly, the low response rate due to the low adoption rates in Australia needs to be noted when considering the data in this table. While statistically these low figures have been accounted for procedurally, the use of the data in terms of wider inferences needs to be done with caution. Secondly, with the exception of the benefit "Reduced our administration costs," the perception of benefits is higher for the non-member respondents than for member respondents. At first glance this appears to refute the earlier studies (Ciappei et al., 2005; Cirillo, 2000; Daniel et al., 2002b; Daniel et al., 2002a; Terziovski, 2003), however, one possible explanation is that many of the benefits tested in this study have been achieved through membership of an alliance and are thus less perceptibly important in e-commerce adoption and use.

Table 15 indicates that there were differences in the ratings of three e-commerce benefits between alliance members and non-members. These were benefits related to increased sales, improved efficiency, and quality of information. However, all three of these were rated higher by the non-members. This implies that membership of an alliance does not necessarily have an important role in achieving benefits through e-commerce implementation.

Finally, Table 16 provides the details for the disadvantages incurred through the adoption and use of e-commerce.

*Table 16. Comparison of e-commerce disadvantages (alliance members vs. non-members): Australia*

| | Mean Members | N Members | Mean Non-Members | N Non-Members | t value | Significance |
|---|---|---|---|---|---|---|
| Deteriorated relations. with business partners. | * | * | * | * | * | * |
| Increased costs. | 1.70 | 10 | 2.53 | 15 | -1.446 | .162 |
| Increased the computer maintenance required. | 1.10 | 10 | 2.07 | 15 | -1.897 | .070 |
| Doubled the amount of work. | * | * | * | * | * | * |
| Reduced the flexibility of the business processes. | 1.30 | 10 | 2.40 | 15 | -2.001 | .057 |
| Raised security concerns. | 2.30 | 10 | 4.13 | 15 | -2.533 | .028 |
| Made us increasingly dependent on this technology. | 2.50 | 10 | 3.53 | 15 | -1.539 | .138 |

Note: * insufficient data

Again, the low response rate due to the low adoption rates in Australia needs to be noted when considering the data in Table 16. Only one disadvantage (security risks) showed a statistically significant difference between respondents that were members of an alliance and respondents that were not. Non-member respondents were far more concerned with security as a disadvantage than were members. A number of studies have suggested that membership of some form of alliance "dampens" the effect of disadvantages. This appears to be the case with the disadvantage security risks, but is not in evidence with any of the other disadvantages tested for.

## Summary of Findings: Australia

The results from the Australian sample, yet again, differ from the Swedish findings. In Australian regional SMEs, several e-commerce criteria, barriers, benefits and disadvantages show significant differences between alliance members and non-members. Where adoption drivers are concerned, four criteria were different between the two groups, with non-members rating these consistently higher in importance than members. Non-members generally viewed pressure from competitors, access to new markets, improved competitiveness, and external support as being more important than members. The latter is particularly unsurprising since one of the benefits of alliance membership is access to resources, which implies that non-members were not concerned about the availability of external support. In fact, they gave this criterion a particularly low rating.

The e-commerce barriers show a different picture although non-members, as expected, rated barriers higher than alliance members. However, this difference was significant in only one instance related to the cost of implementing e-commerce. Non-members assigned a higher level of importance to this barrier than members. Once again, resource availability within an alliance may be the cause of this finding.

E-commerce benefits indicated an unexpected result in that alliance members generally rated the benefits of e-commerce lower than non-members. Three benefits related to increased sales, better quality of information, and internal efficiency showed significant differences. In the case of increased sales, the members gave this benefit a mean rating of only 1.00. As mentioned previously, this could be due to the fact that the benefits were experienced through the alliance itself, rather than through e-commerce per se.

Finally, in relation to the disadvantages of e-commerce adoption, security risks were rated highly by non-members. This is the only disadvantage that showed a significant difference between the two groups. Considering that one of the functions of an alliance is to dissipate negative effects, it is somewhat surprising to isolate only one disadvantage in the results.

*Table 17. Comparison of e-commerce adoption criteria (alliance members vs. non-members): USA*

| Criteria | Mean Members | N Members | Mean Non-Members | N Non-Members | t value | Significance |
|---|---|---|---|---|---|---|
| Demand and/or pressure from customers. | 3.07 | 19 | 3.25 | 42 | -.540 | .591 |
| Pressure from competition. | 2.71 | 19 | 1.74 | 42 | 2.207 | .037 |
| Demand and/or pressure from suppliers. | 3.24 | 19 | 2.74 | 42 | 1.152 | .254 |
| To reduce costs. | 1.52 | 19 | 1.56 | 42 | -.101 | .920 |
| To improve customer service. | 3.41 | 19 | 3.61 | 42 | -.724 | .473 |
| To shorten lead time/reduce stock levels. | 2.59 | 19 | 2.10 | 42 | 1.359 | .180 |
| To increase sales. | 2.81 | 19 | 1.85 | 42 | 2.537 | .012 |
| To improve internal efficiency. | 2.00 | 19 | 1.90 | 42 | .274 | .785 |
| To strengthen relations with business partners. | 2.29 | 19 | 2.00 | 42 | .786 | .435 |
| The possibility of reaching new customers/markets. | 2.24 | 19 | 1.69 | 42 | 1.470 | .147 |
| To improve our competitiveness. | 2.59 | 19 | 2.05 | 42 | 1.274 | .208 |
| We were offered external support to adopt e-commerce. | 3.84 | 19 | 4.16 | 42 | -1.326 | .191 |
| To improve our marketing. | 4.12 | 19 | 4.19 | 42 | -.423 | .674 |
| To improve control. | 3.07 | 19 | 3.25 | 42 | -.540 | .591 |

# USA

Due to the number of responses in the U.S. sample, there was insufficient data to conduct tests for barriers, benefits, or disadvantages. Therefore, Table 17 provides the data for e-commerce adoption criteria only.

An examination of Table 17 shows that two criteria (Pressure from competition and Increased sales) showed a statistically significant difference between member and non-member respondents. In both cases, respondents that indicated membership of some form of strategic alliance rated these criteria as being more important than non-member respondents.

Before examining Table 17 in detail, it is worth noting that like the Australian respondents, the measure of membership of any form of alliance was low. Unlike the Australian respondents, the U.S. responses do not show a higher rating by non-members of the criteria for adoption. In the U.S., it was the members who rated the two statistically significant criteria as being more important. At first glance the results would suggest that membership may lead to a greater awareness, or greater urgency to alleviate pressure from competition and to increase sales. However, this raises the question as to why criteria such as improvement to customer service and improvement to marketing are actually rated higher by non-member respondents.

We will now compare the results across the three locations.

Table 18. Comparison summary between alliance members and non-members across three locations

|  | Sweden | Australia | USA |
|---|---|---|---|
| E-commerce adoption criteria | No differences. | Pressure from competition, access to new markets, improved competitiveness, and external support rated higher by non-members. | Pressure from competition and increased sales rated higher by members. |
| E-commerce barriers | Unsuitability of e-commerce to products/services and lack of advantages rated higher by members. | Financial investment rated higher by non-members. | Insufficient data |
| E-commerce benefits | No differences. | Increased sales, internal efficiency, and better quality of information rated higher by non-members. | Insufficient data |
| E-commerce disadvantages | Reduced flexibility rated higher by non-members. | Security risks rated higher by non-members. | Insufficient data |

# Comparison of Differences Between the Three Locations: A Discussion

A comparison of the results across the three locations shows divergent views. We will examine these in relation to each of the four aspects of e-commerce: criteria, barriers, benefits, and disadvantages. They are also summarised in Table 18, which shows only those aspects of e-commerce, which showed significant differences in a particular location.

In Sweden, there were no statistically significant differences between members and non-members for any of the e-commerce adoption criteria. This is in contrast to the Australian respondents who differed on four criteria, and the U.S. respondents who differed on two criteria. This would appear to suggest that in the Swedish context, belonging to an alliance is not an incentive to adopt e-commerce. Indeed the difference in the criteria means of members and non-members is almost negligible. However, in Australia, SMEs that belong to an alliance showed a difference on four criteria when compared to non-members. These criteria were mainly related to competition/competitiveness, new customers and markets, and availability of external support. All of the non-members rated these criteria higher than members suggesting that belonging to an alliance may afford access to these potential benefits. Australian respondents shared one of the criteria with the U.S.—that of pressure from competitors. However, in the U.S. instance the results were at odds with Australia because it was the members who assigned a higher mean to this criterion implying perhaps that belonging to an alliance increases the pressure from competition. The second criterion in the U.S., which showed any differenced between members and non-members was increased sales, which once again, was rated higher by the members as an incentive to adopt e-commerce.

In examining the barriers, benefits, and disadvantages of e-commerce, we have to exclude the U.S. sample since there were insufficient responses to perform an analysis. In Sweden, all but one of the barriers were rated higher by members than by non-member, however, only two barriers showed a statistically significant difference—the unsuitability of e-commerce and the lack of advantages. By contrast in Australia, only one barrier surfaced (high investment) and it was rated higher by non-members. The findings show that in the Swedish case, members of alliances perceived the barriers as being more important than their counterparts, and the opposite was true for Australia. The explanation may lie in the types of alliances formed by Swedish and Australian SMEs.

In relation to benefits, there were no statistically significant differences between members and non-members; in Sweden however, it was interesting to note that the mean ratings for both groups were quite similar. In Australia, we found three benefits that differed between the two groups. These were related to sales, internal efficiency, and quality of information. In all three, non-members rated the benefits higher and particularly so in the case of internal efficiency, which had a mean rating of 1.80 for members and 3.33 for non-members. This is somewhat unusual although it can be argued that, as non-members, SMEs are more concerned about their internal structures than maintaining relationships with external partners, thus focusing on internal efficiency.

Finally, in Sweden, there was only one disadvantage that showed a statistically significant difference--reduced flexibility of work. Non-members rated this slightly higher than members did as a disadvantage of e-commerce, however, the divergence in views was minor.

Australian SMEs also showed one disadvantage however, it was related to security risks. Non-members reported experiencing higher security risks on average than members of an alliance. Once again, the explanation may be found in the resource sharing between alliance members, including sharing of technical expertise.

We will now take a closer look at the groupings of e-commerce adoption criteria, barriers, benefits, and disadvantages in each of the two groups (members and non-members) with the purpose of answering our third and final question: Do the groupings of e-commerce adoption criteria, barriers, benefits, and disadvantages differ between strategic alliance members and non-members?

# Groupings of E-Commerce Criteria, Barriers, Benefits, and Disadvantages and Alliance Membership

To answer our third question, a combination of correlations and factor analysis was applied to the data. The results of this analysis are shown in the tables next and discussed at the end of each section, by location.

## Sweden

Tables 19 and 20 provide the correlation matrices of the importance ratings for e-commerce adoption criteria. All correlations significant at the .001 level are shown in bold.

The results of Kaiser-Meyer-Olkin MSA (.876 for non-members, .871 for members) and Bartlett's Test of Sphericity ($\chi^2 = 1028$, $p = .000$ for non-members and $\chi^2 = 692$, p = .000 for members) indicated that the data set satisfied the assumptions for factorability.

For non-member respondents a three-factor solution was extracted with Eigenvalues 7.127, 1.366, and 1.095. These factors account for 68.486% of the variance (refer to Table 21).

For member respondents, a two-factor solution was extracted with Eigenvalues 8.101 and 1.360. These account for 67.581% of variance (see Table 22).

For the non-member respondents the resulting components were rotated using the Varimax procedure and a simple structure was achieved as shown in the rotated component matrix in Table 23.

Table 23 shows that six criteria were grouped around a factor termed "internal business and resources" by non-member SMEs. These were related to internal functions within the organisation such as the supply of raw materials, IT resources, costs, lead time, better control, and efficiency. Five criteria loaded on to the marketing factor include customer service improvements, sales, better relations with business partners, competitiveness, and marketing. Two criteria (pressure from customers and competition) were grouped based on the market forces factor.

*Table 19. Adoption criteria correlation matrix for non-members (Sweden)*

| | Demand and/or pressure from customers. | Demand and/or pressure from suppliers. | To reduce costs. | To improve customer service. | To shorten lead time/reduce stock levels. | To increase sales. | To improve internal efficiency. | To strengthen relations with business partners. | The possibility of reaching new customers/markets. | To improve our competitiveness. | We were offered external support to adopt e-commerce. | To improve our marketing. | To improve control. |
|---|---|---|---|---|---|---|---|---|---|---|---|---|---|
| Pressure from competition. | .582 | | | | | | | | | | | | |
| Demand and/or pressure from suppliers. | .233* | .370 | | | | | | | | | | | |
| To reduce costs. | .342 | .405 | .594 | | | | | | | | | | |
| To improve customer service. | .465 | .505 | .450 | .687 | | | | | | | | | |
| To shorten lead time/reduce stock levels. | .217* | .355 | .532 | .660 | .586 | | | | | | | | |
| To increase sales. | .259** | .458 | .413 | .616 | .696 | .562 | | | | | | | |
| To improve internal efficiency. | .161 | .329 | .330 | .516 | .493 | .490 | .459 | | | | | | |
| To strengthen relations with business partners. | .424 | .443 | .488 | .524 | .752 | .593 | .590 | .427 | | | | | |
| The possibility of reaching new customers/markets. | .281** | .454 | .348 | .450 | .688 | .442 | .689 | .367 | .592 | | | | |
| To improve our competitiveness. | .351 | .612 | .428 | .560 | .741 | .606 | .687 | .480 | .706 | .747 | | | |
| We were offered external support to adopt e-commerce. | .082 | .235* | .330 | .343 | .235* | .371 | .302 | .188* | .322 | .172 | .318 | | |
| To improve our marketing. | .238* | .393 | .316 | .328 | .620 | .277** | .608 | .328 | .460 | .800 | .604 | .236* | |
| To improve control. | .258** | .377 | .525 | .615 | .558 | .580 | .469 | .432 | .524 | .436 | .568 | .433 | .313 |

*Note: * significant at 0.05 level    ** significant at 0.01 level*

*Table 20. Adoption criteria correlation matrix for members (Sweden)*

| | Demand and/or pressure from customers. | Demand and/or pressure from suppliers. | To reduce costs. | To improve customer service. | To shorten lead time/reduce stock levels. | To increase sales. | To improve internal efficiency. | To strengthen relations with business partners. | The possibility of reaching new customers/markets. | To improve our competitiveness. | We were offered external support to adopt e-commerce. | To improve our marketing. | To improve control. |
|---|---|---|---|---|---|---|---|---|---|---|---|---|---|
| Pressure from competition. | .742 | | | | | | | | | | | | |
| Demand and/or pressure from suppliers. | .436 | .588 | | | | | | | | | | | |
| To reduce costs. | .606 | .609 | .588 | | | | | | | | | | |
| To improve customer service. | .561 | .513 | .324* | .723 | | | | | | | | | |
| To shorten lead time/reduce stock levels. | .391** | .432 | .606 | .649 | .400 | | | | | | | | |
| To increase sales. | .455 | .291* | .363** | .508 | .555 | .361** | | | | | | | |
| To improve internal efficiency. | .551 | .407 | .416 | .758 | .681 | .577 | .507 | | | | | | |
| To strengthen relations with business partners. | .546 | .522 | .506 | .599 | .608 | .453 | .462 | .612 | | | | | |
| The possibility of reaching new customers/markets. | .499 | .369** | .400 | .427 | .628 | .416 | .769 | .494 | .604 | | | | |
| To improve our competitiveness. | .636 | .602 | .525 | .602 | .613 | .464 | .620 | .622 | .809 | .749 | | | |
| We were offered external support to adopt e-commerce. | .489 | .505 | .696 | .482 | .286* | .523 | .410 | .414 | .488 | .449 | .514 | | |
| To improve our marketing. | .549 | .442 | .409 | .460 | .575 | .443 | .725 | .534 | .587 | .848 | .748 | .441 | |
| To improve control. | .559 | .461 | .468 | .674 | .540 | .704 | .564 | .621 | .593 | .664 | .617 | .592 | .609 |

*Note: * significant at 0.05 level    ** significant at 0.01 level*

The same approach was used for the member respondents. The resulting components were rotated using the Varimax procedure and a simple structure was achieved as shown in the rotated component matrix in Table 24.

Unlike the non-members, the alliance members grouped adoption criteria based on two factors: marketing and internal business/resources. However, while the non-members rated internal business/resources (Eigenvalue 7.127, % var. 50.909%) as being more important, the most important factor for the member respondents (Eigenvalue 8.101, % var. 57.864%)

*Table 21. Total variance explained: Adoption criteria (non-members in Sweden)*

| Component | Eigenvalue | % Variation | Cumulative % |
|---|---|---|---|
| 1 | 7.127 | 50.909 | 50.909 |
| 2 | 1.366 | 9.756 | 60.665 |
| 3 | 1.095 | 7.821 | 68.486 |

*Table 22. Total variance explained: Adoption criteria (members in Sweden)*

| Component | Eigenvalue | % Variation | Cumulative % |
|---|---|---|---|
| 1 | 8.101 | 57.864 | 57.864 |
| 2 | 1.360 | 9.717 | 67.581 |

*Table 23. Rotated component matrix: Adoption criteria (non-members in Sweden)*

| | Component 1: Internal Business and Resources | Component 2: Marketing | Component 3: Market Forces |
|---|---|---|---|
| Demand and/or pressure from customers. | | | .921 |
| Pressure from competition. | | | .733 |
| Demand and/or pressure from suppliers. | .696 | | |
| To reduce costs. | .747 | | |
| To improve customer service. | | .661 | |
| To shorten lead time/reduce stock levels. | .771 | | |
| To increase sales. | | .713 | |
| To improve internal efficiency. | .526 | | |
| To strengthen relations with business partners. | | .517 | |
| The possibility of reaching new customers/markets. | | .895 | |
| To improve our competitiveness. | | .697 | |
| We were offered external support to adopt e-commerce. | .629 | | |
| To improve our marketing. | | .881 | |
| To improve control. | .746 | | |

*Table 24. Rotated component matrix: Adoption criteria (members in Sweden)*

|  | Component 1: Marketing | Component 2: Internal Business & Resources |
|---|---|---|
| Demand and/or pressure from customers. |  | .594 |
| Pressure from competition. |  | .732 |
| Demand and/or pressure from suppliers. |  | .813 |
| To reduce costs. |  | .739 |
| To improve customer service. | .700 |  |
| To shorten lead-time/reduce stock levels. |  | .743 |
| To increase sales. | .828 |  |
| To improve internal efficiency. | .558 | .538 |
| To strengthen relations with business partners. | .603 |  |
| The possibility of reaching new customers/markets. | .895 |  |
| To improve our competitiveness. | .739 |  |
| We were offered external support to adopt e-commerce. |  | .741 |
| To improve our marketing. | .853 |  |
| To improve control. | .564 | .592 |

was marketing. A number of authors (Datta, 1988; O'Donnell et al., 2002; Overby et al., 2001) have suggested that one of the benefits of an alliance is to increase the efficiency of the member business internally. Similarly, advocates of e-commerce adoption (Fletcher, 1994; Turban, Lee, King, & Chung, 2002) have shown that e-commerce requires the business to become internally efficient in order to gain maximum benefit from the adoption and the use of the technology. The results in Tables 23 and 24 would suggest that member respondents have, through their membership, gained a more efficient business (internally), thus rating this need as less important than their non-member counterparts.

Tables 25 and 26 provide the correlation matrices of the importance ratings for e-commerce adoption barriers. All correlations significant at the .001 level are shown in bold.

The results of Kaiser-Meyer-Olkin MSA (.856 for non-members, .852 for members) and Bartlett's Test of Sphericity ($\chi^2 = 404$, $p = .000$ for non-members and $\chi^2 = 331$, p = .000 for members) indicated that the data set satisfied the assumptions for factorability. For both sets of data, again, a two-factor solution was extracted. Tables 27 and 28 show the total variance.

The resulting components were rotated using the Varimax procedure and a simple structure was achieved as shown in the rotated component matrix (see Tables 29 and 30).

An examination of Tables 29 and 30 shows that both members and non-members grouped e-commerce barriers based on two factors: its suitability and the complexity of implementing it. However, while non-members assigned a higher priority on the latter, the members were mainly concerned about organisational issues and how e-commerce would fit in to their business. This is in line with previous research, which shows that alliances dissipate

*Table 25. Adoption barriers correlation matrix for non-members (Sweden)*

| | E-commerce is not suited to our products/services. | E-commerce is not suited to our way of doing business. | E-commerce is not suited to the ways our clients do business. | E-commerce does not offer any advantages to our organisation. | We do not have the technical knowledge in the organisation to implement e-commerce. | E-commerce is too complicated to implement. | E-commerce is not secure. | The financial investment required to implement e-commerce is too high. | We do not have time to implement e-commerce. |
|---|---|---|---|---|---|---|---|---|---|
| E-commerce is not suited to our way of doing business. | .745 | | | | | | | | |
| E-commerce is not suited to the ways our clients do business. | .716 | .801 | | | | | | | |
| E-commerce does not offer any advantages to our organisation. | .759 | .790 | .762 | | | | | | |
| We do not have the technical knowledge in the organisation to implement e-commerce. | .309* | .266* | .295* | .405** | | | | | |
| E-commerce is too complicated to implement. | .476 | .427** | .485 | .479 | .607 | | | | |
| E-commerce is not secure. | .593 | .541 | .579 | .630 | .495 | .851 | | | |
| The financial investment required to implement e-commerce is too high. | -.053 | -.132 | .085 | -.114 | .455 | .488 | .277* | | |
| We do not have time to implement e-commerce. | .329** | .260* | .415** | .386** | .450 | .683 | .626 | .458 | |
| It is difficult to choose the most suitable e-commerce standard with so many different options available. | .266* | .342** | .443 | .292* | .436 | .647 | .582 | .495 | .547 |

*Note: * significant at 0.05 level    ** significant at 0.01 level*

*Table 26. Adoption barriers correlation matrix for members (Sweden)*

| | E-commerce is not suited to our products/services. | E-commerce is not suited to our way of doing business. | E-commerce is not suited to the ways our clients do business. | E-commerce does not offer any advantages to our organisation. | We do not have the technical knowledge in the organisation to implement e-commerce. | E-commerce is too complicated to implement. | E-commerce is not secure. | The financial investment required to implement e-commerce is too high. | We do not have time to implement e-commerce. |
|---|---|---|---|---|---|---|---|---|---|
| E-commerce is not suited to our way of doing business. | .603 | | | | | | | | |
| E-commerce is not suited to the ways our clients do business. | .607 | .566 | | | | | | | |
| E-commerce does not offer any advantages to our organisation. | .455 | .547 | .248* | | | | | | |
| We do not have the technical knowledge in the organisation to implement e-commerce. | .207 | .307* | .320* | .402** | | | | | |
| E-commerce is too complicated to implement. | .297* | .384** | .531 | .314* | .635 | | | | |
| E-commerce is not secure. | .388** | .547 | .546 | .329* | .513 | .718 | | | |
| The financial investment required to implement e-commerce is too high. | -.055 | -.128 | .080 | -.121 | .466 | .477 | .279* | | |
| We do not have time to implement e-commerce. | .298* | .327** | .458 | .217 | .576 | .796 | .594 | .459 | |
| It is difficult to choose the most suitable e-commerce standard with so many different options available. | .380** | .414** | .548 | .329** | .653 | .763 | .631 | .485 | .757 |

*Note:  * significant at 0.05 level     ** significant at 0.01 level*

the negative aspects of e-commerce adoption. Studies (Achrol et al., 1999; Dean et al., 1997; Marchewka et al., 2000) have shown that SME clusters assist members by sharing technical knowledge, talent, and skills. Since non-members do not have access to these resources, they have rated the barriers associated with the difficulty of implementing e-commerce higher. By contrast, the members were assessing e-commerce from a business viewpoint and were not as concerned about the problems associated with adopting the technology, possibly due to having access to the required resources in the alliance they belong to.

Tables 31 and 32 provide the correlation matrices of the ratings for e-commerce benefits. All correlations significant at the .001 level are shown in bold.

The results of Kaiser-Meyer-Olkin MSA (.738, non-members and .836, members) and Bartlett's Test of Sphericity ($\chi^2 = 351$, p = .000, non-members; $\chi^2 = 292$, p = .000, members) indicated that the data set satisfied the assumptions for factorability. Principle Components Analysis was chosen as the method of extraction in order to account for maximum variance in the data using a minimum number of factors. For the non-member respondents, a

*Table 27. Total variance explained: Adoption barriers (non-members in Sweden)*

| Component | Eigenvalue | % Variation | Cumulative % |
|---|---|---|---|
| 1 | 1.538 | 17.086 | 17.086 |
| 2 | 5.218 | 57.974 | 75.060 |

*Table 28. Total variance explained: Adoption barriers (members in Sweden)*

| Component | Eigenvalue | % Variation | Cumulative % |
|---|---|---|---|
| 1 | 4.895 | 54.389 | 54.389 |
| 2 | 1.407 | 15.629 | 70.018 |

*Table 29. Rotated component matrix: Adoption barriers (non-members in Sweden)*

| Barrier | Component 1: Unsuitable | Component 2: Too Difficult |
|---|---|---|
| E-commerce is not suited to our products/services. | .864 | |
| E-commerce is not suited to our way of doing business. | .909 | |
| E-commerce is not suited to the ways our clients do business. | .847 | |
| E-commerce does not offer any advantages to our organisation. | .871 | |
| We do not have the technical knowledge in the organisation to implement e-commerce. | | .704 |
| E-commerce is too complicated to implement. | | .870 |
| E-commerce is not secure. | | .742 |
| The financial investment required to implement e-commerce is too high. | .810 | |
| We do not have time to implement e-commerce. | | .802 |
| It is difficult to choose the most suitable e-commerce standard with so many different options available. | | .776 |

*Table 30. Rotated component matrix: Adoption barriers (members in Sweden)*

| Barrier | Component 1: *Unsuitable* | Component 2: *Too Difficult* |
|---|---|---|
| E-commerce is not suited to our products/services. | .850 | |
| E-commerce is not suited to our way of doing business. | .842 | |
| E-commerce is not suited to the ways our clients do business. | .640 | |
| E-commerce does not offer any advantages to our organisation. | .678 | |
| We do not have the technical knowledge in the organisation to implement e-commerce. | | .765 |
| E-commerce is too complicated to implement. | | .896 |
| E-commerce is not secure. | | .699 |
| The financial investment required to implement e-commerce is too high. | .785 | |
| We do not have time to implement e-commerce. | | .876 |
| It is difficult to choose the most suitable e-commerce standard with so many different options available. | | .848 |

three-factor solution was extracted with Eigenvalues of 3.776, 1.774, and 1.131, and was supported by an inspection of the Screen Plot. These three factors accounted for 66.817% of the total variance as shown in Table 33. For the member respondents, a two-factor solution was extracted with Eigenvalues of 5.083 & 1.683, accounting for 67.657% of the total variance as shown Table 34.

Both sets of components were rotated using the Varimax procedure and a simple structure was achieved as shown in the rotated component matrix in Tables 8.35 and 8.36. In both cases, the factors are independent and uncorrelated, as an orthogonal rotation procedure was used.

An examination of Table 35 shows that for the non-member respondents, three benefits loaded onto the efficiency and costs factor. These were related to lower costs and more efficient internal operations. This factor accounted for 17.741% of variance in the non-member group. However, the non-members assigned the highest priority to the benefits related to inventory and relationships with business partners (such as suppliers). Despite not being members of an alliance, these SMEs experienced improvements to their supply chain functions as a distinct benefit of e-commerce adoption. By contrast, the members did not identify this as a separate benefit at all. The alliance member SMEs grouped their benefits around improved sales functions and more efficient internal operations. This tends to support the notion put forward by Schindehutte and Morris (2001), Datta (1988), and Overby et al. (2000) that membership of an SME cluster assists with the internal efficiency of its members

Finally, Tables 37 and 38 provide the correlation matrices of disadvantages in non-member and member SMEs in Sweden. All correlations significant at the .001 level are shown in bold.

For respondents who were not members of an alliance, the results of Kaiser-Meyer-Olkin MSA (.873) and Bartlett's Test of Sphericity ($\chi^2 = 486.94$, $p = .000$) indicated that the data set satisfied the assumptions for factorability. Principle components analysis was chosen

*Table 31. E-commerce benefits correlation matrix for non-members (Sweden)*

| E-commerce… | Reduced our administration costs. | Reduced our production costs. | Reduced our lead time. | Reduced our stock levels. | Lead to increased sales. | Increased our internal efficiency. | Improved our relations with business partners. | Gave us access to new customers and markets. | Improved our competitiveness. |
|---|---|---|---|---|---|---|---|---|---|
| Reduced our production costs. | .325 | | | | | | | | |
| Reduced our lead time. | .726 | .312 | | | | | | | |
| Reduced our stock levels. | .584 | .178 | .591 | | | | | | |
| Lead to increased sales. | .532 | .325 | .671 | .616 | | | | | |
| Increased our internal efficiency. | .574 | .346 | .614 | .560 | .593 | | | | |
| Improved our relations with business partners. | .646 | .255** | .564 | .409 | .434 | .457 | | | |
| Gave us access to new customers and markets. | .530 | .244** | .534 | .585 | .554 | .501 | .333 | | |
| Improved our competitiveness. | .349 | .248** | .411 | .412 | .368 | .685 | .351 | .571 | |
| Improved the quality of information in our organisation. | .491 | .203* | .557 | .505 | .683 | .519 | .364 | .602 | .489 |

*Note: * significant at 0.05 level     ** significant at 0.01 level*

*Table 32. E-commerce benefits correlation matrix for members (Sweden)*

| E-commerce... | Reduced our administration costs. | Reduced our production costs. | Reduced our lead time. | Reduced our stock levels. | Lead to increased sales. | Increased our internal efficiency. | Improved our relations with business partners. | Gave us access to new customers and markets. | Improved our competitiveness. |
|---|---|---|---|---|---|---|---|---|---|
| Reduced our production costs. | .733 | | | | | | | | |
| Reduced our lead time. | .700 | .780 | | | | | | | |
| Reduced our stock levels. | .624 | .745 | .641 | | | | | | |
| Lead to increased sales. | .326* | .493 | .406 | .546 | | | | | |
| Increased our internal efficiency. | 551 | .759 | .717 | .639 | .402 | | | | |
| Improved our relations with business partners. | .567 | .647 | .563 | .690 | .362** | .658 | | | |
| Gave us access to new customers and markets. | .473 | .590 | .593 | .619 | .325* | .751 | .703 | | |
| Improved our competitiveness. | .384** | .536 | .545 | .420 | .279* | .772 | .716 | .681 | |
| Improved the quality of information in our organisation. | .324* | .456 | .409 | .493 | .471 | .509 | .520 | .629 | .442 |

*Note: * significant at 0.05 level    ** significant at 0.01 level*

*Table 33. Total variance explained: E-commerce benefits (non-members in Sweden)*

| Component | Eigenvalue | % Variance | Cumulative % |
|---|---|---|---|
| 1 | 1.131 | 11.311 | 66.817 |
| 2 | 3.776 | 37.765 | 37.765 |
| 3 | 1.774 | 17.741 | 55.505 |

*Table 34. Total variance explained: E-commerce benefits (members in Sweden)*

| Component | Eigenvalue | % Variance | Cumulative % |
|---|---|---|---|
| 1 | 1.683 | 16.827 | 67.657 |
| 2 | 5.083 | 50.830 | 50.830 |

*Table 35. Rotated component matrix: E-commerce benefits (non-members in Sweden)*

| Benefits | Component 1: Sales | Component 2: Inventory & Relationships | Component 3: Efficiency & Costs |
|---|---|---|---|
| Reduced our administration costs. | | | .867 |
| Reduced our production costs. | | | .452 |
| Reduced our lead time. | | .860 | |
| Reduced our stock levels. | | .850 | |
| Lead to increased sales. | .701 | | |
| Increased our internal efficiency. | | | .853 |
| Improved our relations with business partners. | | .639 | |
| Gave us access to new customers and markets. | .898 | | |
| Improved our competitiveness. | .637 | | |
| Improved the quality of information in our organisation. | .846 | | |

as the method of extraction in order to account for maximum variance in the data using a minimum number of factors. A two factor solution was extracted with Eigenvalues of 5.237 and 1.426 and was supported by the Scree plot. These two factors accounted for 60.566% of the variance as shown in Table 39.

For respondents who were members of an alliance, the results of Kaiser-Meyer-Olkin MSA (.749) and Bartlett's Test of Sphericity ($\chi^2 = 288.49$, $p = .000$) indicated that the data set satisfied the assumptions for factorability. Principle Components Analysis was chosen as the method of extraction in order to account for maximum variance in the data using a minimum number of factors. A three-factor solution was extracted with Eigenvalues of 5.043, 1.636, and 1.005, and was supported by an inspection of the Scree Plot. These three factors accounted for 65.859% of the total variance as shown in Table 40.

In both cases, the resulting components were rotated using a Varimax procedure and a simple structure was achieved (see Tables 41 and 42).

*Table 36. Rotated component matrix: E-commerce benefits (members in Sweden)*

| Benefits | Component 1: Sales | Component 2: Efficiency |
|---|---|---|
| Reduced our administration costs. | | .771 |
| Reduced our production costs. | | .743 |
| Reduced our lead time. | | .822 |
| Reduced our stock levels. | | .501 |
| Lead to increased sales. | .875 | |
| Increased our internal efficiency. | | .646 |
| Improved our relations with business partners. | .720 | |
| Gave us access to new customers and markets. | .927 | |
| Improved our competitiveness. | .876 | |
| Improved the quality of information in our organisation. | .808 | |

*Table 37. E-commerce disadvantages correlation matrix for non-members (Sweden)*

| E-commerce... | Deteriorated relations with our business partners. | Increased costs. | Increased the computer maintenance required. | Doubled the amount of work. | Reduced the flexibility of the business processes. | Raised security concerns. |
|---|---|---|---|---|---|---|
| Increased costs. | .560 | | | | | |
| Increased the computer maintenance required. | .552 | .526 | | | | |
| Doubled the amount of work. | .665 | .657 | .677 | | | |
| Reduced the flexibility of the business processes. | .583 | .496 | .560 | .622 | | |
| Raised security concerns. | .791 | .504 | .508 | .709 | .638 | |
| Made us increasingly dependent on this technology. | .693 | .520 | .516 | .623 | .600 | .748 |

*Note: * significant at 0.05 level    ** significant at 0.01 level*

Non-members grouped e-commerce disadvantages based on the deterioration of their business practices and the resources required to maintain e-commerce. By contrast, alliance members loaded the computer maintenance and increasing dependence on e-commerce technology on to a completely separate factor. They also grouped increased costs together with the doubling of the amount of work in the organisation. However, both members and non-members were in agreement with the ratings assigned to the business practices factor, which was rated the highest. Therefore, we can argue that both groups were concerned about the effects of e-commerce on their business functions and operations.

*Table 38. E-commerce disadvantages correlation matrix for members (Sweden)*

| E-commerce... | Deteriorated relations with our business partners. | Increased costs. | Increased the computer maintenance required. | Doubled the amount of work. | Reduced the flexibility of the business processes. | Raised security concerns. |
|---|---|---|---|---|---|---|
| Increased costs. | .382** | | | | | |
| Increased the computer maintenance required. | .385** | .608 | | | | |
| Doubled the amount of work. | .453 | .622 | .759 | | | |
| Reduced the flexibility of the business processes. | .425 | .588 | .514 | .611 | | |
| Raised security concerns. | .656 | .572 | .582 | .656 | .620 | |
| Made us increasingly dependent on this technology. | .548 | .566 | .578 | .690 | .697 | .853 |

*Note: * significant at 0.05 level    ** significant at 0.01 level*

*Table 39. Total variance explained: E-commerce disadvantages (non-members in Sweden)*

| Component | Eigenvalue | % Variation | Cumulative % |
|---|---|---|---|
| 1 | 5.237 | 47.605 | 47.605 |
| 2 | 1.426 | 12.962 | 60.566 |

*Table 40. Total variance explained: E-commerce disadvantages (members in Sweden)*

| Component | Eigenvalue | % Variation | Cumulative % |
|---|---|---|---|
| 1 | 5.043 | 45.849 | 45.849 |
| 2 | 1.636 | 14.869 | 60.719 |
| 3 | 1.005 | 9.140 | 69.859 |

*Table 41. Rotated component matrix: E-commerce disadvantages (non-members in Sweden)*

| Disadvantage | Component 1: Business Practices | Component 2: Resources |
|---|---|---|
| Deteriorated relations with business partners. | .716 | |
| Increased costs. | | .708 |
| Increased the computer maintenance required. | | .733 |
| Doubled the amount of work. | .538 | |
| Reduced the flexibility of the business processes. | .867 | |
| Raised security concerns. | .780 | |
| Made us increasingly dependent on this technology. | .490 | |

# Summary: Groupings and Alliance Membership in Sweden

The Swedish data shows some distinct differences between alliance members and non-members in relation to how they group e-commerce adoption criteria, barriers, benefits, and disadvantages.

While non-members identified three groups of e-commerce criteria (internal and business resource criteria, marketing criteria, and market forces criteria), the criteria leading to e-commerce adoption by members can be explained by way of two groups (marketing criteria and internal business/resource criteria). Non-members also rated criteria related to improving internal operations and functions as being more relevant, while members ranked marketing criteria as being more important in their decision to adopt e-commerce.

Although both non-members and members grouped e-commerce barriers around two factors (suitability and complexity or difficulty), they assigned different priorities to them. Non-members were more concerned about the difficulties associated with e-commerce adoption, while members assessed the technology from an organisational point of view and ranked issues related to the suitability of e-commerce as being a more important barrier.

In relation to e-commerce benefits, there were differences in both the grouping and the ratings of the factors between members and non-members. Non-members identified three distinct groups of advantages after adopting e-commerce (better sales, improved supply chain functions, and increased efficiency). They ranked the improvements to their supply chain as being the most important. Members, on the other hand, had two groups of benefits—increased sales and improved efficiency—and the latter was thought to be more important.

Finally, although we saw differences between the groupings of e-commerce disadvantages (two for non-members and three for members), their priority ratings matched. Both members and non-members found internal business practices had deteriorated since e-commerce implementation (e.g., through reduced flexibility). There were some interesting differences, however, in the loadings of certain disadvantages, with members identifying a distinct and separate group of problems related to maintaining the technology.

We will now examine the groupings in the Australian context.

# Australia

Due to the low adoption rate of e-commerce, there was insufficient data to examine e-commerce adoption criteria, benefits, or disadvantages in the Australian sample. Tables 43 and 44 provide the correlation matrices for the barriers to e-commerce. All correlations significant at the .001 level are shown in bold.

The results of the Kaiser-Meyer-Olkin MSA (.767 for members, .827 for non-members) and Bartlett's Test for Sphericity ($\chi^2 = 196$ p=.000 for members, $\chi^2 = 540$ p=.000 for non-members) indicated that the data set satisfied the assumptions for factorability. Principle components analysis was chosen as the method of extraction in order to account for maximum variance in the data using a minimum number of factors. For both sets of data, a two-factor solution was extracted. Tables 45 and 46 provide the total variance.

*Table 43. Adoption barriers correlation matrix for non-members (Australia)*

| | E-commerce is not suited to our products/services. | E-commerce is not suited to our way of doing business. | E-commerce is not suited to the ways our clients do business. | E-commerce does not offer any advantages to our organisation. | We do not have the technical knowledge in the organisation to implement e-commerce. | E-commerce is too complicated to implement. | E-commerce is not secure. | The financial investment required to implement e-commerce is too high. | We do not have time to implement e-commerce. |
|---|---|---|---|---|---|---|---|---|---|
| E-commerce is not suited to our way of doing business. | .750 | | | | | | | | |
| E-commerce is not suited to the ways our clients do business. | .749 | .797 | | | | | | | |
| E-commerce does not offer any advantages to our organisation. | .704 | .741 | .727 | | | | | | |
| We do not have the technical knowledge in the organisation to implement e-commerce. | .207* | .160 | .204* | .255* | | | | | |
| E-commerce is too complicated to implement. | .012 | .019 | .085 | .155 | .659 | | | | |
| E-commerce is not secure. | -.044 | -.007 | -.015 | .125 | .433 | .555 | | | |
| The financial investment required to implement e-commerce is too high. | .161 | .159 | .169 | .228* | .486 | .536 | .393 | | |
| We do not have time to implement e-commerce. | -.038 | -.063 | .056 | .094 | .367 | .509 | .352 | .614 | |
| It is difficult to choose the most suitable e-commerce standard with so many different options available. | -.033 | -.050 | -.005 | .119 | .393 | .465 | .377 | .497 | .632 |

Note: * significant at 0.05 level    ** significant at 0.01 level

*Table 44. Adoption barriers correlation matrix for members (Australia)*

| | E-commerce is not suited to our products/services. | E-commerce is not suited to our way of doing business. | E-commerce is not suited to the ways our clients do business. | E-commerce does not offer any advantages to our organisation. | We do not have the technical knowledge in the organisation to implement e-commerce. | E-commerce is too complicated to implement. | E-commerce is not secure. | The financial investment required to implement e-commerce is too high. | We do not have time to implement e-commerce. |
|---|---|---|---|---|---|---|---|---|---|
| E-commerce is not suited to our way of doing business. | .766 | | | | | | | | |
| E-commerce is not suited to the ways our clients do business. | .121 | .835 | | | | | | | |
| E-commerce does not offer any advantages to our organisation. | .492** | .469** | .181 | | | | | | |
| We do not have the technical knowledge in the organisation to implement e-commerce. | .253 | .455** | .313 | .217 | | | | | |
| E-commerce is too complicated to implement. | .139 | .345* | .312 | .197 | .832 | | | | |
| E-commerce is not secure. | -.066 | .061 | .277 | .275 | .468** | .507** | | | |
| The financial investment required to implement e-commerce is too high. | -.017 | .137 | -.044 | -.044 | .601 | .530** | .284 | | |
| We do not have time to implement e-commerce. | .221 | .472** | .268 | .304 | .559** | .552** | .171 | .319 | |
| It is difficult to choose the most suitable e-commerce standard with so many different options available. | .308 | .484** | -.129 | .338 | .488** | .506** | .254 | .115 | .620 |

*Note: * significant at 0.05 level   ** significant at 0.01 level*

The resulting components were rotated using the Varimax procedure and a simple structure was achieved as shown in the rotated component matrix (see Tables 47 and 48).

Apart from the rankings assigned to the different groups of barriers, there are very few differences between alliance members and non-members in Australian regional SMEs in relation to the obstacles to e-commerce adoption. The findings are also similar to the results in Sweden where both categories of SMEs identified two groups of barriers, with suitability being of more concern to members and the complexity of e-commerce being of more importance to non-members.

We will now examine the groupings in the last location before discussing the results and drawing conclusions.

*Table 45. Total variance explained: Adoption barriers (non-members in Australia)*

| Component | Eigenvalue | % Variation | Cumulative % |
|---|---|---|---|
| 1 | 2.972 | 29.716 | 29.716 |
| 2 | 3.776 | 37.765 | 67.480 |

*Table 46. Total variance explained: Adoption barriers (members in Australia)*

| Component | Eigenvalue | % Variation | Cumulative % |
|---|---|---|---|
| 1 | 4.505 | 45.051 | 45.051 |
| 2 | 2.161 | 21.607 | 66.658 |

*Table 47. Rotated component matrix: Adoption barriers (non-members in Australia)*

| Barrier | Component 1: Unsuitable | Component 2: Too Difficult |
|---|---|---|
| E-commerce is not suited to our products/services. | .891 | |
| E-commerce is not suited to our way of doing business. | .891 | |
| E-commerce is not suited to the ways our clients do business. | .882 | |
| E-commerce does not offer any advantages to our organisation. | .818 | |
| We do not have the technical knowledge in the organisation to implement e-commerce. | | .863 |
| E-commerce is too complicated to implement. | | .878 |
| E-commerce is not secure. | | .608 |
| The financial investment required to implement e-commerce is too high. | | .782 |
| We do not have time to implement e-commerce. | | .786 |
| It is difficult to choose the most suitable e-commerce standard with so many different options available. | | .845 |

*Table 48. Rotated component matrix: Adoption barriers (members in Australia)*

| Barrier | Component 1: Unsuitable | Component 2: Too Difficult |
|---|---|---|
| E-commerce is not suited to our products/services. | .895 | |
| E-commerce is not suited to our way of doing business. | .911 | |
| E-commerce is not suited to the ways our clients do business. | .909 | |
| E-commerce does not offer any advantages to our organisation. | .862 | |
| We do not have the technical knowledge in the organisation to implement e-commerce. | | .802 |
| E-commerce is too complicated to implement. | | .881 |
| E-commerce is not secure. | | .760 |
| The financial investment required to implement e-commerce is too high. | | .806 |
| We do not have time to implement e-commerce. | | .679 |
| It is difficult to choose the most suitable e-commerce standard with so many different options available. | | .754 |

# USA

There was insufficient data to examine the e-commerce barriers, benefits, or disadvantages in the U.S. sample. Tables 49 and 50 provide the correlation matrices of the importance ratings for e-commerce adoption criteria. All correlations significant at the .001 level are shown in bold.

The results of the Kaiser-Meyer-Olkin MSA (.333 for members, .536 for non-members and Bartlett's test for Sphericity ($\chi^2 = 189$ p=.000 for members and $\chi^2 = 232$ p=.000 for non-members) indicated that the data set satisfied the assumptions for factorability. It should be noted however, that the Kaiser-Meyer-Olkin value for members was marginally below the optimally accepted values. Principle Components Analysis was chosen as the method of extraction in order to account for maximum variance in the data using a minimum number of factors. A five-factor solution with Eigenvalues 5.480, 2.128, 1.855, 1.344, and 1.031 was chosen for the member respondents. This was supported by an inspection of the Scree plot and accounted for 84.633% of the variance. A four factor solution with Eigenvalues 4.075, 2.343, 1.724, 1.231 was chosen for the non-member respondents. This was supported by an inspection of the Scree plot and accounted for 66.953% of the variance. These results are shown in Tables 51 and 52.

The resulting components were rotated using the Varimax procedure and a simple structure was achieved as shown in the rotated component matrices in Tables 53 and 54.

An examination of Tables 51 and 52 shows that there are substantial differences between the two categories of SMEs. The first obvious difference is that the member respondents loaded onto a five-factor solution while the non-members loaded onto four factors. For the member respondents, customer service was a separate criterion to all others and was solely loaded onto its own factor. By comparison, non-member respondents loaded this criterion

*Table 49. Adoption criteria correlation matrix for non-members (USA)*

| | Demand and/ or pressure from customers. | Demand and/ or pressure from suppliers. | To reduce costs. | To improve customer service. | To shorten lead time/reduce stock levels. | To increase sales. | To improve internal efficiency. | To strengthen relations with business partners. | The possibility of reaching new customers/markets. | To improve our competitiveness. | We were offered external support to adopt e-commerce. | To improve our marketing. | To improve control. |
|---|---|---|---|---|---|---|---|---|---|---|---|---|---|
| Pressure from competition. | .475 | | | | | | | | | | | | |
| Demand and/or pressure from suppliers. | .551* | .191 | | | | | | | | | | | |
| To reduce costs | .062 | .383 | .122 | | | | | | | | | | |
| To improve customer service. | .289 | .100 | .148 | -.247 | | | | | | | | | |
| To shorten lead time/reduce stock levels. | .316 | .526* | .197 | .167 | .527* | | | | | | | | |
| To increase sales. | .290 | .725** | .311 | .240 | .396 | .850 | | | | | | | |
| To improve internal efficiency. | .212 | .521* | -.106 | .262 | -.111 | .150 | .286 | | | | | | |
| To strengthen relations with business partners. | .427 | .611** | .128 | .653** | -.109 | .323 | .403 | .712** | | | | | |
| The possibility of reaching new customers/markets. | .398 | .686** | .306 | .354 | .444 | .526* | .605* | .388 | .590* | | | | |
| To improve our competitiveness. | .480 | .954 | .221 | .378 | .255 | .570* | .732** | .529* | .672** | .833 | | | |
| We were offered external support to adopt e-commerce | .334 | .329 | .265 | .029 | .017 | .533* | .351 | .041 | .073 | .224 | .301 | | |
| To improve our marketing. | .052 | .004 | -.101 | -.582* | -.123 | -.058 | -.113 | .274 | -.301 | -.272 | -.082 | .230 | |
| To improve control. | .607** | .367 | .260 | -.006 | .029 | .200 | .141 | .273 | .209 | -.041 | .242 | .162 | .382 |

Note: * significant at 0.05 level     ** significant at 0.01 level

*Table 50. Adoption criteria correlation matrix for members (USA)*

| | Demand and/or pressure from customers. | Demand and/or pressure from suppliers. | To reduce costs. | To improve customer service. | To shorten lead time/reduce stock levels. | To increase sales. | To improve internal efficiency. | To strengthen relations with business partners. | The possibility of reaching new customers/markets. | To improve our competitiveness. | We were offered external support to adopt e-commerce. | To improve our marketing. | To improve control. |
|---|---|---|---|---|---|---|---|---|---|---|---|---|---|
| Pressure from competition. | .085 | | | | | | | | | | | | |
| Demand and/or pressure from suppliers. | -.031 | .399* | | | | | | | | | | | |
| To reduce costs. | .143 | .654 | .409** | | | | | | | | | | |
| To improve customer service. | -.069 | .031 | .174 | .163 | | | | | | | | | |
| To shorten lead time/reduce stock levels. | .005 | .261 | .204 | .102 | .075 | | | | | | | | |
| To increase sales. | .249 | .385* | .466** | .123 | .093 | .642 | | | | | | | |
| To improve internal efficiency. | .349* | .177 | .441** | .221 | .096 | .297 | .634 | | | | | | |
| To strengthen relations with business partners. | .168 | .366* | .384* | .242 | -.011 | .723 | .665 | .359* | | | | | |
| The possibility of reaching new customers/markets. | .135 | .408** | .371* | .129 | .057 | .554 | .909 | .451** | .644 | | | | |
| To improve our competitiveness. | -.187 | .377* | .183 | .241 | -.091 | .356* | .397* | .208 | .443** | .560 | | | |
| We were offered external support to adopt e-commerce. | .203 | -.343* | -.084 | -.091 | .272 | -.256 | -.188 | .000 | -.150 | -.193 | -.226 | | |
| To improve our marketing. | .034 | .136 | .385* | .301 | .197 | .133 | .095 | .253 | .115 | .036 | -.040 | .468** | |
| To improve control. | .016 | -.221 | .071 | .080 | .247 | -.207 | -.106 | .096 | -.292 | -.131 | -.210 | .387* | .740 |

*Note: * significant at 0.05 level     ** significant at 0.01 level*

with improved marketing and improved control. For member respondents, pressure from customers and pressure from suppliers was loaded onto the same factor (together with improved control). For non-member respondents, pressure from customers was loaded together with better internal efficiency, while pressure from suppliers was grouped with pressure from competition and reduced costs. Non-member respondents loaded reduced stock and increased sales together with stronger relations with business partners, access to new markets, and improvement to competitiveness, thus implying improvements to the complete supply chain. Clearly, in the U.S. sample, there are divergent views between alliance members and non-members about e-commerce adoption criteria. However, there is some agreement in relation to the priority assigned to the first grouping in both categories (competitiveness/supply chain benefits) in that both members and non-members rated these drivers as being the most important.

We will now compare and discuss the key findings across the two locations.

## Comparison of Results: A Discussion

At the outset of this chapter, we identified three questions about SMEs and alliance membership, and the role of alliance membership in e-commerce adoption. We will now compare the answers to those three questions across the three locations and draw some conclusions.

Our first question was concerned with associations between various business characteristics and membership of an alliance. We found a number of associations in Sweden, none in Australia, and two in the U.S. These are summarised in Table 55, which indicates which SMEs are more likely to be members of an alliance.

The limited number of associations is, in itself, interesting because other studies have found a number of links between alliance membership and certain business characteristics. Previous research (Brush, 1997; Carter, 2000; Sandberg, 2003) has suggested that entering into alliances is more difficult for female CEOs than for males. We did not have any results to support this finding in any of the three locations. Other studies (Jorde et al., 1989; Miles et al., 1999; Schindehutte et al., 2001) have suggested that alliances assist SMEs to gain access to various financial, technical, and marketing resources. This would imply that SMEs, which have lower IT skills would be attracted to an alliance. Again, no such evidence was found in our research.

Our second question addressed the differences between alliance members and non-members in relation to e-commerce adoption criteria, barriers, benefits, and disadvantages. We ran a series of t-tailed tests to determine if these differences exist, and indeed, found this to be the case. There is very little agreement between SMEs in the three locations with regards to various aspects of e-commerce and alliance membership, as can be seen in Table 56.

As Table 56 indicates, there were some similarities between the Australian and U.S. SMEs with regards to e-commerce adoption criteria in that both locations showed differences in the pressure from competition criterion. However, while Australian non-members rated this criterion as being more important, in the U.S., it was the members who did so. In general, it was the non-members who rated all of the e-commerce adoption criteria higher than alli-

*Table 51. Total variance explained: Adoption criteria (non-members in USA)*

| Component | Eigenvalue | % Variation | Cumulative % |
|---|---|---|---|
| 1 | 4.075 | 29.107% | 29.107% |
| 2 | 2.343 | 16.739% | 45.846% |
| 3 | 1.724 | 12.313% | 58.159% |
| 4 | 1.231 | 8.794% | 66.953% |

*Table 52. Total variance explained: Adoption criteria (members in USA)*

| Component | Eigenvalue | % Variation | Cumulative % |
|---|---|---|---|
| 1 | 5.480 | 39.139% | 39.139% |
| 2 | 2.138 | 15.273% | 54.412% |
| 3 | 1.855 | 13.251% | 67.664% |
| 4 | 1.344 | 9.603% | 77.267% |
| 5 | 1.031 | 7.366% | 84.633% |

*Table 53. Rotated component matrix: Adoption criteria (non-members in USA)*

| | Component 1: Supply Chain | Component 2: Marketing | Component 3: Market Forces | Component 4: Sales |
|---|---|---|---|---|
| Demand and/or pressure from customers. | | | | .919 |
| Pressure from competition. | | | .834 | |
| Demand and/or pressure from suppliers. | | | .497 | |
| To reduce costs. | | | .870 | |
| To improve customer service. | | .581 | | |
| To shorten lead time/reduce stock levels. | .803 | | | |
| To increase sales. | .902 | | | |
| To improve internal efficiency. | | | | .553 |
| To strengthen relations with business partners. | .765 | | | |
| The possibility of reaching new customers/markets. | .882 | | | |
| To improve our competitiveness. | .524 | | | |
| We were offered external support to adopt e-commerce. | | .572 | | |
| To improve our marketing. | | .781 | | |
| To improve control. | | .843 | | |

*Table 54. Rotated component matrix: Adoption criteria (members in USA)*

| | Component 1:Competitiveness | Component 2: Sales | Component 3: Market forces | Component 4:Marketing & Resources | Component 5: Customer Service |
|---|---|---|---|---|---|
| Demand and/or pressure from customers. | | | .849 | | |
| Pressure from competition. | .787 | | | | |
| Demand and/or pressure from suppliers. | | | .774 | | |
| To reduce costs. | | | | .724 | |
| To improve customer service. | | | | | .946 |
| To shorten lead time/reduce stock levels. | | .692 | | | |
| To increase sales. | | .591 | | | |
| To improve internal efficiency. | .878 | | | | |
| To strengthen relations with business partners. | .849 | | | | |
| The possibility of reaching new customers/markets. | .607 | | | | |
| To improve our competitiveness. | .797 | | | | |
| We were offered external support to adopt e-commerce. | | .887 | | | |
| To improve our marketing. | | | | .929 | |
| To improve control. | | | .693 | | |

*Table 55. Summary of associations between business characteristics and alliance membership*

| | Sweden | Australia | USA |
|---|---|---|---|
| Business age | Younger SMEs | | - |
| Business size | Smaller SMEs | | Mid-sized SMEs (10 to 49 employees) |
| Level of CEO education | Qualified and unqualified CEOs almost equal | None | |
| Existence of enterprise-wide system | None | | - |
| E-commerce adoption | Adopters and non-adopters almost equal | | Adopters |

*Table 56. Summary of differences between members and non-members about e-commerce*

| | Statistically Significant Differences | | |
|---|---|---|---|
| | Sweden | Australia | USA |
| E-Commerce Criteria | No statistically significant differences. | • Pressure from competition.<br>• Possibility of reaching new customers/markets.<br>• Improved competitiveness.<br>• External support. | • Pressure from competition.<br>• Increased sales<br>(both rated more important by members). |
| | Almost all criteria rated more important by non-members. | Most criteria (incl. statistically significant) rated more important by non-members. | Variations between ratings of importance between members and non-members. |
| E-Commerce Barriers | • Not suited to our products/services.<br>• Does not offer any advantages. | High financial investment. | Data unavailable |
| | Almost all barriers rated more important by members. | Almost all barriers rated more important by non-members. | |
| E-Commerce Benefits | No statistically significant differences. | • Increased sales.<br>• Improved internal efficiency.<br>• Improved quality of information. | Data unavailable |
| | Variations between ratings between members and non-members. | Almost all benefits rated higher by non-members. | |
| E-Commerce Disadvantages | Reduced flexibility. | Security concerns. | Data unavailable |
| | Almost all disadvantages rated higher by non-members. | Almost all disadvantages rated higher by non-members. | |

ance members. This may suggest that SMEs outside an alliance react more strongly to the reasons for adopting e-commerce.

Although alliance members and non-members differed in relation to e-commerce barriers in both Sweden and Australia, it was the members who rated the barriers as being more important overall in Sweden. By contrast, in Australia SMEs that did not belong to an alliance experienced the obstacles to e-commerce adoption more strongly. The non-members in Australia also rated almost all of the e-commerce benefits higher, suggesting that belonging to an alliance did not promote advantages from e-commerce. There was more agreement between non-members in Sweden and Australia where SMEs in both locations rated e-commerce disadvantages higher than their member counterparts. This implies that members were less affected by the negative aspects of introducing e-commerce in their organisations.

Our last question was concerned with the groupings of criteria, barriers, benefits, and disadvantages in member and non-member SMEs. The results for the three locations, yet again, show interesting differences. Since the results of e-commerce benefit and disadvantage groupings are only available for Sweden, we will compare the results for criteria and barriers only.

The criteria groupings are only available for Sweden and the U.S. In Sweden, alliance non-members described three overarching reasons for adopting e-commerce, which we have termed internal business/resources, marketing, and market forces. In contrast, members omit the third factor (market forces); this suggesting that strategic alliances are "cushioning" its members from the impact of the external environment (such as pressure from customers, suppliers, and competitors). The factors found for members are more in line with the overall findings (discussed in Chapter IV), which also show a two-factor solution. In contrast, the U.S. respondents show a much more mixed set of results with five factors derived for members and four factors for non-members. While there is some degree of overlap between the Swedish and U.S. results, it is relatively minor and suggests that in the U.S. context, the presence of strategic alliances does not contribute to a clearer picture of the incentives to adopt e-commerce.

Comparing the results of grouping e-commerce barriers in Sweden and Australia (insufficient data from the U.S.) shows that there are similarities in that a two-factor solution was derived in both instances. The two factors are related to the unsuitability of e-commerce and the complexity or difficulties involved. The priorities placed on each grouping of barriers were the same in Sweden and Australia where alliance members placed a higher emphasis on the difficulties associated with implementing e-commerce and non-members placing more priority on the unsuitability of e-commerce. Once again, we have summarised the results in Tables 57 to 60.

# E-Commerce and Strategic Alliances: Implications

At the outset of this chapter, we discussed the benefits of alliances both from a general viewpoint and from the perspective of e-commerce. While previous research shows that SMEs stand to gain in a number of ways by forming alliances with other organisations, our study paints a different picture of the situation in three locations. The differences between

*Table 57. Groupings of e-commerce criteria: A comparison between non-members in Sweden and the USA*

|  | SWEDEN NON-MEMBERS | | | USA NON-MEMBERS | | | |
|---|---|---|---|---|---|---|---|
|  | 1: Internal Business and Resources | 2: Marketing | 3: Market Forces | 1: Supply Chain | 2: Marketing | 3: Market Forces | 4: Sales |
| Demand and/or pressure from customers. |  |  | ✓ |  |  |  | ✓ |
| Pressure from competition. |  |  | ✓ |  |  | ✓ |  |
| Demand and/or pressure from suppliers. | ✓ |  |  |  |  | ✓ |  |
| To reduce costs. | ✓ |  |  |  |  | ✓ |  |
| To improve customer service. |  | ✓ |  |  | ✓ |  |  |
| To shorten lead time/reduce stock levels. | ✓ |  |  | ✓ |  |  |  |
| To increase sales. |  | ✓ |  | ✓ |  |  |  |
| To improve internal efficiency. | ✓ |  |  |  |  |  | ✓ |
| To strengthen relations with business partners. |  | ✓ |  | ✓ |  |  |  |
| The possibility of reaching new customers/markets. |  | ✓ |  | ✓ |  |  |  |
| To improve our competitiveness. |  | ✓ |  | ✓ |  |  |  |
| We were offered external support to adopt e-commerce. | ✓ |  |  |  | ✓ |  |  |
| To improve our marketing. |  | ✓ |  |  | ✓ |  |  |
| To improve control. | ✓ |  |  |  | ✓ |  |  |

these locations in relation to alliances are noticeable and, once again, point to the need for further study in a specific region prior to promoting e-commerce adoption through the use of alliances. By doing this, government organisations can promote the use of alliances as a means to facilitate e-commerce adoption. For example, in our study we found that e-commerce disadvantages were experienced more strongly by non-members than members of an alliance. This would suggest the formation of an alliance between e-commerce adopters in order to dissipate the negative effects of e-commerce implementation and ensure a smoother transition from pre e-commerce to post e-commerce business. Similarly, in Australia e-commerce adoption by SMEs who are not members of an alliance is more likely to be affected by pressure from competition. The differences between SMEs in different locations and with different alliance statuses have been highlighted and summarised in this chapter so that they can be used to promote e-commerce adoption in differing situations.

*Table 58. Groupings of e-commerce criteria: A comparison between alliance members in Sweden and the USA*

| | SWEDEN MEMBERS | | USA MEMBERS | | | | |
|---|---|---|---|---|---|---|---|
| | 1: Marketing | 2: Internal Business & Resources | 1: Competitiveness | 2: Sales | 3: Market forces | 4: Marketing & Resources | 5: Customer Service |
| Demand and/or pressure from customers. | | ✓ | | | ✓ | | |
| Pressure from competition. | | ✓ | ✓ | | | | |
| Demand and/or pressure from suppliers. | | ✓ | | | ✓ | | |
| To reduce costs. | | ✓ | | | | ✓ | |
| To improve customer service. | ✓ | | | | | | ✓ |
| To shorten lead time/reduce stock levels. | | ✓ | | ✓ | | | |
| To increase sales. | ✓ | | | ✓ | | | |
| To improve internal efficiency. | ✓ | ✓ | ✓ | | | | |
| To strengthen relations with business partners. | ✓ | | ✓ | | | | |
| The possibility of reaching new customers/markets. | ✓ | | ✓ | | | | |
| To improve our competitiveness. | ✓ | | ✓ | | | | |
| We were offered external support to adopt e-commerce. | | ✓ | | ✓ | | | |
| To improve our marketing. | ✓ | | | | | ✓ | |
| To improve control. | ✓ | ✓ | | | ✓ | | |

# E-Commerce and Strategic Alliances: Key Findings

## Sweden

- Younger SMEs, smaller SMEs, and SMEs without an enterprise-wide system are more likely to be members of an alliance.

- There were no differences between members and non-members in relation to e-commerce adoption criteria.

- There were differences in two barriers between members and non-members. Members rated the poor suitability of e-commerce to their products/services and the lack of e-commerce benefits as stronger e-commerce barriers than non-members.

- There were no differences between members and non-members in relation to e-commerce benefits.

*Table 59. Groupings of e-commerce barriers: A comparison between non-members in Sweden and Australia*

| | SWEDEN NON-MEMBERS | | AUSTRALIA NON-MEMBERS | |
|---|---|---|---|---|
| | 1: Unsuitable | 2: Too Difficult | 1: Unsuitable | 2: Too Difficult |
| E-commerce is not suited to our products/services. | ✓ | | ✓ | |
| E-commerce is not suited to our way of doing business. | ✓ | | ✓ | |
| E-commerce is not suited to the ways our clients do business. | ✓ | | ✓ | |
| E-commerce does not offer any advantages to our organisation. | ✓ | | ✓ | |
| We do not have the technical knowledge in the organisation to implement e-commerce. | | ✓ | | ✓ |
| E-commerce is too complicated to implement. | | ✓ | | ✓ |
| E-commerce is not secure. | | ✓ | | ✓ |
| The financial investment required to implement e-commerce is too high. | ✓ | | | ✓ |
| We do not have time to implement e-commerce. | | ✓ | | ✓ |
| It is difficult to choose the most suitable e-commerce standard with so many different options available. | | ✓ | | ✓ |

- Non-members cited reduced flexibility as a stronger disadvantage than members.

- Both members and non-members grouped internal business practices criteria as being more important than the other groupings of criteria.

- Barriers related to the unsuitability of e-commerce were ranked more important by alliance members, while those related to the difficulty of implementing e-commerce were thought to be a higher priority by non-members.

- Non-members experienced more benefits related to the functioning of their supply chain, while non-members rated benefits grouped around business efficiency higher.

- Both members and non-members agreed that the groupings of e-commerce disadvantages related to internal business practices were more applicable to their situation than the other groupings.

# Australia

- None of the business characteristics were found to have any effect on alliance membership in Australia.

*Table 60. Groupings of e-commerce barriers: A comparison between alliance members in Sweden and Australia*

| | SWEDEN MEMBERS | | AUSTRALIA MEMBERS | |
|---|---|---|---|---|
| | 1: Unsuitable | 2: Too Difficult | 1: Unsuitable | 2: Too Difficult |
| E-commerce is not suited to our products/services. | ✓ | | ✓ | |
| E-commerce is not suited to our way of doing business. | ✓ | | ✓ | |
| E-commerce is not suited to the ways our clients do business. | ✓ | | ✓ | |
| E-commerce does not offer any advantages to our organisation. | ✓ | | ✓ | |
| We do not have the technical knowledge in the organisation to implement e-commerce. | | ✓ | | ✓ |
| E-commerce is too complicated to implement. | | ✓ | | ✓ |
| E-commerce is not secure. | | ✓ | | ✓ |
| The financial investment required to implement e-commerce is too high. | ✓ | | | ✓ |
| We do not have time to implement e-commerce. | | ✓ | | ✓ |
| It is difficult to choose the most suitable e-commerce standard with so many different options available. | | ✓ | | ✓ |

- Non-members rated pressure from competition, possibility of reaching new markets, improved competitiveness, and external support as more important drivers than members.

- Non-members were reluctant to adopt e-commerce due to the high financial investment involved.

- Increased sales, better internal efficiency, and improved quality of information were benefits experienced more strongly by non-members.

- Security concerns were an important disadvantage for non-members.

- Barriers related to the unsuitability of e-commerce were ranked more important by alliance members, while those related to the difficulty of implementing e-commerce were thought to be a higher priority by non-members.

# USA

- Mid-sized SMEs (10 to 49 employees) and those that had adopted e-commerce were more likely to belong to a business alliance.

- Pressure from competition and increased sales were more important reasons for members to adopt e-commerce.

- Non-members rated e-commerce drivers related to improvements across their supply chain as being more important, unlike members who rated criteria grouped around increasing competitiveness higher.

# References

Achrol, R. S., & Kotler, P. (1999). Marketing in the network economy. *Journal of Marketing, 63*, 146-163.

Blair, T. (2000). *The launch of UK online.* UK Prime Minister, Press release. Retrieved September 11, 2000, from www.open.gov.uk

Brush, C. G. (1997). Women's entrepreneurship. In *Proceedings of the OECD Conference on Women Entrepreneurs in Small and Medium Enterprises*, OECD, Paris.

Carter, S. (2000). Improving the numbers and performance of women-owned businesses: Some implications for training and advisory services. *Education & Training, 42*(4/5), 326-333.

Ciappei, C., & Simoni, C. (2005). Drivers of new product success in the Italian sport show cluster of Montebelluna. *Journal of Fashion Marketing and Management, 9*(1), 20-42.

Cirillo, R. (2000). The new rules: Move beyond "E" ... and eight other strategies for competing in the new economy: A new generation of e-business consultants is playing by a different set of rules. Nine of them to be exact. Are you up to Speed? *Varbusiness, 1612*, 26.

Copp, C. B., & Ivy, R. L. (2001). Networking trends of small tourism businesses in post-socialist Slovakia. *Journal of Small Business Management, 39*(4), 345-353.

Cropper, S. (1996). Collaborative working and the issue of sustainability. In C. Huxham (ed.), *Creating collaborative advantage* (pp. 80-100). London.

Dahlstrand, A. L. (1999). Technology-based SMEs in the Goteborg Region: Their origin and interaction with universities and large firms. *Regional Studies, 33*(4), 379-389.

Daniel, E., & Wilson, H. (2002a). Adoption intentions and benefits realised: A study of e-commerce in UK SMEs. *Journal of Small Business and Enterprise Development, 9*(4), 331-348.

Daniel, E., Wilson, H., & Myers, A. (2002b). Adoption of e-commerce by SMEs in the UK. *International Small Business Journal, 20*(3), 253-268.

Datta, D. (1988). International joint ventures: A framework for analysis. *Journal of General Management, 14*(2), 78-91.

Dean, J., Holmes, S., & Smith, S. (1997). Understanding Business networks: Evidence from manufacturing and service sectors in Australia. *Journal of Small Business Management, 35*(1), 79-84.

Dennis, C. (2000). Networking for marketing advantage. *Management Decision, 38*(4), 287-292.

Drakopoulou-Dodd, S., Jack, S., & Anderson, A. R. (2002). Scottish entrepreneurial networks in the international context. *International Small Business Journal, 20*(2), 213-219.

European Commission. (2000). *European survey of the information society.* European Society Indicators in the Member States of the EU. Retrieved from www.europa. eu.in/ISPO/esis

Fletcher, M. (1994). How bank managers make lending decisions to small firms. In *Proceedings of the 17ᵗʰ ISBA UK National Small Firms Policy and Research Conference.* Sheffield, UK: Sheffield Hallam University.

Gibb, A. (1993). Small business development in Central and Eastern Europe—Opportunity for a rethink. *Journal of Business Venturing, 8,* 461-486.

Golden, P. A., & Dollinger, M. (1993, summer). Cooperative alliances and competitive strategies in small manufacturing firms. *Entrepreneurship Theory and Practice,* 43-56.

Hadjimonolis, A. (1999). Barriers to innovation for SMEs in a small less developed country (Cyprus). *Technovation, 19*(9), 561-570.

Jarratt, D. G. (1998). A strategic classification of business alliances: A qualitative perspective built from a study of small and medium-sized enterprises. *Qualitative Market Research: An International Journal, 1*(1), 39-49.

Johannisson, B., Ramirez-Pasillas, M., & Karlsson, G. (2002, August). Theoretical and methodological challenges bridging firm strategies and contextual networking. *Entrepreneurship and Innovation,* 165-174.

Jorde, T., & Teece, D. (1989). Competition and cooperation: Striking the right balance. *Californian Management Review, 31*(3), 25-38.

Keeble, D., Lawson, C., Moore, B., & Wilkinson, F. (1999). Collective learning processes, networking, and "institutional thickness" in the Cambridge Region. *Regional Studies, 33*(4), 319-332.

Lawrence, K. L. (1997). Factors inhibiting the utilisation of electronic commerce facilities in Tasmanian small-to-medium sized enterprises. In *Proceedings of the 8ᵗʰ Australasian Conference on Information Systems* (pp. 587-597).

MacGregor, R. C., & Bunker, D. J. (1996). Does experience with IT vendors/consultants influence small business computer education requirements. In *Association of Information Systems Proceedings of the Americas Conference on Information Systems,* Phoenix AZ (pp. 31-33).

MacGregor, R., & Vrazalic, L. (2005, December). Electronic commerce adoption and strategic alliance membership: A study of regional SMEs in Sweden. In *Proceedings of the International Business Information Management Conference,* Cairo (pp. 13-15).

Marchewka, J. T., & Towell, E. R. (2000). A comparison of structure and strategy in electronic commerce. *Information Technology and People, 13*(2), 137-149.

Miles, G., Preece, S., & Baetz, M. C. (1999, April, 20-29). Dangers of dependence: The impact of strategic alliance use by small technology based firms. *Journal of Small Business Management.*

Nalebuff, B. J., & Brandenburg, A. M. (1996). *Co-operation*. Philadelphia: Harper Collins Business.

O'Donnell, A., Gilmore, A., Cummins, D., & Carson, D. (2001). The network construct in entrepreneurship research: A review and critique. *Management Decision, 39*(9), 749-760.

Overby, J. W., & Min, S. (2001). International supply chain management in an Internet environment: A network-oriented approach to internationalisation. *International Marketing Review, 18*(4), 392-420.

Ozcan, G. (1995). Small business networks and local ties in Turkey. *Entrepreneurship and Regional Development, 7*(3), 265-282.

Premaratne, S. P. (2001). Networks, resources, and small business growth: The experience in Sri Lanka. *Journal of Small Business Management, 39*(4), 363-371.

Quayle, M. (2002). E-commerce: The challenge for UK SMEs in the Twenty-First Century. *International Journal of Operations and Production Management, 22*(10), 1148-1161.

Sandberg, K. W. (2003). An exploratory study of women in micro enterprises: Gender related difficulties. *Journal of Small Business and Enterprise Development, 10*(4), 408-417.

Schindehutte, M., & Morris, M. H. (2001). Understanding strategic adaptation in small firms. *International Journal of Entrepreneurial Behaviour and Research, 7*(3), 84-107.

Singh, J. P., & Gilchrist, S. M (2002). Three layers of the electronic commerce network: Challenges for the developed and developing worlds. *Info, 4*(2), 31-41.

Taylor, M., & Murphy A. (2004) SMEs and E-business. *Journal of Small Business and Enterprise Development, 11*(3), 280 - 289.

Terziovski, M. (2003). The relationship between networking practices and business excellence: A study of small to medium enterprises (SMEs). *Measuring Business Excellence, 7*(2), 78-92.

Tetteh, E., & Burn, J. (2001). Global strategies for SME-business: Applying the SMALL framework. *Logistics Information Management, 14*(1-2), 171-180.

Tikkanen, H. (1998). The network approach in analysing international marketing and purchasing operations: A case study of a European SME's focal net 1992-95. *Journal of Business and Industrial Marketing, 13*(2), 109-131.

Turban, E., Lee, J., King, D., & Chung, H. (2000). *Electronic commerce: A managerial perspective*. NJ: Prentice Hall.

Veradarajan, P. R., & Cunningham, M. (1995). Strategic alliances: A synthesis of conceptual foundations. *Journal of the Academy of Marketing Science, 23*(4), 282-296.

Walczuch, R., Van Braven, G., & Lundgren, H. (2000). Internet adoption barriers for small firms in the Netherlands. *European Management Journal, 18*(5), 561-572.

Westhead, P., & Storey, D. J. (1996). Management training and small firm performance: Why is the link so weak? *International Small Business Journal, 14*(4), 13-24.

Wheelen, T., & Hunger, J. D. (2002). *Strategic management and business policy*. New York: Prentice Hall.

Yeung, H. W. (1994). Critical reviews of geographical perspectives on business organisations and the organisation of production: Towards a network approach. *Progressive Human Geography, 18*(4), 460-490.

## Chapter IX

# The Role of Gender in E-Commerce Adoption:
## Does Having a Male or Female CEO Affect E-Commerce Use?

One question that inevitably seems to be raised in most areas of business research is the question of gender. The literature is full of studies comparing males to females across everything from ability in mathematics to coping with stress in the workplace. The area of SMEs is no different.

The past 20 years has seen a shift away from the traditional male-dominated economy that centred on manufacturing, toward a more service and retail-based economy that has seen a substantial increase in the participation of females (Cox, 1999; Teltscher, 2002). Not only has there been a rise in the participation of females in the workforce, but the advent of affordable technology has led to a more flexible method of work and a greater global participation by the workforce. A number of studies (Singh, 2001; Teltscher, 2002) have concluded that, compared to the 1990s, there is a more equitable makeup of the workforce particularly in the SME sector. This includes both an increase in the overall level of participation by females as well as increases in the ownership/management of SMEs by females. A number of studies have explored potential determinants of Internet use and found gender to be an influential variable in predicting this use (Butler, 2000; Sexton, Johnson, & Hignite, 2002). Others have developed frameworks to explain gender differences in Internet use and online behaviour (Rodgers & Harris, 2003). In this chapter, we will examine the role of gender in the general ownership/management of SMEs and then consider its role in the adoption and use of e-commerce.

# Background

Perhaps an appropriate opening preface to this section should be the observation by Baker, Aldrich, and Liou (1997) and Carter (2000) that research into gender differences in the ownership/management of SMEs is scarce by comparison to research that has examined SMEs in general. However, that having been said, there are a number of interesting findings in the literature that compare various facets of gender differences in the ownership/management of SMEs. These facets include comparisons of ownership/management statistics and reasons for the movement into the SME sector, finance availability, management style, networking, business types, and success or failure of the business.

Previous research (Brooksbank, 2000; Carter, 2000; Reynolds, Savage, & Williams, 1992) has suggested that the primary motivation for moving into the SME sector is the desire to become self-employed. An examination of the UK labour force figures for the 1990s (Labour Force Survey 1990-1999) shows that while the growth in self-employment in males was 4.73%, the growth in self-employment in females was 19.06%. Studies by Nillson (1997), Brush and Hisrich (1999), and Sandberg (2003) have provided similar figures in Europe, U.S., and Scandinavia.

While early studies (Goffee & Skase, 1985; Hisrich & Brush, 1986; Watkins & Watkins, 1984) concentrated on the motivational similarities (Male vs. Female), studies by Brush (1997), Buttner and Moore (1997), and Carter and Cannon (1992) found that females saw becoming self-employed within the SME sector as a means of circumventing the "glass ceiling."

The growth in the SME sector coupled with the rise of the number of women entering the IT sector has triggered several new research studies in relation to access to finance, management style, alliances, and IT use.

Some of these studies (Carter, 2000; Rosa, Hamilton, Carter, & Bums, 1994; Sandberg, 2003) have examined gender differences both in the acquisition of finance as well as the use of that finance within the SME. A study of 600 UK SMEs (Carter & Rosa, 1998) found that males were more likely to make use of bank loans and overdrafts than females. Indeed, females were less likely to use or rely on financial institutional arrangements including cheaper sources of finance such as extended supplier credit than were their male counterparts. This same study found that female owner/managers used less start-up capital (33%) than males, resulting in fewer employees and long-term disadvantages in terms of their business being able to grow.

Not only has the use of finance been shown to differ between males and females, a number of studies (Carter, 2000; Carter et al., 1998; Fay & Williams, 1993; Fletcher, 1994; Koper, 1993; Rosa et al., 1994; Sandberg, 2003) have shown that the ability to access finance often differs between male and female owner/managers. Many of these studies have concluded that while financial institutions may have a non-discriminatory policy, the application of those policies often prejudice against women through stereotyping.

The increased difficulty of obtaining finance by female owner/managers have impinged on four areas of financing:

- The ability to raise start-up finance (Carter 2000; Koper, 1993)
- Differences in guarantees required to attract financing (Carter, 2000; Sandberg, 2003)
- Attraction of ongoing finance through females' failing to penetrate the informal financial networks (Olm, Carsrud, & Avery, 1988; Sandberg, 2003)
- Sexual stereotyping (Carter, 2000)

An examination of the literature surrounding gender differences and management style in the SME sector provides differing and disparate results. Previous research (Bartol & Butterfield, 1976; Bass, 1981; Maupin, 1990; Powell, 1993) suggests that there are few real differences in leadership styles between men and women. Studies by Johnson and Storey (1993) found female owner/managers to be less confident, less aggressive, and lacking in problem-solving abilities than males. Other more recent studies (McGregor & Tweed, 2001; Verheul, Risseeuw, & Bartelse, 2002) found that female managers of SMEs were more relaxed with giving instructions to staff through informal conversation than were their male counterparts. Indeed, while the male managers stressed the role and use of power, female managers stressed the importance of interpersonal communication. These studies also showed that female managers were more likely to hire external expertise and were more inclined to develop business strategies that were specific to their particular business than were their male counterparts.

A recent study of SMEs in Sweden (Sandberg, 2003) showed that female managers paid more attention to business-to-business links and strategic alliances than males did. The study also showed that female managers were more mindful of both their customers and their staff than were male managers. Similar findings were reported in a study carried out on New Zealand SMEs (McGregor et al., 2001). This study also found that females were significantly better at dealing with the details of the day-to-day business and were far more aware and capable of managing budgets than their male counterparts.

Several studies have examined the role of gender in relation to alliances between SMEs. Early studies (DeWine & Casbolt, 1983; Smeltzer & Fann, 1989) suggest that male networks and alliances are often far more informal than female networks. More recent studies (Brush, 1997; Carter, 2000; Carter et al., 1998; Sandberg, 2003) support these earlier findings adding that females appear to be less welcome in social networks often resulting in a reduced ability to use network partners to gain finance or attract technical or marketing assistance.

Over the years, a number of studies have been carried out that have examined the gender differences in factors such as business size, business age, as well as the number of businesses owned by an owner/manager. Early studies (Kalleberg & Leicht, 1991; Loscocco & Robinson, 1991; Loscocco & Leicht, 1993) have shown that female owned/managed SMEs are usually smaller than those operated by their male counterparts. These studies have shown that these differences in size often translate into differences in turnover and long-term growth potential for the business. Kalleberg and Berg (1987) also found that many female owned/managed SMEs were in less innovative sectors of the market compared to male owned/managed SMEs. Many recent studies (Carter, 2000; Sonfield, Lussier, Corman, & McKinney, 2001) have shown that trend appears to be continuing and note that one of the "spin-offs" of this trend is that males often own several SMEs, while females will, more often than not, stick to a single business.

While there are well documented gender-based differences in the approach to business and business management, studies comparing male success to female success, or indeed male failure to female failure have found no real differences in the likelihood of success or failure dependent on gender (Kolsaker & Payne, 2002; Labich, 1994; Perry, 2002). In a recent study of SMEs in the U.S., Perry (2002) found out that not only was there no relationship between gender and success or failure of an SME, but there were significant gender-based differences in the extent and use of planning, the formulation of enterprise-wide strategies or the implementation of strategies within an SME.

With regards to IT use by different genders, early studies (Gilroy & Desai, 1986; Meier & Lambert, 1991) found that males were less anxious about using computer technology than females. Yet, according to Gebler (2000), in the year 2000 female Internet users exceeded male users. The implications of this event are significant considering the previous research into the use of the Internet by females. Shade (1998) and Sheehan (1999) both found that females were more concerned with privacy and security issues and subsequently more cautious about using the Internet for online shopping and trading. Presumably, the same concerns would apply to female business owners considering e-commerce adoption. Kolsaker et al. (2002) refuted these studies by finding no significant differences between the genders in relation to Internet privacy and security. It should be noted, however, that their study followed the surge of female users after 2000, while the studies by Shade (1998) and Sheehan (1999) preceded the widespread use of the Internet by females.

Although the gap between male and female Internet adoption rates has disappeared resulting in a more gender-balanced use of the Internet, differences remain in how the Internet is actually used. For example, Akhter (2003) found that men were still more likely to use the Internet for shopping than women. This would suggest that males may be more open to e-commerce adoption as business owners because they are more willing to adopt the technology as consumers. However, empirical evidence of such a trend is not available. Although our knowledge of gender differences in relation to *Internet* adoption as users and consumers is broad, our understanding of gender differences in relation to *e-commerce* adoption as business owners is scant and inadequate. The exception is a study of e-commerce and teleworking in 112 Spanish SMEs by Perez, Carnicer, and Sanchez (2002). The authors found that SMEs with female managers were significantly more concerned with the difficulty of using the technology than were their male counterparts. The study also cited cost of the technology and changes to work procedures as being of more concern to female managers. This chapter provides an additional insight into the role of gender in relation to e-commerce adoption in the SME sector.

# Research Questions

Our aim in this chapter is to explore the issues related to gender and e-commerce in several ways. Since we have already examined the associations between gender and other business characteristics in Chapter III, these results will not be replicated here. Instead, the reader is referred to the earlier chapter. In this chapter, we will focus on determining whether the importance assigned to e-commerce adoption criteria, e-commerce barriers, e-commerce benefits, or disadvantages differs between male and female CEOs of SMEs. Our second aim is to determine whether the groupings and priorities of criteria for adoption, barriers to adoption, e-commerce benefits, and disadvantages differ between males and females. Subsequently, the chapter is organised based on the following two questions:

1.   Are there any differences between male and female CEOs in relation to e-commerce adoption criteria, barriers, benefits, and disadvantages?
2.   Do the groupings of e-commerce adoption criteria, barriers, benefits, and disadvantages differ between SMEs with male and female CEOs?

# Methodology

Respondents in all three locations were asked to indicate whether their CEO (owner/manager) was male or female. Chapter III provided a summary of the responses to this question. These are replicated in Table 1 for the benefit of the reader.

Table 1 shows that in all three locations, males made up the majority of the respondents with almost 86% of Swedish CEOs being male and just under 64% of Australian CEOs. The percentage of female respondents is substantially lower than previous studies (Carter, 2000; Nillson, 1997; Sandberg, 2003) who reported that 25%-30% of SMEs were female owned/managed. One possible explanation is that since this study was regionally based, the percentages found in earlier studies may not apply, suggesting that females find it harder to establish and run an SME in a regional setting. However, since the sample size is relatively small, the other explanation is that the results are a function of the number of respondents, rather than indicative of the population. It should also be noted here that there were no associations found between gender and e-commerce adoption (as per the results in Chapter III), which would suggest that gender does not influence e-commerce adoption (i.e., males are just as likely to adopt e-commerce as females and vice versa). Due to the low number of female respondents in the U.S., it was not possible to perform a statistical analysis. Therefore, this data has been excluded from the chapter.

The rest of this chapter is structured as follows. First, we will present the results of the two-tailed t-tests in Sweden and Australia and then the results of the factor analysis. The final part of the chapter will discuss and compare the findings, and present the business implications of the results.

*Table 1. Summary of responses to gender question*

| | Sweden | | Australia | | USA | |
|---|---|---|---|---|---|---|
| | **TOTAL RESPONDENTS** | | | | | |
| | No of responses | % | No of responses | % | No of responses | % |
| Female | 36 | 11.5 | 58 | 36.3 | 17 | 14.7 |
| Male | 269 | 85.9 | 102 | 63.7 | 89 | 76.7 |
| Missing | 8 | 2.6 | 0 | 0 | 10 | 8.6 |
| | **E-COMMERCE ADOPTERS** | | | | | |
| | No of responses | % | No of responses | % | No of responses | % |
| Female | 19 | 10.4 | 7 | 28 | 9 | 14.3 |
| Male | 160 | 87.4 | 18 | 72 | 49 | 77.8 |
| Missing | 4 | 2.2 | 0 | 0 | 5 | 7.9 |
| | **NON-ADOPTERS** | | | | | |
| | No of responses | % | No of responses | % | No of responses | % |
| Female | 17 | 13.1 | 51 | 37.8 | 8 | 15.1 |
| Male | 109 | 83.8 | 84 | 62.2 | 40 | 75.5 |
| Missing | 4 | 3.1 | 0 | 0 | 5 | 9.4 |

# Gender and E-Commerce Adoption

Our first research question was concerned with the differences between males and females in terms of their ratings of various e-commerce aspects. To find out if any such differences existed, the data was subdivided for each location into male-owned and female-owned SMEs. A series of two-tailed t-tests was then applied to the data to determine if there were any statistically significant differences in the ratings of e-commerce adoption criteria, barriers to adoption, benefits derived from e-commerce adoption, or disadvantages incurred through adoption of e-commerce. The results are discussed next.

## Sweden

Table 2 provides the results of the two-tailed t-tests for criteria to adopt e-commerce.

An examination of Table 2 shows that males placed a higher level of importance on all criteria when compared to females. The table also shows that there were statistically significant differences (male vs. female) for 10 of the 14 criteria tested. With the exception of the criterion related to external assistance and support, males rated all criteria in the important

*Table 2. Comparison of e-commerce adoption criteria (males vs. females): Sweden*

| Criteria | Mean Males | N Males | Mean Females | N Fe- males | t value | Significance |
|---|---|---|---|---|---|---|
| Demand and/or pressure from customers. | 2.03 | 160 | 1.42 | 19 | 1.759 | .080 |
| Pressure from competition. | 2.30 | 160 | 1.47 | 19 | 2.281 | .024 |
| Demand and/or pressure from suppliers. | 1.74 | 160 | 1.02 | 19 | 2.719 | .007 |
| To reduce costs. | 3.09 | 160 | 1.95 | 19 | 2.885 | .004 |
| To improve customer service. | 3.73 | 160 | 2.42 | 19 | 2.499 | .021 |
| To shorten lead time/reduce stock levels. | 2.57 | 160 | 1.68 | 19 | 1.744 | .096 |
| To increase sales. | 2.99 | 160 | 1.68 | 19 | 3.207 | .002 |
| To improve internal efficiency. | 3.59 | 160 | 3.21 | 19 | .824 | .420 |
| To strengthen relations with business partners. | 2.94 | 160 | 1.84 | 19 | 2.838 | .005 |
| The possibility of reaching new customers/markets. | 2.99 | 160 | 1.53 | 19 | 3.585 | .000 |
| To improve our competitiveness. | 3.38 | 160 | 2.05 | 19 | 3.230 | .001 |
| We were offered external support to adopt e-commerce. | 1.35 | 160 | 1.02 | 19 | 2.026 | .044 |
| To improve our marketing. | 2.96 | 160 | 1.95 | 19 | 1.996 | .059 |
| To improve control. | 2.63 | 160 | 1.84 | 19 | 2.000 | .047 |

range, while, with the exception of adopting e-commerce to improve internal efficiency, females rated them as unimportant. This raises the question as to the applicability of criteria for adoption for SMEs that are owned/managed by females and highlights the divergent views of male and female CEOs about the reasons why they adopted e-commerce. Table 2 also shows that six criteria (demand and/or pressure from suppliers, reduced costs, increased sales, stronger relations with business partners, new customers/markets, and improved competitiveness) were highly statistically different between males and females. Since males rated the criteria as being more important overall, this would suggest that females were more inclined to view e-commerce as an internal mechanism for improving the business rather than an external tool.

The same analysis was undertaken for e-commerce barriers and the following results were obtained (Table 3).

Unlike the differences shown in the e-commerce criteria, Table 3 indicates that for the regional Swedish respondents there were no significant differences between male and female CEOs in the importance assigned to e-commerce barriers. The mean ratings for males and females are very similar. This suggests that the male and female CEOs of non-adopters have comparable views about e-commerce barriers.

Table 4 provides the Swedish data for the benefits derived from e-commerce adoption.

*Table 3. Comparison of e-commerce adoption barriers (males vs. females): Sweden*

| Barriers | Mean Males | N Males | Mean Females | N Females | t value | Significance |
|---|---|---|---|---|---|---|
| E-commerce is not suited to our products/services. | 2.74 | 109 | 2.65 | 17 | .193 | .847 |
| E-commerce is not suited to our way of doing business. | 2.63 | 109 | 2.53 | 17 | .213 | .832 |
| E-commerce is not suited to the ways our clients do business. | 2.59 | 109 | 2.29 | 17 | .602 | .548 |
| E-commerce does not offer any advantages to our organisation. | 2.39 | 109 | 2.12 | 17 | .576 | .566 |
| We do not have the technical knowledge in the organisation to implement e-commerce. | 2.59 | 109 | 2.65 | 17 | -.125 | .901 |
| E-commerce is too complicated to implement. | 1.98 | 109 | 1.94 | 17 | .096 | .923 |
| E-commerce is not secure. | 2.07 | 109 | 2.00 | 17 | .175 | .862 |
| The financial investment required to implement e-commerce is too high. | 2.29 | 109 | 1.94 | 17 | .781 | .436 |
| We do not have time to implement e-commerce. | 2.46 | 109 | 2.24 | 17 | .470 | .639 |
| It is difficult to choose the most suitable e-commerce standard with so many different options available. | 2.32 | 109 | 2.18 | 17 | .301 | .764 |

An examination of Table 4 shows that 6 of the 10 examined benefits show a significant difference in the rating of importance between male CEOs and female CEOs. As with the criteria, all of the benefits are rated as being more important by the males compared to females. One interesting finding however is the fact that with the exception of the benefit improved relations with business partners, all ratings (male and female) are in the unimportant to very unimportant range. One possible explanation is that while benefits derived from e-commerce do exist, they may be lower than expected by the respondents. This notion is supported by earlier findings (see Riquelme, 2002) and will be discussed in detail in a subsequent chapter.

Table 5 provides the data concerned with disadvantages incurred through the adoption of e-commerce.

An examination of Table 5 shows that only one disadvantage (reduced flexibility) showed any significant difference in how it was rated by male vs. female CEOs. While both males and females rated this disadvantage as unimportant to very unimportant, the males considered the disadvantage more important than did the females.

*Table 4. Comparison of e-commerce benefits (males vs. females): Sweden*

| Benefits | Mean Males | N Males | Mean Females | N Females | t value | Significance |
|---|---|---|---|---|---|---|
| Reduced our administration costs. | 2.83 | 160 | 2.05 | 19 | 2.018 | .045 |
| Reduced our production costs. | 2.79 | 160 | 1.68 | 19 | 1.355 | .177 |
| Reduced our lead time. | 2.16 | 160 | 1.47 | 19 | 1.905 | .058 |
| Reduced our stock levels. | 2.78 | 160 | 2.05 | 19 | 1.435 | .166 |
| Lead to increased sales. | 2.06 | 160 | 1.02 | 19 | 3.463 | .002 |
| Increased our internal efficiency. | 2.53 | 160 | 1.37 | 19 | 3.179 | .002 |
| Improved our relations with business partners. | 3.19 | 160 | 2.68 | 19 | 1.321 | .188 |
| Gave us access to new customers and markets. | 2.83 | 160 | 1.68 | 19 | 3.052 | .003 |
| Improved our competitiveness. | 2.58 | 160 | 1.63 | 19 | 2.424 | .016 |
| Improved the quality of information in our organisation. | 2.06 | 160 | 1.00 | 19 | 4.142 | .000 |

*Table 5. Comparison of e-commerce disadvantages (males vs. females): Sweden*

| Disadvantages | Mean Males | N Males | Mean Females | N Females | t value | Significance |
|---|---|---|---|---|---|---|
| Deteriorated relations with business partners. | 1.26 | 160 | 1.02 | 19 | 1.440 | .152 |
| Increased costs. | 1.88 | 160 | 1.37 | 19 | 1.604 | .110 |
| Increased the computer maintenance required. | 2.09 | 160 | 2.11 | 19 | -.035 | .972 |
| Doubled the amount of work. | 1.83 | 160 | 1.42 | 19 | 1.408 | .161 |
| Reduced the flexibility of the business processes. | 1.77 | 160 | 1.00 | 19 | 2.602 | .010 |
| Raised security concerns. | 1.21 | 160 | 1.02 | 19 | 1.522 | .130 |
| Made us increasingly dependent on this technology. | 1.37 | 160 | 1.00 | 19 | 1.685 | .094 |

# Summary of Findings: Sweden

Our results indicate that there are no differences between male and female CEOs when it comes to e-commerce adoption barriers only. Therefore, where barriers are concerned, being of a specific gender does not necessarily mean more obstacles to e-commerce adoption. There are however, differences between e-commerce criteria, benefits, and disadvantages. Swedish SMEs owned by male CEOs rated 10 different e-commerce adoption drivers as being more important to them than female CEOs. Similarly, six e-commerce benefits were experienced more strongly by male CEOs and only one disadvantage. One explanation is that there were very few female respondents. If this were the case, however, similar results to those in Table 3 would have occurred in the other three tables (i.e., if barriers did not show any significant differences, e-commerce criteria, benefits, and disadvantages also would not have indicated any divergent views). Another important observation is that, almost uniformly (i.e., across genders), the ratings for e-commerce benefits and disadvantages were below the median rating of 3.

We now turn to the results of the Australian study, where the same statistical analysis has been applied.

# Australia

There were insufficient adopters in the Australian study to examine gender-based differences in the criteria for adoption, benefits derived from adoption, or the disadvantages incurred through adoption. Table 6 provides the data for the e-commerce adoption barriers.

Table 6 indicates that only two barriers related to the suitability of e-commerce were statistically significant. In both instances, these barriers were rated as being more important by males. Unlike Sweden, where the ratings of barriers by both male and female CEOs were low, Australian SMEs generally rated the barriers as being important. This is in line with the low rate of e-commerce adoption found in the Australian sample.

We will now compare the results across the two locations.

*Table 6. Comparison of e-commerce adoption barriers (males vs. females): Australia*

| Barriers | Mean Males | N Males | Mean Females | N Females | t value | Significance |
|---|---|---|---|---|---|---|
| E-commerce is not suited to our products/services. | 3.57 | 84 | 2.75 | 51 | -2.963 | .004 |
| E-commerce is not suited to our way of doing business. | 3.64 | 84 | 3.04 | 51 | -2.288 | .024 |
| E-commerce is not suited to the ways our clients do business. | 3.46 | 84 | 3.43 | 51 | -.079 | .937 |
| E-commerce does not offer any advantages to our organisation. | 3.45 | 84 | 3.02 | 51 | -1.624 | .107 |
| We do not have the technical knowledge in the organisation to implement e-commerce. | 3.06 | 84 | 3.18 | 51 | .386 | .700 |
| E-commerce is too complicated to implement. | 2.90 | 84 | 3.24 | 51 | 1.137 | .257 |
| E-commerce is not secure. | 2.86 | 84 | 2.80 | 51 | -.199 | .843 |
| The financial investment required to implement e-commerce is too high. | 2.88 | 84 | 2.92 | 51 | .141 | .888 |
| We do not have time to implement e-commerce. | 2.88 | 84 | 3.27 | 51 | 1.369 | .173 |
| It is difficult to choose the most suitable e-commerce standard with so many different options available. | 2.58 | 84 | 2.84 | 51 | .914 | .362 |

# Comparison of Differences Between the Three Locations: A Discussion

The results previously presented are summarised in Table 7. It should be noted that due to the response rate, it is only possible to perform a comparison between Sweden and Australia and then only on the e-commerce barriers, since insufficient data was available for an analysis of the criteria, benefits and drivers in the Australian study. Table 7 shows only those aspects of e-commerce, which showed significant differences in a particular location between male CEOs and female CEOs.

In Sweden, we found a number of differences between male CEOs and female CEOs in relation to e-commerce criteria, benefits, and disadvantages. However, more importantly, all of these were rated higher or more strongly by male CEOs. Compared to Sweden, which had no significant differences between the ratings of e-commerce barriers by males and females, in Australia, there were differences in the ratings of organisational barriers related to the suitability of e-commerce to the organisation. As mentioned previously, due to the small number of responses, it was not possible to undertake a statistical analysis for the U.S. respondents.

*Table 7. Comparison summary between males and females across three locations*

|  | Sweden | Australia | USA |
|---|---|---|---|
| E-commerce adoption criteria | Pressure from competition, pressure from suppliers, reduced costs, improved customer service, increased sales, stronger relations with partners, possibility of reaching new customers, improved competitiveness, external support, and improved control rated higher by males. | Insufficient data | Insufficient data |
| E-commerce barriers | No differences. | E-commerce not suited to products/services and e-commerce not suited to our way of doing business rated higher by males | Insufficient data |
| E-commerce benefits | Reduced administration costs, increased sales, increased internal efficiency, access to new customers and markets, improved competitiveness, and improved quality of information rated higher by males. | Insufficient data | Insufficient data |
| E-commerce disadvantages | Reduced flexibility rated higher by males. | Insufficient data | Insufficient data |

We will now take a closer look at the groupings of e-commerce adoption criteria, barriers, benefits, and disadvantages in each of the two categories (male and female) with the purpose of answering our second question: Do the groupings of e-commerce adoption criteria, barriers, benefits, and disadvantages differ between SMEs with male and female CEOs?

# Groupings of E-Commerce Criteria, Barriers, Benefits, and Disadvantages and CEO Gender

To answer our second question, a combination of correlations and factor analysis was applied to the data. The results of this analysis are shown in the tables next and discussed at the end of each section, by location.

## Sweden

Tables.8 and 9 provide the correlation matrices of the importance ratings for e-commerce adoption criteria. All correlations significant at the .001 level are shown in bold.

Principle components analysis was chosen as the method of extraction in order to account for maximum variance in the data using a minimum number of factors. For male owned/managed respondents, a three factor solution was extracted with Eigenvalues 7.342, 1.338, and 1.027. This was supported by an examination of the Scree plot. The three factors accounted for 69.340% of the variance. For female owned/managed respondents, a three factor solution was extracted with Eigenvalues 8.818, 1.335 and 1.276. This was supported by an examination of the Scree plot. The three factors accounted for 81.632% of the variance. These results are summarized in Tables 10 and 11.

For both the male and female respondents the resulting components were rotated using the Varimax procedure and a simple structure was achieved as shown in the rotated component matrices in Table 12 and 13.

Both male and female CEOs grouped e-commerce criteria around three factors. While the second factor (related to internal efficiency and availability of external resources) was similar between the two groups, males and females had divergent views about the other groupings. Males assigned a higher level of importance to the criteria related to sales and marketing and grouped pressure from customers and competition separately. Females grouped these two criteria together with the sales and marketing drivers, and subsequently this factor has been re-named "sales and market forces" in the female CEO category. Unlike their male counterparts, female CEOs assigned the highest priority to the relationships factor (dealings with suppliers and business partners). These findings support previous research, which indicates that females are better at managing interpersonal relationships and communication than males.

Another explanation exists for these results. One of the outcomes of adopting e-commerce is the development of business partnerships and the establishment of "virtual networks." If female CEOs in regional Swedish SMEs find it difficult to develop these networks, this

*Table 8. Adoption criteria correlation matrix for males (Sweden)*

| | Demand and/or pressure from customers. | Demand and/or pressure from suppliers. | To reduce costs. | To improve customer service. | To shorten lead time/reduce stock levels. | To increase sales. | To improve internal efficiency. | To strengthen relations with business partners. | The possibility of reaching new customers/markets. | To improve our competitiveness. | We were offered external support to adopt e-commerce. | To improve our marketing. | To improve control. |
|---|---|---|---|---|---|---|---|---|---|---|---|---|---|
| Pressure from competition. | .616 | | | | | | | | | | | | |
| Demand and/or pressure from suppliers. | .288** | .475 | | | | | | | | | | | |
| To reduce costs. | .408 | .492 | .576 | | | | | | | | | | |
| To improve customer service. | .465 | .487 | .373 | .670 | | | | | | | | | |
| To shorten lead time/reduce stock levels. | .334 | .413 | .613 | .656 | .501 | | | | | | | | |
| To increase sales. | .307 | .352 | .396 | .518 | .598 | .479 | | | | | | | |
| To improve internal efficiency. | .339 | .452 | .397 | .665 | .643 | .556 | .507 | | | | | | |
| To strengthen relations with business partners. | .490 | .491 | .490 | .506 | .653 | .555 | .534 | .572 | | | | | |
| The possibility of reaching new customers/markets. | .352 | .399 | .372 | .374 | .632 | .417 | .690 | .444 | .611 | | | | |
| To improve our competitiveness. | .452 | .617 | .483 | .547 | .653 | .547 | .611 | .628 | .728 | .727 | | | |
| We were offered external support to adopt e-commerce. | .220** | .322 | .477 | .331 | .195* | .403 | .316 | .285** | .355 | .257** | .330 | | |
| To improve our marketing. | .331 | .368 | .366 | .322 | .564 | .325 | .636 | .440 | .536 | .810 | .645 | .311 | |
| To improve control. | .335 | .442 | .468 | .600 | .514 | .620 | .459 | .459 | .492 | .486 | .587 | .447 | .392 |

*Note: * significant at 0.05 level    ** significant at 0.01 level*

*Table 9. Adoption criteria correlation matrix for females (Sweden)*

| | Demand and/or pressure from customers. | Demand and/or pressure from suppliers. | To reduce costs. | To improve customer service. | To shorten lead time/reduce stock levels. | To increase sales. | To improve internal efficiency. | To strengthen relations with business partners. | The possibility of reaching new customers/markets. | To improve our competitiveness. | We were offered external support to adopt e-commerce. | To improve our marketing. | To improve control. |
|---|---|---|---|---|---|---|---|---|---|---|---|---|---|
| Pressure from competition. | .811 | | | | | | | | | | | | |
| Demand and/or pressure from suppliers. | .585** | .292 | | | | | | | | | | | |
| To reduce costs. | .625** | .494* | .646** | | | | | | | | | | |
| To improve customer service. | .725 | .720** | .651** | .877 | | | | | | | | | |
| To shorten lead time/reduce stock levels. | .138 | .226 | .219 | .625** | .592** | | | | | | | | |
| To increase sales. | .630** | .698** | .327 | .852 | .843 | .683** | | | | | | | |
| To improve internal efficiency. | .393 | .250 | .354 | .510* | .426 | .481* | .499* | | | | | | |
| To strengthen relations with business partners. | .476* | .521* | .611** | .730 | .864 | .540* | .577** | .273 | | | | | |
| The possibility of reaching new customers/markets. | .541* | .623** | .367 | .754 | .801 | .639** | .920 | .430 | .521* | | | | |
| To improve our competitiveness. | .537* | .767 | .329 | .726 | .862 | .612** | .852 | .329 | .806 | .755 | | | |
| We were offered external support to adopt e-commerce. | .303 | .373 | .176 | .618** | .520* | .581** | .540* | .307 | .611** | .300 | .667** | | |
| To improve our marketing. | .642** | .696** | .340 | .684** | .796 | .560* | .855 | .457* | .469* | .920 | .743 | .333 | |
| To improve control. | .588** | .4450 | .722 | .877 | .809 | .597** | .748 | .520* | .769 | .636** | .711** | .711** | .626** |

*Note: * significant at 0.05 level    ** significant at 0.01 level*

would explain the stronger desire to foster those links. By comparison, male CEOs who may have already established such relations, would naturally be adopting e-commerce to assist in sales and marketing.

Tables 14 and 15 provide the correlation matrices of the importance ratings for e-commerce adoption barriers. All correlations significant at the .001 level are shown in bold.

*Table 10. Total variance explained: Adoption criteria (males in Sweden)*

| Component | Eigenvalue | % Variation | Cumulative % |
|-----------|-----------|-------------|--------------|
| 1 | 7.342 | 52.445 | 52.445 |
| 2 | 1.338 | 9.557 | 62.003 |
| 3 | 1.027 | 7.337 | 69.340 |

*Table 11. Total variance explained: Adoption criteria (females in Sweden)*

| Component | Eigenvalue | % Variation | Cumulative % |
|-----------|-----------|-------------|--------------|
| 1 | 1.335 | 9.534 | 9.534 |
| 2 | 1.276 | 9.112 | 18.646 |
| 3 | 8.818 | 62.985 | 81.632 |

*Table 12. Rotated component matrix: Adoption criteria (males in Sweden)*

| | Component 1: Sales & Marketing | Component 2: Efficiency & Resources | Component 3: Market Forces |
|---|---|---|---|
| Demand and/or pressure from customers. | | | .837 |
| Pressure from competition. | | | .759 |
| Demand and/or pressure from suppliers. | | .749 | |
| To reduce costs. | | .641 | |
| To improve customer service. | .598 | | |
| To shorten lead time/reduce stock levels. | | .751 | |
| To increase sales. | .749 | | |
| To improve internal efficiency. | | .465 | |
| To strengthen relations with business partners. | .553 | | |
| The possibility of reaching new customers/markets. | .894 | | |
| To improve our competitiveness. | .661 | | |
| We were offered external support to adopt e-commerce. | | .724 | |
| To improve our marketing. | .875 | | |
| To improve control. | | .660 | |

*Table 13. Rotated component matrix: Adoption criteria (females in Sweden)*

| | Component 1: Sales & Market Forces | Component 2: Efficiency & Resources | Component 3: Relationships |
|---|---|---|---|
| Demand and/or pressure from customers. | .727 | | |
| Pressure from competition. | .868 | | |
| Demand and/or pressure from suppliers. | | | .933 |
| To reduce costs. | | .613 | |
| To improve customer service. | .638 | | |
| To shorten lead time/reduce stock levels. | | .897 | |
| To increase sales. | .760 | | |
| To improve internal efficiency. | | .450 | |
| To strengthen relations with business partners. | | | .652 |
| The possibility of reaching new customers/markets. | .783 | | |
| To improve our competitiveness. | .643 | | |
| We were offered external support to adopt e-commerce. | | .755 | |
| To improve our marketing. | .847 | | |
| To improve control. | | | .646 |

The results of the Kaiser-Meyer-Olkin MSA (.872 for males, .721 for females) and Bartlett's test of Sphericity ($\chi^2 = 578$, $p = .000$ for males, $\chi^2 = 578$, p=.000 for females) indicated that the data sets satisfied the assumptions for factorability. Principle components analysis was chosen as the method of extraction in order to account for maximum variance in the data using a minimum number of factors. A two-factor solution was extracted with Eigenvalues of 4.594 and 1.436 for males and 1.435 and 5.906 for females. This was supported by an inspection of the Scree Plots. These two factors accounted for 70.994% of the total variance in males and 81.575% in females. Tables 16 and 17 show the total variance.

The resulting components were rotated using the Varimax procedure and a simple structure was achieved as shown in the rotated component matrix (see Tables 18 and 19).

The previous results point to a distinct difference in the way males and females perceive e-commerce adoption barriers. While 55% of male owners felt that e-commerce was too difficult, only 16% of the female respondents rated this as their primary reason not to adopt e-commerce. Instead, 66% of females felt that e-commerce was unsuitable for their business, while 16% of males considered this to be an important e-commerce adoption barrier. Although gender differences have been reported in prior studies, the results of the Swedish study appear to disagree with the results of previous research. Whereas prior studies suggested that males were less anxious about computing technology (Perez et al., 2002; Rodgers et al., 2003; Singh, 2001), this study implies the opposite with males reporting difficulties associated with e-commerce as an adoption barrier.

Tables 20 and 21 provide the correlation matrices of the ratings for e-commerce benefits. All correlations significant at the .001 level are shown in bold.

*Table 14. Adoption barriers correlation matrix for males (Sweden)*

| | E-commerce is not suited to our products/services. | E-commerce is not suited to our way of doing business. | E-commerce is not suited to the ways our clients do business. | E-commerce does not offer any advantages to our organisation. | We do not have the technical knowledge in the organisation to implement e-commerce. | E-commerce is too complicated to implement. | E-commerce is not secure. | The financial investment required to implement e-commerce is too high. | We do not have time to implement e-commerce. |
|---|---|---|---|---|---|---|---|---|---|
| E-commerce is not suited to our way of doing business. | .629 | | | | | | | | |
| E-commerce is not suited to the ways our clients do business. | .600 | .632 | | | | | | | |
| E-commerce does not offer any advantages to our organisation. | .596 | .647 | .443 | | | | | | |
| We do not have the technical knowledge in the organisation to implement e-commerce. | .296** | .320** | .322** | .471 | | | | | |
| E-commerce is too complicated to implement. | .369 | .390 | .507 | .419 | .651 | | | | |
| E-commerce is not secure. | .451 | .506 | .525 | .478 | .550 | .790 | | | |
| The financial investment required to implement e-commerce is too high. | .330 | .360 | .545 | .352 | .578 | .658 | .625 | | |
| We do not have time to implement e-commerce. | .288** | .272** | .450 | .281** | .539 | .729 | .619 | .603 | |
| It is difficult to choose the most suitable e-commerce standard with so many different options available. | .285** | .364 | .500 | .316** | .553 | .664 | .578 | .668 | .645 |

*Note:  * significant at 0.05 level      ** significant at 0.01 level*

*Table 15. Adoption barriers correlation matrix for females (Sweden)*

| | E-commerce is not suited to our products/services. | E-commerce is not suited to our way of doing business. | E-commerce is not suited to the ways our clients do business. | E-commerce does not offer any advantages to our organisation. | We do not have the technical knowledge in the organisation to implement e-commerce. | E-commerce is too complicated to implement. | E-commerce is not secure. | The financial investment required to implement e-commerce is too high. | We do not have time to implement e-commerce. |
|---|---|---|---|---|---|---|---|---|---|
| E-commerce is not suited to our way of doing business. | .989 | | | | | | | | |
| E-commerce is not suited to the ways our clients do business. | .907 | .920 | | | | | | | |
| E-commerce does not offer any advantages to our organisation. | .893 | .882 | .809 | | | | | | |
| We do not have the technical knowledge in the organisation to implement e-commerce. | .320 | .307 | .223 | .282 | | | | | |
| E-commerce is too complicated to implement. | .633** | .607** | .522* | .442 | .456 | | | | |
| E-commerce is not secure. | .739** | .718** | .609** | .540* | .394 | .896 | | | |
| The financial investment required to implement e-commerce is too high. | .606** | .564* | .631** | .584* | .482 | .778 | .655** | | |
| We do not have time to implement e-commerce. | .486* | .450 | .529* | .433 | .315 | .750 | .624** | .915 | |
| It is difficult to choose the most suitable e-commerce standard with so many different options available. | .589* | .542* | .430 | .416 | .426 | .907 | .895 | .618** | .574* |

*Note: * significant at 0.05 level   ** significant at 0.01 level*

The results of the Kaiser-Meyer-Olkin MSA (.919 for males and .455 for females) and Bartlett's Test for Sphericity ($\chi^2 = 1551$, p = .000 for males, $\chi^2 = 389$, p = .000 for females) indicated that both sets of data satisfied the assumptions of factorability. Principle Components Analysis was chosen as the method of extraction in order to account for maximum variance in the data using a minimum number of factors. A two-factor solution was extracted with Eigenvalues 7.711 and 1.307 for males. This was supported by an inspection of the Scree plot. These two factors accounted for 64.411% of the variance. For the females, a single factor with Eigenvalue 10.240 was chosen. This factor accounted for 73.142% of the variance. These results are summarized in Tables 22 and 23.

Both sets of components were rotated using the Varimax procedure and a simple structure was achieved as shown in the rotated component matrix in Tables 24 and 25. In both cases, the factors are independent and uncorrelated, as an orthogonal rotation procedure was used.

Table 16. Total variance explained: Adoption barriers (males in Sweden)

| Component | Eigenvalue | % Variation | Cumulative % |
|---|---|---|---|
| 1 | 4.954 | 55.04 | 55.04 |
| 2 | 1.436 | 15.96 | 71.00 |

Table 17. Total variance explained: Adoption barriers (females in Sweden)

| Component | Eigenvalue | % Variation | Cumulative % |
|---|---|---|---|
| 1 | 1.435 | 15.95 | 15.95 |
| 2 | 5.906 | 65.63 | 81.58 |

Table 18. Rotated component matrix: Adoption barriers (males in Sweden)

| Barrier | Component 1: Too Difficult | Component 2: Unsuitable |
|---|---|---|
| E-commerce is not suited to our products/services. | | .631 |
| E-commerce is not suited to our way of doing business. | | .672 |
| E-commerce is not suited to the ways our clients do business. | | .739 |
| E-commerce does not offer any advantages to our organisation. | | .655 |
| We do not have the technical knowledge in the organisation to implement e-commerce. | .717 | |
| E-commerce is too complicated to implement. | .850 | |
| E-commerce is not secure. | .838 | |
| The financial investment required to implement e-commerce is too high. | .784 | |
| We do not have time to implement e-commerce. | .746 | |
| It is difficult to choose the most suitable e-commerce standard with so many different options available. | .764 | |

*Table 19. Rotated component matrix: Adoption barriers (females in Sweden)*

| Barrier | Component 1: Too Difficult | Component 2: Unsuitable |
|---|---|---|
| E-commerce is not suited to our products/services. | | .914 |
| E-commerce is not suited to our way of doing business. | | .929 |
| E-commerce is not suited to the ways our clients do business. | | .904 |
| E-commerce does not offer any advantages to our organisation. | | .906 |
| We do not have the technical knowledge in the organisation to implement e-commerce. | .591 | |
| E-commerce is too complicated to implement. | .909 | |
| E-commerce is not secure. | .779 | |
| The financial investment required to implement e-commerce is too high. | .787 | |
| We do not have time to implement e-commerce. | .785 | |
| It is difficult to choose the most suitable e-commerce standard with so many different options available. | .850 | |

As can be seen in Table 24 the two factors for males have been termed "financial" and "competitiveness." Six benefits loaded onto the financial factor (which was also deemed to be of higher priority by the respondents) while four loaded onto the competitiveness factor. These two factors are independent and uncorrelated as an orthogonal rotation procedure was used. However, female CEOs did not make any distinctions between the benefits of e-commerce. While it may be argued that the results are a function of the lower than expected numbers of female respondents, it is interesting to note that, in some respects, the results agree with earlier findings (Simon, 2001; Singh, 2001) that suggested that females considered the Internet in relation to the specific task that needs to be achieved, while males took a "broader' view of the Internet.

In deriving the factors for the disadvantages of e-commerce adoption, for both males and females, a single factor solution was extracted. As such, there were no gender-based differences for the disadvantages and they will not be reported.

## Summary: Groupings and Gender in Sweden

Although there were no differences in the groupings of e-commerce disadvantages between male and female CEOs, there were divergent views on e-commerce adoption criteria, barriers and benefits. Both males and females grouped adoption criteria around three factors, although relationships with suppliers and partners were deemed to be more important by females. This is in contrast to males who ranked sales and marketing drivers as being more relevant.

The e-commerce barriers showed differences in the groupings only where priorities were concerned because both categories (i.e., males and females) grouped obstacles to e-commerce

*Table 20. E-commerce benefits correlation matrix for males (Sweden)*

| E-commerce… | Reduced our administration costs. | Reduced our production costs. | Reduced our lead time. | Reduced our stock levels. | Lead to increased sales. | Increased our internal efficiency. | Improved our relations with business partners. | Gave us access to new customers and markets. | Improved our competitiveness. |
|---|---|---|---|---|---|---|---|---|---|
| Reduced our production costs. | .353 | | | | | | | | |
| Reduced our lead time. | .692 | .354 | | | | | | | |
| Reduced our stock levels. | .577 | .251** | .626 | | | | | | |
| Lead to increased sales. | .423 | .333 | .559 | .608 | | | | | |
| Increased our internal efficiency. | .530 | .384 | .637 | .609 | .493 | | | | |
| Improved our relations with business partners. | .654 | .305 | .580 | .512 | .415 | .566 | | | |
| Gave us access to new customers and markets. | .478 | .275 | .540 | .575 | .452 | .579 | .492 | | |
| Improved our competitiveness. | .345 | .277 | .471 | .412 | .340 | .746 | .530 | .609 | |
| Improved the quality of information in our organisation. | .473 | .290 | .473 | .482 | .310 | .636 | .524 | .669 | .645 |

Note: * significant at 0.05 level    ** significant at 0.01 level

*Table 21. E-commerce benefits correlation matrix for females (Sweden)*

| E-commerce… | Reduced our administration costs. | Reduced our production costs. | Reduced our lead time. | Reduced our stock levels. | Lead to increased sales. | Increased our internal efficiency. | Improved our relations with business partners. | Gave us access to new customers and markets. | Improved our competitiveness. |
|---|---|---|---|---|---|---|---|---|---|
| Reduced our production costs. | .749 | | | | | | | | |
| Reduced our lead time. | .808 | .825 | | | | | | | |
| Reduced our stock levels. | .699** | .619** | .610** | | | | | | |
| Lead to increased sales. | .676** | .579** | .728 | .557* | | | | | |
| Increased our internal efficiency. | .761 | .711** | .834 | .601** | .686** | | | | |
| Improved our relations with business partners. | .509* | .478* | .490* | .560* | .373 | .435 | | | |
| Gave us access to new customers and markets. | .659** | .744 | .784 | .865 | .731 | .758 | .493* | | |
| Improved our competitiveness. | .479* | .547* | .554* | .610** | .297 | .583** | .405 | .663** | |
| Improved the quality of information in our organisation. | .696** | .756 | .814 | .814 | .675** | .696** | .554* | .919 | .803 |

*Note: * significant at 0.05 level    ** significant at 0.01 level*

*Table 22. Total variance explained: E-commerce benefits (males in Sweden)*

| Component | Eigenvalue | % Variance | Cumulative % |
|---|---|---|---|
| 1 | 7.711 | 55.076 | 55.076 |
| 2 | 1.307 | 9.335 | 64.411 |

*Table 23. Total variance explained: E-commerce benefits (females in Sweden)*

| Component | Eigenvalue | % Variance | Cumulative % |
|---|---|---|---|
| 1 | 10.240 | 73.142% | 73.142% |

*Table 24. Rotated component matrix: E-commerce benefits (males in Sweden)*

| Benefits | Component 1: Financial & Relationships | Component 2: Competitiveness |
|---|---|---|
| Reduced our administration costs. | .779 | |
| Reduced our production costs. | .473 | |
| Reduced our lead time. | .754 | |
| Reduced our stock levels. | .740 | |
| Lead to increased sales. | .739 | |
| Increased our internal efficiency. | | .706 |
| Improved our relations with business partners. | .638 | |
| Gave us access to new customers and markets. | | .624 |
| Improved our competitiveness. | | .906 |
| Improved the quality of information in our organisation. | | .742 |

*Table 25. Rotated component matrix: E-commerce benefits (females in Sweden)*

| Benefits | Component 1: Sales |
|---|---|
| Reduced our administration costs. | .863 |
| Reduced our production costs. | .866 |
| Reduced our lead time. | .889 |
| Reduced our stock levels. | .855 |
| Lead to increased sales. | .742 |
| Increased our internal efficiency. | .838 |
| Improved our relations with business partners. | .595 |
| Gave us access to new customers and markets. | .926 |
| Improved our competitiveness. | .717 |
| Improved the quality of information in our organisation. | .923 |

adoption around the suitability of e-commerce and the complexity of implementing it in the organisation. This is in line with the findings reported in previous chapters. However, while male CEOs assigned a higher priority to the difficulties of e-commerce adoption, females were more concerned about its suitability to the organisation. This does not agree with previous research that shows males as being more confident users of technology.

Finally, we extracted a two-factor solution for e-commerce benefits reported by male CEOs but only a single factors solution for females. This suggests that women CEOs did not distinguish between the different benefits achieved through e-commerce adoption.

We will now examine the groupings in the Australian context.

## Australia

Due to the low adoption rate of e-commerce, there was insufficient data to examine e-commerce adoption criteria, benefits, or disadvantages in the Australian sample. Tables 26 and 27 provide the correlation matrices for the barriers to e-commerce. All correlations significant at the .001 level are shown in bold.

The results of the Kaiser-Meyer-Olkin MSA (.784 for males and .786 for females) and Bartlett's Test for Sphericity ($\chi^2 = 415$, p = .000 for males, $\chi^2 = 313$, p = .000 for females) indicated that both sets of data satisfied the assumptions of factorability. Principle components analysis was chosen as the method of extraction in order to account for maximum variance in the data using a minimum number of factors. For both males and females a two-factor solution was extracted with Eigenvalues 3.635 and 2.738 for males and 4.440 and 2.586 for females. The Eigenvalues accounted for 63.730% of variance for males and 70.264% for females. Tables 28 and 29 provide the total variance.

The resulting components were rotated using the Varimax procedure and a simple structure was achieved as shown in the rotated component matrix (see Tables 30 and 31).

The previous results show the same groupings of barriers as the Swedish SMEs, however, with one notable difference. Unlike the Swedish SMEs, in Australian organisations males are more concerned about the suitability of e-commerce to their business while females are more concerned with the technical difficulties of e-commerce itself. This is more consistent with previous findings that suggest females have less developed technical skills than males.

We will now compare and discuss the key findings across the two locations.

## Comparison of Results: A Discussion

At the outset of this chapter, we identified two questions about the gender of the CEO in an SME and e-commerce adoption. We will now compare the answers to those two questions across the two locations and draw some conclusions.

Our first question addressed the differences between males and females in relation to e-commerce adoption criteria, barriers, benefits, and disadvantages. We ran a series of t-tailed tests in Australia and Sweden to determine if these differences exist, and indeed, found this

*Table 26. Adoption barriers correlation matrix for males (Australia)*

| | E-commerce is not suited to our products/services. | E-commerce is not suited to our way of doing business. | E-commerce is not suited to the ways our clients do business. | E-commerce does not offer any advantages to our organisation. | We do not have the technical knowledge in the organisation to implement e-commerce. | E-commerce is too complicated to implement. | E-commerce is not secure. | The financial investment required to implement e-commerce is too high. | We do not have time to implement e-commerce. |
|---|---|---|---|---|---|---|---|---|---|
| E-commerce is not suited to our way of doing business. | .810 | | | | | | | | |
| E-commerce is not suited to the ways our clients do business. | .495 | .843 | | | | | | | |
| E-commerce does not offer any advantages to our organisation. | .658 | .744 | .471 | | | | | | |
| We do not have the technical knowledge in the organisation to implement e-commerce. | .358 | .357 | .359 | .458 | | | | | |
| E-commerce is too complicated to implement. | .370 | .349 | .384 | .458 | .684 | | | | |
| E-commerce is not secure. | .301** | .357 | .361 | .495 | .517 | .732 | | | |
| The financial investment required to implement e-commerce is too high. | .406 | .373 | .225* | .449 | .680 | .703 | .477 | | |
| We do not have time to implement e-commerce. | .360 | .325** | .332** | .485 | .604 | .791 | .575 | .712 | |
| It is difficult to choose the most suitable e-commerce standard with so many different options available. | .305** | .311** | .110 | .468 | .627 | .696 | .583 | .674 | .699 |

*Note: * significant at 0.05 level    ** significant at 0.01 level*

*Table 27. Adoption barriers correlation matrix for females (Australia)*

| | E-commerce is not suited to our products/services. | E-commerce is not suited to our way of doing business. | E-commerce is not suited to the ways our clients do business. | E-commerce does not offer any advantages to our organisation. | We do not have the technical knowledge in the organisation to implement e-commerce. | E-commerce is too complicated to implement. | E-commerce is not secure. | The financial investment required to implement e-commerce is too high. | We do not have time to implement e-commerce. |
|---|---|---|---|---|---|---|---|---|---|
| E-commerce is not suited to our way of doing business. | .856 | | | | | | | | |
| E-commerce is not suited to the ways our clients do business. | .754 | .679 | | | | | | | |
| E-commerce does not offer any advantages to our organisation. | .847 | .770 | .823 | | | | | | |
| We do not have the technical knowledge in the organisation to implement e-commerce. | .326 | .209 | .185 | .249 | | | | | |
| E-commerce is too complicated to implement. | .268 | .209 | .397* | .316 | .577** | | | | |
| E-commerce is not secure. | .165 | .135 | .287 | .387 | .369 | .560** | | | |
| The financial investment required to implement e-commerce is too high. | .165 | .092 | .304 | .184 | .570** | .882 | .558** | | |
| We do not have time to implement e-commerce. | .370 | .311 | .446* | .402* | .650 | .971 | .582** | .897 | |
| It is difficult to choose the most suitable e-commerce standard with so many different options available. | .222 | .105 | .335 | .245 | .689 | .910 | .639** | .935 | .911 |

*Note: * significant at 0.05 level    ** significant at 0.01 level*

*Table 28. Total variance explained: Adoption barriers (males in Australia)*

| Component | Eigenvalue | % Variation | Cumulative % |
|---|---|---|---|
| 1 | 2.738 | 27.378 | 27.378 |
| 2 | 3.635 | 36.351 | 63.730 |

*Table 29. Total variance explained: Adoption barriers (females in Australia)*

| Component | Eigenvalue | % Variation | Cumulative % |
|---|---|---|---|
| 1 | 4.440 | 44.403 | 44.403 |
| 2 | 2.586 | 25.861 | 70.264 |

*Table 30. Rotated component matrix: Adoption barriers (males in Australia)*

| Barrier | Component 1: Too Difficult | Component 2: Unsuitable |
|---|---|---|
| E-commerce is not suited to our products/services. | | .902 |
| E-commerce is not suited to our way of doing business. | | .896 |
| E-commerce is not suited to the ways our clients do business. | | .886 |
| E-commerce does not offer any advantages to our organisation. | | .855 |
| We do not have the technical knowledge in the organisation to implement e-commerce. | .774 | |
| E-commerce is too complicated to implement. | .820 | |
| E-commerce is not secure. | .591 | |
| The financial investment required to implement e-commerce is too high. | .749 | |
| We do not have time to implement e-commerce. | .717 | |
| It is difficult to choose the most suitable e-commerce standard with so many different options available. | .668 | |

*Table 31. Rotated component matrix: Adoption barriers (females in Australia)*

| Barrier | Component 1: Too Difficult | Component 2: Unsuitable |
|---|---|---|
| E-commerce is not suited to our products/services. | | .884 |
| E-commerce is not suited to our way of doing business. | | .926 |
| E-commerce is not suited to the ways our clients do business. | | .922 |
| E-commerce does not offer any advantages to our organisation. | | .732 |
| We do not have the technical knowledge in the organisation to implement e-commerce. | .758 | |
| E-commerce is too complicated to implement. | .885 | |
| E-commerce is not secure. | .765 | |
| The financial investment required to implement e-commerce is too high. | .739 | |
| We do not have time to implement e-commerce. | .790 | |
| It is difficult to choose the most suitable e-commerce standard with so many different options available. | .816 | |

to be the case. There is minimal agreement between SMEs with regards to various aspects of e-commerce and gender of the CEO, as can be seen in Table 32.

Table 32 indicates that in Sweden, males consistently rated e-commerce criteria, benefits, barriers, and disadvantages higher than their female counterparts. We also found a number of significant differences in the ratings of the different aspects of e-commerce, which implies the need to consider gender when promoting e-commerce adoption. In the Australian study, we examined the e-commerce barriers only, and unlike Swedish SMEs, which showed no significant differences between males and females, males CEOs in Australian SMEs rated two barriers as being more important than females. These are related to the suitability of e-commerce to the organisation.

Our second question was concerned with the groupings of criteria, barriers, benefits, and disadvantages in SMEs with male and female CEOs. The results for the two locations, yet again, show interesting differences. Since the results of e-commerce criteria, benefits, and disadvantage groupings are only available for Sweden (and have been discussed and sum-marised at length previously), we will compare the results for barriers only.

Comparing the results of grouping e-commerce barriers in Sweden and Australia (insuf-ficient data from the U.S.) shows that there are similarities in that a two-factor solution was derived in both instances. The two factors are related to the unsuitability of e-commerce and the complexity or difficulties involved. However, the priorities placed on each grouping of

*Table 32. Summary of differences between male and female CEOs about e-commerce*

| | Statistically Significant Differences | |
| --- | --- | --- |
| | **Sweden** | **Australia** |
| **E - C o m m e r c e Criteria** | • Pressure from competition.<br>• Pressure from suppliers.<br>• Reduced costs.<br>• Improved customer service.<br>• Increased sales.<br>• Stronger relations with partners.<br>• Possibility of reaching new customers.<br>• Improved competitiveness.<br>• External support.<br>• Improved control. | Data unavailable |
| | All criteria rated more important by males | |
| **E - C o m m e r c e Barriers** | No statistically significant differences. | • E-commerce not suited to products/services.<br>• E-commerce not suited to way of doing business. |
| | Almost all barriers rated more important by males. | Variations between ratings of importance between males and females. Statistically significant barriers rated higher by males. |

*Table 32. Continued*

| | Statistically Significant Differences | |
|---|---|---|
| | **Sweden** | **Australia** |
| **E - C o m m e r c e Benefits** | • Reduced administration costs.<br>• Increased sales.<br>• Increased internal efficiency.<br>• Access to new customers and markets.<br>• Improved competitiveness.<br>• Improved quality of information. | Data unavailable |
| | All benefits rated higher by males. | |
| **E - C o m m e r c e Disadvantages** | Reduced flexibility. | Data unavailable |
| | Almost all disadvantages rated higher by males. | |

barriers differed between Sweden and Australia. While males were more concerned about e-commerce difficulties in Sweden, the opposite was true in the Australian context. We have summarised the results in Tables 33 and 34.

The reason for this may be found in research by Simon (2001) and Singh (2001). Simon (2001) found that females tended to be "less enthralled by technology than males" (Simon 2001 p. 30) and used a more comprehensive information processing scheme when making decisions about technology. In a similar vein, Singh (2001) proposed that females use the Internet as a tool for carrying out activities and not as a technology that must be mastered. Both Simon (2001) and Singh (2001) appear to be suggesting that females are more likely to consider Internet technologies, including e-commerce, in relation to their suitability for a particular activity. In contrast, males view Internet technologies simply as tools, which require time, effort, and resources to learn and implement. This may explain the results of the Swedish study presented here. However, the results from the Australian study are more consistent with previous studies by Shade (1998), Sheehan (1999), and Akhter (2003), which argued that females were more concerned with privacy and security issues, and subsequently more cautious about using the Internet. In general, the Australian results support prior research, which showed females experiencing more difficulties using technology than males.

# E-Commerce and Gender: Implications

The results here suggest that male and female owners of SMEs have divergent views in relation to e-commerce and differ across locations. Clearly, separate and gender-relevant e-commerce adoption programs and strategies must be developed to address these differences and ensure the highest rate of e-commerce adoption. In Sweden, government organisations should target female SMEs with strategies that promote the suitability of e-commerce to their businesses and help them determine the value of e-commerce to their organisation. The same should be done for male CEOs in Australia. In contrast, male CEOs in Sweden have

*Table 33. Groupings of e-commerce barriers: A comparison between males in Sweden and Australia*

| | SWEDEN MALE CEOs | | AUSTRALIA MALE CEOs | |
|---|---|---|---|---|
| | 1: Too Difficult | 2: Unsuitable | 1: Too Difficult | 2: Unsuitable |
| E-commerce is not suited to our products/services. | | ✓ | | ✓ |
| E-commerce is not suited to our way of doing business. | | ✓ | | ✓ |
| E-commerce is not suited to the ways our clients do business. | | ✓ | | ✓ |
| E-commerce does not offer any advantages to our organisation. | | ✓ | | ✓ |
| We do not have the technical knowledge in the organisation to implement e-commerce. | ✓ | | ✓ | |
| E-commerce is too complicated to implement. | ✓ | | ✓ | |
| E-commerce is not secure. | ✓ | | ✓ | |
| The financial investment required to implement e-commerce is too high. | ✓ | | ✓ | |
| We do not have time to implement e-commerce. | ✓ | | ✓ | |
| It is difficult to choose the most suitable e-commerce standard with so many different options available. | ✓ | | ✓ | |

concerns about the complexity of implementing e-commerce and therefore require support in the form of technical or financial assistance to adopt the technology. The same assistance should be extended to female CEOs in Australia. The end result is likely to be a higher rate of e-commerce adoption, which is particularly important in the Australian context.

# E-Commerce and Gender: Key Findings

## Sweden

- There were ten differences between male and female CEOs in relation to e-commerce adoption criteria, all of which were rated higher by males.
- There were no differences between males and females in relation to e-commerce barriers.

*Table 34. Groupings of e-commerce barriers: A comparison between females in Sweden and Australia*

| | SWEDEN FEMALE CEOs | | AUSTRALIA FEMALE CEOs | |
|---|---|---|---|---|
| | 1: Too Difficult | 2: Unsuit-able | 1: Unsuit-able | 2: Too Difficult |
| E-commerce is not suited to our products/services. | | ✓ | | ✓ |
| E-commerce is not suited to our way of doing business. | | ✓ | | ✓ |
| E-commerce is not suited to the ways our clients do business. | | ✓ | | ✓ |
| E-commerce does not offer any advantages to our organisation. | | ✓ | | ✓ |
| We do not have the technical knowledge in the organisation to implement e-commerce. | ✓ | | ✓ | |
| E-commerce is too complicated to implement. | ✓ | | ✓ | |
| E-commerce is not secure. | ✓ | | ✓ | |
| The financial investment required to implement e-commerce is too high. | ✓ | | ✓ | |
| We do not have time to implement e-commerce. | ✓ | | ✓ | |
| It is difficult to choose the most suitable e-commerce standard with so many different options available. | ✓ | | ✓ | |

- There were differences in six e-commerce benefits between male and female CEOs, with males rating these higher than females.
- Males cited reduced flexibility as a stronger disadvantage than females.
- Males were more concerned about sales and marketing groupings of e-commerce criteria, while females assigned a higher priority to building relationships with business partners.
- Barriers related to the unsuitability of e-commerce were ranked more important by females, while those related to the difficulty of implementing e-commerce were thought to be a higher priority by males.
- Males experienced more benefits related to financial issues such as reduced costs and increased sales, while females did not distinguish between any groupings of benefits.
- No gender-based differenced were observed in the groupings of e-commerce disadvantages.

# Australia

- Males were reluctant to adopt e-commerce due to the lack of suitability to their products/services and their way of doing business.

- Barriers related to the unsuitability of e-commerce were ranked more important by males, while those related to the difficulty of implementing e-commerce were thought to be a higher priority by female CEOs.

# References

Akhter, S. H. (2003). Digital divide and purchase intention: Why demographic psychology matters? *Journal of Economic Psychology, 24*, 321-327.

Baker, T., Aldrich, H. E., & Liou, N. (1997). Invisible entrepreneurs: The neglect of women business owners by mass media and scholarly journals in the USA *Entrepreneurship and Regional Development, 9*(3), 221-238.

Bartol, K. M., & Butterfield, D. A. (1976). Sex effects in evaluating leaders. *Journal of Applied Psychology, 61*, 446-454.

Bass, B. M. (1981). Women and leadership. In R. Stogdills (Ed.), *Handbook of leadership: A survey of theory and research*. New York: Free Press.

Brooksbank, D. (2000). Self-employment and small firms. In S. Carter & D. Jones-Evans (Eds.), *Enterprise and small business: Principles, policy, and practice*. London: FT Prentice Hall.

Brush, C. G. (1997). Women's entrepreneurship. In *Proceedings of the OECD Conference on Women Entrepreneurs in Small and Medium Enterprises*, Paris. OECD.

Brush, C. G., & Hisrich, R. (1999). Women owned businesses: Why do they matter? In Z. Acs (Ed.), *Are small firms important? Their role and impact*. Boston: Kluwer Academic Publishers.

Butler, D. (2000). Gender, girls, and computer technology: What's the status now? *Clearing House, 73*(4), 225-229.

Buttner, E. H., & Moore, D. P. (1997, January). Women's organisational exodus to entrepreneurship: Self reported motivations and correlates with success. *Journal of Small Business Management*, 34-47.

Carter, S. (2000). Improving the numbers and performance of women-owned businesses: Some implications for training and advisory services. *Education & Training, 42*(4/5), 326-333.

Carter, S., & Cannon, T. (1992). *Women as entrepreneurs*. London: Academic Press.

Carter, S., & Rosa, P. (1998). The financing of male and female owned businesses. *Entrepreneurship and Regional Development, 10*(3), 225-241.

Cox, B. (1999). *Gender gap narrows, changing landscape for e-commerce*. Internetnews. Retrieved June 8, from www.internetnews.com

DeWine, S. & Casbolt, D. (1983). Networking: External communication systems for female organisational members. *Journal of Business Communication, 20,* 57-67.

Fay, M., & Williams, L. (1993). Sex of applicant and the availability of business start-up finance. *Australian Journal of Management, 16*(1), 65-72.

Fletcher, M. (1994). How bank managers make lending decisions to small firms. In *Proceedings of the 17th ISBA UK National Small Firms Policy and Research Conference.* Sheffield, UK: Sheffield Hallam University.

Gebler, D. (2000). *Rethinking e-commerce gender demographics.* E-Commerce Times. Retrieved October 6, 2006, from www.ecommercetimes.com

Gilroy, F., & Desai, H. (1986). Computer anxiety: Sex, race, and age. *International Journal of Man-Machine Studies, 25,* 711-719.

Goffee, R., & Skase, R. (1985). *Women in charge: The experience of female entrepreneurs.* London: Allen & Unwin.

Hisrich, R., & Brush, C. G. (1986). *The woman entrepreneur: Starting, financing, and managing a successful new business.* Lexington: Lexington Books.

Johnson, S., & Storey, D. (1993). Male and female entrepreneurs and their businesses. In S. Allen & C. Truman (Eds.), *Women in business: Perspectives on women entrepreneurs.* London: Routledge.

Kalleberg, A. L., & Berg, I. (1987). *Work and industry.* New York: Plenum Press.

Kalleberg, A. L., & Leicht, K. T. (1991). Small business success and survival: Individual and structural determinants of organisational performance. *Academy of Management Journal, 34,* 1-26.

Kolsaker, A., & Payne, C. (2002). Engendering trust in e-commerce: A study of gender-based concerns. *Marketing Intelligence & Planning, 20*(4/5), 206-214.

Koper, G. (1993). Women entrepreneurs and the granting of business credit. In S. Allen & C. Truman (Eds.), *Women in business: Perspectives on women entrepreneurs.* London: Routledge.

Labich, K. (1994). Why companies fail. *Fortune, 14,* 52-68.

Litan, R. E., & Rivlin, A. M. (2001). Projecting the economic impact of the Internet. *The American Economic Review, 91*(2), 313-317.

Loscocco, K., & Robinson, J. (1991), Barriers to women's small business success in the United States. *Gender and Society, 5*(4), 511-532.

Loscocco, K.A., & Leicht, K. T. (1993). Gender, work-family linkages, and economic success among small business owners. *Journal of Marriage and the Family, 55,* 875-887.

Maupin, R. (1990). Sex role identity and career success of certified public accountants. *Advances in Public Interest Accounting,* 97-105.

McGregor, J., & Tweed, D. (2001). Gender and managerial competence: Support for theories of androgyny. *Women in Management Review, 16*(6), 279-286.

Meier, S. T., & Lambert, M. E. (1991). Psychometric properties and correlates of three computer aversion scales. *Behaviour Research Methods, Instruments, and Computers, 23*(1), 9-15.

Nillson, P. (1997). Business counselling services directed towards female entrepreneurs—some legitimacy dilemmas. *Entrepreneurship and Regional Development, 9*(3), 239-258.

Olm, K., Carsrud, A. L., & Avery, L. (1988). The role of networks in new venture funding of female entrepreneurs: A continuing analysis. In B. A. Kirchoff, W. A. Long, E. McMullan, K. H. Vespers, & W. E. Wetzel (Eds.), *Frontiers of entrepreneurship research.* Wellesly: Babson College.

Perez, M. P., Carnicer, M. P. L., & Sanchez, A. M. (2002). Differential effects of gender perceptions of teleworking by human resources managers. *Women in Management Review, 17*(6), 262-275.

Perry, S. C. (2002). A comparison of failed and non-failed small businesses in the United States: Do men and women use different planning and decision-making strategies? *Journal of Developmental Entrepreneurship, 7*(4), 415-428.

Powell, G. N. (1993). *Women and men in management.* Newbury Park, CA: Sage Publications.

Reynolds, W., Savage, W., & Williams, A. (1994). *Your own business: A practical guide to success.* ITP.

Riquelme, H. (2002). Commercial Internet adoption in China: Comparing the experience of small, medium, and large business. *Internet Research: Electronic Networking Applications and Policy, 12*(3), 276-286.

Rodgers, S., & Harris, M. A. (2003). Gender and e-commerce: An exploratory study. *Journal of Advertising Research, 43*(3), 322.

Rosa, P., Hamilton, D., Carter, S., & Bums, H. (1994). The impact of gender on small business management: Preliminary findings of a British study. *International Small Business Journal, 12*(3), 25-32.

Sandberg, K. W. (2003). An exploratory study of women in micro enterprises: Gender related difficulties. *Journal of Small Business and Enterprise Development, 10*(4), 408-417.

Sexton, R. S., Johnson, R. A., & Hignite, M. A. (2002). Predicting Internet/e-commerce use. *Internet Research, 12*(5), 402-410.

Shade, L. R. (1998). A gendered perspective on access to the information infrastructure. *The Information Society, 14*, 33-44.

Sheehan, K. (1999). An investigation of gender differences in online privacy concerns and resultant behaviour. *Internet Marketing*, 159-173.

Simon, S. J. (2001). The impact of culture and gender on Web Sites: An empirical study. *The DATA BASE for Advances in Information Systems, 32*(1), 18-37.

Singh, S. (2001). Gender and use of the Internet at home. *New Media & Society, 3*(4), 395-415.

Smeltzer, L. R., & Fann, G. L. (1989, April). Gender differences in external networks of small business owner/managers. *Journal of Small Business Management*, 25-32.

Sonfield, M., Lussier, R., Corman, J., & McKinney, M. (2001). Gender comparisons in strategic decision-making: An empirical analysis of the entrepreneurial strategy matrix. *Journal of Small Business Management, 39*(2), 165-173.

Teltscher, S. (2002). *E-Commerce and Development Report 2002*, United Nations Conference on Trade and Development.

Verheul, I., Risseeuw, P., & Bartelse, G. (2002). Gender differences in strategy and human resource management. *International Small Business Journal, 20*(4), 443-476.

Watkins, J., & Watkins, D. (1984). The female entrepreneur: Backgrounds and determinants of business choice—Some British data. *International Small Business Journal, 2*(4), 21-31.

**Chapter X**

# The Role of Education in E-Commerce Adoption:
## Does the CEO's Level of Education Affect E-Commerce Adoption?

In the previous chapter, we examined the role of gender in e-commerce adoption and found a number of divergent views between male and female CEOs in SMEs located in Sweden and Australia. In this chapter, we will discuss the impact of the CEOs education level on e-commerce use and adoption. Previously (in Chapter III), we determined that there were no associations between the level of the CEO's education and whether an SME had adopted e-commerce or not. However, we will now take a closer look at the relationship between educational qualification and specific aspects of e-commerce such as the criteria, barriers, benefits, and disadvantages.

## Background

Numerous studies (Beaver, 2002; Curran, Stanworth, & Watkins, 1986; Fiol, 2001; Foster & Lin, 2003; Harada, 2002; Hodgetts & Kuratko, 1992; Nandram, 2002) have attempted to define the characteristics of a successful small business entrepreneur, while others (Mazzarol, Volery, Doss, & Thein, 1999; O'Donnell, Gilmore, Cummins, & Carson, 2001; Tetteh &

Burn, 2001; Venkatash & Morris, 2000) have begun to examine the skills necessary to adopt and use e-commerce in the SME sector. As would be expected, these studies have shown that the knowledge and skill of the SME owner/manager contributes to the success of the organisation in general, and also have strong positive links to success with the adoption and use of IT in the organisation, which implies the use of e-commerce.

Studies by MacGregor, Bunker, and Waugh (1998), Tetteh et al. (2001), Tabor (2005), and O'Donnell et al. (2001) found that not only did computer skills reduce apprehension regarding IT or e-commerce adoption and use in SMEs, but they often altered the perception of adoption criteria, barriers, benefits, and disadvantages stemming from e-commerce adoption. In particular, these studies showed that there was a greater appreciation by those that had some computer background and skill, for the need to examine organisational issues prior to e-commerce adoption and use. They further showed that organisational benefits were considered to be more important by those that had a background in computing than those whose skills were low or non-existent. Indeed, those whose background and skills in computer use were low based most of their judgement of benefits and disadvantages in terms of finance, while those that indicated that they had some background (through qualifications) in using computing technology, used a variety of measures when considering benefits and disadvantages incurred with adopting e-commerce.

With more and more businesses adopting and using e-commerce, educationalists were quick to develop a raft of training programs both for owner/managers within various industry sectors and for students who would ultimately fill some of those roles in the future (see Fusilier & Durlabhji, 2003; Mitra & Matlay, 2004). However, there is a growing realisation that skills beyond simple IT are required both for general management as well as successful use of e-commerce (Tabor, 2005). Therefore, it is important to take a more holistic look at the overall educational background and qualifications of the CEO, rather than simply limiting it to IT skills.

# Research Questions

Our aim in this chapter is to explore the issues related to the CEO's level of education and e-commerce in several ways. Since we have already examined the associations between education and other business characteristics in Chapter III, these results will not be replicated here. Instead, the reader is referred to the earlier chapter. In this chapter, we will focus on determining whether the rating assigned to e-commerce adoption criteria, e-commerce barriers, e-commerce benefits, and disadvantages differs between CEOs with different levels of education. Our second aim is to determine whether the groupings and priorities of criteria for adoption, barriers to adoption, e-commerce benefits, and disadvantages differ between these CEOs. Subsequently, the chapter is organised based on the following two questions:

1. Are there any differences between qualified CEOs and those without any formal education in relation to e-commerce adoption criteria, barriers, benefits, and disadvantages?

2.    Do the groupings of e-commerce adoption criteria, barriers, benefits, and disadvantages differ between SMEs with CEOs who have formal qualifications and those without any formal qualifications?

# Methodology

In line with the views of Sambrook (2003), Sambrook and Stewart (2000), and Figueira (2003), the education background was subdivided into three categories--those respondents that did not have any formal educational background, those respondents that had completed some form of high school or trade qualification (considered trained respondents), and those that had some form of university qualification. Respondents in two locations were asked to indicate the level of education of their CEO. Chapter III provided a summary of the responses to this question. These are replicated next for the benefit of the reader.

*Table 1. Summary of responses to education question*

|  | Sweden | | Australia | |
|---|---|---|---|---|
|  | TOTAL RESPONDENTS | | | |
|  | No of responses | % | No of responses | % |
| No formal education. | 37 | 11.8 | 32 | 20 |
| High school/trade qualification. | 118 | 37.7 | 84 | 52.5 |
| University qualification. | 138 | 44.1 | 44 | 27.5 |
| Missing | 20 | 6.4 | 0 | 0 |
|  | E-COMMERCE ADOPTERS | | | |
|  | No of responses | % | No of responses | % |
| No formal education. | 17 | 9.3 | 5 | 20 |
| Trade qualification. | 62 | 33.9 | 11 | 44 |
| University qualification. | 91 | 49.7 | 9 | 36 |
| Missing | 13 | 7.1 | 0 | 0 |
|  | NON-ADOPTERS | | | |
|  | No of responses | % | No of responses | % |
| No formal education. | 20 | 15.4 | 27 | 20 |
| Trade qualification. | 56 | 43.1 | 73 | 54.1 |
| University qualification. | 47 | 36.2 | 35 | 25.9 |
| Missing | 7 | 5.4 | 0 | 0 |

Table 1 shows that in both locations, the majority of respondents had some form of qualification. However, while almost 45% of respondents in Sweden were university graduates, the highest number of respondents in the Australian study had a high school or trade qualification. The number of e-commerce adopters without any formal education in Sweden was quite low, just under 10%, and half of the Australian adopters. In contrast, the level of non-adopters without any formal qualification was comparable (just over 15% in Sweden and 20% in Australia). Based on Table 1 we can conclude the most of the respondents were qualified and therefore capable of making decisions informed by educational training, rather than business experience alone. Due to the low number of responses to this question in the U.S., it was not possible to perform a statistical analysis. Therefore, this data has been excluded from the chapter.

The rest of this chapter is structured as follows. First, we will present the results of the chi-squared tests in Sweden and Australia and then the results of the factor analysis. The final part of the chapter will discuss and compare the findings, and present the business implications of the results.

# Education and E-Commerce Adoption

Our first research question was concerned with the differences between qualified and unqualified CEOs in terms of their ratings of various e-commerce aspects. To find out if any such differences existed, the data was subdivided for each location into three categories of SMEs. A series of chi-squared tests was then applied to the data to determine if there were any statistically significant differences in the ratings of e-commerce adoption criteria, barriers to adoption, benefits derived from e-commerce adoption, or disadvantages incurred through adoption of e-commerce. The results are discussed next.

## Sweden

Tables 2 to 4 provide the results of the chi-squared tests for criteria to adopt e-commerce.

*Table 2. Association between education level and the criterion "demand/pressure from suppliers"*

| Rating | No Formal Education | High School/Trade | University |
|--------|--------------------|--------------------|-----------|
| 1 | 7 | 22 | 41 |
| 2 | 3 | 8 | 18 |
| 3 | 1 | 14 | 9 |
| 4 | 0 | 11 | 5 |
| 5 | 1 | 1 | 2 |

*Note: $p < .05$*

*Table 3. Association between education level and the criterion "improve customer service"*

| Rating | No Formal Education | High School/Trade | University |
|--------|--------------------|-------------------|------------|
| 1 | 0 | 3 | 4 |
| 2 | 2 | 0 | 0 |
| 3 | 2 | 7 | 12 |
| 4 | 5 | 27 | 20 |
| 5 | 4 | 21 | 41 |

Note: p < .001

*Table 4. Association between education level and the criterion "availability of external support"*

| Rating | No Formal Education | High School/Trade | University |
|--------|--------------------|-------------------|------------|
| 1 | 7 | 34 | 54 |
| 2 | 5 | 13 | 10 |
| 3 | 0 | 3 | 9 |
| 4 | 0 | 5 | 1 |
| 5 | 0 | 2 | 1 |

Note: p < .05

An examination of Table 2 provides an interesting and somewhat unexpected result. While the majority of respondents with no formal education rated this criteria as being unimportant in their situation, a large majority of university educated CEOs also showed the same rating. The highest number of respondents who found this criterion to be important was in the high school/trade qualification category (21%). For the university-qualified respondents, one explanation may be that many of them were in the service sector and thus did not rely on suppliers to conduct their business.

Table 3 indicates that it is the high school/trade respondents who have placed the greatest emphasis on the criterion "improvement to customer service." It is also interesting to note that while a small percentage of both the high school/trade respondents and the university respondents placed no importance on this criterion (rating of 1), no respondent that did not have any formal education rated this criterion as 1 (very unimportant).

Table 4 shows that while no non-formally educated respondents and only two university-qualified respondents rated this criterion as having any importance (rating 4 or 5), seven respondents (12.3%) of the high school/trade respondents considered this important. This would tend to be contrary to earlier findings (see for example Mazzarol et al., 1999; O'Donnell et al., 2001; Tetteh et al., 2001; Venkatash et al., 2000).

Perhaps most interesting is the fact that only three criteria showed any association with the education level of the owner/manager. Thus we can conclude that the majority of criteria for e-commerce adoption are not dependent on the level of educational attainment of the owner/manager but are similar for all owner/managers in regional Sweden.

The same analysis was undertaken for e-commerce barriers and the following results were obtained (Table 5).

*Table 5. Association between education level and the barrier "cost too high"*

| Rating | No Formal Education | High School/Trade | University |
|--------|--------------------|--------------------|-----------|
| 1 | 1 | 3 | 13 |
| 2 | 4 | 7 | 7 |
| 3 | 1 | 16 | 7 |
| 4 | 2 | 12 | 6 |
| 5 | 2 | 10 | 3 |

*Note: p < .001*

*Table 6. Association between education level and the disadvantage "higher costs"*

| Rating | No Formal Education | High School/Trade | University |
|--------|--------------------|--------------------|-----------|
| 1 | 4 | 20 | 34 |
| 2 | 1 | 17 | 12 |
| 3 | 6 | 9 | 25 |
| 4 | 2 | 9 | 3 |
| 5 | 1 | 2 | 1 |

*Note: p < .05*

*Table 7. Association between education level and the disadvantage "dependence on e-commerce"*

| Rating | No Formal Education | High School/Trade | University |
|--------|--------------------|--------------------|-----------|
| 1 | 6 | 30 | 55 |
| 2 | 6 | 16 | 11 |
| 3 | 1 | 9 | 8 |
| 4 | 1 | 2 | 0 |
| 5 | 0 | 0 | 0 |

*Note: p < .05*

Only one of the tested barriers showed any significant association with educational level. An examination of Table 5 showed that the barrier that was concerned with the cost of adopting e-commerce was associated with the educational background of the owner/manager. The data shows that 45.8% of the high school/trade respondents felt this to be an important or very important barrier. By comparison, only 25% of the university-qualified respondents felt that this was an important barrier. Unfortunately, the low response rate of the non-qualified respondents makes any comment questionable at best.

While there were no significant differences in any of the benefits derived from e-commerce, two disadvantages showed a significant association with the level of educational background of the owner/manager. These are shown in Tables 6 and 7.

The results indicate that 19% of the high school/trade respondents felt that they were experiencing higher costs through e-commerce adoption. This compares to 5.3% for the university qualified. Studies by Tabor (2005) and Sambrook (2003) suggest that knowledge of business strategies is essential to the successful adoption and use of e-commerce in the SME sector.

While the figures in Table 6 do not directly address the background knowledge in terms of business strategy, the figures do suggest that at least where cost management is concerned, more high school/trade respondents reported problems with ongoing costs of e-commerce than did the university respondents.

While the percentages are very small, Table 7 shows that some high school/trade respondents felt that dependence on e-commerce was a disadvantage.

## Summary of Findings: Sweden

Our results indicate that there are no differences between qualified and unqualified CEOs when it comes to e-commerce benefits only. Therefore, where benefits are concerned, having a formal education does not necessarily imply specific benefits from e-commerce adoption. There are however, differences between e-commerce criteria, benefits, and disadvantages. Three criteria showed a significant difference between the three categories of CEOs, including demand/pressure from suppliers, improved customer services, and availability of external support. In all three cases, it was the high school graduates or CEOs with trade qualifications that rated these as being more important when compared to those CEOs without any qualifications and those with a graduate degree. The same results were evident in the e-commerce barriers where high school/trade qualified CEOs rated high costs as an important barrier. Finally, two e-commerce disadvantages were showed a significant difference between the three CEO categories, and once again, it was the CEOs with high school/trade qualifications that rated higher costs and dependence on e-commerce as being relevant, although it should be noted that the percentages were quite small, and overall, the vast majority of SMEs rated this disadvantage as being inapplicable in their situation.

## Australia

The same statistical analysis was been applied to the Australian data, and no significant differences were found between any of the e-commerce barriers, criteria, benefits, and disadvantages across the three categories of CEOs. This suggests that the educational level of the CEO in the Australian context did not affect any of the reasons why Australian SMEs were or were not adopting e-commerce, or the subsequent advantages and problems that resulted from the adoption.

We will now take a closer look at the groupings of e-commerce adoption criteria, barriers, benefits, and disadvantages in each of the three categories of education (unqualified, trade qualified, and university qualified) with the purpose of answering our second question: Do the groupings of e-commerce adoption criteria, barriers, benefits, and disadvantages differ between CEOs with different levels of education?

# Groupings of E-Commerce Criteria, Barriers, Benefits, Disadvantages, and CEO Education

To answer our second question, a combination of correlations and factor analysis was applied to the data. The results of this analysis are shown in the tables next and discussed at the end of each section, by location.

## Sweden

Tables 8 and 9 provide the correlation matrices of the importance ratings for e-commerce adoption criteria. All correlations significant at the .001 level are shown in bold.

Factor analysis was used to investigate the underlying factors. The results of the Kaiser-Meyer-Olkin MSA (.499 for unqualified CEOs, .836 for trade qualified CEOs, .881 for university qualified CEOs) and Bartlett's test of Sphericity ($\chi^2 = 362$, $p = .000$ for unqualified CEOs, $\chi^2 = 596$, p=.000 for trade qualified CEOs, $\chi^2 = 921$, p=.000 for university qualified CEOs) indicated that the data sets satisfied the assumptions for factorability. Principle Components Analysis was chosen as the method of extraction in order to account for maximum variance in the data using a minimum number of factors. For those respondents that indicated no formal education, a three factor solution was extracted with Eigenvalues 9.641, 1.419, 1.170. This was supported by an inspection of the Scree Plot. These factors account for 87.358% of the variance. For those respondents that indicated high school or trade qualifications, a three-factor solution was extracted with Eigenvalues 6.915, 1.941, and 1.131. This was also supported by an inspection of the Scree Plot. These factors account for 71.332% of the variance. Finally, for those respondents that indicated a university qualification, a two-factor solution was extracted with Eigenvalues 7.844 and 1.125. These factors account for 64.064% of the variance. The results are summarized in Tables 11 to 13.

For all three categories of respondents, the resulting components were rotated using the Varimax procedure and a simple structure was achieved as shown in the rotated component matrices in Table 14 to 16.

Both unqualified and high school/trade qualified CEOs grouped e-commerce criteria around three factors. While there were some similarities between the first groupings, which was predominantly related to sales criteria, there were more divergent views between the second and third groupings. CEOs with no formal qualifications grouped pressure from competitors and suppliers, as well as the availability of external support together, while CEOs that had a high school or trade qualification rated a similar grouping as the least significant but included pressure from customers and competitors as part of it. The third grouping was the mostly widely divergent, with unqualified CEOs putting together a variety of criteria related to competitiveness and efficiency together in contrast to their counterparts who grouped drivers mainly related to improvements in their supply chain together.

In contrast to these two categories of CEOs, owners/managers with a university qualification grouped criteria based on two factors: sales/marketing and supply chain/market forces. While there are some parallels between these respondents and the other two categories of respondents in relation to the first grouping, the second grouping consisted of criteria related

*Table 8. Adoption criteria correlation matrix for unqualified CEOs (Sweden)*

| | Demand and/or pressure from customers. | Demand and/or pressure from suppliers. | To reduce costs. | To improve customer service. | To shorten lead time/reduce stock levels. | To increase sales. | To improve internal efficiency. | To strengthen relations with business partners. | The possibility of reaching new customers/markets. | To improve our competitiveness. | We were offered external support to adopt e-commerce. | To improve our marketing. | To improve control. |
|---|---|---|---|---|---|---|---|---|---|---|---|---|---|
| Pressure from competition. | .632** | | | | | | | | | | | | |
| Demand and/or pressure from suppliers. | .503* | .792 | | | | | | | | | | | |
| To reduce costs. | .545* | .786 | .646** | | | | | | | | | | |
| To improve customer service. | .843 | .747 | .518* | .790 | | | | | | | | | |
| To shorten lead time/reduce stock levels. | .663** | .520* | .445 | .547* | .681** | | | | | | | | |
| To increase sales. | .853 | .545* | .443 | .579* | .800 | .724** | | | | | | | |
| To improve internal efficiency. | .627** | .572* | .313 | .530* | .701** | .466 | .582* | | | | | | |
| To strengthen relations with business partners. | .768 | .726** | .751 | .633** | .733** | .776 | .802 | .525* | | | | | |
| The possibility of reaching new customers/markets. | .892 | .477* | .421 | .434 | .799 | .612** | .854 | .573* | .744 | | | | |
| To improve our competitiveness. | .695** | .887 | .716** | .817 | .842 | .478* | .734** | .655** | .734** | .623** | | | |
| We were offered external support to adopt e-commerce. | .693** | .790 | .802 | .648** | .656** | .767 | .757 | .496* | .943 | .655** | .751 | | |
| To improve our marketing. | .860 | .458 | .445 | .467 | .799 | .648** | .931 | .573* | .792 | .953 | .686** | .693** | |
| To improve control. | .575* | .654** | .181 | .714** | .820 | .567* | .678** | .678* | .482* | .549* | .711** | .486* | .530* |

Note: * significant at 0.05 level   ** significant at 0.01 level

*Table 9. Adoption criteria correlation matrix for trade qualified CEOs (Sweden)*

| | Demand and/or pressure from customers. | Demand and/or pressure from suppliers. | To reduce costs. | To improve customer service. | To shorten lead time/reduce stock levels. | To increase sales. | To improve internal efficiency. | To strengthen relations with business partners. | The possibility of reaching new customers/markets. | To improve our competitiveness. | We were offered external support to adopt e-commerce. | To improve our marketing. | To improve control. |
|---|---|---|---|---|---|---|---|---|---|---|---|---|---|
| Pressure from competition. | .683 | | | | | | | | | | | | |
| Demand and/or pressure from suppliers. | .000 | .279* | | | | | | | | | | | |
| To reduce costs. | .341* | .579 | .616 | | | | | | | | | | |
| To improve customer service. | .500 | .530 | .330** | .638 | | | | | | | | | |
| To shorten lead time/reduce stock levels. | .022 | .222 | .668 | .567 | .401** | | | | | | | | |
| To increase sales. | .350** | .435 | .401** | .669 | .667 | .476 | | | | | | | |
| To improve internal efficiency. | .284* | .444 | .339** | .662 | .723 | .543 | .657 | | | | | | |
| To strengthen relations with business partners. | .364** | .392** | .412** | .523 | .680 | .603 | .584 | .634 | | | | | |
| The possibility of reaching new customers/markets. | .353** | .431 | .171 | .371** | .620 | .338** | .665 | .530 | .579 | | | | |
| To improve our competitiveness. | .439 | .532 | .303* | .481 | .726 | .409** | .700 | .622 | .637 | .805 | | | |
| We were offered external support to adopt e-commerce. | .048 | .151 | .419** | .266* | .046 | .352** | .190 | .178 | .172 | .047 | .120 | | |
| To improve our marketing. | .422** | .458 | .246 | .318* | .546 | .261* | .566 | .514 | .495 | .763 | .695 | .198 | |
| To improve control. | .180 | .417** | .387** | .527 | .256* | .558 | .458 | .495 | .393** | .311* | .441 | .533 | .326** |

Note: * significant at 0.05 level   ** significant at 0.01 level

*Table 10. Adoption criteria correlation matrix for university qualified CEOs (Sweden)*

| | Demand and/or pressure from customers. | Demand and/or pressure from suppliers. | To reduce costs. | To improve customer service. | To shorten lead time/reduce stock levels. | To increase sales. | To improve internal efficiency. | To strengthen relations with business partners. | The possibility of reaching new customers/markets. | To improve our competitiveness. | We were offered external support to adopt e-commerce. | To improve our marketing. | To improve control. |
|---|---|---|---|---|---|---|---|---|---|---|---|---|---|
| Pressure from competition. | .630 | | | | | | | | | | | | |
| Demand and/or pressure from suppliers. | .476 | .515 | | | | | | | | | | | |
| To reduce costs. | .473 | .405 | .558 | | | | | | | | | | |
| To improve customer service. | .469 | .512 | .467 | .761 | | | | | | | | | |
| To shorten lead time/reduce stock levels. | .406 | .443 | .583 | .713 | .563 | | | | | | | | |
| To increase sales. | .322** | .335** | .438 | .594 | .628 | .489 | | | | | | | |
| To improve internal efficiency. | .290** | .318*** | .424 | .602 | .528 | .525 | .457 | | | | | | |
| To strengthen relations with business partners. | .495 | .493 | .509 | .539 | .723 | .508 | .541 | .456 | | | | | |
| The possibility of reaching new customers/markets. | .371 | .425 | .594 | .550 | .685 | .497 | .735 | .416 | .628 | | | | |
| To improve our competitiveness. | .456 | .605 | .556 | .588 | .696 | .594 | .653 | .526 | .809 | .770 | | | |
| We were offered external support to adopt e-commerce. | .298** | .333** | .400 | .416 | .322** | .413 | .402 | .310** | .456 | .375 | .466 | | |
| To improve our marketing. | .325 | .404 | .505 | .463 | .620 | .386 | .667 | .404 | .554 | .839 | .691 | .356** | |
| To improve control. | .437 | .411 | .602 | .673 | .670 | .651 | .547 | .505 | .591 | .662 | .668 | .434 | .527 |

*Note: \* significant at 0.05 level   \*\* significant at 0.01 level*

*Table 11. Total variance explained: Adoption criteria (unqualified CEOs in Sweden)*

| Component | Eigenvalue | % Variation | Cumulative % |
|---|---|---|---|
| 1 | 9.641 | 68.865 | 68.865 |
| 2 | 1.419 | 10.138 | 79.002 |
| 3 | 1.170 | 8.356 | 87.358 |

*Table 12. Total variance explained: Adoption criteria (trade qualified CEOs in Sweden)*

| Component | Eigenvalue | % Variation | Cumulative % |
|---|---|---|---|
| 1 | 6.915 | 49.393 | 49.393 |
| 2 | 1.941 | 13.862 | 63.255 |
| 3 | 1.131 | 8.077 | 71.332 |

*Table 13. Total variance explained: Adoption criteria (university qualified CEOs in Sweden)*

| Component | Eigenvalue | % Variation | Cumulative % |
|---|---|---|---|
| 1 | 7.844 | 56.029 | 56.029 |
| 2 | 1.125 | 8.035 | 64.064 |

to external (market) pressures as well as supply chain efficiencies. Once again, the differences within the SME sector are highlighted.

Tables 17 and 19 provide the correlation matrices of the importance ratings for e-commerce adoption barriers. All correlations significant at the .001 level are shown in bold.

The results of the Kaiser-Meyer-Olkin MSA (.784 for unqualified CEOs, .867 for trade qualified CEOs, .816 for university qualified CEOs) and Bartlett's test of Sphericity ($\chi^2$ = 172, $p$ = .000 for unqualified CEOs, $\chi^2$ = 338, p=.000 for trade qualified CEOs and $\chi^2$ = 327, p=.000 for university qualified CEOs) indicated that the data sets satisfied the assumptions for factorability. Principle components analysis was chosen as the method of extraction in order to account for maximum variance in the data using a minimum number of factors. For all three sets of respondents, a two-factor solution was extracted with Eigenvalues 6.556 and 1.393 (for the unqualified CEOs), 5.587 and 1.345 (for the trade qualified CEOs) and Eigenvalues 5.340 and 1.784 (for university qualified CEOs). This was supported by an inspection of the Scree Plot. These factors account for 79.489% of the variance, 69.328% of the variance and 71.243% of the variance respectively. The results are shown in Tables 20 to 22.

The resulting components were rotated using the Varimax procedure and a simple structure was achieved as shown in the rotated component matrix (see Tables 23 and 25).

The results for the e-commerce barriers show a higher degree of similarity between the three categories of CEOs. All three grouped the barriers along the same lines and all three assigned a higher priority to those barriers related to the complexity of implementing e-commerce in the organization, as opposed to the suitability of doing so.

Tables 26 and 28 provide the correlation matrices of the ratings for e-commerce benefits. All correlations significant at the .001 level are shown in bold.

The results of the Kaiser-Meyer-Olkin MSA (.713 for unqualified CEOs, .885 for trade qualified CEOs, .920 for university qualified CEOs) and Bartlett's test of Sphericity ($\chi^2 =$ 270, $p$ = .000 for unqualified CEOs, $\chi^2$ = 565, p=.000 for trade qualified CEOs, $\chi^2$ = 1104, p = .000 for university qualified CEOs) indicated that the data sets satisfied the assumptions for factorability. Principle components analysis was chosen as the method of extraction in order to account for maximum variance in the data using a minimum number of factors. For the unqualified CEOs, a two-factor solution was extracted with Eigenvalues 8.986 and 1.619. These factors account for 75.752% of the total variance. A three factor solution was extracted for the trade qualified CEOs with Eigenvalues 7.410, 1.456 and 1.027. These factors account for 70.666% of the total variance. For the university qualified respondents, a two-factor solution was extracted with Eigenvalues 8.740 and 1.249. These factors account for 71.349% of the total variance. The results are shown in Tables 29 to 31.

All three sets of components were rotated using the Varimax procedure and a simple structure was achieved as shown in the rotated component matrix in Tables 32 and 34. In all cases, the factors are independent and uncorrelated as an orthogonal rotation procedure was used.

With the e-commerce benefits, there are both differences in the number of groupings as well as the priorities assigned to them. Both CEOs without any qualifications and those with a university degree grouped benefits around two factors. However, while the former grouped efficiency and sales benefits together and rated these as being the most applicable, the latter rated efficiency and competitiveness together, and gave this grouping the highest priority. In contrast, SMEs with a CEO who had high school or trade qualifications grouped e-commerce benefits based on three factors with the main difference being the benefits related to sales and supply chain issues (such as stock levels) which loaded on to a separate factor. However, this category of SMEs rated competitiveness and increased market share as being the most applicable adoption criteria.

Finally, Tables 35 and 37 provide the correlation matrices of the ratings for e-commerce disadvantages. All correlations significant at the .001 level are shown in bold.

The results of the Kaiser-Meyer-Olkin MSA (.790 for unqualified CEOs, .892 for trade qualified CEOs, .906 for university qualified CEOs) and Bartlett's test of Sphericity ($\chi^2 =$ 236, $p$ = .000 for unqualified CEOs, $\chi^2$ = 500, p=.000 for trade qualified CEOs, $\chi^2$ = 736, p = .000 for university qualified CEOs) indicated that the data sets satisfied the assumptions for factorability. Principle components analysis was chosen as the method of extraction in order to account for maximum variance in the data using a minimum number of factors. For the unqualified CEOs and university qualified respondents, a single factor solution was extracted and therefore will not be reported. For the trade qualified respondents, a two-factor solution was extracted with Eigenvalues 6.776 and 1.147. This was supported by an inspection of the Scree plot and accounted for 72.030% of the variance. This is shown in Table 38.

*Table 14. Rotated component matrix: Adoption criteria (unqualified CEOs in Sweden)*

|  | Component 1: Sales | Component 2: External Drivers | Component 3: Competitiveness & Efficiency |
|---|---|---|---|
| Demand and/or pressure from customers. | .795 |  |  |
| Pressure from competition. |  | .756 |  |
| Demand and/or pressure from suppliers. |  | .941 |  |
| To reduce costs. |  |  | .677 |
| To improve customer service. |  |  | .691 |
| To shorten lead time/reduce stock levels. | .656 |  |  |
| To increase sales. | .834 |  |  |
| To improve internal efficiency. |  |  | .711 |
| To strengthen relations with business partners. | .688 |  |  |
| The possibility of reaching new customers/markets. | .897 |  |  |
| To improve our competitiveness. |  |  | .636 |
| We were offered external support to adopt e-commerce. |  | .749 |  |
| To improve our marketing. | .909 |  |  |
| To improve control. |  |  | .890 |

*Table 15. Rotated component matrix: Adoption criteria (trade qualified CEOs in Sweden)*

|  | Component 1: Sales & Competitiveness | Component 2: Supply Chain | Component 3: Market Forces |
|---|---|---|---|
| Demand and/or pressure from customers. |  |  | .855 |
| Pressure from competition. |  |  | .789 |
| Demand and/or pressure from suppliers. |  | .769 |  |
| To reduce costs. |  | .627 |  |
| To improve customer service. | .806 |  |  |
| To shorten lead time/reduce stock levels. |  | .729 |  |
| To increase sales. | .754 |  |  |
| To improve internal efficiency. | .722 |  |  |
| To strengthen relations with business partners. | .740 |  |  |
| The possibility of reaching new customers/markets. | .859 |  |  |
| To improve our competitiveness. | .835 |  |  |
| We were offered external support to adopt e-commerce. |  | .743 |  |
| To improve our marketing. | .710 |  |  |
| To improve control. |  | .727 |  |

Table 16. Rotated component matrix: Adoption criteria (university qualified CEOs in Sweden)

| | Component 1: Sales & Marketing | Component 2: Supply Chain & Market Forces |
|---|---|---|
| Demand and/or pressure from customers. | | .821 |
| Pressure from competition. | | .783 |
| Demand and/or pressure from suppliers. | | .623 |
| To reduce costs. | | .579 |
| To improve customer service. | .696 | |
| To shorten lead time/reduce stock levels. | | .627 |
| To increase sales. | .828 | |
| To improve internal efficiency. | .502 | |
| To strengthen relations with business partners. | .615 | |
| The possibility of reaching new customers/markets. | .877 | |
| To improve our competitiveness. | .734 | |
| We were offered external support to adopt e-commerce. | .367 | |
| To improve our marketing. | .846 | |
| To improve control. | .623 | |

The resulting components were rotated using a Varimax procedure and a simple structure was achieved as shown in the rotated component matrix (see Table 39).

While SMEs with unqualified and university qualified CEOs did not differentiate between different groupings of e-commerce disadvantages, those with high school/trade qualifications did distinguish between two factors: business practices and resources/workloads. The greater importance was placed on the business practices factor (Eigenvalue 6.776, % var. 61.604%). This factor included deterioration of relations with business partners, reduced flexibility of work, security risks, and dependence on e-commerce. It is interesting to note that although conventional wisdom would associate security risks with an additional workload, the Swedish respondents mapped this to changes in the business practices.

## Summary: Groupings and Gender in Sweden

Although there were no differences in the groupings of e-commerce barriers between CEOs with different levels of education (all of the CEOs grouped barriers around two factors: the difficulties associated with implementing e-commerce and the unsuitability of the technology), there were divergent views on e-commerce adoption criteria, benefits, and disadvantages. Both unqualified and high school/trade qualified CEOs grouped e-commerce criteria around three factors, however, university graduates only identified two groupings. All three CEOs were in agreement that the criteria related predominantly to sales were the most important. There was a somewhat similar result when it came to e-commerce benefits with all of the

*Table 17. Adoption barriers correlation matrix for unqualified CEOs (Sweden)*

| | E-commerce is not suited to our products/services. | E-commerce is not suited to our way of doing business. | E-commerce is not suited to the ways our clients do business. | E-commerce does not offer any advantages to our organisation. | We do not have the technical knowledge in the organisation to implement e-commerce. | E-commerce is too complicated to implement. | E-commerce is not secure. | The financial investment required to implement e-commerce is too high. | We do not have time to implement e-commerce. |
|---|---|---|---|---|---|---|---|---|---|
| E-commerce is not suited to our way of doing business. | .881 | | | | | | | | |
| E-commerce is not suited to the ways our clients do business. | .486** | .535** | | | | | | | |
| E-commerce does not offer any advantages to our organisation. | .550** | .508** | .279 | | | | | | |
| We do not have the technical knowledge in the organisation to implement e-commerce. | -.026 | -.050 | -.234 | .084 | | | | | |
| E-commerce is too complicated to implement. | .076 | .027 | .032 | .075 | .628 | | | | |
| E-commerce is not secure. | .125 | .074 | .100 | .212 | .231 | .634 | | | |
| The financial investment required to implement e-commerce is too high. | -.161 | -.110 | .128 | -.243 | .479** | .576 | .268 | | |
| We do not have time to implement e-commerce. | -.335* | -.333 | -.118 | -.310 | .587 | .517** | .329 | .587 | |
| It is difficult to choose the most suitable e-commerce standard with so many different options available. | -.047 | .072 | -.050 | -.137 | .721 | .796 | .476** | .626 | .638 |

*Note:  * significant at 0.05 level     ** significant at 0.01 level*

*Table 18. Adoption barriers correlation matrix for trade qualified CEOs (Sweden)*

| | E-commerce is not suited to our products/services. | E-commerce is not suited to our way of doing business. | E-commerce is not suited to the ways our clients do business. | E-commerce does not offer any advantages to our organisation. | We do not have the technical knowledge in the organisation to implement e-commerce. | E-commerce is too complicated to implement. | E-commerce is not secure. | The financial investment required to implement e-commerce is too high. | We do not have time to implement e-commerce. |
|---|---|---|---|---|---|---|---|---|---|
| E-commerce is not suited to our way of doing business. | .655 | | | | | | | | |
| E-commerce is not suited to the ways our clients do business. | .526 | .562 | | | | | | | |
| E-commerce does not offer any advantages to our organisation. | .532 | .646 | .353** | | | | | | |
| We do not have the technical knowledge in the organisation to implement e-commerce. | .104 | .227 | .032 | .439** | | | | | |
| E-commerce is too complicated to implement. | .033 | .129 | .246 | .149 | .419** | | | | |
| E-commerce is not secure. | .237 | .462 | .243 | .239 | .244 | .456 | | | |
| The financial investment required to implement e-commerce is too high. | .161 | .015 | .199 | .099 | .361** | .418** | .247 | | |
| We do not have time to implement e-commerce. | -.092 | -.068 | .057 | .002 | .275* | .610 | .121 | .353** | |
| It is difficult to choose the most suitable e-commerce standard with so many different options available. | .041 | .084 | .161 | .193 | .365** | .467 | .228 | .425** | .521 |

*Note: * significant at 0.05 level    ** significant at 0.01 level*

*Table 19. Adoption barriers correlation matrix for university qualified CEOs (Sweden)*

| | E-commerce is not suited to our products/services. | E-commerce is not suited to our way of doing business. | E-commerce is not suited to the ways our clients do business. | E-commerce does not offer any advantages to our organisation. | We do not have the technical knowledge in the organisation to implement e-commerce. | E-commerce is too complicated to implement. | E-commerce is not secure. | The financial investment required to implement e-commerce is too high. | We do not have time to implement e-commerce. |
|---|---|---|---|---|---|---|---|---|---|
| E-commerce is not suited to our way of doing business. | .791 | | | | | | | | |
| E-commerce is not suited to the ways our clients do business. | .667 | .699 | | | | | | | |
| E-commerce does not offer any advantages to our organisation. | .694 | .675 | .460** | | | | | | |
| We do not have the technical knowledge in the organisation to implement e-commerce. | .284 | .091 | .037 | .196 | | | | | |
| E-commerce is too complicated to implement. | .574 | .388** | .392** | .435** | .537 | | | | |
| E-commerce is not secure. | .616 | .426** | .446** | .519 | .324* | .804 | | | |
| The financial investment required to implement e-commerce is too high. | .367* | .362* | .487** | .180 | .357* | .666 | .513 | | |
| We do not have time to implement e-commerce. | .445** | .232 | .364* | .269 | .473** | .730 | .651 | .651 | |
| It is difficult to choose the most suitable e-commerce standard with so many different options available. | .360* | .377** | .412* | .153 | .483** | .727 | .563 | .730 | .621 |

*Note: * significant at 0.05 level    ** significant at 0.01 level*

*Table 20. Total variance explained: Adoption barriers (unqualified CEOs in Sweden)*

| Component | Eigenvalue | % Variation | Cumulative % |
|---|---|---|---|
| 1 | 6.556 | 65.556 | 65.556 |
| 2 | 1.393 | 13.932 | 79.489 |

*Table 21. Total variance explained: Adoption barriers (trade qualified CEOs in Sweden)*

| Component | Eigenvalue | % Variation | Cumulative % |
|---|---|---|---|
| 1 | 5.587 | 55.875 | 55.875 |
| 2 | 1.345 | 13.454 | 69.328 |

*Table 22. Total variance explained: Adoption barriers (university qualified CEOs in Sweden)*

| Component | Eigenvalue | % Variation | Cumulative % |
|---|---|---|---|
| 1 | 5.340 | 53.398 | 53.398 |
| 2 | 1.784 | 17.844 | 71.243 |

*Table 23. Rotated component matrix: Adoption barriers (unqualified CEOs in Sweden)*

| Barrier | Component 1: Too Difficult | Component 2: Unsuitable |
|---|---|---|
| E-commerce is not suited to our products/services. | | .890 |
| E-commerce is not suited to our way of doing business. | | .936 |
| E-commerce is not suited to the ways our clients do business. | .644 | |
| E-commerce does not offer any advantages to our organisation. | | .892 |
| We do not have the technical knowledge in the organisation to implement e-commerce. | .651 | |
| E-commerce is too complicated to implement. | .894 | |
| E-commerce is not secure. | .768 | |
| The financial investment required to implement e-commerce is too high. | .845 | |
| We do not have time to implement e-commerce. | .888 | |
| It is difficult to choose the most suitable e-commerce standard with so many different options available. | .795 | |

*Table 24. Rotated component matrix: Adoption barriers (trade qualified CEOs in Sweden)*

| Barrier | Component 1: Too Difficult | Component 2: Unsuitable |
|---|---|---|
| E-commerce is not suited to our products/services. | | .844 |
| E-commerce is not suited to our way of doing business. | | .813 |
| E-commerce is not suited to the ways our clients do business. | | .747 |
| E-commerce does not offer any advantages to our organisation. | | .667 |
| We do not have the technical knowledge in the organisation to implement e-commerce. | .758 | |
| E-commerce is too complicated to implement. | .845 | |
| E-commerce is not secure. | .634 | |
| The financial investment required to implement e-commerce is too high. | .713 | |
| We do not have time to implement e-commerce. | .819 | |
| It is difficult to choose the most suitable e-commerce standard with so many different options available. | .782 | |

*Table 25. Rotated component matrix: Adoption barriers (university qualified CEOs in Sweden)*

| Barrier | Component 1: Too Difficult | Component 2: Unsuitable |
|---|---|---|
| E-commerce is not suited to our products/services. | | .862 |
| E-commerce is not suited to our way of doing business. | | .903 |
| E-commerce is not suited to the ways our clients do business. | | .770 |
| E-commerce does not offer any advantages to our organisation. | | .819 |
| We do not have the technical knowledge in the organisation to implement e-commerce. | .689 | |
| E-commerce is too complicated to implement. | .844 | |
| E-commerce is not secure. | .656 | |
| The financial investment required to implement e-commerce is too high. | .778 | |
| We do not have time to implement e-commerce. | .830 | |
| It is difficult to choose the most suitable e-commerce standard with so many different options available. | .836 | |

*Table 26. E-commerce benefits correlation matrix for unqualified CEOs (Sweden)*

| E-commerce… | Reduced our administration costs. | Reduced our production costs. | Reduced our lead time. | Reduced our stock levels. | Lead to increased sales. | Increased our internal efficiency. | Improved our relations with business partners. | Gave us access to new customers and markets. | Improved our competitiveness. |
|---|---|---|---|---|---|---|---|---|---|
| Reduced our production costs. | .509 | | | | | | | | |
| Reduced our lead time. | .572 | .590 | | | | | | | |
| Reduced our stock levels. | .381** | .605 | .428 | | | | | | |
| Lead to increased sales. | .289* | .512 | .426 | .485 | | | | | |
| Increased our internal efficiency. | .187 | .451 | .351** | .306** | .271* | | | | |
| Improved our relations with business partners. | .711 | .524 | .412 | .409 | .251* | .370** | | | |
| Gave us access to new customers and markets. | .238* | .319** | .309** | .371** | .467 | .541 | .256* | | |
| Improved our competitiveness. | -.020 | .332** | .182 | .161 | .109 | .792 | .179 | .343** | |
| Improved the quality of information in our organisation. | .228* | .276* | .318** | .236* | .591 | .387** | .286* | .471 | .280* |

*Note: * significant at 0.05 level    ** significant at 0.01 level*

*Table 27. E-commerce benefits correlation matrix for trade qualified CEOs (Sweden)*

| E-commerce... | Reduced our administration costs. | Reduced our production costs. | Reduced our lead time. | Reduced our stock levels. | Lead to increased sales. | Increased our internal efficiency. | Improved our relations with business partners. | Gave us access to new customers and markets. | Improved our competitiveness. |
|---|---|---|---|---|---|---|---|---|---|
| Reduced our production costs. | .632 | | | | | | | | |
| Reduced our lead time. | .686 | .608 | | | | | | | |
| Reduced our stock levels. | .322** | .579 | .441 | | | | | | |
| Lead to increased sales. | .257* | .329** | .426 | .649 | | | | | |
| Increased our internal efficiency. | .454 | .622 | .569 | .510 | .274* | | | | |
| Improved our relations with business partners. | .555 | .472 | .538 | .364** | .237* | .429 | | | |
| Gave us access to new customers and markets. | .398** | .326** | .426 | .420 | .225 | .384** | .519 | | |
| Improved our competitiveness. | .230 | .195 | .249* | .180 | .071 | .612 | .432 | .460 | |
| Improved the quality of information in our organisation. | .270* | .344** | .395** | .472 | .432 | .282* | .298* | .411 | .189 |

*Note:  * significant at 0.05 level     ** significant at 0.01 level*

Table 28. E-commerce benefits correlation matrix for university qualified CEOs (Sweden)

| E-commerce... | Reduced our administration costs. | Reduced our production costs. | Reduced our lead time. | Reduced our stock levels. | Lead to increased sales. | Increased our internal efficiency. | Improved our relations with business partners. | Gave us access to new customers and markets. | Improved our competitiveness. |
|---|---|---|---|---|---|---|---|---|---|
| Reduced our production costs. | .710 | | | | | | | | |
| Reduced our lead time. | .728 | .751 | | | | | | | |
| Reduced our stock levels. | .665 | .716 | .629 | | | | | | |
| Lead to increased sales. | .495 | .619 | .569 | .541 | | | | | |
| Increased our internal efficiency. | .555 | .660 | .621 | .548 | .542 | | | | |
| Improved our relations with business partners. | .665 | .603 | .549 | .521 | .396 | .530 | | | |
| Gave us access to new customers and markets. | .597 | .572 | .563 | .655 | .548 | .674 | .517 | | |
| Improved our competitiveness. | .437 | .592 | .517 | .483 | .384 | .811 | .507 | .632 | |
| Improved the quality of information in our organisation. | .500 | .538 | .473 | .488 | .660 | .595 | .509 | .665 | .578 |

Note: * significant at 0.05 level     ** significant at 0.01 level

CEO categories viewing competitiveness as a high priority; however, once again there were differences between the groupings themselves. Unqualified and university qualified CEOs grouped benefits according to two factors, while trade qualified CEOs identified three groups of benefits, the third being related to supply chain issues. Finally, this same category of CEOs was the only one to distinguish between two groups of e-commerce disadvantages. The others did not show any distinct groupings, loading all of the disadvantages onto a single factor. This suggests that unqualified and university qualified CEOs did not distinguish between the different disadvantages experienced through e-commerce adoption.

We will now examine the groupings in the Australian context.

## Australia

Due to the low adoption rate of e-commerce, there was insufficient data to examine e-commerce adoption criteria, benefits, or disadvantages in the Australian sample. Tables 40 and 41 provide the correlation matrices for the barriers to e-commerce for two categories of respondents since only six respondents indicated they did not have any formal education and had not adopted e-commerce. All correlations significant at the .001 level are shown in bold.

The results of the Kaiser-Meyer-Olkin MSA (.692 for trade qualified CEOs, .610 for university qualified CEOs) and Bartlett's test of Sphericity ($\chi^2 = 144$, p=.000 for trade qualified CEOs and $\chi^2 = 226$, p=.000 for university qualified CEOs) indicated that the data sets satisfied the assumptions for factorability. Principle components analysis was chosen as the

*Table 29. Total variance explained: E-commerce benefits (unqualified CEOs in Sweden)*

| Component | Eigenvalue | % Variation | Cumulative % |
|---|---|---|---|
| 1 | 8.986 | 64.186 | 64.186 |
| 2 | 1.619 | 11.566 | 75.752 |

*Table 30. Total variance explained—e-commerce benefits (trade qualified CEOs in Sweden)*

| Component | Eigenvalue | % Variation | Cumulative % |
|---|---|---|---|
| 1 | 1.027 | 7.338 | 7.338 |
| 2 | 7.410 | 52.930 | 60.268 |
| 3 | 1.456 | 10.398 | 70.666 |

*Table 31. Total variance explained: E-commerce benefits (university qualified CEOs in Sweden)*

| Component | Eigenvalue | % Variation | Cumulative % |
|---|---|---|---|
| 1 | 1.249 | 8.919 | 8.919 |
| 2 | 8.740 | 62.430 | 71.349 |

*Table 32. Rotated component matrix: E-commerce benefits (unqualified CEOs in Sweden)*

| Benefits | Component 1: Efficiency & Sales | Component 2: Costs & Relationships |
|---|---|---|
| Reduced our administration costs. | | .936 |
| Reduced our production costs. | | .679 |
| Reduced our lead time. | .664 | |
| Reduced our stock levels. | .727 | |
| Lead to increased sales. | .782 | |
| Increased our internal efficiency. | .643 | |
| Improved our relations with business partners. | | .697 |
| Gave us access to new customers and markets. | .914 | |
| Improved our competitiveness. | .810 | |
| Improved the quality of information in our organisation. | .791 | |

*Table 33. Rotated component matrix: E-commerce benefits (trade qualified CEOs in Sweden)*

| Benefits | Component 1: Efficiency & Relationships | Component 2: Competitiveness & Market Share | Component 3: Sales & Supply Chain |
|---|---|---|---|
| Reduced our administration costs. | .807 | | |
| Reduced our production costs. | .797 | | |
| Reduced our lead time. | .757 | | |
| Reduced our stock levels. | | | .672 |
| Lead to increased sales. | | | .872 |
| Increased our internal efficiency. | .687 | | |
| Improved our relations with business partners. | .631 | | |
| Gave us access to new customers and markets. | | .729 | |
| Improved our competitiveness. | | .838 | |
| Improved the quality of information in our organisation. | | | .688 |

*Table 34. Rotated component matrix: E-commerce benefits (university qualified CEOs in Sweden)*

| Benefits | Component 1: Costs & Sales | Component 2: Competitiveness & efficiency |
|---|---|---|
| Reduced our administration costs. | .839 | |
| Reduced our production costs. | .780 | |
| Reduced our lead time. | .771 | |
| Reduced our stock levels. | .764 | |
| Lead to increased sales. | .707 | |

*Table 34. Continued*

| Benefits | Component 1: Costs & Sales | Component 2: Competitiveness & efficiency |
|---|---|---|
| Increased our internal efficiency. | | .753 |
| Improved our relations with business partners. | .673 | |
| Gave us access to new customers and markets. | | .598 |
| Improved our competitiveness. | | .903 |
| Improved the quality of information in our organisation. | .554 | |

method of extraction in order to account for maximum variance in the data using a minimum number of factors. For the trade qualified CEOs, a two-factor solution was extracted with Eigenvalues 4.512 and 2.845. These factors account for 73.571% of the variance. For the university qualified CEOs, a three factor solution was extracted with Eigenvalues 4.323, 2.425, and 1.139. These factors account for 78.876% of the variance. The results are shown in Tables 42 and 43.

The resulting components were rotated using the Varimax procedure and a simple structure was achieved as shown in the rotated component matrix (see Tables 44 and 45).

Unlike their Swedish counterparts, Australian SMEs did differ in their views of how e-commerce barriers are grouped. Those CEOs with a high school/trade qualification grouped barriers around the same factors as their Swedish counterparts and assigned a high priority to the complexity of implementing e-commerce. However, CEOs with a university qualification were more concerned about barriers related to suitability. In addition, they viewed certain

*Table 35. E-commerce disadvantages correlation matrix for unqualified CEOs (Sweden)*

| E-commerce... | Deteriorated relations with our business partners. | Increased costs. | Increased the computer maintenance required. | Doubled the amount of work. | Reduced the flexibility of the business processes. | Raised security concerns. |
|---|---|---|---|---|---|---|
| Increased costs. | .327** | | | | | |
| Increased the computer maintenance required. | .404 | .403 | | | | |
| Doubled the amount of work. | .346** | .378** | .600 | | | |
| Reduced the flexibility of the business processes. | .265* | .376** | .462 | .444 | | |
| Raised security concerns. | .640 | .271* | .295* | .432 | .308** | |
| Made us increasingly dependent on this technology. | .706 | .291* | .325** | .439 | .398 | .803 |

Note: * significant at 0.05 level    ** significant at 0.01 level

*Table 36. E-commerce disadvantages correlation matrix for trade qualified CEOs (Sweden)*

| E-commerce... | Deteriorated relations with our business partners. | Increased costs. | Increased the computer maintenance required. | Doubled the amount of work. | Reduced the flexibility of the business processes. | Raised security concerns. |
|---|---|---|---|---|---|---|
| Increased costs. | .251* | | | | | |
| Increased the computer maintenance required. | .297* | .594 | | | | |
| Doubled the amount of work. | .417 | .599 | .725 | | | |
| Reduced the flexibility of the business processes. | .378** | .324** | .343** | .434 | | |
| Raised security concerns. | .604 | .332** | .403 | .566 | .562 | |
| Made us increasingly dependent on this technology. | .301* | .343** | .409 | .444 | .445 | .520 |

Note: * significant at 0.05 level    ** significant at 0.01 level

*Table 37. E-commerce disadvantages correlation matrix for university qualified CEOs (Sweden)*

| E-commerce... | Deteriorated relations with our business partners. | Increased costs. | Increased the computer maintenance required. | Doubled the amount of work. | Reduced the flexibility of the business processes. | Raised security concerns. |
|---|---|---|---|---|---|---|
| Increased costs. | .486 | | | | | |
| Increased the computer maintenance required. | .454 | .388 | | | | |
| Doubled the amount of work. | .583 | .567 | .608 | | | |
| Reduced the flexibility of the business processes. | .518 | .552 | .529 | .680 | | |
| Raised security concerns. | .752 | .502 | .437 | .683 | .593 | |
| Made us increasingly dependent on this technology. | .792 | .515 | .455 | .690 | .648 | .888 |

Note: * significant at 0.05 level    ** significant at 0.01 level

*Table 38. Total variance explained: E-commerce disadvantages (trade qualified CEOs in Sweden)*

| Component | Eigenvalue | % Variation | Cumulative % |
|-----------|-----------|-------------|--------------|
| 1 | 6.776 | 61.604 | 61.604 |
| 2 | 1.147 | 10.426 | 72.030 |

*Table 39. Rotated component matrix: E-commerce disadvantages (trade qualified CEOs in Sweden)*

| Disadvantage | Component 1: Business Practices | Component 2: Resources & Workload |
|--------------|-------------------------------|----------------------------------|
| Deteriorated relations with business partners. | .694 | |
| Increased costs. | | .840 |
| Increased the computer maintenance required. | | .742 |
| Doubled the amount of work. | | .726 |
| Reduced the flexibility of the business processes. | .757 | |
| Raised security concerns. | .843 | |
| Made us increasingly dependent on this technology. | .770 | |

technical barriers related to IT expertise, complexity, and security as being a separate and distinct group of barriers from those related to resources (finances and time) and selecting the most suitable e-commerce standard. This implies that CEOs with a graduate qualification were more aware of the business and organisational issues that affected e-commerce implementation, rather than the technical ones.

# Comparison of Results: A Discussion

At the outset of this chapter, we identified two questions about the level of education of the CEO in an SME and e-commerce adoption. We will now compare the answers to those two questions across the two locations and draw some conclusions.

Our first question addressed the differences between unqualified, high school/trade qualified and university qualified CEOs in relation to e-commerce adoption criteria, barriers, benefits, and disadvantages. We ran a series of chi-squared tests in Australia and Sweden to determine if these differences exist, and indeed, found this to be the case in relation to criteria, barriers, and disadvantages. A summary of these can be seen in Table 46.

Table 46 indicates that in Sweden, CEOs with high school/trade qualification consistently rated e-commerce criteria, barriers, and disadvantages higher than counterparts. However, it should be noted that the percentages of CEOs who did this were small and this is only in comparison to the other categories of CEOs. There were no such differences in the Australian study, implying that the education level of the CEO has no bearing on any of the aspects of e-commerce. This raises the inevitable question as to the homogeneity of the SME sector.

Our second question was concerned with the groupings of criteria, barriers, benefits, and disadvantages in SMEs with the CEOs' education level. The results for the two locations, yet again, show interesting differences. Since the results of e-commerce criteria, benefits, and disadvantage groupings are only available for Sweden (and have been discussed and summarised at length previously), we will compare the results for barriers only.

While all three groups of respondents in the Swedish study loaded the barriers onto two factors (too difficult and unsuitable) and declared the former as being of more importance, the Australian university-educated respondents loaded the barriers onto three factors, making a distinction between technical difficulties and resource difficulties as barriers. Similarly, while all three groups in the Swedish study and the high school/trade respondents in the Australian study rated the technical barriers far more important, the Australian university-educated respondents considered that organizational barriers (related to the suitability of e-commerce) were more important. This is in line with the expectation that university level educated respondents would have the required technical skills to overcome these types of e-commerce barriers. We have summarised the results in Tables 47 and 48. (There were insufficient responses by unqualified CEOs in Australia and therefore these have been excluded.)

## E-Commerce and CEO Education: Implications

Our results suggest that the level of education of an SME owner/manager is associated with e-commerce in general and more specifically, with various aspects of e-commerce (criteria, barriers, and disadvantages). However, we have found divergent views between the two locations in relation to these associations. Once again, the homogeneity of the SME sector has been shown to be a fallacy. Despite the inherent differences between the two locations examined in this chapter, we can not confidently state that SME owners with the same level of education will treat e-commerce the same way. This is yet another issue we need to take into account in promoting e-commerce adoption. Similarly, this has implications for the level of educational training required to adopt e-commerce successfully.

## E-Commerce and CEO Education: Key Findings

### Sweden

- There were three differences between the different CEOs in relation to e-commerce adoption criteria, all of which were rated higher by high school/trade qualified CEOs.

*Table 40. Adoption barriers correlation matrix for trade qualified CEOs (Australia)*

| | E-commerce is not suited to our products/services. | E-commerce is not suited to our way of doing business. | E-commerce is not suited to the ways our clients do business. | E-commerce does not offer any advantages to our organisation. | We do not have the technical knowledge in the organisation to implement e-commerce. | E-commerce is too complicated to implement. | E-commerce is not secure. | The financial investment required to implement e-commerce is too high. | We do not have time to implement e-commerce. |
|---|---|---|---|---|---|---|---|---|---|
| E-commerce is not suited to our way of doing business. | .721 | | | | | | | | |
| E-commerce is not suited to the ways our clients do business. | .499* | .755 | | | | | | | |
| E-commerce does not offer any advantages to our organisation. | .578** | .751 | .641** | | | | | | |
| We do not have the technical knowledge in the organisation to implement e-commerce. | .172 | .288 | .244 | .411 | | | | | |
| E-commerce is too complicated to implement. | -.070 | .168 | .191 | .241 | .646** | | | | |
| E-commerce is not secure. | -.115 | .140 | .103 | .218 | .414 | .644** | | | |
| The financial investment required to implement e-commerce is too high. | .010 | .165 | .081 | .350 | .617** | .846 | .458* | | |
| We do not have time to implement e-commerce. | -.196 | -.102 | -.127 | .051 | .582** | .559** | .427 | .689** | |
| It is difficult to choose the most suitable e-commerce standard with so many different options available. | -.072 | .189 | .252 | .257 | .617** | .942 | .622** | .797 | .593** |

*Note:  * significant at 0.05 level    ** significant at 0.01 level*

*Table 41. Adoption barriers correlation matrix for university qualified CEOs (Australia)*

| | E-commerce is not suited to our products/services. | E-commerce is not suited to our way of doing business. | E-commerce is not suited to the ways our clients do business. | E-commerce does not offer any advantages to our organisation. | We do not have the technical knowledge in the organisation to implement e-commerce. | E-commerce is too complicated to implement. | E-commerce is not secure. | The financial investment required to implement e-commerce is too high. | We do not have time to implement e-commerce. |
|---|---|---|---|---|---|---|---|---|---|
| E-commerce is not suited to our way of doing business. | .855 | | | | | | | | |
| E-commerce is not suited to the ways our clients do business. | .203 | .880 | | | | | | | |
| E-commerce does not offer any advantages to our organisation. | .809 | .829 | .326 | | | | | | |
| We do not have the technical knowledge in the organisation to implement e-commerce. | .156 | .119 | .224 | .127 | | | | | |
| E-commerce is too complicated to implement. | .076 | .145 | .221 | .035 | .751 | | | | |
| E-commerce is not secure. | .096 | .060 | .228 | .007 | .548** | .401* | | | |
| The financial investment required to implement e-commerce is too high. | .392* | .394* | -.003 | .317 | .446* | .297 | .386* | | |
| We do not have time to implement e-commerce. | .225 | .274 | .213 | .384* | .369* | .412* | .185 | .711 | |
| It is difficult to choose the most suitable e-commerce standard with so many different options available. | .188 | .051 | -.213 | .257 | .217 | .093 | .198 | .369* | .504** |

*Note : * significant at 0.05 level     ** significant at 0.01 level*

*Table 42. Total variance explained: Adoption barriers (trade qualified CEOs in Australia)*

| Component | Eigenvalue | % Variation | Cumulative % |
|---|---|---|---|
| 1 | 4.512 | 45.123 | 45.123 |
| 2 | 2.845 | 28.447 | 73.571 |

*Table 43. Total variance explained: Adoption barriers (university qualified CEOs in Australia)*

| Component | Eigenvalue | % Variation | Cumulative % |
|---|---|---|---|
| 1 | 2.425 | 24.251 | 24.251 |
| 2 | 4.323 | 43.234 | 67.485 |
| 3 | 1.139 | 11.391 | 78.876 |

*Table 44. Rotated component matrix: Adoption barriers (trade qualified CEOs in Australia)*

| Barrier | Component 1: Too Difficult | Component 2: Unsuitable |
|---|---|---|
| E-commerce is not suited to our products/services. | | .824 |
| E-commerce is not suited to our way of doing business. | | .932 |
| E-commerce is not suited to the ways our clients do business. | | .834 |
| E-commerce does not offer any advantages to our organisation. | | .839 |
| We do not have the technical knowledge in the organisation to implement e-commerce. | .742 | |
| E-commerce is too complicated to implement. | .932 | |
| E-commerce is not secure. | .703 | |
| The financial investment required to implement e-commerce is too high. | .887 | |
| We do not have time to implement e-commerce. | .783 | |
| It is difficult to choose the most suitable e-commerce standard with so many different options available. | .919 | |

*Table 45. Rotated component matrix: Adoption barriers (university qualified CEOs in Australia)*

| Barrier | Component 1: Technical | Component 2: Unsuitable | Component 2: Too Difficult |
|---|---|---|---|
| E-commerce is not suited to our products/services. | | .918 | |
| E-commerce is not suited to our way of doing business. | | .947 | |
| E-commerce is not suited to the ways our clients do business. | | .953 | |
| E-commerce does not offer any advantages to our organisation. | | .911 | |
| We do not have the technical knowledge in the organisation to implement e-commerce. | .886 | | |
| E-commerce is too complicated to implement. | .846 | | |
| E-commerce is not secure. | .711 | | |
| The financial investment required to implement e-commerce is too high. | | | .635 |
| We do not have time to implement e-commerce. | | | .857 |
| It is difficult to choose the most suitable e-commerce standard with so many different options available. | | | .833 |

- There was one difference between the CEOs in relation to e-commerce barriers. The high financial investment required was rated as being more important by high school/ trade qualified CEOs.

- There were no differences between the CEOs in relation to e-commerce benefits.

- High school/trade qualified CEOs cited higher costs and dependence on e-commerce as a stronger disadvantage; however, this is only in comparison to the other CEOs.

- All three categories of CEOs were the most concerned about criteria related to sales, however, they grouped these differently.

- All three categories of CEOs grouped e-commerce barriers based on two factors (difficulties and suitability) and all the thought that the obstacles related to difficulties were more important.

- Competitiveness was given the top priority by all three categories of CEOs as an e-commerce benefit they experienced; however, they grouped the benefits differently.

- Only the high school/trade qualified CEOs distinguished between two groups of e-commerce disadvantages related to business practices and resources/workloads. The other categories did not separate the problems associated with e-commerce into distinct groups.

*Table 46. Summary of differences between unqualified, high school/trade qualified, and university qualified CEOs in Sweden and Australia*

| | Statistically Significant Differences | |
|---|---|---|
| | Sweden | Australia |
| E-Commerce Criteria | • Demand/pressure from suppliers.<br>• Improved customer service.<br>• External support.<br>Significant criteria rated more important by high school/trade qualified CEOs. | No statistically significant differences. |
| E-Commerce Barriers | • High financial investment.<br>Significant barriers rated more important by high school/trade qualified CEOs. | No statistically significant differences. |
| E-Commerce Benefits | No statistically significant differences. | No statistically significant differences. |
| E-Commerce Disadvantages | • High costs.<br>• Dependence on e-commerce.<br>Significant disadvantages rated more applicable by high school/trade qualified CEOs | No statistically significant differences. |

*Table 47. Groupings of e-commerce barriers: A comparison between high school/trade qualified CEOs in Sweden and Australia*

| | SWEDEN TRADE QUALIFIED CEOs | | AUSTRALIA TRADE QUALIFIED CEOs | |
|---|---|---|---|---|
| | 1: Too Difficult | 2: Unsuitable | 1: Too Difficult | 2: Unsuitable |
| E-commerce is not suited to our products/services. | | ✓ | | ✓ |
| E-commerce is not suited to our way of doing business. | | ✓ | | ✓ |
| E-commerce is not suited to the ways our clients do business. | | ✓ | | ✓ |
| E-commerce does not offer any advantages to our organisation. | | ✓ | | ✓ |
| We do not have the technical knowledge in the organisation to implement e-commerce. | ✓ | | ✓ | |
| E-commerce is too complicated to implement. | ✓ | | ✓ | |
| E-commerce is not secure. | ✓ | | ✓ | |
| The financial investment required to implement e-commerce is too high. | ✓ | | ✓ | |
| We do not have time to implement e-commerce. | ✓ | | ✓ | |
| It is difficult to choose the most suitable e-commerce standard with so many different options available. | ✓ | | ✓ | |

*Table 48. Groupings of e-commerce barriers: A comparison between university qualified CEOs in Sweden and Australia*

| | SWEDEN UNIVERSITY QUALIFIED CEOs | | AUSTRALIA UNIVERSITY QUALIFIED CEOs | | |
| --- | --- | --- | --- | --- | --- |
| | 1: Too Difficult | 2: Unsuitable | 1: Technical | 2: Unsuitable | 3:Too Difficult |
| E-commerce is not suited to our products/ services. | | ✓ | | ✓ | |
| E-commerce is not suited to our way of doing business. | | ✓ | | ✓ | |
| E-commerce is not suited to the ways our clients do business. | | ✓ | | ✓ | |
| E-commerce does not offer any advantages to our organisation. | | ✓ | | ✓ | |
| We do not have the technical knowledge in the organisation to implement e-commerce. | ✓ | | ✓ | | |
| E-commerce is too complicated to implement. | ✓ | | ✓ | | |
| E-commerce is not secure. | ✓ | | ✓ | | |
| The financial investment required to implement e-commerce is too high. | ✓ | | | | ✓ |
| We do not have time to implement e-commerce. | ✓ | | | | ✓ |
| It is difficult to choose the most suitable e-commerce standard with so many different options available. | ✓ | | | | ✓ |

## Australia

• There were no differences between the CEOs in relation to any aspects of e-commerce.

• Barriers related to the unsuitability of e-commerce were ranked more important by university qualified CEOs who also identified three distinct groups of obstacles, unlike their high school/trade qualified counterparts who aligned themselves with the Swedish respondents.

# References

Beaver, G. (2002). *Small business, entrepreneurship, and enterprise development.* Harlow: Pearson Education.

Curran, J., Stanworth, J., & Watkins, D. (1986). *The survival of the small firm* (Vol. 1). *The Economics of Survival and Entrepreneurship.* Aldershot: Gower Publishing.

Figueira, E. (2003). *Evaluating the effectiveness of e-learning strategies for small and medium enterprises.* Retrieved from www.theknownet.com/ ICT_SMEs_seminars/ Figueira.html

Fiol, C. M. (2001). Revisiting an identity-based view of sustainable competitive advantage. *Journal of Management, 27*(5), 691-699.

Foster, J., & Lin, A. (2003). Individual differences in learning entrepreneurship and their implications for Web-based instruction in e-business and e-commerce. *British Journal of Educational Technology, 34*(4), 455.

Fusilier, M., & Durlabhji, S. (2003). No downturn here: Tracking e-business programs in higher education. *Decision Sciences, 1*(1), 73-98.

Harada, N. (2002). Who succeeds as an entrepreneur? An analysis of the post-entry performance of new firms in Japan. *Japan in the World Economy, 44*(1), 1-13.

Hodgetts, R. M., & Kuratko, D. F. (1992). *Effective small business management.* Orlando: Harcourt Brace & Jovanovich.

MacGregor, R. C., Bunker, D. J., & Waugh, P. (1998). Electronic commerce and small/medium enterprises (SME's) in Australia: An electronic data interchange (EDI) pilot study. In *Proceedings of the 11th International Bled Electronic Commerce Conference,* Slovenia.

Mazzarol, T., Volery, T., Doss, N., & Thein, V. (1999). Factors influencing small business start-ups. *International Journal of Entrepreneurial Behaviour and Research, 5*(2), 48-63.

Mitra, J., & Matlay, H. (2004, February). Entrepreneurial and vocational education and training: Lessons from eastern and central Europe. *Industry and Higher Education,* 53.

Nandram, S. S (2002). Behavioural attributes of entrepreneurial success and failure: New perspectives gained through critical incident techniques. In *Proceedings of the Conference on Small Business and Entrepreneurial Development,* Nottingham (pp. 321-330).

O'Donnell, A., Gilmore, A., Cummins, D., & Carson, D. (2001). The network construct in entrepreneurship research: A review and critique. *Management Decision, 39*(9), 749-760.

Sambrook, S. (2003). E-learning in small organisations. *Education & Training, 45*(8/9), 506-516.

Sambrook, S., & Stewart, J. (2000). Factors influencing learning in European oriented organisations: Issue for management. *Journal of European Industrialised Training, 24*(2/3/4), 209-219.

Tabor, S. W. (2005). Achieving significant learning in e-commerce education through small business consulting projects. *Journal of Information Systems Education, 16*(1), 19-26.

Tetteh, E., & Burn, J. (2001). Global strategies for SME-business: Applying the SMALL framework. *Logistics Information Management, 14*(1-2), 171-180.

Venkatash, V., & Morris, M. G. (2000). Why don't men ever stop to ask for directions? Gender, social influence, and their role in technology acceptance and usage behavior. *MIS Quarterly, 24*(1).

Chapter XI

# Interaction of Adoption Factors:
## Do SMEs Achieve the Desired Benefits from E-Commerce Adoption?

For each of the three locations, the previous chapters have examined the four different aspects of e-commerce adoption (criteria, barriers, benefits, and disadvantages) both as a complete set and also by different categories of SMEs, depending on whether they were members of a business alliance, on the gender of their CEO, and on the CEO's level of education. The results reported are indicative of the diversity of the SME sector and represent a useful starting point when developing programs or initiatives to promote e-commerce adoption in SMEs. We will examine their implications further in the final chapter. In this chapter, we aim to determine whether four different aspects of e-commerce adoption actually affect one another. Therefore, this chapter will examine the interaction between the criteria, benefits, and disadvantages of e-commerce in those SMEs that have adopted the technology. The following chapter will consider the interaction of barriers and potential drivers in organisations that do not use e-commerce.

While many SMEs are driven to adopt e-commerce for various external and internal reasons, as we have already seen, the question that remains unanswered is whether any of the reasons that drive this adoption have any bearing on the subsequent benefits and disadvantages experienced following the implementation of e-commerce. If an SME adopts e-commerce to increase sales, does it actually achieve this goal through e-commerce? Our primary aim in this chapter, therefore, is to examine whether the varying priorities placed on criteria for e-commerce adoption are associated with the positive or negative outcomes of this adoption.

This chapter will present the results of a series of linear regressions, which were applied to e-commerce benefits and disadvantages in order to determine whether their rating was statistically significantly associated with the rating of any of the e-commerce adoption criteria. Linear regression was used as it was shown that many of the criteria were strongly correlated (see Chapter IV). A full list of e-commerce criteria, benefits, and disadvantages used in this chapter can be found in Chapters IV, VI, and VII respectively. Unfortunately, there were few responses to the questions concerning benefits and disadvantages from the U.S. sample, rendering insufficient data to effectively apply any statistical measure. The same analysis will be preformed on certain categories of SMEs (following the sub-division of the data) in order to determine whether the interactions between criteria and benefits and criteria and disadvantages differ within these various categories. These results are presented in the final sections of the chapter.

## E-Commerce Criteria and Benefits in Sweden

We found a number of statistically significant associations in the Swedish sample between e-commerce criteria and benefits. Nine of the ten benefits tested showed a significant association with one or more e-commerce adoption drivers. These are shown in Tables 1 to 9, which also indicate the relevant p value, and will now be discussed.

Table 1 shows that three criteria (reduced costs, improvements to internal efficiency, and stronger relations with business partners) are associated with the benefit of lower administration costs. The results show that there is a strong association (significance levels of .000 and .001 respectively) between the criteria "reducing costs" and "improving internal efficiency" and lower administration costs. A less significant association (.033) was found with the criterion "strengthening relations with business" partners. In all cases, those that

*Table 1. Regression table for lower administration costs*

| Dependant variable lower administration costs | | |
|---|---|---|
| | Beta | p value |
| Reduce cost. | .370 | .000 |
| Improve internal efficiency. | .278 | .001 |
| Strengthen relations with business partners. | .204 | .003 |
| R Squared | | .427 |
| Adjusted R squared | | .363 |
| p value for the complete regression table | | .000 |

*Table 2. Regression table for reduced lead time*

| Dependant variable reduced lead time | | |
|---|---|---|
| | Beta | p value |
| Reduce cost. | .441 | .000 |
| Strengthen relations with business partners. | .261 | .007 |
| R Squared | | .415 |
| Adjusted R squared | | .348 |
| p value for the complete regression table | | .000 |

*Table 3. Regression table for reduced stock*

| Dependant variable reduced stock | | |
|---|---|---|
| | Beta | p value |
| Pressure from competition. | .175 | .022 |
| Shorter lead time/reduced stock. | .742 | .000 |
| R Squared | | .622 |
| Adjusted R squared | | .579 |
| p value for the complete regression table | | .000 |

placed a higher level of importance on these criteria also assigned a higher importance to the benefit of lower administration costs. This would imply that the expectations of e-commerce were met, although not for production costs.

If we compare these results to those in Chapter IV's Table 14, it can be seen that two of the criteria (reduced costs and improved internal efficiency) were loaded together under the internal operations factor. The third criterion (stronger relations with business partners) was loaded onto the second factor termed (marketing and partnerships). This raises a number of questions. If, as shown in Table 4.14, e-commerce criteria in Sweden were loaded onto two factors, why are only some of these associated with the benefit of lower administration costs. Alternatively, if all three criteria are associated with this benefit, why are they loaded onto different factors? Clearly, as with all subsequent findings, it is important not only to examine the factors upon which criteria are loaded, but we also need to examine the "consequences" of these criteria.

Table 2 provides the data for the benefit "reduced lead time." It indicates that two criteria (reduced costs and strengthening relations with business partners) were significantly associated with the benefit of reduced lead time. Again, those respondents that placed a higher level of importance on these criteria as reasons for adopting e-commerce also reported a higher level in reduced lead time as a result of the adoption. It is interesting to note that reducing lead time, as the reason for adopting e-commerce had no statistically significant association with the matching (actual) benefit. Most authors (see for example Tetteh & Burn, 2001; Turban, Lee, King, & Chung, 2002) have stressed the need to examine the organisation holistically in order to maximise the benefits derivable from e-commerce adoption and use. The data in Table 2 (and indeed Tables 1 to 9) shows that the achievement of a perceived benefit does not rely on a single criterion, on which an organisation should concentrate, but on paying heed to various criteria in order to achieve the desired goal.

The findings in Table 3 show that two criteria (pressure from competition and shorter lead time/reduced stock) were statistically significantly associated with reduced stock. A significantly high Beta value (.742) was derived for the criterion "shorter lead time," suggesting that those respondents that had wished to achieve a reduction in their stock levels through the adoption of e-commerce had achieved that goal. A less significant association was derived from the criterion "pressure from competition."

While the association between the reduced stock criterion and the same benefit obvious, the association with pressure from competition is not. One possibility is that part of the "push" to adopt and use e-commerce, initiated by comparison with other competitive firms, has been to save money through the reduction of excess stock. However, if this were the case, we would expect the criterion pressure from competition to feature in other regression tables. This was not the case.

An examination of Table 4 shows that no less than six criteria were statistically significantly associated with the benefit of increased sales. The strongest association appears to be between increased sales and shorter lead time/reduced stock (.000). This would suggest that the ability for e-commerce to reduce the time taken between sale and delivery was the greatest asset to securing and increasing sales volume. The association between the increased sales criterion and the matching benefit was far less significant (.033), suggesting that a desire for increased sales through e-commerce did not necessarily materialise or other factors were more important than simply addressing sales on its own. Of particular interest is the negative Beta value (-.279) between improved competitiveness and increased sales. The data would suggest that those that had placed a high priority on improving competitiveness, in fact reported a lower benefit of increased sales than those that assigned a lower importance to this criterion. One possible explanation is that while sales may have increased for these respondents, they may have been below the anticipated levels when decisions to adopt e-commerce had been initially taken. Three other criteria showed some significance with

*Table 4. Regression table for increased sales*

| Dependant variable increased sales | | |
|---|---|---|
| | Beta | p value |
| Demand/pressure from suppliers. | .175 | .034 |
| Shorter lead time/reduced stock. | .333 | .000 |
| Increase sales. | .189 | .033 |
| Strengthen relations with business partners. | .186 | .036 |
| Improved competitiveness. | -.279 | .009 |
| Improved control. | .209 | .021 |
| R Squared | .517 | |
| Adjusted R squared | .460 | |
| p value for the complete regression table | .000 | |

*Table 5. Regression table for increased internal efficiency*

| Dependant variable increased internal efficiency | | |
|---|---|---|
| | Beta | p value |
| Reduced costs. | .185 | .035 |
| Increased sales. | .197 | .015 |
| Strengthen relations with business partners. | .212 | .010 |
| New customers/markets. | .239 | .025 |
| Improved control. | .276 | .004 |
| R Squared | .570 | |
| Adjusted R squared | .521 | |
| p value for the complete regression table | .000 | |

increased sales. While two of these (strengthen relations with business partners and improved control) may have been expected, there is no obvious reason for the association between pressure from suppliers and the benefit of increased sales. This is particularly unexpected when the criterion demand/pressure from customers showed no association.

Table 5 shows that five criteria (reduced costs, increased sales, stronger relations with partners, new customers/markets, and improved control) are significantly associated with the benefit of improved internal efficiency. Before considering these, it is interesting to note that this benefit was not associated with the matching criterion. Again, it may be argued that improvement to internal efficiency is a combination of many factors, rather than a simple desire to make such improvements in isolation. The Beta values for all of the criteria in Table 5 are positive, indicating that the higher the level placed on these as criteria for adopting e-commerce, the stronger the perception of having achieved the benefit of improving internal efficiency. Of particular interest is the fact that the highest level of association (.004) with the benefit-improved internal efficiency is the criterion "improved control." Those SMEs that adopted e-commerce in order to improve their internal controls experienced improvements to their efficiency, which implies that the benefit materialised in the form of a more efficient organisation, which has a direct bearing on control.

*Table 6. Regression table for improved relations with business partners*

| Dependant variable improved relations with business partners | | |
|---|---|---|
| | Beta | p value |
| Reduce costs. | .308 | .003 |
| Improve internal efficiency. | .385 | .000 |
| Improved control. | .234 | .031 |
| R Squared | .411 | |
| Adjusted R squared | .345 | |
| p value for the complete regression table | .000 | |

*Table 7. Regression table for new customers and markets*

| Dependant variable new customers and markets | | |
|---|---|---|
| | Beta | p value |
| Improve internal efficiency. | -.161 | .035 |
| Strengthen relations with business partners. | .445 | .000 |
| R Squared | | .511 |
| Adjusted R squared | | .455 |
| p value for the complete regression table | | .000 |

Three criteria were significantly associated with the benefit of having improved relations with business partners as a result of e-commerce adoption. This benefit was reported by SMEs who said they adopted e-commerce to reduce costs (.003 significance), improve internal efficiency (.000 significance), and improve control (.031 significance). The data suggests that those respondents who placed higher priority on improving internal efficiency and reducing cost (and to a lesser extent improving control) reported having stronger relations with business partners as a result of adopting e-commerce into their businesses. Two findings emerge that are interesting. Firstly, while strengthening relations with business partners is considered as part and parcel with sales, marketing, and customer services, none of these criteria had any statistically significant effect on better business relationships. Secondly, there was no association between developing relations with business partners as the reason to adopt e-commerce and the same benefit.

Two criteria were significantly associated with the e-commerce benefit of having access to new customers and markets. While new customers and markets are synonymous with improvements to marketing and improvements to competitiveness, no statistically significant association was found between these and the outcome of gaining new customers and markets. The negative Beta value found for the criterion "improve internal efficiency" suggests that those respondents who placed a greater emphasis on improving their internal efficiency did not necessarily report gaining new customers and markets. There are a number of possibilities to explain this. One possibility is that emphasis on improvements to internal efficiency might detract from reaching new customers and markets. An alternative may be that those that were looking to reach new customers and markets simply placed a lower level of im-

*Table 8. Regression table for improved competitiveness*

| Dependant variable improved competitiveness | | |
|---|---|---|
| | Beta | p value |
| New customers and markets. | .361 | .001 |
| Improve marketing. | .318 | .001 |
| R Squared | | .556 |
| Adjusted R squared | | .505 |
| p value for the complete regression table | | .000 |

*Table 9. Regression table for improved quality of information*

| Dependant variable improved quality of information | | |
|---|---|---|
| | Beta | p value |
| Demand/pressure from suppliers. | .439 | .000 |
| Reduced costs. | .335 | .000 |
| Strengthen relations with business partners. | .327 | .000 |
| Improve marketing. | .245 | .007 |
| R Squared | | .584 |
| Adjusted R squared | | .537 |
| p value for the complete regression table | | .000 |

portance on internal efficiency as a reason for adopting e-commerce. While this is not clear, the data show that there is no association between the new customers and markets criterion and related benefit. Finally, the data suggests that the benefit of new customers and markets was best achieved by those respondents who strove to strengthen their relations with their business partners (.000 significance).

Table 8 shows that there was a significant association (.001) between two criteria (access new customers and markets and improve marketing) and the benefit of improved competitiveness. Again, the data shows that there was no statistically significant association between the decision to improve competitiveness through e-commerce and the actual benefit of improved competitiveness. However, the results do suggest that improvement to competitiveness is a combination of several factors.

Four criteria had a statistically significant association with improved quality of information as a benefit of e-commerce. Conventional wisdom would have suggested that improvements to the quality of information were associated with improvements to internal efficiency and control; however, these associations were not in evidence in the Swedish data. Indeed, the data shows that those respondents that placed a high level of importance on the marketing-oriented aspects of e-commerce reported, among other benefits, a higher level of improvement to the quality of their information under an e-commerce approach to their day-to-day activities. While the relationships between the reduced costs and improved marketing and improved quality of information as a benefit remain unclear, a number of studies (Chaffey, 2004; Klein & Krcmar, 2006) have shown that improvements to information are associated with suppliers' demands and strengthening relations with business partners.

# Summary of Criteria and Benefits in Sweden

The results of the statistical analysis in Sweden indicate some associations between e-commerce adoption criteria and the benefits experienced following e-commerce adoption. For the most part, however, there were few "direct" associations. Table 10 provides a summary of all the associations between criteria and benefits in Sweden. Those criteria which are relevant to the associated benefit are shown in bold (those of direct relevance are underlined and those which are indirectly relevant are shown in italics).

Table 10 shows that those SMEs, which set out to reduce costs and improve their internal efficiency may experience lower administration costs, while those, which aim to reduce their stock levels and increase sales, also may achieve the same benefit. However, for the other criteria, there was no direct association between the reason for adopting e-commerce and the subsequent benefit. Instead, SMEs are likely to achieve a related benefit. For example,

*Table 10. Summary of criteria and benefits (Sweden)*

| Criteria (We adopted e-commerce because of/to…) | Benefit (We experienced these benefits after e-commerce adoption…) | Type of association |
|---|---|---|
| Reduce cost | Lower administration costs | + |
| Improve internal efficiency | | + |
| Strengthen relations with business partners | | + |
| Reduce cost | Reduced lead time | + |
| Strengthen relations with business partners | | + |
| Pressure from competition | Reduced stock | + |
| Shorten lead time/reduced stock levels | | + |
| Demand/pressure from suppliers | Increased sales | + |
| Shorten lead time/reduced stock levels | | + |
| Increase sales | | + |
| Strengthen relations with business partners | | + |
| Improve competitiveness | | - |
| Improve control | | + |
| Reduce costs | Increased internal efficiency | + |
| Increase sales | | + |
| Strengthen relations with business partners | | + |
| Access new customers/markets | | + |
| Improve control | | + |
| Reduce cost | Improved relations with business partners | + |
| Improve internal efficiency | | + |
| Improve control | | + |
| Improve internal efficiency | Access to new customers and markets | - |
| Strengthen relations with business partners | | + |
| Access new customers/markets | Improved competitiveness | + |
| Improve marketing | | + |
| Demand/pressure from suppliers | Improved quality of information | + |
| Reduce cost | | + |
| Strengthen relations with business partners | | + |
| Improve marketing | | + |

those SMEs, which wanted to improve their marketing by implementing e-commerce, may have achieved better quality of information in the organisation as a result, which can contribute towards improved marketing. There were also some negative associations. Those respondents who placed a greater emphasis on improving their internal efficiency did not necessarily report gaining new customers and markets and those that had placed a high priority on improving competitiveness, in fact reported a lower benefit of increased sales than those that assigned a lower importance to this criterion.

The key finding here is that the reasons why SMEs adopt e-commerce do not necessarily materialise into corresponding benefits. We will discuss the implications of this later. In the next section, we will examine the association between e-commerce criteria and disadvantages.

## E-Commerce Criteria and Disadvantages in Sweden

Three of the seven disadvantages tested for provided statistically significant associations with one or more criteria for the adoption of e-commerce. These are show in Tables 11 to 13.

Table 11 shows that only one criterion (demand/pressure from customers) was significantly associated with the disadvantage of higher costs. The data suggests that those respondents who felt that they had been "forced" into the adoption of e-commerce by their customer base, also reported that the outcome of that adoption was having to deal with the increased costs associated with e-commerce. This result matches earlier findings with EDI adoption in SMEs (see MacGregor et al., 1998).

*Table 11. Regression table for higher costs*

| Dependant variable higher costs | | |
|---|---|---|
| | Beta | p value |
| Demand/pressure from customers. | .222 | .037 |
| R Squared | | .183 |
| Adjusted R squared | | .090 |
| p value for the complete regression table | | .026 |

*Table 12. Regression table for security risks*

| Dependant variable security risks | | |
|---|---|---|
| | Beta | p value |
| External support. | .294 | .002 |
| R Squared | | .207 |
| Adjusted R squared | | .117 |
| p value for the complete regression table | | .008 |

*Table 13. Regression table for dependence on e-commerce*

| Dependant variable dependence on e-commerce | | |
|---|---|---|
| | Beta | p value |
| External support. | .195 | .033 |
| R Squared | | .215 |
| Adjusted R squared | | .126 |
| p value for the complete regression table | | .005 |

Only one criterion (access to external support) was associated with experiencing security risks. The data shows that there is a very high level of association (.002) between these two factors, suggesting that those who placed a greater importance on the availability of external assistance also had higher misgivings concerning the security of the resulting systems they were using. If we equate the need for external assistance with lack of IT skills, this result is not unexpected.

Table 13 provides the data for the disadvantage "dependence on e-commerce." Once again, the same criterion was associated with a dependence on e-commerce. Those who placed a greater importance on the availability of external assistance had higher misgivings concerning their dependence on e-commerce as a day-to-day necessity for their business.

# Summary of Criteria and Disadvantages in Sweden

The results of the statistical analysis in Sweden indicate some associations between e-commerce adoption criteria and the disadvantages experienced following e-commerce adoption. However, there were no direct associations. Table 14 provides a summary of all the associations between criteria and disadvantages in Sweden.

We will now examine the situation in Australia.

*Table 14. Summary of criteria and disadvantages (Sweden)*

| Criteria (We adopted e-commerce because of/to…) | Disadvantages (We experienced these problems after e-commerce adoption…) | Type of Association |
|---|---|---|
| Demand/pressure form customers. | Higher costs | + |
| Availability of external support. | Security concerns | + |
| | Dependence on e-commerce | + |

# E-Commerce Criteria and Benefits in Australia

We found a smaller number of statistically significant associations in the Australian sample between e-commerce criteria and benefits. Five of the ten benefits tested showed a significant association with one or more e-commerce adoption drivers. These are shown in Tables 15 to 19, which also indicate the relevant p value, and will be discussed. It should be noted at the outset that there were no significant associations between criteria and any of the disadvantages for the Australian data.

*Table 15. Regression table for lower administration costs*

| Dependant variable lower administration costs | | |
|---|---|---|
| | Beta | p value |
| Reduced costs. | .750 | .004 |
| Improved internal efficiency. | .778 | .018 |
| R Squared | | .860 |
| Adjusted R squared | | .664 |
| p value for the complete regression table | | .012 |

*Table 16. Regression table for lower production costs*

| Dependant variable lower production costs | | |
|---|---|---|
| | Beta | p value |
| Reduced costs. | .524 | .033 |
| Shorten lead time and reduce stock. | .628 | .013 |
| Increased sales. | -1.130 | .020 |
| R Squared | | .839 |
| Adjusted R squared | | .615 |
| p value for the complete regression table | | .012 |

*Table 17. Regression table for reduced stock*

| Dependant variable reduced stock | | |
|---|---|---|
| | Beta | p value |
| Demand/pressure from customers. | -.555 | .047 |
| Demand/pressure from suppliers. | .729 | .006 |
| Improve control. | -.731 | .035 |
| R Squared | | .869 |
| Adjusted R squared | | .685 |
| p value for the complete regression table | | .009 |

Table 15 shows that two criteria (reduced costs and improvements to internal efficiency) are associated with the benefit of lowering administration costs. The data shows that there is a strong association (significance levels of .004) between the desire to reduce costs and lower administration costs as the resulting benefit. The data shows that there is a less significant level association (.018) with expected improvements to internal efficiency. A comparison with the Swedish results (see Table 1) shows that both reduced costs and improvements to internal efficiency are associated the benefit of lower administration costs. However, in the Swedish study, a third criterion (stronger relations with business partners) was also associated with this benefit. This is not apparent in the Australian study.

An examination of Table 16 shows that two criteria appear to be associated with the benefit "lower production costs." As would be expected, these criteria (reduced costs and shorter lead time/reduced stock) are connected with the lowering of costs of production. It is interesting to note that while the Australian respondents provided a link between criteria for adoption and this benefit, no such link was found in the Swedish study.

While the criterion demand/pressure from suppliers provided a positive Beta value (.729), the criterion demand/pressure from customers provided a negative Beta (-.555). This suggests that those respondents who placed a higher level of importance on suppliers achieved a correspondingly higher level of benefit in the form of reduced stock. However, those that placed a higher level of importance on customers achieved a lower level of benefit in the form of reducing their stock levels than those who placed a lower level of importance on this particular criterion. The table also shows that the association between improvements to control and reduced stock produced a negative Beta value. Again, we can conclude that those respondents who aimed to improve their control likewise reported a lower level of stock reduction. A comparison with the Swedish findings (Table 3) shows that pressure from competition and shortened lead time/reduced stock were associated with the benefit "reduced stock."

An examination of Table 18 shows that one criterion was statistically associated with improved relations with business partners. It is interesting to compare this result to the Swedish results (see Table 6). In both cases, there was a highly statistically significant association between the criterion "improved internal efficiency" and the benefit "improved relations with business partners" (both results showed a p value of .000). In both cases, there was no relationship between the criterion "improved relations with business partners" and the matching benefit. However, the Swedish results showed that two other criteria (reduced costs and improved control) were associated with this benefit, while no such association was found in the Australian study.

*Table 18. Regression table for improved relations with business partners*

| Dependant variable improved relations with business partners | | |
|---|---|---|
| | Beta | p value |
| Improved internal efficiency. | 1.121 | .000 |
| R Squared | | .913 |
| Adjusted R squared | | .792 |
| p value for the complete regression table | | .001 |

*Table 19. Regression table for new customers and markets*

| Dependant variable new customers and markets | | |
|---|---|---|
| | Beta | p value |
| Strengthen relations with business partners. | .849 | .001 |
| R Squared | | .853 |
| Adjusted R squared | | .646 |
| p value for the complete regression table | | .015 |

Only one criterion was statistically associated with access to new customers and markets. Again, it is interesting to compare this result to the Swedish results (see Table 7). In both cases, there was a highly statistically significant association between the criterion "strengthen relations with business partners" and the benefit of gaining access to new customers and markets (the Australian results showed a p value of .001, while the Swedish results showed a p value of .000). In both cases, there was no relationship between the criterion "new customers and markets" and the matching benefit.

## Summary of Criteria and Benefits in Australia

The results of the statistical analysis in Sweden indicate some associations between e-commerce adoption criteria and the benefits experienced following e-commerce adoption. For the most part, however, there were few direct associations. Table 10 provides a summary of all the associations between criteria and benefits in Sweden. Those criteria which are relevant to the associated benefit are shown in bold (those of direct relevance are underlined and those which are indirectly relevant are shown in italics).

Table 20 shows, once again, that there were few direct associations between e-commerce criteria and benefits. The ones that did emerge were related to costs, as those SMEs, which were likely to adopt e-commerce in order to reduce costs are also likely to experience lower administration and lower production costs as e-commerce benefits. Table 20 also indicates that those SMEs, which experienced reduced stock levels following e-commerce adoption, decided to implement e-commerce because of pressure from suppliers, amongst other things. Those SMEs, which improved their relationships with business partners were aiming to improve their internal efficienct through e-commerce, while those that gained access to new markets were using the technology in order to strengthen their business relationships.

We also sub-divided the data into different categories depending on several business characteristics and examined the associations between criteria and benefits, and criteria and disadvantages in each category. These results will be discussed next.

*Table 20. Summary of criteria and benefits (Australia)*

| Criteria (We adopted e-commerce because of/to…) | Benefit (We experienced these benefits after e-commerce adoption…) | Type of association |
|---|---|---|
| Reduce cost | Lower administration costs | + |
| Improve internal efficiency | | + |
| Reduce cost | Lower production costs | + |
| Shorten lead time/reduced stock levels | | + |
| Increase sales | | - |
| Demand/pressure from customers | Reduced stock | - |
| Demand/pressure from suppliers | | + |
| Improve marketing | | + |
| Improve control | | - |
| Improve internal efficiency | Improved relations with business partners | + |
| Strengthen relations with business partners | Access to new customers and markets | + |

# E-Commerce Criteria and Benefits/Disadvantages Associations and Strategic Alliance Membership

Owing to the large number of statistically significant results, the data will be presented in summarised form, showing only those criteria-benefits and criteria-disadvantages in each category, which are associated and the type of association (positive or negative—shown in brackets). Tables 21 and 22 show the associations by alliance membership. The data shown is for Sweden only due to the low number of adopters in Australia and insufficient data in the U.S. study.

Table 21 shows substantial differences in the relationships between criteria and benefits depending on whether the respondent was a member of a strategic alliance or not. While both members and non-members showed a significant association between improvements to internal efficiency as a criterion and the benefit of lower administration costs, the non-members also showed an association with other criteria (reduce costs, shorten lead time and reduce stock, and strengthen relations with business partners). One of the criteria (shorten lead time and reduce stock) produced a negative relationship, suggesting that those that place a higher level of importance on this criterion perceived a lower level of benefit than those that placed less importance on the same criterion. The results raise a number of questions. If, as might be first concluded, alliance members had less to attain through e-commerce adoption and use (having achieved some benefits through their membership), why had they not achieved improvements to internal efficiency? Secondly, and equally importantly, why did non-members who actually placed a lesser level of importance on shorter lead time and reduced stock lower their administration costs when no such association was found for members.

*Table 21. Membership of a strategic alliance-criteria/benefits*

| Benefit of e-commerce | Criteria for non-members | Criteria for members |
|---|---|---|
| Lower administration costs. | To reduce costs (+). | To improve internal efficiency (+). |
| | To shorten lead time and reduce stock (-). | |
| | To improve internal efficiency (+). | |
| | To strengthen relations with business partners (+). | |
| Lower production costs. | Demand/pressure from suppliers (-). | |
| | To reduce costs (+). | |
| Reduced lead time. | To reduce costs (+). | Demand/Pressure from Suppliers (-). |
| | To improve internal efficiency (+). | To strengthen relations with business partners (+). |
| | To strengthen relations with business partners (+). | |
| Reduced stock. | To shorten lead time and reduce stock (+). | Pressure from competition (+). |
| | | To shorten lead time and reduce stock (+). |
| | | To improve control (+). |
| Increased sales. | To shorten lead time and reduce stock (+). | To increase sales (+). |
| | To strengthen relations with business partners (+). | To improve competitiveness (-). |
| | To improve control (+). | |
| Increased internal efficiency. | To increase sales (+). | To reduce costs (+). |
| | To improve internal efficiency (+). | To improve marketing (+). |
| Improved relations with business partners. | To reduce costs (+). | To shorten lead time and reduce stock (+). |
| | To improve internal efficiency (+). | To improve internal efficiency (+). |
| | | To improve marketing (+). |
| Access to new customers/markets. | To improve internal efficiency (-). | To strengthen relations with business partners (+). |
| | To strengthen relations with business partners (+). | |
| Improved competitiveness. | To improve customer service (-). | To reach new customers/markets (+). |
| | To increase sales (+). | |
| | To improve marketing (+). | |
| Improved quality of information. | Demand/pressure from suppliers (+). | Demand/pressure from suppliers (+). |
| | To reduce costs (+). | To strengthen relations with business partners (+). |
| | To strengthen relations with business partners (+). | To improve marketing (+). |

*Table 22. Membership of a strategic alliance: Criteria/disadvantages*

| Disadvantage of e-commerce | Criteria for non-members | Criteria for members |
|---|---|---|
| Deterioration of relations with business partners. | Pressure from competition (+). | None |
| Higher costs. | Demand/pressure from customers (+). | |
| Doubling of work. | Demand/pressure from customers (+). | |
| Dependence on e-commerce. | Availability of external support (+). | |

An examination of the benefit of reduced lead time, again, raises some questions. While it may be expected that non-members may need to place emphasis on reducing costs and improving internal efficiency (that may not be required by member respondents), why do both members and non-members need to strengthen relations with business partners in order to reduce lead time. One of the obvious benefits of alliance membership is the implied relationships with business partners. Yet, the findings suggest that reduced lead time requires both members and non-members to place importance on strengthening relations with business partners.

The benefit of reduced stock is interesting. Where both groups indicated that the higher the level of importance placed on reducing stock and lead time, the higher the perceived benefit in terms of reduced stock, alliance members also showed that they needed to place a high level of importance on pressure from competition in order to achieve this. A number of studies (Achrol & Kotler. 1999; Christopher, 1999; O'Donnell, Gilmore, Cummins, & Carson, 2002) suggest that external pressure is dissipated through the structure and membership of an alliance. This appears not to be the case for the benefit of reduced stock.

If we examine the benefit of increased internal efficiency, it is interesting to note that non-member respondents were the only group that showed an association with the corresponding criterion. For non-members, increased internal efficiency was associated with a higher level of importance placed on increasing sales, while for member respondents it was associated with higher levels of importance, having been placed on reducing costs and improving marketing.

Neither members nor non-members associated the benefit-improved relations with business partners with the criterion to strengthen relations with business partners. However, both associated the benefit with importance being placed on improving internal efficiency. It is interesting to note that while member respondents associated improved relations with business partners with shortening lead time and reducing stock, non-members associated it with importance being placed on reduction of costs.

Table 21 also shows that both member and non-member respondents associated access to new customers/markets with the criterion strengthen relations with business partners. This again raises the question as to why member respondents felt that they needed to place the same level of importance on this criterion for the adoption of e-commerce as non-members and why this strengthened relationship had not been achieved through alliance membership.

The benefit-improved competitiveness was associated with three criteria by non-member respondents. These were improved customer service, increased sales, and improved marketing. However, it interesting to note that the criterion improved customer service provided a negative Beta value. This suggests that those that placed a higher level of importance on this criterion perceived a lower level of benefit in terms of improved competitiveness than those that placed a lower level of importance on it. One possible explanation is that the actual increase in competitiveness was far less than the anticipated increase.

The final benefit improved quality of information and provides an interesting finding. Both the member and non-member respondents showed that the higher the level of importance placed on demand/pressure from suppliers, the higher the perceived improvement to the quality of information. While not actually examined, this result would suggest that most respondents, be they members of an alliance or not, had introduced an "upstream" purchasing function within their e-commerce operation. As such, demand and pressure from suppliers would necessitate improvement to the quality of information. This does, however, raise the question as to why criteria such as improvements to internal efficiency and improvements to control were not associated with the benefit improvement to the quality of information.

A number of studies (Achrol et al., 1999; Christopher, 1999; O'Donnell et al., 2002) suggest that external pressure is dissipated through the structure and membership of an alliance. An examination of Table 22 would support this notion, particularly external forces that are in the form of pressure from customers or competition, with which alliance members show no association.

# E-Commerce Criteria and Benefits/Disadvantages Associations and Business Size

Tables 23 and 24 show the associations by business size. The data shown is for Sweden only due to the low number of adopters in Australia and insufficient data in the U.S. study. Due to space restrictions, the criteria have been abbreviated.

Table 23 provides a very interesting finding. While clearly benefits to e-commerce adoption and use were gained by all facets of the SME sector in Sweden (see Chapter VI), Table 23 shows that for the most part it is the very small businesses (1-9 employees) that show associations between benefits and decisions made in the adoption process (criteria). Only three benefits (reduced stock, new customers and markets, and improved quality of information) showed associations with the criteria used in the adoption process.

Two benefits, however, should be examined in detail. The benefit-improved relations with business partners (1-9 employees) shows a negative association with the criterion improved control. In other words, those that placed less importance on this criterion reported higher levels of benefit in terms of improved relations with business partners than those that placed a high level of importance on the criterion. Again, this may be explained by the suggestion that the actual level of benefit may not have reached that anticipated by the respondents. Not so easily explained is the negative association between the benefit new customers and markets and the criteria increased sales and increased customer service (> 49 employees).

Three disadvantages (deterioration of relations with business partners, higher costs, and dependence on e-commerce) were associated with one or more criteria, according to Table

*Table 23. Business size: Criteria/benefits*

| Benefit of e-commerce | 1 to 9 employees | 10 to 19 employees | 20 to 49 employees | More than 49 employees |
|---|---|---|---|---|
| Lower administration costs. | Reduced costs (+). | | | |
| | Internal efficiency (+). | | | |
| | Improve control (+). | | | |
| Lower production costs. | Shorter lead time (+). | | | |
| | Internal efficiency (+). | | | |
| Reduced lead time. | Reduced costs (+). | | | |
| | Competitiveness (-). | | | |
| Reduced stock. | Customer service (+). | | Shorter lead time (+). | |
| | Shorter lead time (+). | | | |
| | Increase sales (-). | Shorter lead time (+). | Improve marketing (+). | |
| | Internal efficiency (+). | | | |
| | Improve control (+). | | | |
| Increased sales. | Shorter lead time (+). | | | |
| | Increase sales (+). | | | |
| Increased internal efficiency. | Internal efficiency (+). | | | |
| | Relations with business partners (+). | | | |
| | Improve marketing (+). | | | |
| Improved relations with business partners. | Reduced costs (+). | | | |
| | Customer service (+). | | | |
| | Improve control (-). | | | |

*continued on following page*

*Table 23. Continued*

| Access to new customers/markets. | Relations with business partners (+). | | | Customer service (-). |
|---|---|---|---|---|
| | Improve control (+). | | | Increased sales (-). |
| Improved competitiveness. | Increased sales (+). | | | |
| | Internal efficiency (+). | | | |
| Improved quality of information. | Demand/pressure from suppliers (+). | Demand/pressure from suppliers (+). | | |
| | Reduced costs (+). | Reduced costs (+). | | |
| | Relations with business partners (+). | Increased sales (+). | | |
| | Improved marketing (+). | External support (+). | | |
| | | Improved marketing (-). | | |

24. Two of the disadvantages (higher costs and dependence on e-commerce) were found in the smaller businesses (1-9 employees or 10-19 employees), while the disadvantage of deteriorating relations with business partners was found in the larger SMEs (> 49 employees). Six criteria were positively associated with the disadvantage deterioration of relations with business partners and four criteria were negatively associated with this disadvantage. One of these associations is worth noting. The data shows that those respondents that placed a high level of importance on improving relations with business partners noted a deterioration in that relationship. It is interesting to note that there are no associations with deterioration of business partners for smaller SMEs. One possibility is that larger businesses may be expected to have a large number of business partners. Changes to business partner relationships through e-commerce would be noticeable by the business and would perhaps be negative.

# E-Commerce Criteria and Benefits/Disadvantages Associations and Business Sector

Tables 25 and 26 show the associations by business sector. The data shown is for Sweden only due to the low number of adopters in Australia and insufficient data in the U.S. study. Due to space restrictions, the criteria have been abbreviated.

*Table 24. Business size: Criteria/disadvantages*

| Disadvantages of e-commerce | 1 to 9 employees | 10 to 19 employees | More than 49 employees |
|---|---|---|---|
| Deterioration of relations with business partners. | | | Pressure from competition (+). |
| | | | Pressure from suppliers (+). |
| | | | Reduced costs (-). |
| | | | Shorter lead time (+). |
| | | | Increased sales (+). |
| | | | Improve internal efficiency (-). |
| | | | Relations with business partners (+). |
| | | | New customers/markets (+). |
| | | | Improve competitiveness (-). |
| | | | External support (-). |
| Higher costs. | Customer service (-). | | |
| Dependence on e-commerce. | Customer service (-). | Shorter lead time (+). | |
| | External support (+). | External support (+). | |
| | | Marketing (-). | |
| | | Improve control (-). | |

There are a number of differences that can be seen across the three business sectors in Table 25. Three of these, however, are worthy of mention. The benefit reduced lead time was associated with four criteria (strengthen relations with business partners, new customers/markets, improved competitiveness, and improved marketing). Two of these, however, showed a negative association with the benefit. A similar finding can be seen for the benefits increased sales (industrial sector) and access to new customers and markets (retail and service sectors). The results clearly show that while both criteria and benefits may be applicable to many sectors of the SME community, their interaction appears to be unique to specific sectors.

Table 26 shows that two disadvantages were associated with the perceived importance of criteria, but only for the industrial sector. Again, this should not be read as saying that there were no disadvantages for the other sectors, but that these disadvantages were not statistically significantly associated with any of the e-commerce criteria.

*Table 25. Business sector: Criteria/benefits*

| Benefit of e-commerce | Industrial | Service | Retail |
|---|---|---|---|
| Lower administration costs. | Improve control (+). | | |
| Lower production costs. | Shorter lead time (+). | Shorter lead time(+). | |
| Reduced lead time. | Relations with business partners (+). | | |
| | New customers/markets (+). | | |
| | Competitiveness (-). | | |
| | Improved marketing (-). | | |
| Reduced stock. | Shorter lead time(+). | Shorter lead time (+). | Shorter lead time (+). |
| | | Increased Sales (-). | |
| Increased sales. | Competitiveness (-). | | Internal efficiency (+). |
| | External support (+). | | |
| Increased internal efficiency. | Reduced costs (+). | | |
| Access to new customers/markets. | Relations with business partners (+). | Customer Service (-). | Pressure from competition (+). |
| | | Improve control (+). | Shorter lead time (-). |
| | | | Marketing (+). |
| Improved competitiveness. | New customers/markets (+). | Increased sales (+). | New customers/markets (+). |
| | | External support (-). | |
| Improved quality of information. | Demand/pressure from suppliers (+). | Demand/pressure from suppliers (+). | Pressure from competition (+). |
| | Relations with business partners (+). | Reduced costs (+). | Reduced costs (+). |

# E-Commerce Criteria and Benefits/Disadvantages Associations and Market Focus

Table 27 shows the associations by market focus. The data shown is for Sweden only due to the low number of adopters in Australia and insufficient data in the study. Due to space restrictions, the criteria have been abbreviated. There were no significant associations with disadvantages.

An examination of Table 27 shows that the association between e-commerce benefits and criteria is vastly different depending on whether the business is trading locally or nationally.

*Table 26. Business sector: Criteria/disadvantages*

| Disadvantages of e-commerce | Industrial |
| --- | --- |
| Deterioration of relations with business partners. | Pressure from competition (+). |
|  | Demand/pressure from suppliers (+). |
| Higher costs. | Improved customer service (-). |
|  | Improved competitiveness (+). |
|  | Improved marketing (+). |

As might be expected, businesses that are trading locally have different requirements and different outcomes than those looking to a wider marketplace. Three associations, however, are worth noting. The benefit increased sales shows that local respondents that placed a higher level of importance on increased competitiveness also noted a lower level of benefit than those that placed less emphasis on the criterion. Again, one possibility is that the actual level of the benefit was lower than the anticipated level. However, this raises the question as to why this was only perceived in the local market.

The benefit increased internal efficiency (national) shows a negative association with improved customer services. There are two possible reasons for this—that the effort of improving customer services distracted the respondents from improving the internal efficiency of the business or that the perceived benefit was lower than expectations. Again, both possibilities raise questions as to why this only appeared to occur to national level respondents and not local level respondents. The benefit-improved quality of information (local) was negatively associated with the criterion improved internal efficiency. Again, this is interesting because it appears to have only occurred at the local market level

# E-Commerce Criteria and Benefits/Disadvantages Associations and Type of E-Commerce

Table 28 shows the associations by type of e-commerce. The data shown is for Sweden only due to the low number of adopters in Australia and insufficient data in the U.S. study. Due to space restrictions, the criteria have been abbreviated. There were no significant associations with disadvantages.

Table 28 compares B2B and B2C respondents. As might be expected, B2B respondents associated many of the benefits with criteria involving their dealings with other businesses (pressure from suppliers, pressure from competition, etc). B2C businesses, by comparison were more concerned with internal efficiency, increased sales, etc. Three associations are worth noting: increased internal efficiency (B2B) is negatively associated with the criterion improvement to competitiveness; improved quality of information (B2B) is negatively associated with increased internal efficiency; and improvement to competitiveness (B2B) is negatively associated with new customers/market. In all cases, as for previous tables, the most reasonable explanation is that actual benefits fell well short of anticipated benefit levels.

*Table 27. Market focus: Criteria/benefits*

| Benefit of e-commerce | Local | National |
|---|---|---|
| Lower administration costs. | Reduce costs (+). | Reduce costs (+). |
| | Internal efficiency (+). | Relations with business partners (+). |
| Lower production costs. | Shorter lead time (+). | Reduced costs (+). |
| Reduced lead time. | Reduced costs (+). | Relations with business partners (+). |
| Reduced stock. | Shorter lead time (+). | Pressure from competition (+). |
| | Increase sales (-). | Shorter lead time (+). |
| Increased sales. | Improved competitiveness (-). | Shorter lead time (+). |
| | | External support (+). |
| Increased internal efficiency. | | Reduced costs. |
| | | Improve customer service (-). |
| Improved relations with business partners. | Internal efficiency (+). | Reduced costs (+). |
| | | Internal efficiency (+). |
| Access to new customers/ markets. | Relations with business partners (+). | Relations with business partners (+). |
| | Improve control (+). | |
| Improvements to competitiveness. | | New customers/markets (+). |
| Improved quality of information. | Demand/pressure from suppliers (+). | Demand/pressure from suppliers (+). |
| | Reduced costs (+). | Reduced costs (+). |
| | Internal efficiency (-). | Relations with business partners (+). |
| | Improved marketing (+). | Improved marketing (+). |

# Comparison of the Two Locations and Implications

Table 29 summarises the findings across the two locations for the purposes of comparison. Clearly, the most obvious difference is the number of criteria associated with the benefits of e-commerce adoption. While the Swedish study found nine criteria associated with benefits, the Australian found only five.

Those SMEs, which experienced lower administration costs (in Sweden and Australia) and lower production costs (in Australia), also set out to reduce their costs through e-commerce adoption. An additional association exists between the first benefit and improvements to internal efficiency as a driver. This would suggest that SMEs generally to experience cost reductions and efficiencies as a result of e-commerce use.

Similarly, those SMEs in Sweden, which reduced their stock levels as a result of e-commerce, listed this as a reason why they chose to implement e-commerce in the first place. In Australia, this was manifested differently through the "demand/pressure from suppliers" criterion.

Swedish SMEs, which increased their sales through e-commerce, wanted to use the technology to do so, but also to improve their supply chain and strengthen relations with business

*Table 28. E-commerce types: Criteria/benefits*

| Benefit of e-commerce | B2C | B2B |
|---|---|---|
| Lower administration costs. | Internal efficiency (+). | |
| Lower production costs. | | Pressure from competition (+). |
| | | External support (+). |
| Reduced stock. | | Pressure from competition (+). |
| | | Demand/Pressure from suppliers (-). |
| | | Shorter lead time (+). |
| Increased sales. | Internal efficiency (+). | |
| | Shorter lead time (+). | |
| Increased internal efficiency. | | Pressure from competition (+). |
| | | Increased sales (+). |
| | | Improved competitiveness (-). |
| Access to new customers/markets. | | Relations with business partners (+). |
| Improvements to competitiveness. | Increased sales (+). | New customers/markets (-). |
| Improved quality of information. | | Demand/pressure from suppliers (+). |
| | | Internal efficiency (-). |

partners. However, they did not rate improving competitiveness as a major driver. Those SMEs, which experienced more efficient operations, were likely to adopt e-commerce in order to reduce costs and improve their internal controls.

SMEs in Sweden and in Australia, which had better business relationships as a result of e-commerce both set out to improve internal efficiency, instead. Similarly, the both groups of SMEs, which gained access to new customers and markets may have originally wanted to improve relations with their partners.

Finally, in the Swedish study, SMEs that said they had improved their competitiveness through e-commerce, initially adopted the technology to access new customers and markets and improve their marketing. Meanwhile, those that had better information did not implement e-commerce for this reason at all.

From the previous, we can conclude that there was some commonality between the reasons why SMEs adopted e-commerce and the subsequent benefits. Although reduced costs, increased sales, and reduced stock levels are likely to materialise from being the initial motivators for e-commerce adoption, in other instances the association is less clear.

The implications of this are significant because the results indicate that it is not always possible to achieve what SMEs set out to do through e-commerce adoption. It is important to ensure that SMEs have an unambiguous picture of what they can expect from e-commerce adoption in order to avoid problems later when some of the potential benefits do not materialise. This chapter contains some of the most useful findings of the studies in Australia and Sweden, because it allows government organisations to realistically manage the expectations of SMEs when promoting e-commerce adoption, and also to highlight that the expected benefits of e-commerce do not necessarily materialise and instead some unexpected benefits may occur as a result.

To provide a more detailed picture, we subdivided the Swedish data by alliance membership (members and non-members), business size, business sector, market focus, and type of e-commerce (B2C or B2B). Once again, the results were as diverse as the different types of SMEs. Clearly, in developing any type of program to convince SMEs to adopt e-commerce it is not only important to clearly show the types of benefits they can expect to achieve and the disadvantages that are likely to occur, but it is also critical to avoid a blanket approach, as these benefits and disadvantages are not uniform across the SME sector. Any attempt to promote certain benefits over others may result in those benefits failing to appear, this creating a negative perception of e-commerce technology. Considering the resources SMEs require to implement e-commerce, this must be managed carefully and adequate support needs to be provided to SMEs.

# E-Commerce Criteria and Resulting Benefits/Disadvantages: Key Findings

## Sweden

- There were nine associations between the reasons why SMEs adopted e-commerce and the resulting benefits in Sweden.
- SMEs, which experienced lower administration costs, reduced stock levels, and increased sales had likely adopted e-commerce for these very reasons.
- For all of the other drivers and resulting benefits, the association was not so clear cut.
- Those SMEs, which adopted e-commerce due to the availability of external support may become dependent on the technology, and those, which were forced into adoption by their customers, are likely to experience higher costs as a result.

## Australia

- There were five associations between the reasons why SMEs adopted e-commerce and the resulting benefits in Australia.
- SMEs, which experienced lower administration and production costs had likely adopted e-commerce for this very reason.
- Those SMEs, which had lower stock levels following e-commerce adoption, may have adopted the technology due to pressure from their suppliers.

*Table 29. Comparison of associations between adoption drivers and e-commerce benefits in Sweden and Australia*

| Benefit (We experienced these benefits after e-commerce adoption...) | Criteria (Sweden) (We adopted e-commerce because of/to...) | Criteria (Australia) (We adopted e-commerce because of/to...) |
|---|---|---|
| Lower administration costs. | Reduce cost (+).<br>Improve internal efficiency (+).<br>Strengthen relations with business partners (+). | Reduce cost (+).<br>Improve internal efficiency (+). |
| Lower production costs. | | Reduce cost (+).<br>Shorten lead time/reduced stock levels (+).<br>Increase sales (-). |
| Reduced lead time. | Reduce cost (+).<br>Strengthen relations with business partners (+). | |
| Reduced stock. | Pressure from competition (+).<br>Shorten lead time/reduced stock levels (+). | Demand/pressure from customers (-).<br>Demand/pressure from suppliers (+).<br>Improve marketing (+).<br>Improve control (-). |
| Increased sales. | Demand/pressure from suppliers (+).<br>Shorten lead time/reduced stock levels (+).<br>Increase sales (+).<br>Strengthen relations with business partners (+).<br>Improve competitiveness (-).<br>Improve control (+). | |
| Increased internal efficiency. | Reduce costs (+).<br>Increase sales (+).<br>Strengthen relations with business partners (+).<br>Access new customers/markets (+).<br>Improve control (+). | |
| Improved relations with business partners. | Reduce cost (+).<br>Improve internal efficiency (+).<br>Improve control (+). | Improve internal efficiency (+). |
| Access to new customers and markets. | Improve internal efficiency (-).<br>Strengthen relations with business partners (+). | Strengthen relations with business partners (+). |

*continued on following page*

*Table 29. Continued*

| Benefit (We experienced these benefits after e-commerce adoption…) | Criteria (Sweden) (We adopted e-commerce because of/to…) | Criteria (Australia) (We adopted e-commerce because of/to…) |
|---|---|---|
| Improved competitiveness. | Access new customers/markets (+). Improve marketing (+). | |
| Improved quality of information. | Demand/pressure from suppliers (+). Reduce cost (+). Strengthen relations with business partners (+). Improve marketing (+). | |

- For the other drivers and resulting benefits, the association was not so clear cut.
- There were no associations between the reasons why SMEs adopted e-commerce and the resulting disadvantages in Australia.

# References

Achrol, R. S., & Kotler, P. (1999). Marketing in the network economy. *Journal of Marketing, 63*, 146-163.

Chaffey, D. (2004). *E-business and e-commerce management: strategy, implementation, and practice*. NJ: Prentice Hall.

Christopher, M. L. (1999). Creating the agile supply chain. In D. L. Anderson (Ed.), *Achieving supply chain excellence through technology* (pp. 28-32). San Francisco: Montgomery Research Inc.

Klein, A., & Krcmar, H. (2006). DCXNET e-transformation at Daimler/Chrysler. *Journal of Information Technology, 21*(1), 52-65.

MacGregor, R. C., Bunker, D. J., & Waugh, P. (1998). Electronic commerce and small/medium enterprises (SME's) in Australia: An electronic data interchange (EDI) pilot study. *Proceedings of the 11th International Bled Electronic Commerce Conference*, Slovenia.

O'Donnell, A., Gilmore, A., Cummins, D., & Carson, D. (2001). The network construct in entrepreneurship research: A review and critique. *Management Decision, 39*(9), 749-760.

Tetteh, E., & Burn, J. (2001). Global strategies for SME-business: Applying the SMALL framework. *Logistics Information Management, 14*(1-2), 171-180.

Turban, E., Lee, J., King, D., & Chung, H. (2000). *Electronic commerce: A managerial perspective*. NJ: Prentice Hall.

## Chapter XII

# Current Barriers and Future Drivers:
## Why SMEs Don't Use E-Commerce Today and What Potential Benefits May Lead Them to Use E-Commerce in the Future

In line with the ever-increasing globalisation of business and business dealings, governments, particularly those in developed countries, are beginning to look at mechanisms to build international competitive advantage. Taylor and Murphy (2004) conclude, however, that much of the governmental effort is preoccupied with information and communications technology, believing that simple adoption of these technologies will assure competitive advantage over rival economies. This has been the case in SMEs.

Maskell, Eskilinen, Hannibalsson, Malmberg, and Vatne (1998) suggest that aside from the obvious political mileage gained through having SMEs "wired to the global market place," most governments believe that knowledge and learning are still able to be manipulated locally to achieve global advantage. Unfortunately, however, this is often translated into the simplistic "all ICT good, no ICT bad" (Taylor et al., 2004, p. 281), particularly where SMEs are concerned.

Despite the advocacy by governments that it is becoming a critical necessity for SMEs to become involved in e-business, studies in Europe, the U.S. and Australia (Buckley & Montes, 2002; Dixon et al., 2002; Martin & Matlay, 2001) have found that they are less engaged with ICTs than their larger counterparts and, indeed, invest less in these technologies per employee than larger firms. Recent studies (OECD, 2002; Taylor et al., 2004) have found that while over 20% of SMEs purchase through the Web and more than 30% sell through the Web, the value of these purchases and sales only account for 2% of the total purchases and sales.

As already noted, many policies either fail to note the non-homogeneous nature of the SME sector, or they are based on the simplistic view that technology will weld organisations and markets together, despite the apparent differences in those organisations and markets (Dixon et al., 2002). The results, then, are policies promoting the benefits of ICTs without due recourse to the barriers that have prevented non-adopters from adopting and using these technologies.

Previous research (Riquelme, 2002; Vrazalic et al., 2003; Quayle, 2002; Elliot & Boshoff, 2005; Beck et al., 2005; Webster et al., 2005; Simpson & Docherty, 2004; Xanthidis & Nicholas, 2004) has examined the barriers to e-commerce adoption. However, no study has examined the drivers that may induce future adoption of these same technologies by those same SMEs. It is argued that for government agencies to be able to develop policies and initiatives to assist SMEs with adopting e-commerce in the future, it is essential that current concerns and potential future inducements are factored into those policies and initiatives.

In the previous chapter, we examined the e-commerce adopters and showed a number of associations between the reasons that SMEs adopt e-commerce and the benefits and disadvantages that they subsequently experience. In this chapter, we will examine the non-adopter respondents. Our aim is to determine whether any of the adoption barriers are associated with the reasons that may lead SMEs to use e-commerce—in other words, the potential drivers that would motivate an SME to adopt e-commerce technology.

In each of the three studies, respondents that had not adopted e-commerce were asked to rate the importance of a set of ten barriers (as described in Chapter V). The respondents were also asked to rate the importance of a set of fourteen criteria that may induce them to introduce e-commerce adoption in the future (the same criteria as those listed for e-commerce adopters in Chapter IV were used). A series of linear regressions was then applied to the data to determine the extent and nature of any associations between current barriers and future drivers or criteria. We wanted to determine whether there was any association between the present reasons for not using e-commerce and the possible reasons that may lead to e-commerce adoption in the future.

The findings will be presented from each of the three countries—Sweden, Australia, and U.S. This will be followed by a detailed discussion of the findings and their effect on policy decisions.

# E-Commerce Barriers and Potential Drivers in Sweden

We found a number of statistically significant associations in the Swedish sample between e-commerce barriers and criteria. Twelve of the fourteen criteria tested showed a significant association with one or more e-commerce adoption barriers. These are shown in Tables 1 to 12, which also indicate the relevant p value and will now be discussed.

As expected, Table 1 shows that those respondents who rated the unsuitability of e-commerce to the way their clients did business, may, in the future adopt e-commerce if their customers did demand their use of the technology. No other barriers were associated with this future criterion. While this outcome might be expected, it nonetheless is an important finding. A number of studies of e-commerce barriers in the SME sector (Adebanjo, Kehoe, Galligan, & Mahoney, 2006; Eid, 2005; Kaynak, Tatoglu, & Kula, 2005; Kelliher & Henderson, 2006; Miller, 2005; Stockdale & Standing, 2006) have concluded that many SMEs have been reluctant to engage in e-commerce because a large percentage of their clientele prefer not to use e-commerce to do business. Thus while advocates of e-commerce point to new customers and markets, these businesses rely and remain loyal to their current customers rather than risking the possibility of losing these and perhaps replacing them with different customers

Table 2 shows that two barriers were significantly associated with pressure from competition. "E-commerce is not suited to our way of doing business" provided a negative Beta value. This suggests that those respondents that rated this barrier as very important were not likely to rate pressure from competition as important. In other words, the criterion "pressure from competition" was not a mitigating reason for adoption for those who considered that e-commerce was not suited to their way of doing business as being important. The barrier "e-commerce is not suited to the way our clients do business" provided a highly significant positive Beta value. This suggests that those that placed a high level of importance on this barrier would, in the future, place a high level of importance on adopting e-commerce due to pressure from competition. In other words, if competition were likely to "woo" clients away because of e-commerce, then this would force the business to adopt and use it. While this is

*Table 1. Regression table for demand and/or pressure from customers*

| Dependant variable demand and/or pressure from customers | | |
|---|---|---|
| | Beta | p value |
| E-commerce is not suited to the ways our clients do business. | .339 | .010 |
| R Squared | | .266 |
| Adjusted R squared | | .204 |
| p value for the complete regression table | | .000 |

*Table 2. Regression table for pressure from competition*

| Dependant variable pressure from competition | | |
|---|---|---|
| | Beta | p value |
| E-commerce is not suited to our way of doing business. | -.301 | .023 |
| E-commerce is not suited to the ways our clients do business. | .418 | .001 |
| R Squared | | .333 |
| Adjusted R squared | | .276 |
| p value for the complete regression table | | .000 |

not the case, they have resisted e-commerce. These two associations place the business in a difficult position. On the one hand, e-commerce does not suit the business operation and pressure from competition will not alter this view. However, if there is a change in the way their customers work in the future, this might pre-empt a change of thinking.

An examination of Table 3 provides an interesting finding. While, as might be expected, the barrier "E-commerce is not suited to the ways our clients do business" returned a positive Beta value (i.e., those that placed a high level of importance on it, also placed a high level of importance on demand and/or pressure from suppliers). The barrier "We do not have the technical knowledge in the organisation to implement e-commerce" also returned a positive Beta value. This second barrier suggests that those that placed a high level of importance on this barrier would likewise place a high level of importance on adopting e-commerce because of the demand and/or pressure from suppliers, even though their technical knowledge was limited. It is interesting to note that no such association was found for demand by customers (Table 1) or demand from competition (Table 2). One possible explanation is that pressure from suppliers might be accompanied by the necessary technical expertise to overcome difficulties by the respondents.

*Table 3. Regression table for demand/pressure from suppliers*

| Dependant variable demand and/or pressure from suppliers | | |
|---|---|---|
| | Beta | p value |
| E-commerce is not suited to the ways our clients do business. | .400 | .002 |
| We do not have the technical knowledge in the organisation to implement e-commerce. | .254 | .019 |
| R Squared | .319 | |
| Adjusted R squared | .261 | |
| p value for the complete regression table | .000 | |

*Table 4. Regression table for reduced costs*

| Dependant variable to reduce costs | | |
|---|---|---|
| | Beta | p value |
| E-commerce is not suited to the ways our clients do business. | .288 | .021 |
| We do not have the technical knowledge in the organisation to implement e-commerce. | .253 | .018 |
| The financial investment required to implement e-commerce is too high. | .261 | .033 |
| R Squared | .338 | |
| Adjusted R squared | .282 | |
| p value for the complete regression table | .000 | |

Table 4 shows that three barriers were significantly associated with reduced costs as an adoption driver. In all cases, these returned positive Beta values. This suggests that those SMEs, which placed a high level of importance on any or all of the barriers, were likely to place a high level of importance on reduced costs. Despite the high financial investment to adopt e-commerce, the respondents would outlay the necessary funds if they were sufficiently convinced that e-commerce would reduce costs. This suggests that at present respondents are not convinced that e-commerce will reduce costs. The association between the barrier "lack of technical knowledge" and the future criterion "reduced costs" is an interesting one. While not tested, one possible conclusion is that the perception of cost reduction may require a degree of technical knowledge. The final association was between the barrier "e-commerce is not suited to the way our clients work" and the future criterion "reduced costs." This suggests that if respondents were convinced that costs could be reduced, this may override client consideration.

Table 5 provides a somewhat unexpected outcome. One barrier (e-commerce is not suited to our products/services) was associated with the desire to use e-commerce to improve customer service. However, the Beta value was highly significant and negative. This suggests that

*Table 5. Regression table for improved customer service*

| Dependant variable to improve customer service | | |
|---|---|---|
| | Beta | p value |
| E-commerce is not suited to our products/services. | -.460 | .001 |
| R Squared | | .222 |
| Adjusted R squared | | .156 |
| p value for the complete regression table | | .001 |

*Table 6. Regression table for increased sales*

| Dependant variable to increase sales | | |
|---|---|---|
| | Beta | p value |
| E-commerce is not suited to our products/services. | -.501 | .000 |
| E-commerce does not offer any advantages to our organisation. | .290 | .023 |
| R Squared | | .210 |
| Adjusted R squared | | .143 |
| p value for the complete regression table | | .001 |

those respondents who placed a high level of importance on e-commerce not being suited to our products/services were not likely to place a high level of importance on improving customer service as a driver for adoption. The data shows that for Swedish respondents, improvement to customer service does not mitigate the concerns about e-commerce not being suited to their products and services.

While it might be expected that increases in sales may, in the future, mitigate current concerns regarding the advantages of e-commerce (positive Beta .290, p < .05), a second barrier (e-commerce is not suited to our products/services) returned a highly significant negative Beta value. This suggests that those who placed a high level of importance on this barrier are very unlikely to place a high level of importance on increased sales as a reason to adopt e-commerce in the future. This can be thought of in two ways. Those that may in the future adopt e-commerce to increase sales are not worried that e-commerce does not suit their products and services, while those that believe that e-commerce does not suit their products and services are not going to alter their views on the possibility of increased sales. Clearly, e-commerce does not suit all businesses. Table 6 shows that many of the Swedish SMEs have recognised this.

The data in Table 7 suggests that those that placed a high level of importance on e-commerce not being suited to the ways their clients do business and/or not having the time to implement e-commerce are likely to place a high level of importance on improving internal

*Table 7. Regression table for improved internal efficiency*

| Dependant Variable To improve internal efficiency | | |
|---|---|---|
| | Beta | p value |
| E-commerce is not suited to the ways our clients do business. | .294 | .022 |
| We do not have time to implement e-commerce. | .241 | .041 |
| R Squared | .300 | |
| Adjusted R squared | .241 | |
| p value for the complete regression table | .000 | |

*Table 8. Regression table for strengthen relations with business partners*

| Dependant variable to strengthen relations with business partners | | |
|---|---|---|
| | Beta | p value |
| E-commerce is not suited to the ways our clients do business. | .289 | .024 |
| E-commerce is too complicated to implement. | -.332 | .042 |
| We do not have time to implement e-commerce. | .318 | .007 |
| R Squared | .305 | |
| Adjusted R squared | .246 | |
| p value for the complete regression table | .000 | |

efficiency as a reason for adopting e-commerce in the future. The reverse of this is likewise quite interesting. Those respondents that did not place much importance on either or both of these barriers are not likely to place a high level of importance on the criterion improving internal efficiency either.

Table 8 provides the data for the future criterion "Strengthen relations with business partners." While it may be expected that the barrier "E-commerce is not suited to the ways our clients do business" would be associated with the desire to strengthen relations with business partners, the data in Table 8 shows that two other barriers are similarly associated with the future criterion. The barrier "E-commerce is too complicated to implement" is associated with the same criterion but the Beta value returned is negative. This implies that those SMEs, which placed a high level of importance on this barrier are not likely to place a high level of importance on the using e-commerce to strengthen relations with business partners at some future time. Put another way, strengthening of relations with business partners does not appear to mitigate problems concerned with the complications of the technology itself. This is an important finding, which suggests that despite organisational and financial benefits, there is a strong technical barrier for many SMEs to adopt e-commerce. Only those that do not have that technical "fear" (low perception of importance on e-commerce is too complicated to implement) are amenable to the organisational gains of future adoption. The third bar-

*Table 9. Regression table for access to new customers/markets*

| Dependant variable access to new customers/markets | | |
|---|---|---|
| | Beta | p value |
| E-commerce is not suited to the ways our clients do business. | .365 | .002 |
| We do not have time to implement e-commerce. | .338 | .002 |
| R Squared | | .436 |
| Adjusted R squared | | .389 |
| p value for the complete regression table | | .000 |

*Table 10. Regression table for external support*

| Dependant variable external support | | |
|---|---|---|
| | Beta | p value |
| E-commerce is not suited to our way of doing business. | -.271 | .044 |
| E-commerce is not suited to the ways our clients do business. | .290 | .022 |
| We do not have the technical knowledge in the organisation to implement e-commerce. | .230 | .034 |
| R Squared | | .315 |
| Adjusted R squared | | .257 |
| p value for the complete regression table | | .000 |

rier, associated with the criterion is "We do not have time to implement e-commerce." The data suggests that strengthening of relations with business partners is a mitigating reason to overcome current lack of time involved in adopting and using e-commerce.

An examination of Table 9 shows that two barriers (e-commerce is not suited to the ways our clients do business and we do not have time to implement e-commerce) are positively associated with access to new customers and markets as an adoption driver. While the first of these barriers might be expected, the second is unexpected. The data suggests that those who placed a high level of importance on this barrier are more likely to adopt e-commerce for the reason of reaching new customers and markets than those who did not place a high level of importance on the current time constraints. This finding may also suggest that many businesses are not sufficiently convinced that they can or will reach new customers and markets and use the excuses that they have not had time or it is not how their customers do business as reasons why they have not adopted the technology.

The data shows that those SMEs, which did not have the requisite knowledge to adopt e-commerce, might adopt in the future if there was some form of technical support. An examination of the data in Table 10 shows that two other barriers (e-commerce is not suited to our way of doing business and e-commerce is not suited to the ways our clients do business) were also associated with the availability of external support as a potential driver. The data shows that those that placed a high level of importance on the barrier "E-commerce is not suited to our way of doing business" are not likely to adopt e-commerce even if external support is available. The data also shows that those organisations, which placed a high level of importance on e-commerce not being suited to the ways their clients do business, might adopt e-commerce in the future if external assistance was available.

*Table 11. Regression table for improved marketing*

| Dependant variable to improve marketing | | |
|---|---|---|
| | Beta | p value |
| The financial investment required to implement e-commerce is too high. | .247 | .044 |
| We do not have time to implement e-commerce. | .289 | .012 |
| R Squared | | .337 |
| Adjusted R squared | | .280 |
| p value for the complete regression table | | .000 |

*Table 12. Regression table for improved control*

| Dependant variable to improve control | | |
|---|---|---|
| | Beta | p value |
| We do not have the technical knowledge in the organisation to implement e-commerce. | .293 | .003 |
| R Squared | | .433 |
| Adjusted R squared | | .384 |
| p value for the complete regression table | | .000 |

This association between external support and e-commerce not suiting the way clients work is unexpected and not easily explained. Respondents appear to be using the "excuse" that it does not suit their clientele but indicating that with sufficient assistance they will adopt in spite of their clients.

Table 11 provides the data for the future criterion "Improve our marketing." Two barriers (financial investment and time) were associated with this criterion and that both returned a positive Beta value. The data suggests that respondents who placed a high level of importance on either the financial investment required to implement e-commerce and/or the time to implement e-commerce were likely to place a high level of importance on adopting e-commerce to improve their marketing. An interesting "alternate" view is that those that placed a low level of importance on one or both of these barriers was likely to place a low level of importance on the criterion as well. This seems to suggest that other barriers are in effect, despite there being no significant associations with those barriers.

An examination of Table 12 shows that one barrier (lack of technical knowledge in the organisation) is highly significantly associated with improved control as an e-commerce driver. The data shows that those that rated the technical knowledge barrier as being important are likely to assign the same importance to the criterion "Improvement to control" in the future adoption of e-commerce.

# Summary of Barriers and Potential Drivers in Sweden

As can be seen, the Swedish data has presented a number of unexpected findings. Thus, despite the advocacy by governments and academics that e-commerce will provide SMEs with a number of potential benefits, the data suggests that these benefits may only be associated with certain current barriers faced by the SME sector and specific drivers must be targeted for specific SMEs only. The data also shows that some criteria do not mitigate current barriers to e-commerce adoption. These, in the main, are showing up as negative Beta results. For convenience, Table 13 summarises the findings of the Swedish study.

We will now examine the situation in Australia.

*Table 13. Summary of barriers and potential criteria (Sweden)*

| Future criteria (*We would adopt e-commerce because of/to...*) | Barriers (*We currently do not use e-commerce because of...*) | Type of association |
|---|---|---|
| Demand and/or pressure from customers. | E-commerce is not suited to the ways our clients do business. | + |
| Pressure from competition. | E-commerce is not suited to our way of doing business. | - |
| | E-commerce is not suited to the ways our clients do business. | + |

*continued on following page*

*Table 13. Continued*

| Future criteria (*We would adopt e-commerce because of/to...*) | Barriers (*We currently do not use e-commerce because of...*) | Type of as-sociation |
|---|---|---|
| Demand and/or pressure from suppliers. | E-commerce is not suited to the ways our clients do business . | + |
| | We do not have the technical knowledge in the organisation to implement e-commerce. | + |
| Reduce costs. | E-commerce is not suited to the ways our clients do business . | + |
| | We do not have the technical knowledge in the organisation to implement e-commerce. | + |
| | The financial investment required to implement e-commerce is too high. | + |
| Improve customer service. | E-commerce is not suited to our products/services. | - |
| Increase sales. | E-commerce is not suited to our products/services. | - |
| | E-commerce does not offer any advantages to our organisation. | + |
| Improve internal efficiency. | E-commerce is not suited to the ways our clients do business. | + |
| | We do not have time to implement e-commerce. | + |
| Strengthen relations with business partners. | E-commerce is not suited to the ways our clients do business. | + |
| | E-commerce is too complicated to implement. | - |
| | We do not have time to implement e-commerce. | + |
| Possibility of reaching new customers/markets. | E-commerce is not suited to the ways our clients do business. | + |
| | We do not have time to implement e-commerce. | + |
| Availability of external support. | E-commerce is not suited to our way of doing business. | - |
| | E-commerce is not suited to the ways our clients do business. | + |
| | We do not have the technical knowledge in the organisation to implement e-commerce. | + |
| Improve marketing. | The financial investment required to implement e-commerce is too high. | + |
| | We do not have time to implement e-commerce. | + |
| Improve control. | We do not have the technical knowledge in the organisation to implement e-commerce. | + |

# E-Commerce Barriers and Potential Drivers in Australia

Unlike Sweden, only four future criteria showed a significant association with current barriers to e-commerce adoption in Australia. These are shown in Tables 14 to 17, which also indicate the relevant p value, and will now be discussed.

Two barriers (e-commerce does not offer any advantages to our organisation and it is difficult to choose the most suitable e-commerce standard with so many different options available) were associated with pressure from competition. The data shows that those that placed a high level of importance on one or both barriers were likely to place a high level of importance on the criterion as well in any future decision to adopt e-commerce. It is interesting to compare the data with Sweden (see Table 2), that showed associations with e-commerce is not suited to our way of doing business nor the way our clients did business. While it may be argued that the Australians not seeing any advantage to their organisation may have included concerns about products, services, and clientele, it seems that the Swedish respondents were more "in tune" with their methods of business and their customers than the Australian respondents.

*Table 14. Regression table for pressure from competition*

| Dependant variable the pressure from competition | | |
|---|---|---|
| | Beta | p value |
| E-commerce does not offer any advantages to our organisation. | .319 | .024 |
| It is difficult to choose the most suitable e-commerce standard with so many different options available. | .752 | .035 |
| R Squared | | .288 |
| Adjusted R squared | | .191 |
| p value for the complete regression table | | .001 |

*Table 15. Regression table for reduced costs*

| Dependant variable to reduce costs | | |
|---|---|---|
| | Beta | p value |
| E-commerce is not suited to the ways our clients do business. | .514 | .005 |
| R Squared | | .345 |
| Adjusted R squared | | .256 |
| p value for the complete regression table | | .000 |

Table 15 provides an unexpected result. The data shows that those that placed a high level of importance on not adopting e-commerce because it was not suited to the ways their clients did business, were also likely to place a high level of importance on adopting e-commerce because it reduced costs. Similarly, those that placed a low level of importance on this barrier would probably place a low level of importance on reducing costs through e-commerce adoption. A comparison to the Swedish respondents (see table 4) shows that while both nominated e-commerce not suiting the way their clients did business, the Swedish respondents were also concerned with costs and their technical ability

Three barriers (e-commerce is not suited to our way of doing business, e-commerce is not suited to the ways our clients do business, and e-commerce does not offer any advantages to our organisation) are associated with improved customer service as a potential driver. Two barriers have returned a positive Beta value, indicating that those that placed a high level of importance on one or both of these barriers, were also likely to place a high level of importance on the future criterion as well. One barrier (e-commerce is not suited to our way of doing business) returned a negative Beta value indicating that those that placed a high level of importance on this barrier were not likely to place a high value on the future criterion of improving customer service. Put another way, improvement to customer service appears not to be a mitigating reason to overcome the fact that e-commerce is not suited to their way of doing business.

*Table 16. Regression table for improved customer service*

| Dependant variable to improve customer service | | |
|---|---|---|
| | Beta | p value |
| E-commerce is not suited to our way of doing business. | -.332 | .035 |
| E-commerce is not suited to the ways our clients do business. | .397 | .031 |
| E-commerce does not offer any advantages to our organisation. | .287 | .037 |
| R Squared | .317 | |
| Adjusted R squared | .225 | |
| p value for the complete regression table | .000 | |

*Table 17. Regression table for improved marketing*

| Dependant variable to improve our marketing | | |
|---|---|---|
| | Beta | p value |
| E-commerce is not suited to the ways our clients do business. | .677 | .001 |
| R Squared | .225 | |
| Adjusted R squared | .120 | |
| p value for the complete regression table | .018 | |

Table 17 provides the data for the future criterion, "improve our marketing." The table shows that those that placed a high level of importance on the fact that e-commerce was not suited to the way their customers did business, would, in the future place a high level of importance on improvement to marketing, through e-commerce adoption. A comparison with the Swedish respondents (see Table 11) shows that while the Australian respondents appeared to be concerned with their clients, the Swedish respondents were simply concerned with cost and time.

# Summary of Barriers and Potential Drivers in Australia

Table 18 summarises the findings of the Australian study. As can be seen, only four future criteria were associated with current barriers. This suggests that many of the benefits suggested by advocates as a reason to adopt e-commerce do not address current concerns by SME owner/managers in regional Australia.

We will now examine the situation in the U.S.A..

*Table 18. Summary of barriers and potential criteria (Australia)*

| Future criteria (We would adopt e-commerce because of/to...) | Barriers (We currently do not use e-commerce because of...) | Type of association |
|---|---|---|
| Pressure from competition. | E-commerce does not offer any advantages to our organisation. | + |
| | It is difficult to choose the most suitable e-commerce standard with so many different options available. | + |
| Reduce costs. | E-commerce is not suited to the ways our clients do business. | + |
| Improve customer service. | E-commerce is not suited to our way of doing business. | - |
| | E-commerce is not suited to the ways our clients do business. | + |
| | E-commerce does not offer any advantages to our organisation. | + |
| Improve marketing. | E-commerce is not suited to the ways our clients do business. | + |

# E-Commerce Barriers and Potential
# Drivers in the USA

Eight future criteria showed a significant association with current barriers to e-commerce adoption in the U.S. These are shown in Tables 19 to 26, which also indicate the relevant p value, and will now be discussed.

Table 19 provides two unexpected findings. While the positive association between the barrier "E-commerce does not offer any advantages to our organisation" and the criterion "Demand and/or pressure from customers" would be expected, two barriers returned a negative Beta value. Thus those respondents that placed a high level of importance on their lack of technical knowledge in the organisation to implement e-commerce and/choosing the most suitable standard would be expected to place little importance on this criterion. This suggests that despite customer pressure, the U.S. respondents are very concerned with the

*Table 19. Regression table for demand and/or pressure from customers*

| Dependant variable demand and/or pressure from customers | | |
|---|---|---|
| | Beta | p value |
| E-commerce does not offer any advantages to our organisation. | .503 | .022 |
| We do not have the technical knowledge in the organisation to implement e-commerce. | -.634 | .011 |
| It is difficult to choose the most suitable e-commerce standard with so many different options available. | -1.365 | .007 |
| R Squared | .717 | |
| Adjusted R squared | .528 | |
| p value for the complete regression table | .005 | |

*Table 20. Regression table for pressure from competition*

| Dependant variable the pressure from competition in the line of business | | |
|---|---|---|
| | Beta | p value |
| E-commerce does not offer any advantages to our organisation. | .462 | .043 |
| E-commerce is not secure. | 1.084 | .029 |
| We do not have time to implement e-commerce. | 1.406 | .011 |
| It is difficult to choose the most suitable e-commerce standard with so many different options available. | -1.994 | .001 |
| R Squared | .682 | |
| Adjusted R squared | .471 | |
| p value for the complete regression table | .012 | |

technical aspects of e-commerce. Indeed, only those that do not have technical concerns would opt to use e-commerce in the future if their customers demanded it. A comparison with the Swedish findings (see table 1) shows that the Swedish respondents were concerned with their customers, while the U.S. respondents were concerned with technical problems.

While it may be expected that respondents who placed a high level of importance on "E-commerce does not offer any advantages to our organisation" and/or "We do not have time to implement e-commerce" would also place a high level of importance on adopting e-commerce because of pressure from competition, the other two associations are completely unexpected. The data shows a positive association with security issues. This implies that respondents that placed a high level of importance on security issues of e-commerce would also place a high level of importance on adopting e-commerce because of competition. The data also shows that the barrier "It is difficult to choose the most suitable e-commerce standard with so many different options available" returned a negative Beta value, implying that those that placed a high level of importance on this barrier would place a low level of importance on pressure from competition as a driver to adopt e-commerce.

*Table 21. Regression table for demand/pressure from suppliers*

| Dependant variable demand/pressure from suppliers | | |
|---|---|---|
| | Beta | p value |
| E-commerce does not offer any advantages to our organisation. | .570 | .013 |
| E-commerce is not secure. | 1.072 | .026 |
| It is difficult to choose the most suitable e-commerce standard with so many different options available. | -1.615 | .002 |
| R Squared | .702 | |
| Adjusted R squared | .504 | |
| p value for the complete regression table | .008 | |

*Table 22. Regression table for reduced costs*

| Dependant variable to reduce costs | | |
|---|---|---|
| | Beta | p value |
| We do not have the technical knowledge in the organisation to implement e-commerce. | -.504 | .042 |
| It is difficult to choose the most suitable e-commerce standard with so many different options available. | -.978 | .047 |
| R Squared | .702 | |
| Adjusted R squared | .503 | |
| p value for the complete regression table | .008 | |

Again, a comparison with the Swedish and Australian respondents (see Tables 2 and 14) shows a number of interesting differences. While the Swedish respondents are concerned with their customers, both the U.S. and Australian respondents are concerned with advantages to their organisation and the diversity of e-commerce standards. However, where the Australian SMEs that are concerned with standards indicated they would adopt e-commerce because of pressure from competition, the U.S. respondents would not. The U.S. SMEs were the only group that associated time and security issues with the future criterion pressure from competition.

As with Table 20, two associations with the criterion "Demand/pressure from suppliers" are unexpected, and, indeed, similar to those in Table 20. Again, the data shows a positive association with security issues. This implies that respondents who placed a high level of importance on security issues of e-commerce would also place a high level of importance on adopting e-commerce because of competition. The data also shows that the barrier "It is difficult to choose the most suitable e-commerce standard" returned a negative Beta value, implying that those that placed a high level of importance on this barrier would place a low level of importance on the criterion "Demand and/or pressure from suppliers."

Comparing the U.S. findings to the Swedish responses (see Table 2) shows that the U.S. respondents are very concerned with standards of e-commerce and e-commerce security. No such associations were found in the Swedish data.

Table 22 provides the data for the criterion "Reduce costs." Like the previous two tables, this table shows that two technical barriers were associated with the reduced costs criterion and both returned negative Beta values. Those respondents that placed a high level of importance on not having the technical knowledge in the organisation to implement e-commerce and/or difficulties choosing the most suitable e-commerce standard would not be expected to place a high level of importance on adopting e-commerce to reduce costs. Put another way, reduction of costs through e-commerce adoption is not a mitigating driver for either of the two barriers.

*Table 23. Regression table for improved customer service*

| Dependant variable to improve customer service | | |
|---|---|---|
| | Beta | p value |
| E-commerce does not offer any advantages to our organisation. | .514 | .006 |
| We do not have the technical knowledge in the organisation to implement e-commerce. | -.688 | .001 |
| E-commerce is not secure. | .928 | .017 |
| It is difficult to choose the most suitable e-commerce standard with so many different options available. | -1.392 | .001 |
| R Squared | | .811 |
| Adjusted R squared | | .685 |
| p value for the complete regression table | | .000 |

A comparison of the findings with the Swedish and Australian studies (see Tables 4 and 15) shows that the Australian respondents have only associated organisational issues with the future criterion reduce costs. By comparison, the Swedish respondents associated organisational and technical issues with the future criterion (unsuitability with clients, lack of expertise and higher costs), while the U.S. respondents only associated technical difficulties (lack of expertise and lack of standards) with this future criterion.

The data in Table 23 shows a positive association with security issues. This implies that respondents that placed a high level of importance on security issues of e-commerce would also place a high level of importance on adopting e-commerce because they could improve their customer service. Table 23 also shows that two technical barriers were associated with the criterion reduced costs and both returned negative Beta values. Thus, those respondents that placed a high level of importance on we not having the technical knowledge in the organisation to implement e-commerce and/or difficulties choosing the most suitable e-commerce standard would not be expected to place a high level of importance on the improving their customer service through e-commerce. The two negative Beta values in this table suggest that there is a strong set of technical barriers in play for the U.S. non-adopters. Despite the ability, through e-commerce adoption and use, to improve customer services, respondents are "restricted" by lack of standards and lack of expertise.

A comparison with the Swedish and Australian findings (see Tables 5 and 16) shows that while both were concerned with organisational issues, the U.S. respondents were concerned with technical issues.

Like the previous future criterion, Table 24 shows that the barrier, "Too many choices" is associated with this criterion, but has returned a negative Beta value. Again, this suggests that those that placed a high level of importance on this barrier would place a low level of importance on the reaching new customers and markets through e-commerce use. Clearly, the future possibility of reaching new customers and markets is not a mitigating criterion to overcome the difficulty of having too many options available. A comparison with the Swedish responses (see Table 9) shows that while they associated this criterion with lack of time and unsuitability with the way their clients worked, the U.S. respondents were concerned with technical issues.

*Table 24. Regression table for access to new customers/markets*

| Dependant variable access to new customers/markets | | |
|---|---|---|
| | Beta | p value |
| It is difficult to choose the most suitable e-commerce standard with so many different options available. | -1.256 | .027 |
| R Squared | .615 | |
| Adjusted R squared | .358 | |
| p value for the complete regression table | .046 | |

While it may be expected that respondents that placed a high level of importance on e-commerce not offering any advantages to their organisation and/or not having the time to implement e-commerce would also place a high level of importance on adopting e-commerce to improve their marketing, the negative Beta value for the e-commerce standards barrier suggests that those that placed a high level of importance on this barrier would place a low level of importance on the criterion "Improvements to marketing."

A comparison with the Swedish and Australian responses (see Table 11 and 12.17) shows that while the Australian respondents were concerned with e-commerce not being suited to the way their clients did business, the Swedish and U.S. respondents were associating this criterion with the lack of time barrier. The Swedish respondents also associated this criterion with high costs, while the U.S. respondents were concerned with lack of standards

Finally, Table 26 provides the data for the improved control criterion. Two barriers (e-commerce is not suited to our way of doing business and e-commerce does not offer any advantages to our organisation) are associated with this criterion. The data shows that those that placed a high level of importance on either "E-commerce is not suited to our way of doing business" and/or "E-commerce does not offer any advantages to our organisation" would also place a high level of importance on this criterion.

*Table 25. Regression table for improved marketing*

| Dependant variable to improve marketing | | |
|---|---|---|
| | Beta | p value |
| E-commerce does not offer any advantages to our organisation. | .591 | .005 |
| We do not have time to implement e-commerce. | 1.092 | .019 |
| It is difficult to choose the most suitable e-commerce standard with so many different options available. | -1.664 | .001 |
| R Squared | .763 | |
| Adjusted R squared | .604 | |
| p value for the complete regression table | .001 | |

*Table 26. Regression table for improved control*

| Dependant variable to improve control | | |
|---|---|---|
| | Beta | p value |
| E-commerce is not suited to our way of doing business. | .681 | .021 |
| E-commerce does not offer any advantages to our organisation. | .593 | .005 |
| R Squared | .754 | |
| Adjusted R squared | .590 | |
| p value for the complete regression table | .002 | |

Comparisons with Swedish findings (see Table 12) are interesting. For all other comparisons, it has been the U.S. respondents that have been concerned with technical barriers, while the Swedish respondents have associated future criteria with both organisational as well as technical barriers. The criterion improved control is the reverso of this. While the Swedish respondents associated it with lack of technical knowledge, the U.S. respondents associated it with non suitability with the way business was conducted and lack of perceptual advantages to the business

# Summary of Barriers and Potential Drivers in the USA

Table 27 summarises the findings of the U.S. study. As can be seen, eight future criteria were associated with current barriers. Of particular interest is the recurring theme of too many e-commerce options as a barrier, which is significant for seven of the eight criteria.

*Table 27. Summary of barriers and potential criteria (USA)*

| Future criteria (We would adopt e-commerce because of/to…) | Barriers (We currently do not use e-commerce because of…) | Type of association |
|---|---|---|
| Demand and/or pressure from customers. | E-commerce does not offer any advantages to our organisation. | + |
| | We do not have the technical knowledge in the organisation to implement e-commerce. | - |
| | It is difficult to choose the most suitable e-commerce standard with so many different options available. | - |
| Pressure from competition. | It is difficult to choose the most suitable e-commerce standard with so many different options available. | - |
| | E-commerce does not offer any advantages to our organisation. | + |
| | E-commerce is not secure. | + |
| | We do not have time to implement e-commerce. | + |
| Demand and/or pressure from suppliers. | E-commerce does not offer any advantages to our organisation. | + |
| | E-commerce is not secure. | + |
| | It is difficult to choose the most suitable e-commerce standard with so many different options available. | - |
| Reduce costs. | We do not have the technical knowledge in the organisation to implement e-commerce. | - |
| | It is difficult to choose the most suitable e-commerce standard with so many different options available. | - |

*continued on following page*

*Table 27. Continued*

| Future criteria (We would adopt e-commerce because of/to...) | Barriers (We currently do not use e-commerce because of...) | Type of association |
|---|---|---|
| Improve customer service. | E-commerce does not offer any advantages to our organisation. | + |
| | We do not have the technical knowledge in the organisation to implement e-commerce. | - |
| | E-commerce is not secure. | + |
| | It is difficult to choose the most suitable e-commerce standard with so many different options available. | - |
| Possibility of reaching new customers/markets. | It is difficult to choose the most suitable e-commerce standard with so many different options available. | - |
| Improve marketing. | E-commerce does not offer any advantages to our organisation. | + |
| | We do not have time to implement e-commerce. | + |
| | It is difficult to choose the most suitable e-commerce standard with so many different options available. | - |
| Improve control. | E-commerce is not suited to our way of doing business. | + |
| | E-commerce does not offer any advantages to our organisation. | + |

# Comparison of the Three Locations and Implications

Table 28 summarises the findings across the three locations for the purposes of comparison. Clearly, the most obvious difference is the number of future criteria associated with current barriers to e-commerce adoption. While the Swedish study found twelve future criteria associated with current barriers, the Australian found only four and the U.S. found eight associations.

While those SMEs in Sweden who are currently not using e-commerce because it did not suit their clients way of doing business, are likely to adopt the technology following pressure from customers in the U.S. It is SMEs, which do not see any advantages from e-commerce and do not have the required technical skills that may bow to pressure from customers. The implication is that pressure from customers is sufficient to stir the SMEs into action to overcome the technical difficulties they face and adopt e-commerce.

Swedish SMEs, which do not believe that e-commerce is suited to their customers' way of doing business, may adopt the technology if their competitors do. Australian and U.S. SMEs would only bow to pressure from competition despite the fact that they see no advantages in e-commerce. In the U.S., pressure from competition would also be a strong incentive to overcome security concerns and resource constraints related to time. Once again, the emphasis in Australia and the U.S. is on technical barriers, which would only be surmounted

*Table 28. Comparison of associations between current barriers and potential drivers across three locations*

| Future criteria (We would adopt e-commerce because of/to...) | Barriers (Sweden) (We currently do not use e-commerce because of...) | Barriers (Australia) (We currently do not use e-commerce because of...) | Barriers (U.S.A.) (We currently do not use e-commerce because of...) |
|---|---|---|---|
| Demand and/or pressure from customers. | It is not suited to the ways our clients do business (+). | | It does not offer any advantages (+). We do not have the technical knowledge to implement e-commerce (-). It is difficult to choose the most suitable e-commerce standard with so many different options available (-). |
| Pressure from competition. | It is not suited to our way of doing business (-). It is not suited to the ways our clients do business (+). | It does not offer any advantages (+). It is difficult to choose the most suitable e-commerce standard with so many different options available (+). | It is difficult to choose the most suitable e-commerce standard with so many different options available (-). It does not offer any advantages (+). It is not secure (+). We do not have time to implement e-commerce (+). |
| Demand and/or pressure from suppliers. | It is not suited to the ways our clients do business (+). We do not have the technical knowledge to implement e-commerce (+). | | It does not offer any advantages (+). It is not secure (+). It is difficult to choose the most suitable e-commerce standard with so many different options available (-). |
| Reduce costs. | It is not suited to the ways our clients do business (+). We do not have the technical knowledge to implement e-commerce (+). The financial investment required is too high (+). | It is not suited to the ways our clients do business (+). | We do not have the technical knowledge to implement e-commerce (-). It is difficult to choose the most suitable e-commerce standard with so many different options available (-). |
| Improve customer service. | It is not suited to our products/services (-). | It is not suited to our way of doing business (-). It is not suited to the ways our clients do business (+). It does not offer any advantages (+). | It does not offer any advantages (+). We do not have the technical knowledge to implement e-commerce (-). It is not secure (+). It is difficult to choose the most suitable e-commerce standard with so many different options available (-). |
| Increase sales. | It is not suited to our products/services (-). It does not offer any advantages to our organisation (+). | | |

376  MacGregor & Vrazalic

*Table 28. Continued*

| Future criteria (We would adopt e-commerce because of/to…) | Barriers (Sweden) (We currently do not use e-commerce because of…) | Barriers (Australia) (We currently do not use e-commerce because of…) | Barriers (U.S.A.) (We currently do not use e-commerce because of…) |
|---|---|---|---|
| Improve internal efficiency. | It is not suited to the ways our clients do business (+). We do not have time to implement e-commerce (+). | | |
| Strengthen relations with business partners. | It is not suited to the ways our clients do business (+). It is too complicated to implement (-). We do not have time to implement e-commerce (+). | | |
| Possibility of reaching new customers/markets. | It is not suited to the ways our clients do business (+). We do not have time to implement e-commerce (+). | | It is difficult to choose the most suitable e-commerce standard with so many different options available(-). |
| Availability of external support. | It is not suited to our way of doing business (-). It is not suited to the ways our clients do business (+). We do not have the technical knowledge to implement e-commerce (+). | | |
| Improve marketing. | The financial investment required is too high (+). We do not have time to implement e-commerce (+). | It is not suited to the ways our clients do business (+). | It does not offer any advantages (+). We do not have time to implement e-commerce (+). It is difficult to choose the most suitable e-commerce standard with so many different options available (-). |
| Improve control. | We do not have the technical knowledge to implement e-commerce (+). | | It is not suited to our way of doing business (+). It does not offer any advantages (+). |

if competitors surged ahead. The fear of being "left behind" would drive these SMEs to e-commerce adoption.

In Sweden, SMEs that do not use e-commerce because it is not aligned with the way their customers do business and due to a lack of technical knowledge, would be prompted into action if their suppliers demanded it. Meanwhile, in the U.S.A., SMEs that did not see any advantages to e-commerce and also felt that it was not secure are likely to jump on the e-commerce bandwagon if their suppliers pressured them to do it.

Australian and Swedish SMEs, which do not find e-commerce suited to their client's way of doing business may adopt the technology if it reduced their costs. In Sweden, lower costs would also be a strong incentive to overcome technical and financial barriers. However, in the U.S., those SMEs, which are unsure about e-commerce standards and which do not have the technical knowledge are less likely to adopt e-commerce to reduce costs.

Even though they felt that e-commerce did not offer them any benefits, SMEs in Australia and the U.S.A. are likely to implement the technology if it improved their customer services. This would also be a sufficiently strong driver for SMEs in the U.S.A. to overcome their technical barriers related to security. In Sweden, however, those SMEs, which feel that e-commerce is not suited to the types of products and services they offer are not likely to implement e-commerce in order to improve customer service.

Only SMEs in Sweden would overcome barriers related to the perception that e-commerce does not offer any advantages in return for increased sales. Likewise, the same SMEs are likely to find time to implement e-commerce if it would lead to improvements in internal efficiency, stronger relations with business partners, and access to new customers and markets. The same SMEs may adopt e-commerce if external support was provided in order to overcome the lack of technical knowledge in the organisation.

Both Swedish and U.S. SMEs would find the time to implement e-commerce if it improved their marketing. The formed would also overcome the financial hurdles associated with e-commerce adoption. By contrast, in Australia SMEs, which did not believe e-commerce was suited to their way of doing business would consider adopting the technology if it lead to improvements in marketing.

While most of the U.S. SMEs would tend to overcome various technical barriers in order to achieve certain benefits from e-commerce and Swedish SMEs would do the same for organisational barriers, this is not the case where control is concerned. Swedish SMEs, in this instance, would surmount their lack of technical knowledge in order to improve control of their organisation through e-commerce. By contrast, U.S. SMEs that are not convinced e-commerce is suited to their way of doing business and offers no advantages would do the same.

It should also be noted that the barrier related to too many e-commerce standards was significantly negatively associated with all of the potential criteria for the U.S. study. Those SMEs that placed a high level of importance on this barrier tended to place a low level of importance on pressure from customers, competitors, and suppliers as well as reduced costs, improved customer services, access to new customers and markets, and improved marketing as potential incentives to adopt e-commerce.

From the previous, we can conclude that there was virtually no commonality with the barriers that were associated with the criteria across the three locations. For the most part, in the

Swedish and Australian studies, associations were found with barriers that would normally be termed organisational. By comparison, the U.S. owner/managers associated lack of knowledge and too many e-commerce options (technical barriers) with many of the future criteria and in a negative way. It is also interesting to note the security issue was only apparent in the U.S. study and, indeed, rather than being "negatively" associated with future criteria as might be expected—returned positive associations.

Clearly, as already mentioned, government initiatives need to understand and take note of current concerns of SME owner/managers in order to assist them in future uses of e-commerce. Equally clear is the fact that the nature of these concerns differs from location to location and cannot simply be transported in a "global" fashion. The data from the three studies shows that where one location, Sweden, is primarily concerned with "organisational fit," a similar location, the U.S. is more concerned with technical problems in the adoption and use of e-commerce. Therefore, different incentives and approaches are required for Swedish and Australian SMEs when compared to SMEs located in regional areas in the U.S.

# E-Commerce Barriers and Potential Drivers: Key Findings

## Sweden

- There were twelve associations between current barriers and potential drivers to e-commerce adoption in Sweden.
- For the most part, Swedish SMEs are willing to overcome organisational obstacles (related to the suitability of e-commerce) in order to achieve potential benefits from e-commerce.

## Australia

- There were only four associations between current barriers and potential drivers to e-commerce adoption in Australia.
- Like their Swedish counterparts, Australian SMEs would surmount organisational barriers if they faced pressure from competitors, and if e-commerce was likely to reduce their costs, and improve their customer service and marketing.

## USA

- There were eight associations between current barriers and potential drivers to e-commerce adoption in the U.S.

- U.S. SMEs were distinct from Swedish and Australian organisations because they were more likely, for the most part, to overcome technical hurdles such as security and lack of technical knowledge in order to reap the benefits of e-commerce.

# References

Adebanjo, D., Kehoe, D., Galligan, P., & Mahoney, F. (2006). Overcoming the barriers to e-cluster development in a low product complexity business sector. *International Journal of Operations & Production Management, 26*(8), 924-939.

Beck, R., Wigand, R. T., & Konig, W. (2005). The diffusion and efficient use of electronic commerce among small and medium-sized enterprises: An international three-industry survey. *Electronic Markets, 15*(1), 38-52.

Buckley, P., & Montes, S. (2002). *Main street in the digital age: How small and medium businesses are using the tools of the new economy.* Economics and Statistics Administration, Department of Commerce, Washington (U.S.A.).

Dixon, T., Thompson, B., & McAllister, P. (2002). *The value of ICT for SMEs in the UK: A critical review of literature.* Report for the Small Business Service Research Programme, The College of Estate Management, Reading.

Eid, R. (2005). International Internet marketing: A triangulation study of drivers and barriers in the business-to-business context in the United Kingdom. *Market Intelligence & Planning, 23*(3), 266-280.

Elliot, R., & Boshoff, C. (2005). The influence of organisational factors in small tourism businesses on the success of Internet marketing. *Management Dynamics, 14*(3), 44-58.

Kaynak, E., Tatoglu, E., & Kula, V. (2005). An analysis of the factors affecting the adoption of electronic commerce by SMEs: Evidence from an emerging market. *International Marketing Review, 22*(6), 623-640.

Kelliher, F., & Henderson, J. B. (2006). A learning framework for the small business environment. *Journal of European Industrial Training, 30*(7).

Martin, L. M., & Matlay, H. (2001). "Blanket" approaches to promoting ICT in small firms: Some lessons from the DTI ladder adoption model in the UK. *Internet Research: Electronic Networking Applications and Policy, 11*(5), 399-410.

Maskell, P., Eskilinen, H., Hannibalsson, I., Malmberg, A., & Vatne, E. (1998). *Competitiveness, localised learning and regional development: Specialisation and prosperity in small open economies.* London: Routledge.

Miller, H. (2005). Information quality and market share in electronic commerce. *Journal of Services Marketing, 19*(2), 93-102.

OECD. (2002). *Measuring the information economy 2002.* Paris: OECD.

Quayle, M. (2002). E-commerce: The challenge for UK SMEs in the Twenty-First Century. *International Journal of Operations and Production Management, 22*(10), 1148-1161.

Riquelme, H. (2002). Commercial Internet adoption in China: Comparing the experience of small, medium, and large business. *Internet Research: Electronic Networking Applications and Policy, 12*(3), 276-286.

Simpson, M., & Docherty, A. J. (2004). E-commerce adoption support and advice for UK SMEs. *Journal of Small Business and Enterprise Development, 11*(3), 315-328.

Stockdale, R., & Standing, C. (2006). A classification model to support SME e-commerce adoption initiatives. *Journal of Small Business and Enterprise Development, 13*(3), 381-394.

Taylor, M., & Murphy, A. (2004). SMEs and e-business. *Journal of Small Business and Enterprise Development, 11*(3), 280-289.

Vrazalic, L., Stern, D., MacGregor, R., Carlsson, S., & Magnusson, M. (2003). Barriers to e-commerce adoption in SMEs: Underlying factors from a Swedish study. In *Proceedings of the Australian Conference on Information Systems (ACIS)*, Perth.

Webster, B., Walker, E., & Brown, A. (2005). Australian small business participation in training activities. *Education & Training, 47*(8/9), 552-561.

Xanthidis, D., & Nicholas, D. (2004). Evaluating Internet usage and ecommerce growth in Greece. *New Information Perspectives, 56*(6), 356-366.

**Chapter XIII**

# E-Commerce Adoption in Sweden, Australia, and the USA:
## A Comparison

The preceding chapters have examined the adoption of e-commerce as well as the various aspects of e-commerce implementation (criteria, barriers, benefits, and disadvantages) and the business characteristics affecting those aspects (including alliance membership, gender, and the level of education). The key finding in all of these chapters has been the divergence of views about e-commerce that SMEs located in seemingly similar environments have. There appears to be very little agreement amongst SMEs about e-commerce. Different categories of SMEs adopt e-commerce for different reasons, they experience different benefits and they face a diverse set of problems. By now, the reader must be aware that despite the three locations appearing to match in terms of infrastructure and OECD rating, the findings from each location are very dissimilar. To complete our analysis and paint a complete picture of e-commerce adoption in the three different locations, in this chapter we will statistically compare the actual ratings of each of the four aspects of e-commerce adoption (criteria, barriers, benefits, and disadvantages) between Sweden, Australia, and the U.S. In order to do this, a series of paired two-tailed t-tests were applied to the data to determine the differences in ratings of the four aspects of adoption. As previously noted, due to insufficient responses, it is not possible to examine the benefits or disadvantages for the U.S. sample.

# A Comparison of E-Commerce Criteria

Tables 1 to 3 provide the comparisons of ratings e-commerce adoption criteria in Sweden/Australia, Sweden/U.S., and Australia/U.S. respectively.

A comparison of Tables 1, 2, and 3 shows that only three of the fourteen criteria are rated similarly (i.e., there are no significant differences between the three locations). These are improved customer services, demand/pressure from competition, and shorter lead time/reduced stock. The latter two criteria were considered by all three respondent locations as being unimportant, while the former was considered as important by all respondent locations.

Several studies (Reimenschneider & Mykytyn, 2000; Power & Sohal, 2002) have suggested that many SMEs nominate "Demand and/or pressure from customers" as one of the primary reasons for adopting e-commerce into their day-to-day activities. The data in Tables 1 to 3 shows that this driver was considered moderately important by the U.S. respondents and unimportant by the Swedish respondents, while the Australian respondents were equivocal regarding its importance as a driver for e-commerce adoption. Tables 1 and 2 show that there were significant differences ($p = .018$ and $p = .000$ respectively) between the Swedish and Australian respondents and the Swedish and U.S. respondents. This would suggest that decisions concerning e-commerce adoption are often affected by "external businesses or agencies" in U.S. SMEs, while decisions concerning adoption are more often "internally generated" in Sweden and Australia.

Tables 1 to 3 also show that the criterion "Demand/pressure from suppliers" was considered very unimportant by both the Swedish and Australian respondents, while it was considered moderately important by the U.S. respondents. Tables 2 and 3 show that there were significant differences ($p = .000$ and $p = .002$ respectively) between U.S. and Swedish and U.S.

*Table 1. Paired two-tailed t-test for the rating of importance of criteria (Sweden/Australia)*

| N Sweden = 183<br>N Australia = 25 | Mean Sweden | Mean Australia | t value | significance |
|---|---|---|---|---|
| Demand and/or pressure from customers. | 1.94 | 2.68 | -2.386 | .018 |
| Pressure from competition. | 2.22 | 2.68 | -1.417 | .158 |
| Demand and/or pressure from suppliers. | 1.63 | 1.76 | -.441 | .660 |
| To reduce costs. | 2.96 | 3.48 | -1.452 | .148 |
| To improve customer service. | 3.58 | 3.68 | -.281 | .779 |
| To shorten lead time/reduce stock levels. | 2.48 | 2.60 | -.324 | .746 |
| To increase sales. | 2.82 | 3.56 | -2.022 | .044 |
| To improve internal efficiency. | 3.53 | 3.76 | -.685 | .494 |
| To strengthen relations with business partners. | 2.80 | 1.00 | 5.533 | .000 |
| The possibility of reaching new customers/markets | 2.81 | 3.48 | -1.800 | .073 |
| To improve our competitiveness. | 3.21 | 3.56 | -.951 | .343 |
| We were offered external support to adopt e-commerce. | 1.29 | 1.52 | -.985 | .326 |
| To improve our marketing. | 2.84 | 3.40 | -1.490 | .138 |
| To improve control. | 2.53 | 3.36 | -2.406 | .017 |

*Table 2. Paired two-tailed t-test for the rating of importance of criteria (Sweden/USA)*

| N Sweden = 183<br>N U.S.A. = 63 | Mean Sweden | Mean U.S.A. | t value | significance |
|---|---|---|---|---|
| Demand and/or pressure from customers. | 1.94 | 3.20 | -5.960 | .000 |
| Pressure from competition. | 2.22 | 2.07 | .655 | .513 |
| Demand and/or pressure from suppliers. | 1.63 | 2.91 | -6.309 | .000 |
| To reduce costs. | 2.96 | 1.58 | 5.817 | .000 |
| To improve customer service. | 3.58 | 3.56 | .098 | .922 |
| To shorten lead time/reduce stock levels. | 2.48 | 2.26 | .883 | .378 |
| To increase sales. | 2.82 | 2.16 | 2.647 | .009 |
| To improve internal efficiency. | 3.53 | 1.95 | 6.874 | .000 |
| To strengthen relations with business partners. | 2.80 | 2.12 | 2.876 | .004 |
| The possibility of reaching new customers/markets. | 2.81 | 1.88 | 3.716 | .000 |
| To improve our competitiveness. | 3.21 | 2.25 | 3.722 | .000 |
| We were offered external support to adopt e-commerce. | 1.29 | 4.05 | -17.961 | .000 |
| To improve our marketing. | 2.84 | 3.89 | -4.190 | .000 |
| To improve control. | 2.53 | 4.16 | -7.219 | .000 |

*Table 3. Paired two-tailed t-test for the rating of importance of criteria (Australia/USA)*

| N Australia = 25<br>N U.S.A. = 63 | Mean Australia | Mean U.S.A. | t value | significance |
|---|---|---|---|---|
| Demand and/or pressure from customers. | 2.68 | 3.20 | -1.582 | .118 |
| Pressure from competition. | 2.68 | 2.07 | 1.728 | .088 |
| Demand and/or pressure from suppliers. | 1.76 | 2.91 | -3.141 | .002 |
| To reduce costs. | 3.48 | 1.58 | 5.824 | .000 |
| To improve customer service. | 3.68 | 3.56 | .459 | .648 |
| To shorten lead time/reduce stock levels. | 2.60 | 2.26 | 1.015 | .313 |
| To increase sales. | 3.56 | 2.16 | 4.037 | .000 |
| To improve internal efficiency. | 3.76 | 1.95 | 5.644 | .000 |
| To strengthen relations with business partners. | 1.00 | 2.12 | -3.701 | .000 |
| The possibility of reaching new customers/markets. | 3.48 | 1.88 | 4.578 | .000 |
| To improve our competitiveness. | 3.56 | 2.25 | 3.582 | .001 |
| We were offered external support to adopt e-commerce. | 1.52 | 4.05 | -9.619 | .000 |
| To improve our marketing. | 3.40 | 3.89 | -1.609 | .111 |
| To improve control. | 3.36 | 4.16 | -1.582 | .118 |

and Australian respondents. A number of studies (Poon & Strom, 1997; Raisch, 2001) have suggested that pressure from suppliers is a strong motivator for many SMEs adopting and using e-commerce. Our results suggest that this may be dependent on the location of the SMEs being investigated.

The results in Tables.1 to 3 concerning the criterion "Reduced costs" are particularly interesting. Studies by Abell and Lim (1996), Raisch (2001), and Auger and Gallaugher (1997) have suggested that one of the strongest motivators for adoption of e-commerce is the reduction of costs within the business. The findings here show that Australian respondents rated this criterion as very important, thus supporting these earlier results. By comparison, however, the Swedish respondents placed little importance on reducing costs while the U.S. respondents thought that it was very unimportant.

One of the fundamental incentives for e-commerce adoption, both in the government literature and academic findings is the ability to increase sales. An examination of the data in Tables 1 to 3 shows that while the Australian respondents appear to recognize this as a reason for adoption, the U.S. and Swedish respondents are, at best, equivocal regarding the importance of increasing their volume of sales. Indeed, the comparison of the Australian and Swedish responses was moderately significant (p = .009), while the comparison with the U.S. responses was very high (p = .000).

Porter (2001) suggested that one of the bi-products of e-commerce adoption was the improvement to internal efficiency of the organisation. An examination of Tables 1 to 3 shows that both the Swedish and Australian respondents agreed and considered this criterion as very important (ratings 3.53 and 3.76 respectively). By comparison, the U.S. respondents considered it unimportant (rating it 1.95).

Other studies (Evans & Wurster, 1997; Poon & Swatman, 1997; Raymond, 2001) have suggested that many SMEs adopt e-commerce in an effort to strengthen relations with business partners. While the Swedish and U.S. respondents see some merit in strengthening relations with business partners, the Australian respondents rated this as extremely unimportant. A recent study (MacGregor, 2004) suggested that unlike many European cultures, Australian SME owner/managers are strongly independent regarding strengthening of relations with a business partner as a disincentive. This appears to be the case in this study.

The ability to reach new customers and markets is another important incentive to implement e-commerce. While the Australian respondents appear to recognize this as a good reason for adoption (mean rating 3.48), the U.S. respondents considered this as an unimportant reason (mean rating 1.88).

A number of studies (Raymond, 2001; Reimenschneider et al., 2000; Turban, Lee, King, & Chung, 2000) have suggested that SMEs adopt e-commerce to improve their competitiveness. An examination of Tables 1 to 3 show that while the Swedish and Australian respondents considered this criterion important, the U.S. respondents considered it relatively unimportant. Indeed, a comparison between Swedish and U.S. and Australian and U.S. respondents produced highly significant differences in the ratings (p = .000 and p = .001 respectively).

The criterion, the availability of external support, provides some interesting comparisons. While the Swedish and Australian respondents considered it very unimportant (mean rating of 1.29 and 1.52 respectively), the U.S. respondents considered this to be of high importance (mean rating 4.05) as a reason for adopting e-commerce.

*Table 4. Summary of e-commerce adoption criteria in Sweden, Australia, and the USA*

|  | Sweden | Australia | USA |
|---|---|---|---|
| Demand and/or pressure from customers. | ✗ | ? | ✓ |
| Pressure from competition. | ✗ | ✗ | ✗ |
| Demand and/or pressure from suppliers. | ✗ | ✗ | ? |
| To reduce costs. | ? | ✓ | ✗ |
| To improve customer service. | ✓ | ✓ | ✓ |
| To shorten lead time/reduce stock levels. | ✗ | ✗ | ✗ |
| To increase sales. | ? | ✓ | ✗ |
| To improve internal efficiency. | ✓ | ✓ | ✗ |
| To strengthen relations with business partners. | ? | ✗ | ✗ |
| The possibility of reaching new customers/markets. | ? | ✓ | ✗ |
| To improve our competitiveness. | ✓ | ✓ | ✗ |
| We were offered external support to adopt e-commerce. | ✗ | ✗ | ✓ |
| To improve our marketing. | ? | ✓ | ✓ |
| To improve control. | ✗ | ✓ | ✓ |

✓ Rated important

✗ Rated unimportant

? Neutral

The criterion, improvement to marketing, was considered "similar" (i.e., no significant differences) by both the Swedish and Australian respondents. By comparison, the U.S. respondents considered this criterion to be of some importance. Indeed, there was a highly significant difference ($p = .000$) between the U.S. responses and the Swedish responses. Of interest is the fact that while the U.S. respondents considered this criterion to be of importance, they did not consider similar criteria (increase sales, reaching new customers/markets, or improve competitiveness) as being important.

The final criterion is improving control inside the organisation. An examination of the data in Tables 1 to 3 shows that the Swedish respondents were, at best, equivocal regarding the importance of improving control. By comparison, the Australian thought that this criterion was important, while the U.S. respondents thought that it was very important.

A summary of these findings is provided in Table 4. The criteria, which showed no significant differences are highlighted in bold italics.

# A Comparison of E-Commerce Barriers

Tables 5 to 7 provide the comparisons of ratings e-commerce adoption barriers in Sweden/Australia, Sweden/U.S.A., and Australia/U.S.A. respectively.

Before we examine the data in Tables.5 to.7 as individual barriers, one interesting finding is that in all cases, the rating of barriers by the Swedish respondents is lower than either the Australian or U.S. respondents. One possible explanation is the interaction between SMEs, educational institutions, and government agencies in Sweden, which appears to be far more concentrated than in countries such as Australia or the U.S.A.. Recent studies (Barry, Berg, & Chandler, 2003; Dobers & Strannegard, 2001; Klofsten, 2000; MacGregor, 2004) have pointed to the strong links between SMEs, government, and education institutions in Sweden. These links, which involve educational courses, entrepreneurial initiatives, and technology proliferation, it is argued, have not only resulted in a higher uptake of e-commerce technology in regional SMEs, but a reduction in the perception of barriers to the adoption and use of e-commerce.

A number of recent studies in Hong Kong (Kendall & Kendall, 2001), New Zealand (Abell et al., 1996), UK (Eid, Trueman, & Ahmed, 2002), U.S. (Tambini, 1999), and Greece (Hadji-monolis, 1999) have suggested that the barrier "E-commerce doesn't fit with products/services" is one that often results in SMEs deciding against the adoption and use of the technology. An examination of Tables 5 to 7 shows that it is important to both the Australian and U.S. respondents (mean = 3.26 and 3.91 respectively), while is of little importance as a barrier to the Swedish respondents. Indeed, the differences in the means of ratings of importance of this criterion between the Swedish and Australian and Swedish and U.S. respondents is highly statistically significant (p = .014 and p = .000 respectively).

*Table 5. Paired two-tailed t-test for the rating of importance of barriers (Sweden/Australia)*

| N Sweden = 130<br>N Australia = 135 | Mean Sweden | Mean Australia | t value | significance |
|---|---|---|---|---|
| E-commerce is not suited to our products/services. | 2.72 | 3.26 | -2.481 | .014 |
| E-commerce is not suited to our way of doing business. | 2.61 | 3.42 | -3.865 | .000 |
| E-commerce is not suited to the ways our clients do business. | 2.55 | 3.45 | -3.442 | .001 |
| E-commerce does not offer any advantages to our organisation. | 2.35 | 3.29 | -4.628 | .000 |
| We do not have the technical knowledge in the organisation to implement e-commerce. | 2.57 | 3.10 | -2.433 | .016 |
| E-commerce is too complicated to implement. | 1.97 | 3.03 | -5.309 | .000 |
| E-commerce is not secure. | 2.08 | 2.84 | -3.954 | .000 |
| The financial investment required to implement e-commerce is too high. | 2.23 | 2.90 | -3.217 | .001 |
| We do not have time to implement e-commerce. | 2.46 | 3.03 | -2.691 | .008 |
| It is difficult to choose the most suitable e-commerce standard with so many different options available. | 2.28 | 2.68 | -1.905 | .058 |

*Table 6. Paired two-tailed t-test for the rating of importance of barriers (Sweden/USA)*

| N Sweden = 130<br>N U.S.A. = 53 | Mean Sweden | Mean U.S.A. | t value | significance |
|---|---|---|---|---|
| E-commerce is not suited to our products/services. | 2.72 | 3.91 | -4.127 | .000 |
| E-commerce is not suited to our way of doing business. | 2.61 | 3.77 | -3.935 | .000 |
| E-commerce is not suited to the ways our clients do business. | 2.55 | 3.51 | -3.261 | .001 |
| E-commerce does not offer any advantages to our organisation. | 2.35 | 3.04 | -2.485 | .014 |
| We do not have the technical knowledge in the organisation to implement e-commerce. | 2.57 | 3.43 | -3.007 | .003 |
| E-commerce is too complicated to implement. | 1.97 | 3.47 | -5.865 | .000 |
| E-commerce is not secure. | 2.08 | 3.20 | -4.334 | .000 |
| The financial investment required to implement e-commerce is too high. | 2.23 | 3.21 | -3.606 | .000 |
| We do not have time to implement e-commerce. | 2.46 | 2.96 | -1.775 | .078 |
| It is difficult to choose the most suitable e-commerce standard with so many different options available. | 2.28 | 2.98 | -2.457 | .015 |

*Table 7. Paired two-tailed t-test for the rating of importance of barriers (Australia/USA)*

| N Australia = 135<br>N U.S.A. = 53 | Mean Australia | Mean U.S.A. | t value | significance |
|---|---|---|---|---|
| E-commerce is not suited to our products/services. | 3.26 | 3.91 | -2.638 | .009 |
| E-commerce is not suited to our way of doing business. | 3.42 | 3.77 | -1.434 | .153 |
| E-commerce is not suited to the ways our clients do business. | 3.45 | 3.51 | -.163 | .870 |
| E-commerce does not offer any advantages to our organisation. | 3.29 | 3.04 | 1.020 | .309 |
| We do not have the technical knowledge in the organisation to implement e-commerce. | 3.10 | 3.43 | -1.218 | .225 |
| E-commerce is too complicated to implement. | 3.03 | 3.47 | -1.692 | .092 |
| E-commerce is not secure. | 2.84 | 3.20 | -1.486 | .139 |
| The financial investment required to implement e-commerce is too high. | 2.90 | 3.21 | -1.234 | .219 |
| We do not have time to implement e-commerce. | 3.03 | 2.96 | .285 | .776 |
| It is difficult to choose the most suitable e-commerce standard with so many different options available. | 2.68 | 2.98 | -1.177 | .241 |

Other studies (Bakos & Brynjolfsson, 2000; Farhoomand, Tuunainen, & Yee, 2000; Hadjimonolis, 1999; Mehrtens, Cragg, & Mills, 2001; Sawhney & Zabin, 2002) have shown that the barrier "E-commerce doesn't fit with the way we do business," is also nominated by owner/managers as a reason for deciding against the adoption of e-commerce. Again, an examination of Tables 5 to 7 shows that is important to both the Australian and U.S. respondents (mean = 3.42 and 3.77 respectively), while is of little importance as a barrier to the Swedish respondents (mean = 2.61). This would tend to support the notion that the strong links between SMEs, government and education institutions in Sweden may have reduced the impact of this as a barrier to the Swedish respondents.

Studies by Bakos et al. (2000), Kulmala et al. (2002), and Hadjimonolis (1999) have put forward the notion that SME owner/managers believe that their customers prefer face-to-face business dealings rather than buying and selling over the Internet. An examination of the Australian and U.S. data in Tables 5 to 7 would suggest that this notion applies. Again, the data for the Swedish respondents (mean = 2.55) implies that this is less of a problem to be faced by Swedish owner/managers.

A number of recent studies in the U.S. (Chau & Hui, 2001; Lee & Runge, 2001) and Greece (Hadjimonolis, 1999) have suggested that despite government involvement and incentives, many SME owner/managers see little advantage to their business in adopting e-commerce. For the Australian and U.S. respondents, this has been an important consideration in their decision-making against the adoption of e-commerce (mean = 3.29 and 3.04 respectively).

Farhoomand et al. (2000) and Mirchandani and Motwani (2001) suggested that one of the biggest problems facing the SME community was the lack of technical know-how particularly where e-commerce adoption and use was concerned. Again, it is interesting to note that while the Swedish respondents rated these as unimportant (means = 2.57 and 1.97), both the

*Table 8. Summary of e-commerce adoption barriers in Sweden, Australia, and the USA*

| | Sweden | Australia | U.S.A. |
|---|---|---|---|
| E-commerce is not suited to our products/services. | ? | ✓ | ✓ |
| E-commerce is not suited to our way of doing business. | × | ✓ | ✓ |
| E-commerce is not suited to the ways our clients do business. | × | ✓ | ✓ |
| E-commerce does not offer any advantages to our organisation. | × | ✓ | ? |
| We do not have the technical knowledge in the organisation to implement e-commerce. | × | ? | ✓ |
| E-commerce is too complicated to implement. | × | ? | ✓ |
| E-commerce is not secure. | × | ? | ✓ |
| The financial investment required to implement e-commerce is too high. | × | ? | ✓ |
| We do not have time to implement e-commerce. | × | ? | ? |
| It is difficult to choose the most suitable e-commerce standard with so many different options available. | × | ? | ? |

✓ Rated important

× Rated unimportant

? Neutral

Australian (means 3.10 and 3.03) and U.S. respondents (means 3.43 and 3.47) considered these major drawbacks to the adoption and use of e-commerce.

The problems of security with e-commerce have received substantial media hype. Studies by Aldridge, White, and Forcht (1997), Purao and Campbell (1998), Oxley and Yeung (2001), and Reimenschneider et al. (2001) have suggested that for the SME owner/managers, the fear of security failure has often prevented the adoption of IT, particularly e-commerce. An examination of the data in Tables 5 to 7 shows that while there is little real concern by the Swedish or Australian respondents, the problems of security still presents a major stumbling block for the U.S. regional respondents.

Other barriers to e-commerce include lack of finance (see Hadjimonolis, 1999; Purao et al., 1998; Ratnasingam, 2000; Reimenschneider et al., 2001) and lack of time (see MacGregor et al., 2004). Tables 5 to 7 show that the U.S. respondents are most concerned with lack of available finance to adopt and use e-commerce, while it is the Australian respondents that are most concerned with the lack of adequate time to develop, implement, and use e-commerce.

A summary of these findings is provided in Table 8.

# A Comparison of E-Commerce Benefits

Table 9 provides a comparison of the Swedish and Australian ratings of benefits derived from e-commerce adoption.

*Table 9. Paired two-tailed t-test for the rating of importance of benefits (Sweden/Australia)*

| | Mean Sweden | N Sweden | Mean Australia | N Australia | t value | significance |
|---|---|---|---|---|---|---|
| Reduced our administration costs. | 2.74 | 183 | 3.20 | 25 | -1.342 | .181 |
| Reduced our production costs. | 2.67 | 183 | 2.12 | 25 | .810 | .419 |
| Reduced our lead time. | 2.08 | 183 | 2.24 | 25 | -.496 | .621 |
| Reduced our stock levels. | 2.71 | 183 | 2.32 | 25 | 1.070 | .286 |
| Lead to increased sales. | 1.93 | 183 | 1.84 | 25 | .264 | .792 |
| Increased our internal efficiency. | 2.40 | 183 | 2.72 | 25 | -.977 | .329 |
| Improved our relations with business partners. | 3.14 | 183 | 3.64 | 25 | -1.475 | .142 |
| Gave us access to new customers and markets. | 2.69 | 183 | 1.00 | 25 | 6.143 | .000 |
| Improved our competitiveness. | 2.45 | 183 | 2.88 | 25 | -1.220 | .224 |
| Improved the quality of information in our organisation. | 1.93 | 183 | 3.28 | 25 | -4.317 | .000 |

Only two benefits showed any statistically significant differences between the Swedish and Australian respondents. While the Swedish respondents saw some improvement in terms of access to new customers and markets, the Australian respondents, unanimously found no changes. By comparison, while the Swedish respondents saw little real change in terms of improvement to the quality of their information, the Australian respondents found this to be a quite important benefit from the adoption and use of e-commerce. One possible explanation for the lower than expected results for the Swedish respondents in terms of improving the quality of information might be that as many had been involved in government funded educational initiatives (see Barry et al., 2003; Dobers et al., 2001; Klofsten, 2000; MacGregor, 2004), the quality of information may not have been directly attributed to the adoption of e-commerce.

## A Comparison of E-Commerce Disadvantages

Table 10 provides the comparison of the ratings of disadvantages incurred through the adoption of e-commerce between the Swedish and Australian respondents.

Two disadvantages, "Security risks" and "Dependence on e-commerce" showed a statistically significant difference in the perception of importance between the Australian and Swedish respondents. In both cases, while the Swedish respondents considered these as very unimportant, the Australian respondents perceived these disadvantages as important (mean = 3.40 and 3.12). Increased workload also showed a statistically significant difference, however, both Swedish and Australian SMEs gave this disadvantage a low rating. The other disadvantages did not show a statistically significant differences.

*Table 10. Paired two-tailed t-test for the rating of importance of disadvantages (Sweden/Australia)*

|  | Mean Sweden | N Sweden | Mean Australia | N Australia | t value | significance |
|---|---|---|---|---|---|---|
| Deteriorated relations with our business partners. | 1.22 | 183 | * | * | * | * |
| Increased costs. | 1.81 | 183 | 2.20 | 25 | -1.376 | .170 |
| Increased the computer maintenance required. | 2.08 | 183 | 1.68 | 25 | 1.368 | .173 |
| Doubled the amount of work. | 1.78 | 183 | 1.20 | 25 | 2.232 | .027 |
| Reduced the flexibility of the business processes. | 1.67 | 183 | 1.96 | 25 | -1.094 | .275 |
| Raised security concerns. | 1.16 | 183 | 3.40 | 25 | -10.562 | .000 |
| Made us increasingly dependent on this technology. | 1.30 | 183 | 3.12 | 25 | -8.158 | .000 |

*Note: * Insufficient data*

# Comparison of Three Locations: Implications

Once again, we see some distinct and divergent differences between the three locations in relation to e-commerce criteria, barriers, benefits, and disadvantages. The implications of this are clear: the SME sector is not homogeneous and tailored programs must be developed in different locations (and indeed in different types of SMEs depending on their size, sector, market focus, etc.) if we are to promote and encourage the use of e-commerce in regional areas. The results of this study are an unambiguous message to government organisations seeking to develop regional areas through SMEs and e-commerce, to invest in well-structured, localised, and customised technology programs in partnership with commercial providers of e-commerce solutions. Only through adapted and targeted partnerships between the SME community, local government organisations, and e-commerce software developers will we begin to see an improvement in e-commerce use. This is particularly relevant in the Australian context where the adoption rates remain alarmingly low.

# Comparison of Three Locations: Key Findings

## Criteria

- Only three of the fourteen criteria are rated similarly. These are "Improvement to customer service," "Pressure from competition," and "Shorter lead time and reduced stock."
- "Demand and/or pressure from customers" was rated as moderately important by the U.S. respondents and unimportant by the Swedish respondents, while the Australian respondents were equivocal regarding its importance.
- "Pressure from suppliers" was considered very unimportant by both the Swedish and Australian respondents and moderately important by the U.S. respondents.
- Australian respondents rated "Reduced costs" as very important. By comparison, however, the Swedish respondents placed little importance on reducing costs while the U.S. respondents thought that it was very unimportant.
- While the Australian respondents recognize "Increased sales" as a driver for adoption, the U.S. and Swedish respondents are, at best, equivocal regarding the importance of increasing their volume of sales.
- Both the Swedish and Australian respondents agreed and considered "Improvements to internal efficiency" as very important. By comparison, the U.S. respondents considered it unimportant.
- While the Swedish and U.S. respondents see some merit in strengthening relations with business partners as a driver, the Australian respondents rated this as extremely unimportant.
- Australian respondents considered reaching new markets and customers as a good reason for adoption, but the U.S. respondents considered this as an unimportant reason.

- Swedish and Australian respondents considered "Improved competitiveness" as important, but the U.S. respondents considered it relatively unimportant.
- The availability of external support was thought to be very unimportant by the Swedish and Australian respondents. In contrast, the U.S. respondents considered this to be of high importance as a reason for adopting e-commerce.
- The criterion, improvement to marketing was considered "similar" by both the Swedish and Australian respondents. By comparison, the U.S. respondents considered this criterion to be of some importance.
- Swedish SMEs were, at best, equivocal regarding the importance of improving internal controls. By comparison, the Australians thought that this criterion was important, while the U.S. respondents thought that it was very important.

## Barriers

- The rating of barriers by the Swedish respondents is lower than either the Australian or U.S. respondents.
- Both the Australian and U.S. respondents rated unsuitability of e-commerce to their products/services, their customers and the business itself highly as barriers, while these were of little importance to the Swedish respondents.
- For the Australian and U.S. respondents, lack of advantages has been an important consideration in their decision making to decide against the adoption of e-commerce.
- Swedish respondents rated lack of technical skills as unimportant, but both the Australian and U.S. respondents considered these major drawbacks to the adoption and use of e-commerce.
- There is little real concern by the Swedish or Australian respondents about security. However, this still presents a major stumbling block for the U.S. regional respondents.
- U.S. respondents are most concerned with lack of available finance to adopt and use e-commerce, while it is the Australian respondents that are most concerned with the lack of adequate time to develop, implement, and use e-commerce.

## Benefits

- Only two benefits showed any statistically significant differences between the Swedish and Australian respondents: Improvement in terms of new customers and markets (rated highly in Sweden) and in terms of quality of information (rated highly in Australia).

## Disadvantages

- Three disadvantages showed statistically significant differences. Of these, the Swedish SMEs considered "Security risks" and "Dependence on e-commerce" as very unimportant, while the Australian respondents perceived these disadvantages as important. The third disadvantage (doubling of workload) was given a low rating by both the Swedish and the Australian SMEs.

# References

Abell, W., & Lim, L. (1996). Business use of the Internet in New Zealand: An exploratory study. In *Proceedings of AUSWeb 96*. Retrieved from http//www.scu.edu.au/sponsored/ausweb96

Aldridge, A., White, M., & Forcht, K. (1997). Security considerations of doing business via the Internet: Cautions to be considered. *Internet Research-Electronic Networking Applications and Policy, 7*(1), 9-15.

Auger, P., & Gallaugher, J. M. (1997). Factors affecting adoption of an Internet-based sales presence for small businesses. *The Information Society, 13*(1), 55-74.

Bakos, Y., & Brynjolfsson, E. (2000). Bundling and competition on the Internet. *Marketing Science, 19*(1), 63-82.

Barry, J., Berg, E., & Chandler, J. (2003). Managing intellectual labour in Sweden and England. *Cross Cultural Management, 10*(3), 3-22.

Dobers, P., & Strannegard, L. (2001). Loveable networks—A story of affection, attraction, and treachery. *Journal of Organisational Change Management, 14*(1), 28-49.

Chau, P. Y. K., & Hui, K. L. (2001). Determinants of small business EDI adoption: An empirical investigation. *Journal of Organisational Computing and Electronic Commerce, 11*(4), 229-252.

Eid, R., Trueman, M., & Ahmed, A. M. (2002). A cross-industry review of B2B critical success factors. *Internet Research: Electronic Networking Applications and Policy, 12*(2), 110-123.

Evans, P. B., & Wurster, T. S. (1997). Strategy and the new economics of information. *Harvard Business Review*, Sept-Oct, 70-82.

Farhoomand, A. F., Tuunainen, V. K., & Yee, L. W. (2000). Barriers to global electronic commerce: A cross-country study of Hong Kong and Finland. *Journal of Organisational Computing and Electronic Commerce, 10*(1), 23-48.

Hadjimonolis A. (1999) Barriers to innovation for smes in a small less developed country (Cyprus). *Technovation, 19*(9), 561 – 570.

Kendall, J. E., & Kendall, K. E. (2001). A paradoxically peaceful coexistence between commerce and ecommerce. *Journal of Information Technology, Theory, and Application, 3*(4), 1-6.

Klofsten, M (2000). Training entrepreneurship at universities: A Swedish case. *Journal of European Industrial Training, 24*(6), 337-344.

Kulmala H. I., Paranko J. & Uusi-Rauva E. (2002). The role of cost management in network relationships. *International Journal of Production Economics, 79*(1), 33 - 43.

Lee, J., & Runge, J. (2001). Adoption of information technology in small business: Testing drivers of adoption for entrepreneurs. *Journal of Computer Information Systems*, *42*(1), 44-57.

MacGregor, R. C. (2004). The role of formal networks in the ongoing use of electronic commerce technology in regional small business. *Journal of Electronic Commerce in Organisations*, *2*(1), 1-14.

Mehrtens, J., Cragg, P. B., & Mills, A. M. (2001). A model of Internet adoption by SMEs. *Information and Management*, *39*, 165-176.

Mirchandani, D. A., & Motwani, J. (2001). Understanding small business electronic commerce adoption: An empirical analysis. *Journal of Computer Information Systems*, *41*(3), 70-73.

Oxley, J. E., & Yeung, B. (2001). E-commerce readiness: Institutional environment and international competitiveness. *Journal of International Business Studies*, *32*(4), 705-723.

Poon, S., & Strom, J. (1997). Small business use of the Internet: Some realities. In *Proceedings of the Association for Information Systems Americas Conference*, Indianapolis, IN.

Poon, S., & Swatman, P. (1997). The Internet for Small businesses: An enabling infrastructure. In *Proceedings of the 5th Internet Society Conference* (pp. 221-231).

Porter, M. (2001, March). Strategy and the Internet. *Harvard Business Review*, 63-78.

Power, D. J., & Sohal, A. S. (2002). Implementation and U.S.A.ge of electronic commerce in managing the supply chain: A comparative study of ten Australian companies. *Benchmarking: An International Journal*, *9*(2), 190-208.

Purao, S., & Campbell, B. (1998). Critical concerns for small business electronic commerce: Some reflections based on interviews of small business owners. In *Proceedings of the Association for Information Systems Americas Conference*, Baltimore (pp. 325-327).

Raisch, W. D. (2001). *The e-marketplace: Strategies for success in B2B*. New York: McGraw-Hill.

Ratnasingham, P. (2000). The influence of power on trading partners in electronic commerce. *Internet Research*, *10*(1), 56-62.

Raymond, L. (2001). Determinants of Web site implementation in small business. *Internet Research: Electronic Network Applications and Policy*, *11*(5), 411-422.

Reimenschneider, C. K., & McKinney, V. R. (2001). Assessing beliefs in small business adopters and non-adopters of Web-based e-commerce. *Journal of Computer Information Systems*, *42*(2), 101-107.

Reimenschneider, C. K., & Mykytyn, P. P. Jr. (2000). What small business executives have learned about managing information technology. *Information & Management*, *37*, 257-267.

Sawhney, M., & Zabin, J. (2002). Managing and measuring relational equity in the network economy. *Journal of the Academy of Marketing Science*, *30*(4), 313-332.

Tambini, A. M. (1999). E-shoppers demand e-service. *Discount Store News, 11*(38).

Turban, E., Lee, J., King, D., & Chung, H. (2000). *Electronic commerce: A managerial perspective*. NJ: Prentice Hall.

## Chapter XIV

# Implications for E-Commerce Adoption by SMEs:
## How Can These Results Help with E-Commerce Adoption by SMEs?

The preceding chapters have examined the adoption of e-commerce in SMEs located in regional areas of three developed countries—Sweden, Australia, and the U.S. We have presented detailed empirical evidence of the effects of business characteristics on e-commerce adoption, as well as the underlying reasons for implementing e-commerce or failing to do so. For those SMEs that have pursued this technology, we have derived the key benefits and disadvantages. This chapter will summarise the findings on a macro level (country by country and by the various aspects of e-commerce), draw conclusions, and discuss the implications of these findings.

Although this book is primarily aimed at researchers in the field since it is an attempt to provide a broader view of e-commerce adoption in the context of the studies that have been done to date, it also serves as a useful reference guide for government organisations, which are involved in promoting e-commerce adoption as well as e-commerce solution providers. Most importantly, however, we have not focused in detail on the technical issues surrounding the introduction and use of e-commerce. Instead of examining protocols, hardware and Internet security issues, we have concentrated on the organisational issues involved in e-commerce implementation.

More than just a technology, e-commerce represents a fundamental shift in the way SMEs do business. It implies a new set of business processes, as well as shift from operations to corporate strategy. Taking into account the characteristics of the SME sector, which were presented in Chapter I's Table 1, it becomes obvious why this shift is a major challenge for the SME sector. With limited resources, little time, small numbers of employees, and short-range planning, SMEs are not always in a position to take advantage of the opportunities created by the online environment. As we have seen in the results from the study presented here, this is particularly true of SMEs in regional areas where even simple e-commerce requirements such as the availability of a broadband connection are not always straightforward. It, therefore, becomes important to develop an understanding of the issues that regional SMEs face so that adequate support can be provided to encourage higher rates of participation by SMEs in the Internet economy. The present chapter aims to assist by accentuating the key results, which may prove beneficial in this endeavour.

The results of the research will be summarised by discussing each country separately in order to extract the major findings. In doing this, we will also discuss the implications of these findings for government organisations, in particular.

# E-Commerce in Sweden

Swedish regional SMEs shy away from e-commerce for two main reasons: the unsuitability of the technology to their business and the complexity of implementing e-commerce. Their main concern is with the latter. Some of the difficulties associated with e-commerce implementation include a lack of technical knowledge, security concerns, not enough time, and insufficient financial resources. This suggests that Swedish SMEs would benefit from technical and financial support, as well as support that will reduce the administrative load and allow them to spend more time on e-commerce. Our findings show that, for the most part, Swedish regional SMEs are willing to overcome organisational barriers (related to the suitability of e-commerce); however, the technical barriers may pose a significant hindrance. Clearly, Swedish SMEs are aware of the inherent value of e-commerce, but require the relevant skills and resources to implement it. With an adoption rate of more than 50%, this is an obstacle they seem to be overcoming. This can also be seen in the low ratings that Swedish SMEs gave to e-commerce barriers overall.

We also found that SMEs, which were members of an alliance rated the unsuitability and lack of perceived benefits as stronger barriers than non-members. This may suggest that belong to an alliance could dampen some of the technical difficulties. By contrast, gender did not play a role in e-commerce barriers in Sweden, as both males and females rated barriers similarly. There was only a very minor influence by the level of education of the CEO with high school or trade qualified SME owners/managers reporting the high financial investment as a barrier of some importance.

**Implications**

Swedish regional SMEs appear to be concerned by the technical aspects of e-commerce implementation, although only to some extent. To promote e-commerce adoption, programs should focus on providing practical support in the form of technical skills and financial incentives.

The number of adopters in Sweden is significantly higher than in Australia. This suggests that there is a fertile environment for e-commerce created through support groups, government programs, as well as the general economy. A prime example is the recently launched "Portalen Handelsplats Wemland," which is a portal for SMEs in the Varmland region providing practical e-commerce advice and information. The portal is described in more detail by Peterson and Borg (2005). It is through initiatives such as these that SMEs in Sweden have been able to implement e-commerce successfully and reap the benefits.

The key criteria that prompted these SMEs to adopt e-commerce are improved marketing and business relationships, and more streamlined internal operations. However, the size and market focus of the SME did play a role in this with larger SMEs trading at a local or regional level showing some inclination to bow to external pressures from competitors or suppliers. To some extent, the potential advantages were achieved in the form of improved competitiveness, efficiency and also lower inventory costs. However, at the same time, the SMEs reported more pressure on their resources as well as changes to the way they do business as a result. Although a number of SMEs in Sweden were members of an alliance, there were no differences between members and non-members in relation to e-commerce drivers or the benefits achieved. However, non-members did report less flexibility as a bigger problem than non-members.

Males and females also differed on the reasons why they adopted e-commerce and the subsequent benefits, with men rating most of the adoption criteria and benefits as being more important. Where men were more concerned about implementing e-commerce to develop their sales and marketing, females wanted to build relationships with business partners. As a result, male CEOs reported more benefits related to financial issues such as reduced costs, while female CEOs did not distinguish between any benefits in particular.

Regardless of the level of education of the CEO, achieving competitiveness was a priority benefit for all SME owners/managers. In most cases, SMEs in Sweden experienced the benefits expected to achieve. Those businesses, which set out to lower costs, reduce stock levels, and increase sales through e-commerce are likely to experience the same. However, those SMEs which were pressured into e-commerce by their customers, experienced higher costs.

398 MacGregor & Vrazalic

---

**Implications**

Swedish regional SMEs, which have adopted e-commerce did so primarily for marketing reasons and to improve their efficiency. To a certain extent, they were able to achieve these benefits; however, they experienced resource constraints as a result. These results were dissimilar for SMEs of different sizes, as well as those, which had a specific market focus. SMEs owned by male CEOs and those that were members of an alliance also experienced e-commerce differently. This implies the need to extract the "lessons learned" from successful e-commerce adopters and develop targeted programs and initiatives, which can be applied to non-adopters. Creating clusters, networks, or alliances of SMEs from the same category (e.g., SMEs of the same size) may also facilitate e-commerce adoption.

---

# E-Commerce in Australia

Like their Swedish counterparts, Australian SMEs rejected e-commerce for two key reasons: the difficulties associated with e-commerce and a misalignment with the organisation. However, unlike Sweden, Australian SMEs did show differences depending on whether their CEO was male or female, as well as differences based on their sector and market focus. In general, SMEs with a male CEO and those operating at a local/regional level were more concerned with organisational issues such as the suitability of e-commerce and its benefits. Industrial respondents, on the other hand, were less worried about the complexity of an e-commerce system, possibly due to the nature of their business.

SMEs, which did not join any type of alliance, indicated that cost was an important factor in their decision not to use e-commerce. This suggests that alliances may diminish the effects of financial constraints in Australia through pooling of resources and knowledge. Male CEOss were also more concerned about the unsuitability of e-commerce than female CEOs. University educated CEOs, were also more concerned about organisational issues, implying that they had the pre-requisite skills and knowledge to implement e-commerce but are not convinced of the organisational benefits. However, when asked what would drive them to adopt e-commerce, the Australian respondents agreed that they would surmount these organisational barriers given sufficient pressure from competition, as well as the likelihood the e-commerce would reduce costs and improve marketing.

---

**Implications**

Once again, the need for custom-made programs to different segments of the SME sector becomes evident in Australia. Programs specifically targeted at overcoming organisational barriers (as opposed to technical ones) in certain categories of SMEs would suit the Australian context more. This is in contrast to the Swedish findings, where SMEs require more technical training and support.

---

Australian SMEs adopted e-commerce for three main reasons: improving internal operations, developing business relationships and marketing strategies, and in response to external pressures. Non-members of an alliance rated pressure from competition as a more important barrier than members, suggesting that SMEs can find "strength in numbers" through clusters and networks.

The benefits, which Australian SMEs experienced were, for the most part, a reflection of what they intended. Respondents classified these around three main factors: costs and competitiveness, operations and partnerships, and sales/marketing. Those SMEs, which adopted e-commerce to reduce costs, specifically, are likely to achieve this benefit whereas those that had lower stock levels are likely to have adopted e-commerce due to pressure from their suppliers.

In the Australian scenario, non-members of an alliance actually experienced certain benefits more strongly than members including increased sales, better internal efficiency, and improved quality of information. So, although an alliance may dissipate the financial barriers to e-commerce adoption and cushion the impact from competition, it does not necessarily translate into more gains post e-commerce adoption. There is an indication, though, that security threats were a bigger concern for non-members than members.

---

**Implications**

Alliances may play an important role in promoting e-commerce adoption in Australia; however, their role appears to diminish after adoption. This suggests a carefully managed clustering approach in the pre e-commerce phase may meet with success in regional SMEs in Australia. The effects of external forces, such as suppliers is also an important factor in the Australian context and the role of some support programs may simply be to facilitate this relationship as e-commerce is implemented.

---

# E-Commerce in the USA

Whereas Sweden and Australia were concerned with the difficulties of e-commerce implementation and its unsuitability, regional SMEs in the U.S. added one more factor to the reasons why they shy away from e-commerce--cost and security. SMEs in the U.S. with smaller numbers of employees were particularly worried about these issues suggesting that they require not only financial support but any type of initiative must allay their security fears. However, U.S. SMEs did show an inclination to overcome these hurdles in order to reap the benefits of e-commerce. This is in contrast to Swedish and Australian SMEs, which were more likely to surmount organisational issues.

---

**Implications**

E-commerce adoption initiatives in the U.S. should focus specifically on emphasising the security of the technology and providing financial assistance to SMEs, which are worried about spiralling costs and the security threats. SMEs in the U.S. identified these as a distinct reason for avoiding e-commerce, in addition to issues of unsuitability and complexity.

---

SMEs in the U.S.A. were more ambivalent about the reasons they adopt e-commerce. We found four main factors including improved internal operations, better marketing, improved customer service, and reasons related to costs and competitiveness. However, it was the older SMEs, which were more concerned about maintaining business partnerships and thus adopting e-commerce to please their suppliers and also to improve their marketing. These drivers were also important for SMEs, which were not members of an alliance, whereas alliance members had a desire to improve their competitiveness primarily.

---

**Implications**

Since age and membership alliance had some effect on the reasons why U.S. SMEs adopted e-commerce, any program or initiative should take these business characteristics into account.

---

In Chapter XIII, we examined the ratings of criteria, benefits, disadvantages, and barriers across the three locations in order to draw comparisons. The similarities were far and few in between with only three criteria being rated comparably by SMEs in all three regions. There were related to improvements to customer services, pressure from competition, and better inventory management. Only the Australian respondents placed some importance on adopting e-commerce to reduce costs, and at the same time they rated improvements of relationships with business partners as being insignificant in their decision making process. The Swedish and U.S. SMEs were much more open to using e-commerce to develop relationships. In line with their willingness to overcome technical barriers such as security, U.S. SMEs saw the availability of external support as being an important e-commerce driver.

Table 1 provides a general but very concise summary of our findings. We note that this table should be treated with caution because above all, our research has highlighted the differences within the SME sector both inside one region and across similar regional areas. The benefits and disadvantages of e-commerce are not shown because of the insufficient data in the U.S. study.

*Table 1. Concise summary of findings across three locations*

|           | Barriers                                                                                                   | Criteria                                                        |
|-----------|------------------------------------------------------------------------------------------------------------|----------------------------------------------------------------|
| Sweden    | Mainly technical, but rated as being of low importance.                                                     | Primarily internal drivers (efficiency and better marketing).  |
| Australia | Technical barriers but dependent on the category of the business. In some categories organisational barriers dominate. | Internal drivers as well as external pressures.                |
| U.S.A.    | Mainly technical and related to security issues.                                                            | Mainly internal drivers but not clearly defined.               |

# Final Remarks

Perhaps the most significant result from our study is that any form of e-commerce support program or initiative must be conceived and implemented at, at least, a regional level. SMEs in similar regional areas have shown some remarkable differences in how they approach and view e-commerce. A "one size fits all" approach at a federal level is clearly out of the question. Furthermore, any type of program that focuses on technical issues such as Internet access and Web site implementation, alone, rather than organisational and strategic aspects of e-commerce is unlikely to succeed. This focus has dominated programs to date and is evident in the survey results distributed through official reports, which describer simple measures of online participation, such as having a Web site. As Matlay and Addis (2003) point out, there is little independent verification of these results, which tend to portray a "rosy" picture of technology use by SMEs. Taylor and Murphy (2004) add that the level of engagement of SMEs with the digital economy is still "rudimentary" at best.

Alternative approaches have emerged, but with only limited success. For example, there has been an attempt to promote e-commerce adoption by increasing the levels of interaction between higher education institutions (HEIs) and SMEs. Matlay et al. (2003) describe this trend, but caution that "there is a need […] for designated funding to meet the substantial costs for those HEIs that actively seek to be associated with the SME sector" (p. 324). Their research found that SMEs did not have confidence in e-commerce or the expertise of HEI consultants to assist with the implementation of e-commerce. Clearly, if this type of approach is to work, there is a need to first bridge a major cultural gap between business and academia.

The diversity of the SME sector has been highlighted previously (for example, see Lawson, Alcock, Cooper, & Burgess, 2003; Taylor et al., 2004), however, it appears that we are not taking heed of this diversity. As Taylor et al. (*ibid*) point out, "we need a better understanding of how [*SMEs*] recognise and develop business opportunities in general" (p. 288). Our study has attempted to contribute to this understanding. It has also shown that what is required

*Figure 1. Key requirements for successful e-commerce adoption*

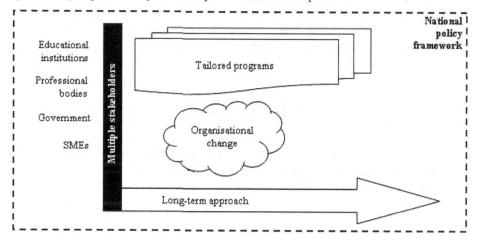

is a multi-faceted approach involving several different stakeholders. While government organisations must continue to play a key role in facilitating e-commerce adoption, a different angle of approach is required. First and foremost, these organisations must take into consideration the findings of numerous research studies, which have shown the differences in e-commerce adoption in the SME sector and develop tailored or custom-made programs for specific segments of this sector. Secondly, they must engage the help of organisations such as professional bodies, industry associations, and tertiary education institutions. These organisations can assist with the development of innovative e-commerce adoption programs aimed at certain categories of SMEs and provide different levels of support, as required.

Furthermore, as Fillis et al. (2004) suggest, any formal or linear conceptualisations of e-commerce development must be abandoned since they do not reflect the "nonlinear, sometimes chaotic pattern of actual smaller firm behaviour" (p. 359). E-commerce adoption is not a neat, simple, or "clean" process. It requires a long-term strategy to implement organisational change and involves multiple stakeholders. Therefore any limited term programs (e.g., those, which conclude after one or two years) that just offer technical or financial support are unlikely to have much effect or, indeed, prove sustainable. Figure 1 depicts the key requirements for successful e-commerce adoption in the SME sector based on the findings of this research, and previous studies.

Figure 1 emphasises the need for tailored programs, which can be developed with the assistance of educational institutions engaged in SME and e-commerce research and which take a long-term perspective. These programs, however, are simply catalysts for a deeper organisational change process that an SME must undertake with the support from multiple stakeholders. The entire e-commerce adoption process must be situated in the context of a relevant national policy framework, which rewards SMEs for adopting e-commerce through favourable taxation and other incentives. This will also serve to increase awareness about e-commerce and its benefits, which is more critical than simply providing an advisory or support service (Simpson & Docherty, 2004).

Promoting e-commerce use in the SME sector is a daunting tasks with many challenges, not in the least those created by the heterogeneity of the sector. Even developed countries, such as Australia, with high levels of Internet penetration and mature technology infrastructures, face an uphill battle to convince the very organisations that make up the cornerstone of their economies to embrace a different way of doing business. The road ahead appears to be long and fraught with difficulties, however, with the long-term support and commitment by multiple stakeholders, and government organisations in particular, SMEs will be able to make a significant business impact in the online environment.

# References

Fillis, I., Johansson, U., Wagner, B. (2004), A conceptualisation of the opportunities and barriers to e-business development in the smaller firm, *Journal of Small Business Enterprise Development, 10*(3), 336-44.

Lawson, R., Alcock, C., Cooper, J., & Burgess, L. (2003). Factors affecting the adoption of electronic commerce technologies by SMEs: An Australian study. *Journal of Small Business and Enterprise Development, 11*(2), 265-276.

Martin, L. M., & Matlay, H. (2001). "Blanket" approaches to promoting ICT in small firms: Some lessons from the DTI ladder adoption model in the UK. *Internet Research: Electronic Networking Applications and Policy, 11*(5), 399-410.

Matlay, H., & Addis, M. (2003). Adoption of ICT and e-commerce in small businesses: An HEI-based consultancy perspective. *Journal of Small Business and Enterprise Development, 10*(3), 321-335.

Peterson, U. O., & Borg, U. (2005). Portalen handelplats wermland: Practical E-commerce for Värmland's businesses and municipalities *ISD 2005 14th International Conference on Information Systems Development*. Karlstad, Sweden.

Simpson, M., & Docherty, A. J. (2004). E-commerce adoption support and advice for UK SMEs. *Journal of Small Business and Enterprise Development, 11*(3), 315-328.

Taylor, M., & Murphy, A. (2004). SMEs and E-business. *Journal of Small Business and Enterprise Development, 11*(3), 280 – 289.

# About the Authors

**Robert MacGregor** is an associate professor in the School of Information Technology and Computer Science at the University of Wollongong, Australia. He is also the former head of discipline in information systems. His research expertise lies in the areas of information technology (IT) and electronic commerce (e-commerce) in small to medium enterprises (SMEs). He has authored a number of journal and conference publications examining the use and adoption of IT in SMEs. MacGregor is also the founding editor of the *Australasian Journal of Information Systems* and was conference chair of the Australian Conference of Information Systems (1992). In his spare time, he writes music. His most recent work is the symphony "Alba."

**Lejla Vrazalic** is an associate professor in information systems at the University of Wollongong, Dubai (UOWD). She is also the chair of the UOWD Research Committee and coordinator of the Program for the Enhancement of Learning and Teaching (PELT). Her research interests are in human computer interaction and e-commerce, and she was awarded the University Medal in 1999 for her research. Vrazalic received the Vice Chancellors Award for Outstanding Contribution to Teaching and Learning (OCTAL) (2004) and a Carrick Citation for Outstanding Contributions to Student Learning (2006). She is also the recipient of the Australian Prime Minister's Award for Excellence in Business Community Partnerships (NSW) (2004) for her work on community portals in Australia.

# Index

**A**

Australia  68,  111,  124,  174

**B**

business
  -to-business (B2B)  43
  -to-consumer (B2C)  43,  97
  age  32,  76
  characteristics  133,  163
    Australian findings  68–74
    Swedish findings  46–66
    U.S. findings  74–81
  sector  46
  size  46,  76,  102,  168,  188

**C**

communication  181
computer knowledge  33

**D**

digital literacy  404

**E**

education level  139
electronic
  commerce (e-commerce)  1–2,  8–
      24,  13–24,  129–155,  257–
      288,  291–327,  328–354,  356–
      378,  381–392,  395–402
    adoption  27
    business strategy  1
    definition  13
    types
      business-to-business (B2B)  43
      business-to-customer (B2C)  43
  data interchange (EDI)  14

**F**

face-to-face  185

**G**

gender  34, 50, 77, 90, 256
glass ceiling  257
global choice  15

**H**

homogeneous approach  42

**I**

Illawarra region  28
information
  and communication technologies
    (ICTs)  1, 7, 355
  technology (IT)  11–24, 12–24
    adoption  2
    online (ITOL)  7
internal efficiency  121
Internet adoption  259
inventory  167

**K**

knowledge-based economy  1

**M**

management style  4

**P**

partial e-commerce  13
product planning  34, 49, 170
pure e-commerce  13

**R**

regional areas  7–8, 26
  Illawarra Region (Australia)  28
  Salt Lake County (U.S.A.)  29–30
  Varmland region (Sweden)  27–28
return on investment (ROI)  9

**S**

Salt Lake County  29
sample size formula  37–39
security  147, 156
self designing partnership  201
small to medium enterprises (SMEs)
    1–17, 25–39, 42–82, 87–
    126, 129–155, 160–177, 180–
    197, 200–254, 256–288, 291–
    327, 328–354, 355–378, 395–402
  characteristics of  3–6
  definition  2–3
  e-commerce adoption  26–39, 86
    Australian implications  398–399
    barriers  129–155, 328
    benefits  86, 160–177, 328
    CEO education  291–327
    CEO gender  256–288
    disadvantages  86, 180–197, 328
    strategic alliance  200–254
    U.S. implications  399–401
strategic alliance  201
  dominated alliance  204
  equal partner alliance  204
  functional alliance  203
  industrial
    alliance  203
    district alliance  203
  intermarket alliance  204
  internal alliance  204
  intra
    -inter-industry alliance  203
    -interorganisational alliance  203
  membership  49
  motivational alliance  203
  opportunity alliance  204
  resource-based alliance  203
  role  201–205
  vertical alliance  204
  virtual organisations alliance  203

strategic postures
  Analyser posture  204
  Defender posture  204
  Prospector posture  204
  Reactor posture  204
survey instrument  43
  business age  32,  43
  business sector  32–33,  43
  business size  31–32,  43
  CEO education  34,  43
  CEO gender  34,  43
  e-commerce adoption barriers  135
  e-commerce adoption benefits
     163–164
  e-commerce adoption disadvantages
     183–184
  enterprise-wide business system
     34,  43
  IT skill level  43
  level of IT skill  33
  market focus  33,  43
  product planning  34,  43
  SME alliance membership  34–41
  strategic alliance membership  43
Sweden  46,  98,  118,  124,  135,  165
Swedish Business Development
     Agency (NUTEK)  7

**T**

Tasmania  88

**U**

unemployment  7

**V**

Varimax procedure  167
virtual network  267

**W**

World Bank  121